THE VALIANT WOMAN
De muliere forti

A Medieval Commentary
on Proverbs 31:10-31
by St. Albert the Great, OP, (c. 1200-1280)
And Especially Useful for Preachers

Translated with Introduction by
Benedict M. Ashley, OP, and Dominic M. Holtz, OP

NEW PRIORY PRESS
EXPLORING THE DOMINICAN VISION

Copyright © 2013 by the Dominican Province of St. Albert the Great (U.S.A.)
All rights reserved. Published by New Priory Press,
2005 South Ashland Avenue, Chicago, IL 60608-2903
Cover Design: Susan Webb
NewPrioryPress.com

COMMENDATION

I was delighted to see that a scholar had taken on the introduction and translation of this important work. Some debate about the authorship of this text has occurred, but a recent article by Daniel M. Callus (*New Blackfriars* 13/146 [July 2007]:278-87) makes a strong case for Albertine authorship. Given the importance of Albert (the teacher of no less a figure than Thomas Aquinas) and the recent attention given to women in medieval Christianity, it will be particularly interesting to show readers how a male Dominican thought about gender and, in particular, women in the high Middle Ages. In addition, we have here an expert translation from the Latin. I therefore recommend publication with the highest enthusiasm.

John P. Doyle, Ph.D.
Prof. of Philosophy Emeritus,
Dept. of Philosophy, St. Louis University

Douay [Vulgate] Text of Proverbs 31:10-31

Who shall find a valiant woman?
   far and from the uttermost coasts is the price of her.

The heart of her husband trusteth in her,
   and he shall have no need of spoils.

She will render him good, and not evil,
   all the days of her life.

She hath sought wool and flax,
   and hath wrought by the counsel of her hands.

She is like the merchant's ship,
   she bringeth her bread from afar.

And she hath risen in the night,
   and given a prey to her household,
     and victuals to her maidens.

She hath considered a field, and bought it:
   with the fruit of her hands she hath planted a vineyard.

She hath girded her loins with strength,
   and hath strengthened her arm.

She hath tasted and seen that her traffic is good:
   her lamp shall not be put out in the night.

She hath put out her hand to strong things,
   and her fingers have taken hold of the spindle.

She hath opened her hand to the needy,
   and stretched out her hands to the poor.

She shall not fear for her house in the cold of snow:
    for all her domestics are clothed with double garments.

She hath made for herself clothing of tapestry:
    fine linen, and purple is her covering.

Her husband is honourable in the gates,
    when he sitteth among the senators of the land.

She made fine linen, and sold it,
    and delivered a girdle to the Canaanite.

Strength and beauty are her clothing,
    and she shall laugh in the latter day.

She hath opened her mouth to wisdom,
    and the law of clemency is on her tongue.

She hath looked well to the paths of her house,
    and hath not eaten her bread idle.

Her children rose up, and called her blessed:
    her husband, and he praised her.

Many daughters have gathered together riches:
    thou hast surpassed them all.

Favour is deceitful, and beauty is vain:
    the woman that feareth the Lord, she shall be praised.

Give her of the fruit of her hands:
    and let her works praise her in the gates.

CONTENTS

COMMENDATION iii
VULGATE TEXT iv
INTRODUCTION xi
EDITOR'S NOTES xv

OUTLINE OF CHAPTER I xv
CHAPTER I Aleph א 2
    Who shall find a valiant woman?
    far and from the uttermost coasts is the price of her. v. 10

OUTLINE OF CHAPTER II 22
CHAPTER II Beth ב 23
    The heart of her husband trusteth in her,
    and he shall have no need of spoils. v.11

OUTLINE OF CHAPTER III 33
CHAPTER III Ghimel ג 34
    She will render him good, and not evil,
    all the days of her life. v.12

OUTLINE OF CHAPTER IV 44
CHAPTER IV Daleth ד 46
    She hath sought wool and flax,
    and hath wrought by the counsel of her hands. v.13

OUTLINE OF CHAPTER V 59
CHAPTER V He ה 61
    She is like the merchant's ship,
    she bringeth her bread from afar. v.14

OUTLINE OF CHAPTER VI 73
CHAPTER VI Vau ו 74
    And she hath risen in the night, and given a prey
    to her household, and victuals to her maidens. v.15

OUTLINE OF CHAPTER VII 81

CHAPTER VII Zain ז **84**

    She hath considered a field, and bought it:
        with the fruit of her hands she hath planted a vineyard. v.16

OUTLINE OF CHAPTER VIII 103

CHAPTER VIII Heth ח **104**

    She hath girded her loins with strength,
        and hath strengthened her arm. v.17

OUTLINE OF CHAPTER IX 111

CHAPTER IX Tet ט **113**

    She hath tasted and seen that her traffic is good:
        her lamp shall not be put out in the night. v.18

OUTLINE OF CHAPTER X 122

CHAPTER X Jod י **124**

    She hath put out her hand to strong things, a
        nd her fingers have taken hold of the spindle. v.19

OUTLINE OF CHAPTER XI 146

CHAPTER XI Caph כ **147**

    She hath opened her hand to the needy,
        and stretched out her hands to the poor. v.20

OUTLINE OF CHAPTER XII 157

CHAPTER XII Lamed ל **160**

    She shall not fear for her house in the cold of snow:
        for all her domestics are clothed with double garments. v.21

OUTLINE OF CHAPTER XIII 179

CHAPTER XIII Mem מ **180**

    She hath made for herself clothing of tapestry:
        fine linen, and purple is her covering. v.22

OUTLINE OF CHAPTER XIV 184

CHAPTER XIV Nun נ **185**

    Her husband is honourable in the gates,
        when he sitteth among the senators of the land. v.23

OUTLINE OF CHAPTER XV 195

CHAPTER XV Samech ס **196**

    She made fine linen, and sold it,
        and delivered a girdle to the Canaanite. v.24

OUTLINE OF CHAPTER XVI 209

CHAPTER XVI Ain ע **213**

    Strength and beauty are her clothing,
        and she shall laugh in the latter day. v.25

OUTLINE OF CHAPTER XVII 265

CHAPTER XVII Peh פ **265**

    She hath opened her mouth to wisdom,
        and the law of clemency is on her tongue. v.26

OUTLINE OF CHAPTER XVIII 274

CHAPTER XVIII Sade צ **276**

    She hath looked well to the paths of her house,
        and hath not eaten her bread idle. v.27

OUTLINE OF CHAPTER XIX 295

CHAPTER XIX Coph ק **298**

    Her children rose up, and called her blessed:
        her husband, and he praised her. v.28

OUTLINE OF CHAPTER XX 331

CHAPTER XX Res ר **332**

    Many daughters have gathered together riches:
        thou hast surpassed them all. v.29

OUTLINE OF CHAPTER XXI 342

CHAPTER XXI Sin ש 342

    Favour is deceitful, and beauty is vain:
        the woman that feareth the Lord, she shall be praised. v.30

OUTLINE OF CHAPTER XXII 347

CHAPTER XXII Thau ת 348

    Give her of the fruit of her hands:
        and let her works praise her in the gates. v.31

SCRIPTURAL INDEX 359

NON-SCRIPTURAL INDEX 370

x

INTRODUCTION

This massive medieval commentary on Proverbs 31:10-31 is attributed in early manuscripts to St. Albert the Great along with certain other works no longer considered to be authentic. Formerly, however, scholars held that *De Muliere Forti* was certainly an authentic work of Albert the Great. Thus P. J. Meersseman, O.P In his 1931 *Introductio In Opera Omnia B. Albert Magni, O.P* (Beyaert, Bruges, p. 88) who also reviewed numerous Mariological works which he judged to be wrongly attributed to Albert, thought there could be no doubt about this work. I was delighted to see that a scholar had taken on the introduction and translation of this important work. So did Daniel M. Callus (*New Blackfriars* 13/146 [July 2007]: 278-87).

Later scholars, however, notably Bernhard Geyer and Albert Fries, concluded it was not authentic. Geyer pointed out that (1) all but one MS containing it is dated after the 13th century; (2) even in this MS the note of ascription is by a later hand; (3) this dating was secondary to that of Albert's Bible commentaries written late in his career; (4) the work is unlike Albert's other writings. To these doubts Fries added that (5) the ecclesiology of the work does not resembled that in Albert's authentic works; (6) the principal MS is in the handwriting of another Dominican, Guerric of St. Quentin (d. 1245); (6) the transmission of this work along with other works of doubtful authorship makes it also questionable.

Nevertheless, Winfried Faser, *Das werke Des Albertus Magnus In inhrer Hanscriftlichen: uberlierferung* (Aschendorff, 1982) for the Cologne Edition considered it at least probably authentic and it is listed as to be included in vol. XVIII of the plan for the Cologne Edition. Yet the editors of the critical edition of his works, called the "Cologne edition" being prepared by the Albertus Magnus Institut in Bonn, Germany now under the directorship of Dr. Ludger Honnefelder has decided to include it in that edition. The chief editor Dr. Dr. Henryk Anzulewicz has indicated to me in correspondence that its authenticity and that of several other Albertine works has proved difficult to determine. Since then Ms. Susana Bullido del Barrio also of the Institut has graciously sent me a very extensive study with a vast bibliography she has made of the authenticity of *De Muliere Forti*, now published in *Subsidia Albertina II: Via Alberti: Texte – Quellen–Interpretationen Herausgegeben*, edited by Ludger Honnefelder, Hannes Möhle, and Susana Bullido del Barrio (Munster; Aschendorff), 'Non est in aliquo opere modus nobilior'– De muliere forti ein Werk. In this article she seems to show that none of these seven objections against the work's authenticity of recent schoolars survive criticism. Yet she also concludes, as did Anzulewicz, that "for the present" the question remains open and cannot be settled until the critical edition appears. In translating De Muliere Forti, however, we have noted a number of features that seem positive arguments for its authenticity.

First, as Bullido del Barrio quotes in the title of her article, we came to agree with the opinion of the Dominican Peter of Prussia who in a biography of Albert c. 1486 said of this work, "In hoc Libro continentur materiae aliquae solemnissimae pro Praedicatoribus: si quis enim habuerit huius Libri practicam, cognoscet quantae virtutis sit; quia ad diuidendum unam auctoritatem, non est in aliquo Opere alicuius Doctoris modus nobilior.

Second, De Muliere Forti is free of the absurdities found in the others works attributed to Albert in vol. 37 of the Borgnet edition, such as the Mariale that asks such fantastic questions as whether Our Lady had red or black hair (q. 19) and whether she knew arithmetic and geometry, qq. 107-108. The Biblia Mariana (Borgnet 37, p. 394-395) does refer to this poem but only very briefly and may be influenced by De Muliere Forti, but the theology and ethics of the poem are profound and similar to those of Albert's authentic works.

Third, this work is, as Bullido del Barrio also notes, obviously written by a Dominican since it cites the Rule of St. Augustine used by the Order of Preachers and is much concerned with their preaching mission. It seems to be, as she points out, intended as a "Handbook for Preachers" closely related to Albert's remarkable commentaries on the Four Gospels. The positive opinions of Meersseman and Callus, both Dominicans, as well as thorough scholars of this literature supports this view.

Fourth, and very significantly, Albert's certainly authentic biblical commentaries show that Albert was very fond of this acrostic poem of Proverbs 31:10-31. In the Commentary on Luke he quotes this poem in various places 38 times and often connects it with the Church and with Mary as it also does. The Commentary on Matthew uses it with much the same frequency, although it is used much less while in the Commentaries on Mark and John. An early authentic work De Bono also contains several quotes from this biblical poem.

Fifth *De Muliere Forti* shows a marked interest in what today we call "the theology of the body," calling attention to the structure, functions, and symbolism of bodily organs such as the feet, the hands, the arms, the loins, the breast, the womb, etc. Only in one instance, like the *Mariale*, it comes close to absurdity by assigning symbolism not only to the five fingers of the Valiant Woman's hand, but also to her hand's fifteen joints and ten nails (!), Albert treats these as symbols of the various virtues or skills with which in all his works he is especially concerned.

Sixth, Albert throughout his authentic works has a mathematical bent, loving to enumerate two, three, four, etc. items. This of course is characteristic of medieval scholasticism, but is not found in St. Thomas Aquinas and others scholastics so constantly as in Albert's writings.

Thus the attribution of *The Valiant Woman* to Albert is very probable. Because of the complexity of the works' divisions, of which medievals were so fond, we have editorially added an outline to introduce each chapter.

Benedict M. Ashley, O.P.

Aleph Capitlm.j. § primus
Incipit liber domini Alber
ti magni ordinis predicatorū. de muliere forti. In quo continentur alique materie solennissime p̄ predicatoribus. Si em̄ habuerint huius libri practicā: cognoscent quāte uirtutis sit.

A

Audes ecclesie descri
bit Salomon in figura mulieris fortis p̄ xxij. capl̄a scd̄m numerū litterarū hebraicarū. In quibus tali utitur metro: ut cuiuslibet capituli sentētie littera sibi p̄escripta scd̄m interpretatōem eiusdem littere videatur alludere. Simile aūt metrū fecit Hieremias in trenis: plangendo incendiū templi. & Hierusalem sub quadruplici ꝑnexione litterarū. Quia uero in primo capl̄o loq̄i Salomon de inuētōe mulieris fortis & inquisitione. que inquisitio est in tentatione. ideo prescribīt huic capitulo hec littera. ALEPH que interpretatur doctrina tentationū. vel mille. & ꝑ iū gātur ambe interpretatōes. tūc idem est qd̄ doctrina mille tentationum. Beatus autē Hieronymus in quadam glosa sup̄ Gene. dicit q̄ millenarius perfectus & quadratus est numerus. intelligens hoc de perfectiōe cubi quadrati. id est corporis. cuius quadratura est in longū latū et ꝓfundum Est em̄ millenarij longitudo. x. que a philosophis radix appellatur. Latitudo autē huius numeri habet ex ductu longitudinis in seipsam. id est si decies . x. accipiātur. hoc est centū Profunditas uero eiusd̄e numeri prouenit ex ductu longitudinis in latitudinē. hoc est sicut. x. multiplicant centenariū. sic decies. x. decies Et vult significare in hoc Salomon p̄sectā tentatiōe hui⁹ mulieris scd̄m qd̄raturā qt̄tuor affectionū naturaliū. que sunt seminariū omnis uirtutis & om̄is uicij

	Spes	
Sunt aūt iste	Metus	Tentatio aūt est p̄ p̄batōe; militie
affectiones	Meror	in qua pugnamus contra dyabo
	Gaudium	lum. mūdum & carnem

In hac em̄ milicia uix fortis inuenitur. & precipue mulier. quia sicut dicit Salomon. vij. Ecc̄i. Virū de mille vnū repperi. mulierē ex omnibus non inueni. intelligens hoc non de sexu: sed potius de resolutis in molliciem ꝯcupiscentie carnalis. De

a ij

EDITOR'S NOTES

The *Catechism of the Catholic Church* identifies the different senses of scripture: "The literal and the spiritual, the latter being subdivided into the allegorical, moral and anagogical senses. The profound concordance of the four senses guarantees all its richness to the living reading of Scripture in the Church."#115

St. Albert's *De muliere forti* is a wonderful example of the spiritual-allegorical way of scriptural interpretation. The literal sense of Proverbs 31:10-31 is a hymn of praise for the virtuous housewife and mother, praised for her strength, her fortitude and loyalty to her husband. The title, simply means "On the Strong Woman [*de muliere forti*]." The Douay Rheims English translation elegantly translates *forti* as "valiant," and so it has come to be known in the English-speaking world and in this translation.

The twenty two verses, vv. 10-31, each begin with a letter of the Hebrew alphabet. Albert's commentary ingeniously finds a connection between the "meaning" of the letters and the verse which follows.

Division is the process used to analyze an image, for its various meanings, and so to unpack its hidden contents. This philosophical tool is wonderfully adapted by the spiritual-allegorical interpreter of Sacred Scripture, and using the valid principle of letting Scripture explain Scripture, Albert finds proof-texts from Scriptures and the Fathers of the Church to validate his elaborate divisions.

In order to keep the reader from getting lost, Fr. Benedict Ashley has provided the reader with elaborate outlines for each chapter, roadmaps through the side streets of St. Albert's quest for meaning. These are not found in the manuscripts, although the diagrams of divisions are in the source texts.

The work is divided into twenty-two chapters following the two-line verses of the poem. The manuscripts subdivide the chapters into paragraphs. We use the paragraph sign, §, to show these subdivisions.

This translation is based on the Douay Rheims English translation (1582-1609) which closely follows the Vulgate Latin used in the middle ages. It matches the Latin text well, but it echoes an archaic vocabulary: e.g. saith for says; teacheth, burneth, and "goeth, and selleth all that he hath, and buyeth that field.(Matthew 13:41)." In the translation, these archaisms have been retained. After a little experience with them, we hope they should not bother the reader.

There is discrepancy in naming and numbering the parts of the Bible. The Vulgate refers to four books of *Kings*, while the common canon today calls the first two books, *1* and *2 Samuel*, and the third and fourth, 1 and 2 Kings. The Vulgate's *Ecclesiasticus* is the current *Sirach*, and the *Apocalypse* is now *Revelations*. Contemporary psalters split the Vulgate's Psalm 9 into two: 9 and 10. So from this point on until Psalm 146, the Vulgate numbering is one less than the contemporary. At that point the Vulgates splits 146 into two, 146 & 147, from there ending the discrepancy. This translation uses the modern bible names and the modern enumeration of the Psalter.

Square brackets [ ] in the translation have several uses.
- The expansion or amplification of a scriptural text which is given only a shorter reference in the manuscripts.
- A brief explanatory phrase, by the translator, used in apposition, to clarify the text.
- A "note" of reference from the translator. In these instances the type font has been reduced to identify this "footnote."

One might ask, "Who is this Valiant Woman?" In the first Chapter Albert points out "why the Church, or the faithful soul, is called a "woman." A scan of the use of the name Valiant Woman reveals a preponderance of references to a Bride or a Wife of Christ, and secondarily to the Church. The virtues and gifts of the Bride-Wife indicate one who is bravely accomplishing her duties, which still require fortitude in the struggle. One can see how this community context can easily be adapted to the mystical adventure of the soul, the "anima," in serving her Beloved. References to the Virgin Mary are only two, and are peripheral, as examples of virtue, but not as the Valiant Woman herself.

Finally, we must acknowledge the inspiration of the translator, Fr. Benedict M. Ashley, O.P., whose own "Barefoot Journeying" – the title of his autobiography – came to an end. He died in Chicago, on February 23, 2013, as this book was in preparation. The "Valiant Woman" was one of his favorite projects. May its publication honor his memory.

Fr. Albert G. Judy, O.P.
Editor

OUTLINE OF CHAPTER I

"Who shall find a valiant woman?
Far and from the uttermost coasts is the price of her." (v.10)

§1. Acrostic Letter Aleph א signifies "doctrine of a thousands tests" by Solomon's square that roots all virtues & vices in hope, fear, sorrow, joy and tests a person for resolution against physical desires.
    1) "Who shall find a Valiant Woman?"
        1) By definition: a woman generates within herself by the seed of another
        2) As a women her bodily members differ from a man in four ways
            1) She receives the seed (Church's zeal for souls).
            2) She guards child in her womb (Church's preaching).
            3) She feeds child on her blood (Church's piety & charity for its members).
            4) She gives thanks, nourishing the Church at her two breasts of:
                1) Invitation to growth in virtue
                2) Comfort that promotes perseverance

§ 2) Why she is sought? For her strength or virtue of fortitude
    1) Difficulties She must overcome
        1) Temptations of the devil
        2) Endurance
        3) She must not fail in either
    2) Strength to overcome five strong forces:
        1) God is overcome by charity
        2) Kingdom of God is overcome by actual merit ("violence")
        3) Devil is overcome by grace
        4) Kingdom of Devil is overcome by voluntary poverty
        5). Self is overcome by meekness and patience

§3) The Dignity of her Husband, Christ, the God-Man who seeks her
    1) Some are not lost but are sought and found in the Resurrection
    2) The lost are found, Jesus seeks his sheep
    3) The found, not known to be lost, yet are found by God who chose us by the
        grace of merit
    4) the Valiant Woman raises her hand in business
        1) To give her the grace needed because humanity ungratefully denied Him.
        2) Sin removed he garment of virtues.
        3) It turned her from spiritual joy to carnal pleasure.
        4) She was sold into the slavery of sin.

§4) For what the Valiant Woman, the Church, now found clothed in grace and
    merits, is praised.
    1) When? In time and at the end of the world
    2) In nature humanity in the God-Man is supreme in all creation
    3) God's trace is in creation, his image in intelligent creatures, but He
        transcends all

4) The greatness of the reward:,
  1) Of nature: Divinity infinitely exceeds humanity
  2) Humanity exceeds other visible creatures by its Soul:
    1) intellect
    2) will
  3) Beatitude whose goals are
    1) In the truth of the good
    2) In its universality
    3) In its unfailing
      1) Redemption
      2) Kingdom
      3) Crown

CHAPTER I

"Who shall find a valiant woman? far and from the uttermost coasts is the price of her." (Proverbs 31:10)

§ 1

ALEPH א. Solomon praises the Church under the symbol of a Valiant Woman in twenty-two verses according to the number of the Hebrew letters in which such a meter is used that the sentiment of each verse seems to allude to the meaning of the letter assigned to it. In the biblical Lamentations Jeremiah uses the same meter under a fourfold list of letters bewailing the burning of the Temple and of Jerusalem. Since, however, Solomon in this poem speaks of the search for and the finding of a Valiant Woman, which search is a kind of test, therefore to this chapter is assigned this letter Aleph (א) that is interpreted either "teaching of test" or a "thousand." If both meanings are joined they mean "doctrine of a thousand tests." St. Jerome, however, in a certain Gloss on Genesis says that 1000 is a perfect, four-squared number, that is, a body whose fourfoldness is in its length, breadth, and depth, because the length of a thousand is the number 10 that by philosophers is called its "root," while its depth is from the extension of its length in breadth, that is, as 10 times 100 and thus 10 times 10 times 100. And Solomon wants by this to signify the perfect testing of this Valiant Woman according to the square of the four natural affections that are the roots of all virtues and vices.

These are the four affections...	Hope
	Fear
	Sorrow
	Joy

Testing, however, is through proving us in a battle in which we fight against the devil, the world, and the flesh. In this warfare it is not easy to find a strong person, especially a woman, for as Solomon says in Ecclesiastes 7:29, "One man among a thousand I have found, a woman among them all I have not found." This, however, is not to be understood as applying to gender, but rather as to resolution with regard to the weakness of carnal concupiscence, for of this battle Job 7:1 says, "The life of man upon earth is a warfare," because through the training of such trials God proves his Saints and, as it says in Wisdom 3:5, "He has found them worthy of himself."

The meaning of the verse that follows this letter is to be gathered from two phrases of which one is a question about this woman who is being sought, where it says: Proverbs 31:10 "**Who shall find a valiant woman?**" The other is about the high praise of the woman who is sought, and this is described as in the phrase "**Far and from the uttermost coasts is the price of her.**" In the first of these phrases four points should be noted. The first is that she is a "woman." The second is "What does she have that she should be sought?" and the answer is that she is "strong." The third is the dignity of the one who seeks her, and this is noted through the question, "Who?" The fourth thing to be noted is the diligence of the search which is indicated by "shall find her?"

Let us return to the first point and consider why the Church, or the faithful soul, is called a "woman." And we can investigate this in two ways: one by a definition, namely, that a woman is a person who generates within herself from the seed of another while the man generates in another by his own seed. The former fits the Church, that is, as Revelation 21:9 says, the "Bride of the Lamb," because whatever is conceived by the Church in her chaste womb is not from herself but from God, from the seed of the grace of Christ who is her Bridegroom, as the Apostle says in II Corinthians 3:5, "Not that we are sufficient to think any thing of ourselves, as of ourselves: but our sufficiency is from God" and as he asks in Galatians 3:5, "Therefore who gives you the Spirit and produces the virtues in you?" as if to say, "No one but Christ." John 1:16 also says, "And of his fullness we all have received, and grace for grace" and Isaiah 26:17-18 says, "So are we become in thy presence, O Lord. We have conceived, and been as it were in labor and have brought forth the spirit," that is, of salvation.

For a second reason, the Church and the faithful soul are called a "woman" in view of the service of the four bodily members or instruments by which a woman differs from a man. The first instrument is for her reception of the seed. The second is for the conservation and development of the conception in her womb. The third is her care of the unborn child as it develops. The fourth is for her service in raising the child once it is born. The first instrument is the semen, the second the womb, the third the supply of blood, the fourth her breasts.

And in the Church these four spiritual instruments are...	Zeal for souls Preaching Piety Thanksgiving

Through "zeal for souls" the Church conceives the salvation of converts. Through "preaching" she shapes, as if with the hand of teaching, the conceived child. Then "piety," which as St. Augustine says, "is good will to all who bear God's image," supplies the matter for the baby lest this be insufficient for its formation. Yet she does not ask about the size of the child she is begetting but only about its health. Fourth, "thanksgiving," signifies that from one part of herself as from one breast flows milk that invites to a better life and from another part as from the other breast flows the milk of admonition that the child should persevere in the gifts it has already received from God. Thus two kinds of milk nourish the little one, namely, milk that enables it to grow toward maturity and milk that enables it to persevere throughout life.

The Song of Songs 7:1 says, "The joints of thy thighs are like a necklace, that are made by the hand of a skillful workman". By "thighs" here is meant the zeal for souls, because, as St. Isidore says in his book *On Etymologies,* the term "necklace" (*monile*) is derived either from "warning" (*monendo*) or "shielding" (*muniendo*) because it is given by the bridegroom to his bride as a reminder of her husband when he is absent. And thus the Church has zeal through which she recalls her commitment to her Spouse and love by which she always seeks to bear fruit to his seed, remembering what is written in Genesis 38:7-10 about Er and Onan, the sons of Judah. Er sinned in that he did not plant his seed in its proper vessel and therefore was slain by God. The other sinner was Onan who "knowing that the children should not be his, when he had intercourse with his dead brother's wife, spilled his seed upon the ground" and thus was also slain by God. "Er" is a name that means "rising confusion" and signifies those who in accordance to the great gifts given them do not seek to grow in their zeal for souls but only for some evil purpose, as the Apostle says in II Corinthians 2:17, "adulterating the word of God." But "Onan," which means "grief of grace," signifies those who are vain and blown up with pride and want to be born sons of grace only to gain praise for themselves, not receiving the seed as zeal for soul but rather in the zeal of vanity and self-praise, preaching, as in II Corinthians the Apostle says 4:5, "themselves not God" (II Corinthians 4:5). Both these men were slain by the Lord because they had been condemned to the punishment of eternal death. A "necklace" is derived from "shielding" because it is given by a husband to shield his wife's bosom lest some adulterer shamefully touch her breasts. Thus again the zeal of modesty guards both one's soul and the Church, as Psalm 69:10 says, "For the zeal of thy house hath eaten me up."

And as for the "womb" that means "preaching" the Apostle says in Galatians. 4:19 "My little children, of whom I am in labor again, until Christ be formed in you." And note that birthing is impeded by two defects of the womb; one is that it has too much moisture so that the semen cannot remain in it and the other is that it has too tight closure so that the semen cannot penetrate it. And so it is spiritually in preaching the Word of God, since by too great wordiness the seed [of truth] is prevented from bearing fruit, as is Leviticus 15:2-4 says, "And the Lord spoke to Moses and Aaron, saying: Speak to the children of Israel, and say to them: The man that hath an issue of seed, shall be unclean. And then shall he be judged subject to this evil, when a filthy humor, at every moment, cleaveth to his flesh, and gathereth there. Every bed on which he sleepeth shall be unclean, and every place on which he sitteth." A "filthy seminal humor" is a sermon that does not fit the time or is not suited to those who hear it. The "bed on which he sleepeth" is what such preachers indulge in, namely, indecency and buffoonery.

The shutting up or closure of the womb occurs when the preached word that might profit many is closed by a damnable silence, as Ezekiel 3:18-21 says, "If, when I say to the wicked, Thou shalt surely die: thou declare it not to him, nor speak to him, that he may be converted from his wicked way, and live: the same wicked man shall die in his iniquity, but I will require his blood at thy hand. But if thou give warning to the wicked, and he be not converted from his wickedness and from his evil way: he indeed shall die in his iniquity, but thou hast delivered thy soul. Moreover if the just man shall turn away from his justice, and shall commit iniquity: I will lay a stumbling-block before him, he shall die, because thou hast not given him warning: he shall die in his sin, and his justices which he hath done, shall not be remembered: but I will require his blood at thy hand. But if thou warn the just man, that the just may not sin and he doth not sin: living he shall live, because thou hast warned him, and thou hast delivered thy soul."

The third way in which a woman differs from a man is as a source of blood, which above we said symbolizes "piety" or "good will to all who bear God's image," and such is according to St. Augustine one of the gifts of the Holy Spirit. From this fount flows the blood of love of neighbor in regards to which the Valiant Woman abounds with all that is needed for the formation of the children of Christ, as is noted in the words of the Apostle, II Corinthians 5:13-14, "For whether we be transported in mind, it is to God, or whether we be sober, it is for you. For the charity of Christ presseth us," that is, whatever we draw from the unfathomable mind of God and whatever we are able to do in ordinary practice we do wholly for you, O Lord, because the love Christ urges us on. For as the abundance of blood urges a woman to give birth to children so the abundance of charity urges us to spiritual rebirth. And therefore in II Corinthians 6:11-12 the Apostle says, "Our mouth is open to you, O ye Corinthians, our heart is enlarged. You are not straitened in us."[modern translation: "We have spoken freely to you, Corinthians, and opened wide our hearts to you. We are not withholding our affection from you"] As if he were to say "The mouth of piety is open to you and the heart of charity toward you is broad and abundant, nothing in us is narrow or restricted in its power of expression that would lead me to do any less for your formation in Christ. And this is what he says in Acts 20:26-27, "Wherefore I take you to witness this day that I am clear from the blood of all men. For I have not spared to declare unto you all the counsel of God." And note that Aristotle says in *History of Animals*, VII, c. 1 that, the 'menstrual discharge of young women is always white.' For elderly women cease to be fertile, as we read in Genesis 18:11, "It had ceased to be with Sarah after the manner of women." And thus two things spiritually corrupt the fount of blood so that it loses its proper color, which should be red with the flame of the fire of the love of God. Thus one cause for the blood to lack redness is youthful immaturity, while the other cause is greed that freezes charity. Of the first cause Jeremiah 31:19 says, "I am confounded and ashamed, because I have borne the reproach of my youth." And of the second Matthew 24:12 says, "And because iniquity hath abounded, the charity of many shall grow cold."

The fourth way in which a woman differs from a man is that she nurtures in Christ little newborn children and this we call "thanksgiving" and for this she has two breasts, from one of which, the invitation to better things, flows the Valiant Woman's milk nourishing spiritual life, from her other breast flows the comforting milk that is perseverance in the life that the child has accepted. And this is what the Apostle means in when he says in I Corinthians 3:1-2, "And I, brethren, could not speak to you as unto spiritual, but as unto carnal. As unto little ones in Christ I gave you milk to drink, not meat" and the Song of Songs 4:11 says, "Honey and milk are under thy tongue," which the Psalmist 45:3 glosses by saying, "Grace is poured abroad in thy lips; therefore hath God blessed thee for ever."

And thus is answered the question why the Church or the faithful soul is called the "Woman."

§ 2

The second question is, What disposition is sought in the Woman? And the answer is *fortitude* as indicated by the phrase "The Valiant Woman." The Woman is said to be strong because of two things involved in fortitude, one is the difficulty of its act or operation; the other is its great strength in overcoming what is very difficult.

The first of these questions is threefold: What must she overcome? What she has to bear it doing so? And why in meeting either of these does she not fail?

The first of these questions concerns meeting the very strong temptations of the enemy and of this Job 3:8 says, "Let them curse it [the day I was born] who curse the day, who are ready to raise up Leviathan." "Leviathan" is interpreted "their increase" and signifies the devil who persuades men to damnation. The Valiant Woman endures the devil's attacks against her when through her works of virtue she challenges him to the contest of temptation. And this is what is said in Genesis 3:15, "And she shall crush they [the serpent's] head," since the terror of the serpent is its head. The fortitude such a battle requires is exemplified in Genesis 32:24-30 by Jacob's wrestle with the Angel in which Jacob is blessed by the Angel and thus strengthened against his brother Esau. For in verse 18 the Angel says to Jacob, "If thou hast been strong against God, how much more shalt thou prevail against men?" Yet the Angel also weakened the sinews of Jacob's thigh. This has a threefold significance as regards those who strongly carry on a spiritual battle: first, they gain the blessing of grace against the devil; and second, they gain the power of virtue against the world; and third, they weaken the concupiscence of the loins, since these are the site of sensual pleasure.

The second aspect of the act of fortitude is that it strongly sustains a person against adversity, since as the Apostle says, II Timothy 3:12, "All that will live godly in Christ Jesus shall suffer persecution." Thus the woman described in II Maccabees 7:20-27 was strong indeed: "That mother was to be admired above measure, and worthy to be remembered by good men, who beheld her seven sons slain in the space of one day, and bore it with a good courage, for the hope that she had in God. And she bravely exhorted every one of them in her own language, being filled with wisdom; and joining a man's heart to a woman's thought." Hence one of her sons was also strong, since in verses 10-12 it is related of him that when he was mocked, "He quickly put forth his tongue, and courageously stretched out his hands and said with confidence, 'These I have from heaven, but for the laws of God I now despise them, because I hope to receive them again from him.' So that the king and they that were with him wondered at the young man's courage, because he esteemed the torments as nothing."

The third point to note is that fortitude both meets difficulties and endures them and does this for a long time. Of which Isaiah 40:29-31 says, "It is he [God] that giveth strength to the weary, and increaseth force and might to them that are not. You shall faint, and labour, and young men" that is, those living like young men engaged in youthful actions, "shall fall by infirmity," that is, by lust. "But they that hope in the Lord shall renew their strength, they shall take wings as eagles, they shall run and not be weary, they shall walk and not faint." And by "take wings" is indicated that fortitude is always new, as Psalmist in 76:11 relates, "And I said, Now have I begun, this is the change of the right hand of the most High." And Isaiah 40:31 says, "They shall take wings as eagles," for an eagle is said to renew its wings so that they recover their first strength. Similarly Psalm 103:5 says, "Thy youth shall be renewed like the eagle's" that is, shall regain its strength. Hence it follows [in the quote from Isaiah above] "They shall run and not be weary." They run in the strenuous effort of work and of suffering and also sustain these for a long time, never overcome by their labors. Also they fly with the swiftness of unfailing desire since they know that only those who persevere will be saved.

The high degree of the Valiant Woman's strength is shown by the fact that it conquers five very strong forces:

Fortitude conquers...	God
	The Kingdom of God
	The Devil
	The Kingdom of the Devil
	One's Self

God is conquered by the drive of charity, the Kingdom of God by the merit of good deeds, the Devil by the abjection of humility, the Kingdom of the Devil by the profession of voluntary poverty, and one's own will through the tranquility of patience and of meekness. And of the first of these the Song of Songs, 8:2 says, "I will take hold of thee, and bring thee into my mother's house, there thou shalt teach me, and I will give thee a cup of spiced wine and new wine of my pomegranates." To take hold of God is to capture him by the power of love and thus, as it were, to bring him in one's mother's house, that is, the house of the body that we have from our first mother, Eve. Similarly the Song of Songs further 3:4 says, "I will not let him go, till I bring him into my mother's house, and into the chamber of her that bore me," that is, into the secret place of my conscience, which is the chamber of maternal grace so that there God is held by the soul in a chaste embrace and enjoyed with kisses not by the contact of fleshly lips but in a spiritual union, as the Apostle says, I Corinthians, 6:17, "Who is joined to the Lord is one spirit with Him." And hence it follows in the quote above, "there thou shalt teach me," since when interior delight is held fast in the mind by the sweet chain of love, soon the intelligence is also opened to the teaching of truth, as John 16:13 says, "When he, the Spirit of truth, is come, he will teach you all truth" and I John 2:20 says, "You have the unction from the Holy One and know all things." "The new wine of my pomegranates" is compared to the exceeding happiness of the Saints, since in a pomegranate are separate seeds, as the Saints are distinguished in their eternal happiness according to differences of merit, as Psalm 149:5 says, "The Saints shall rejoice in glory, they shall be joyful in their beds." And the Lord says the same in John 14:2, "In my Father's house there are many mansions."

Concerning the victory over the Kingdom of God Matthew 11:12 says, "And from the days of John the Baptist until now, the kingdom of heaven suffereth violence and the violent bear it away." And Jesus in Matthew 7:14 says, "How narrow is the gate, and strait is the way that leadeth to life, and few there are that find it!" and hence elsewhere in Luke 13:24 Jesus says, "Strive to enter by the narrow gate." Therefore violence and fortitude are necessary to gain the Kingdom of Heaven.

As to the fortitude of the Devil, who can conquer him? Since in Matthew 12:29 Jesus says, "How can any one enter into the house of the strong, and rifle his goods, unless he first bind the strong? And then he will rifle his house." The Devil is indeed strong; his house is the heart of the sinner and his riches are sins; but the Valiant Woman binds him with the chains of the grace of the sacraments; and his "goods," namely, sins [he persuades men to commit], through the power of grace she destroys. Of this aspect of fortitude Job 41:24 says, "There is no power upon earth that can be compared with him," the Leviathan," who was made to fear no one." Yet this speaks about the Devil's power "upon earth," while the power and fortitude of this Valiant Woman is not of earth but of heaven.

The Kingdom of the Devil is in the spectacles and pomp and riches of this world, all of which through voluntary poverty the Woman overcomes according to what Jesus says in the Gospel of John 16:33, "I have overcome the world" and elsewhere in John 14:30, "The prince of this world cometh, and in me he hath not any thing." Also in Matthew 4:5 we read how Satan took Jesus to a very high mountain and showed him all the kingdoms of the world and their glory and said that he would give them all to Jesus if only Jesus would, out of greed, fall down and adore him, but Jesus answered, "Begone, Satan, for it is written: 'The Lord thy God shalt thou adore, and him only shalt thou serve.'"

Fifthly, one conquerors one's self through patience and fortitude, as the Lord says in Matthew 5:4,"Blessed are the meek; for they shall possess the land," since nobody simply by nature owns the land except the meek and patient, as the Lord says, Luke 21:19, "In your patience you will possess your souls," and in Proverbs

16:32 Solomon says, "He who rules his soul is stronger...than he that taketh cities." These therefore are the ways in which the Woman is called Strong [Valiamt].

§ 3

Next to be considered is the dignity of the one who asks this question, which is implied by the word, "*Who* shall find?" St. Jerome says that in the Sacred Scriptures this word "Who?" sometime means impossibility, as for example Isaiah 53:8 says, "Who shall declare his generation?" This speaks of Jesus' eternal origin and also of the impossibility of answering this question, confronted by which, as St. Ambrose says, "the voice, not only of men but of angels, is silent."

Sometimes, however, this question notes a difficulty as is evident in Sirach 31:8-9, "Blessed is the rich man that is found without blemish, and that hath not gone after gold, nor put his trust in money nor in treasures. Who is he, and we will praise him?", as if to say, "It is hard to find such a one" and it is in this sense that the question "**Who shall find a Valiant Woman**?" should be asked since it is not easy to find such a Woman. As St. Anselm says in his book *Cur Deus Homo* (Why God Became Man), "Two things are required for man, condemned as he is, to find salvation, that someone satisfy for his sin who is able to satisfy for it, and this is God alone. For the creature, who has received all that is and can be, ought to satisfy its Creator for what it has received, but a [sinful] creature cannot do this. And therefore he who through a woman finds justification ought to be both God and man, so that although as man he is a debtor, as God he is able to satisfy that debt." Hence Isaiah 7:14 says [of the Savior], "His name shall be called Emmanuel" which means "God with us," that is, God in our human nature; and Job 33:23-24 says, "If there shall be an angel speaking for him, one among thousands, to declare man's uprightness, God shall have mercy on him, and shall say, Deliver him, that he may not go down to corruption," which passage should be punctuated so as to mean, "If there is an angel, even one among thousands, to speak for him words of redemption, he will obtain mercy, that is, the God-Man," for Christ is this "angel" sent into world who according to the Septuagint translators in Isaiah 9:6 is called "the great Angel of Counsel."

Thus Christ according his eternal generation is the image and likeness of God the Father, but as Man he is that ultimate creature of

God which is also the image and likeness of God. Hence the God-Man is in a sense two likenesses and two images, namely, Man and Son of God. Hence he alone can speak for our redemption. Therefore it is said of him at the end of Revelation 22:13, "I am Alpha and Omega, the First and the Last, the Beginning and the End," the Beginning as God, the End as man, since the end of creatures is man, who was created last.

And thus is answered any question about the dignity of the one who asks, "Who shall find a Valiant Woman?"

§ 4

The next question is, "How diligent is this search?" as indicated by the words "**shall find**" and this question has a fourfold answer:

First, when what is not lost yet is searched for and found, as it is narrated in Genesis 36:24, that, "This is Ana that found the hot waters in the wilderness, when he fed the asses of Sebeon, his father."

Second when what is really lost is nevertheless recovered as related in I Samuel 9:20 of the asses of Cis, father of Saul, "And as for the asses, which were lost three days ago, be not solicitous, because they are found."

Third, sometimes what is searched and found through study is merely what is not known, as Jeremiah 15:16 says, "Thy words were found, and I did eat them."

Fourth sometimes what is not sought is found by luck as it says in Isaiah 65:1, "They have found me that sought me not."

In all these four ways the Valiant Woman is "found" through the work of redemption. She is found, however, because Christ searches for her when he searches to bring salvation through her. The first way of being found is in the resurrection, since we lost the resurrection in Adam, because if he had not sinned we would not have died and would have not needed to rise from the dead. Concerning this Deuteronomy 32:10 says, "He found him in a desert land, in a place of horror, and of vast wilderness." For this desert is our earthly flesh, liable even when we are still alive to the necessity of death. The "place of horror" is the dead body producing from itself a horrible odor of putrefaction; but the "vast wilderness" is when the body is already reduced to ashes. It is there that the Resurrection will find us.

The second way of being "found" brings us to Redemption, as is shown in three parables in Luke 15, of which the first concerns the hundred sheep of which only one is lost. The ninety-nine are left in desert so that the lost one, a human sinner, can be found. The second parable is about a woman who had had ten coins of which she sought the lost one and found it by lighting a lamp and searching the house. The third parable is that of the Prodigal Son, who "was dead and is come to life again; he was lost, and is found."

The third way of being "found" is when God finds in us the grace of merit. Of course he knew us even before we merited, but then he did not yet know us with approval. Thus in Luke 13:27, God says of certain persons, "I know you not... Depart from me, all ye workers of iniquity." For this way of "finding" see also Psalm 89:21, "I have found David my servant, with my holy oil I have anointed him," that is, I have found David as my servant and so that he might fulfill the work assigned to him I have anointed him with the oil of grace.

In a fourth way God "finds" us only by our reputation, since he considers himself very happy when he "finds" us as forgiven. This is symbolized in Genesis 27:20 where Isaac gives his benediction to his son Jacob [thinking he is his brother, the hunter Esau] because of the venison he has brought him:"And Isaac said to his son, How couldst thou find it so quickly, my son? He answered: It was the will of God, that what I sought came quickly in my way." Here Isaac stands for God the Father whose blinded eyes are the prophets, because, as Psalm 18:12 says, God hides himself in the "dark waters in the clouds of the air," that is, he hides his truth in the Prophet's sayings, but greater than the prophets is God's Son. The older son Esau is the first Adam to whom God commanded that he should offer to him food from his hunting with bow and arrow, that is, in wisdom and teaching. But to hunt Esau went into pathless forest, that is, this world of greed. But his younger son, Jacob is the second Adam, the Christ, who at the request of his mother, who is the mercy that made this Son of God become incarnate, went out to the neighboring herd of swine and there got two skins, that is, the body and soul of sinners, thinking himself happy that he so quickly found what he sought. In this way Adam (Jacob) obtained the blessing which we ought to possess by hereditary right, so that as by the sin of the first Adam we lost the blessing of grace that God our Father gave us, while through the Second Adam, Christ or Jacob we have recovered this grace and therefore we bless God (as did the blind Isaac) for that act of gracious benediction.

It should be noted, however, that God "seeks" a Valiant Woman in two ways and in two ways also "seeks and finds her." First God seeks her to give her grace, as is indicated in Genesis 37:14 when Joseph seeks his brothers and finds them in Dothain which means "sufficient deficiency" and signifies the state of sin where Joseph (Christ) is mistreated by his brothers, that is, by humankind. He was mistreated first by mockery; second by stripping him of his outer garment and his tunic of many colors; third by throwing him into a cistern; and fourth by selling him to the Ishmaelites traveling to Egypt. And thus a sinner insults Christ spiritually. For through ingratitude a sinner despises the Holy Spirit, as the Apostle says in Hebrews 10:28-29, "A man making void the Law of Moses dieth without any mercy under two or three witnesses. How much more, do you think he deserveth worse punishments who hath trodden underfoot the Son of God and hath esteemed the blood of the testament unclean, by which he was sanctified, and hath offered an affront to the Spirit of grace?" Joseph's many colored outer garment is decorated with a variety of virtues and his tunic is long enough to cover his whole body with the beauty of honesty. This tunic was by his brothers stained with the blood of a young goat, that is, the dishonesty of sin, because a sinner is symbolized by a goat, and his sin by blood, since as Matthew 25:33 relates Christ the Judge "shall set the sheep on his right hand, but the goats on his left." Third, Joseph is thrown into the cistern when spiritual joy is turned into carnal pleasure; for the Spirit flows like a fountain of cool water, as Psalm 35:10 says. "For with you Lord is the fountain of life." The flesh, although it seems to contain the refreshment of pleasure, actually pours out, as from an emptied cistern, rivulets of misery in pains and sorrows, as the Lord complains in Jeremiah 2:11-13, "Be astonished, O ye heavens, at this, and ye gates thereof, be very desolate, saith the Lord. For my people have done two evils. They have forsaken me, the fountain of living water, and have digged to themselves cisterns, broken cisterns that can hold no water." These "heavens" are the angels and the "gates of heaven" are Saints through whose example we enter the heavens. God calls on these blessed beings in approval of their merits and in condemnation of the sins of others who have not followed their example. Fourth, Jacob (Christ) was sold to the merchants of Egypt and this happens when the goods of grace are postponed and the mind is concerned only with worldly goods, as when Judas sold the Treasure of all Treasures, Jesus Christ, for thirty pieces of silver. Thus first Christ "finds" the Woman in that he seeks to give her grace.

Second he "seeks and finds" her to give her the virtue of fidelity by subjecting her to trials, as it is said in Wisdom 3:5-6, "Afflicted in few things, in many they shall be well rewarded, because God hath tried them, and found them worthy of himself. As gold in the furnace, he hath proved them, and as a victim of a holocaust, he hath received them." And this is also signified in Genesis 32:1 when God tries Abraham with regard to the sacrifice of his son, thus providing us with an example of fidelity; and as Jesus says in Matthew 24:45-47, "Who, thinkest thou, is a faithful and wise servant, whom his lord hath appointed over his family, to give them meat in season? Blessed is that servant, whom when his lord shall come he shall find so doing. Amen I say to you, he shall place him over all his goods "

The Valiant Woman, on her part, seeks God for two reasons, for his help and for his embrace, for his help in trials, as it is says in Psalm 105:4, "Seek ye the Lord, and be strengthened, seek his face evermore," and as Isaiah 55:6 says, "Seek ye the Lord, while he may be found, call upon him, while he is near." She also seeks his embrace in devotion, of which the Song of Songs 3:1-2 says, "In my bed by night I sought him whom my soul loveth: I sought him, and found him not. I will rise, and will go about the city, in the streets and the broad ways I will seek him whom my soul loveth: I sought him, and I found him not," and then in verse. 4, "When I had a little passed by them, I found him whom my soul loveth: I held him, and I will not let him go, till I bring him into my mother's house, and into the chamber of her that bore me." The "bed" is contemplation; the "night" is the obscurity of meditation, because as the Apostle says, II Corinthians 5:7, "For we walk by faith and not by sight." The vision of faith is in a mirror and is obscure, since, as Wisdom 9:15 says, "The corruptible body is a load upon the soul, and the earthly habitation presseth down the mind that museth upon many things." In these nights of meditation the Valiant Woman seeks the Bridegroom to embrace him, yet does not find him, since he does not show himself to his Bride, but remains as it were a stranger. And about this Jeremiah 14:8 asks the Lord, "Why wilt thou be as a stranger in the land, and as a wayfaring man refusing to here remain?" Therefore the bride "rises" by raising up her mind from all care for the body to the contemplation of eternal truths and "goes about the city in the streets," that is, meditates on the ranks of the Saints living in the joy of their eternal rewards, and on the "broad ways," that is, on the ranks of the Angels in their hierarchy. For the "broad ways" are in Greek *platé*, which means "wide."

The Valiant Woman is "seeking to see" the delight of her soul, which can only mean pondering on the glory of the Saints, as if one were to raise one's mental sight by some instrument with which one reaches out to touch the inaccessible light in which God dwells. And therefore those who thus teach others are called the "watchmen" who guard the city, meaning the Angels who are deputed to guard the Church which is the city of the heavenly Jerusalem. For the Angels purify human souls so that they are able more freely to contemplate the boundless light, as Isaiah 6:6-7 says, "One of the seraphim flew to me, and in his hand was a live coal, which he had taken with the tongs off the altar. And he touched my mouth, and said: Behold this hath touched thy lips, and thy iniquities shall be taken away, and thy sin shall be cleansed." Here the "burning coal" is truth. The "tongs," formed of two arms that press together, is the consideration of faith pressing against intelligence as they are connected with each other by the key of divine revelation. The "altar" is the sublimity of eternal bliss as that touches the mouth of the heart and soul through the illuminating ministry of Angels and its two lips are the reason and the will. The heart is cleansed of the iniquity that is the inclination of desire and appetite for worldly things and its longing for depravity and when it is thus cleansed is made such a heart as that of which Jesus says in Matthew 5:8, "Blessed are the clean of heart, they shall see God." What follows in the Song of Songs 3:4, "When I had a little passed by them" means that the beatitude of God is not seen unless the mind is raised above all that is created and there finds and holds on to God only by constant prayer and through fervent devotion and will not let Him go even if He seems to want to depart until that prayer brings the lover into the "house" of the heart, that is the house of the mother of wisdom and in the chamber of conscience where dwells the mother of all good, that is, where grace dwells.

§ 5

What follows is the high praise of the Valiant Woman once she has thus been found, which consists in these words Proverbs, 31:10, **"Far and from the uttermost coasts is the price of her."**

This word "far" can be taken in four ways...	in time in nature in human knowledge in the value of the reward

The price is "far away" in time in two senses: first, as to the end of the world, when the reward will be for the body in its resurrection and of this Ecclesiastes 11:1 says, "Cast thy bread upon the running waters, for after a long time thou shalt find it again." Second, God predestined that the price of redemption should be paid [by Christ on the Cross] in the "last days" [of history] that are also called the "fullness of time" in Galatians 4:4-5, "But when the fullness of the time was come, God sent his Son, made of a woman, made under the law That he might redeem them who were under the law." And of that time that is "far away" in both senses mentioned Numbers 24:23 says, "Alas, who shall live when God shall do these things?" as if to say, "That time is far away for us." And also in Habakkuk 2:2-3, "And the Lord answered me, and said: "Write the vision, and make it plain upon tables, that he that readeth it may run over it. For as yet the vision is far off, and it shall appear at the end, and shall not lie, if it make any delay, wait for it, for it shall surely come and it shall not be slack." And by "vision" Habakkuk meant the revelation God made of the price of redemption and the price of glorification.

Second, this price is "far away" in nature, as is evident, because the price of the Valiant Woman is God who is the beginning of all things, while the Valiant Woman is the goal of all creatures, since beginning and the end are by nature maximally distant. This is what is said in Ecclesiastes 24:44, "For I make doctrine to shine forth to all as the morning light, and I will declare it afar off." For the doctrine, which is, as it were, the morning light is the doctrine of creation that reveals God in his creatures. But this is narrated [in the six days of Genesis] up to the creation of humanity, since, as St. Gregory says, "man stands out from all other beings," for he stands with the stones, lives with the trees, senses with the animals, and thinks with the Angels. Similarly Isaiah 55:9 says, "For as the heavens are exalted above the earth, so are my ways exalted above your ways, and my thoughts above your thoughts." For in the first place is the heavens and the last place is the earth and thus God is first in nature and man last, as is well said in Genesis 24:63 where it is told that Isaac raising his eyes saw approaching "far away" the camel on which Rebecca was riding toward him. Here Isaac stands for the Son of God and Rebecca for the Church, because "Rebecca" is interpreted "she who has received much" and signifies the Church which has received all the gifts of grace. The "camel" on which she rides, because of its hump signifies the flesh which is now hump-backed because of the infirmity and mortality into which we have fallen. Jacob sees her at a distance because of the distance of our original dignity from our fallen nature, and this is what is said in Exodus 20:18, "And all the people saw the voices and the flames, and the sound of the trumpet, and the mount smoking; and being terrified and struck with fear, they stood afar off." The "mountain" is the eminence of the divine nature, God, the "smoke" is the emanation of the creature from the divine nature, not of course from its essence, but from God's will, for as St. John Damascene says, "Creature exist as the work of the divine will." The "voices" are the precepts and commandments of the Law. And the "sounds of the trumpet" are the voices of the prophets by which we know the height and the depth of the divine nature and are "struck with fear" and wonder because we then know our distance from God who is our price [or reward].

The "price" of the Valiant Woman is "far away" in third sense as regards our knowledge of God since we know him so little, since as says Job 36:25-26, "All men see him, every one beholdeth afar off. Behold, God is great, exceeding our knowledge, the number of his years is inestimable," that is, unlimited. And this is what Genesis 22:4 means when it says of Abraham that "And on the third day, lifting up his eyes, he saw the place afar off," that is, that distant mountain called the "Mountain of Vision." For the "three days" are the three divine revelations by which we know God: the first is through his traces when we know him through irrational creatures, second is through his image when we know him through rational creatures, and third is when we know God in himself, but then we see him at a distance and therefore obscurely.

The fourth "far away' from God regards our reception of our price [or reward], although God who is our reward is omnipresent, as is it is said in Joshua 1:3-4, "I will deliver to you every place that the sole of your foot shall tread upon, as I have said to Moses. From the desert, and from Lebanon unto the great river Euphrates, all the land of the Hittites, unto the great sea toward the going down of the sun, shall be your border." The "desert" is the world because it is not a place to live in but to travel through. Lebanon, means the community of the Saints in heaven since "Lebanon" means "clothed in white" and the Saints will be clothed both with the white garment of body and of soul. The Great River is the Euphrates, a name that means either "rising" or "fertile," and signifies the glory of the human Christ who grew and bore fruit to the glory of all the Saints.

The land of Heth is the hell of the damned, because "Heth" means "dreadful." The "great sea" is the depth of the misery of the demons. The "land of the setting sun" is the habitation of those who are dead in original sin because the light of the vision of God no longer rises on them. And thus those that tread the path of meditation receive the reward of rejoicing at the justice of seeing the condemned punished and the pious rewarded.

The ultimate ends of nature are of three sorts...	of Nature
	of the Soul
	of Beatitude

The ultimate ends or extremes of nature are divinity and humanity, as was said, since one can go no further than God as the beginning and on the part of creatures one can go no further to the end than humanity, as Wisdom 8:1 says, "She [Wisdom] reacheth, therefore, from end to end mightily, and ordereth all things sweetly." This should be understood to be true first as to the Incarnation, second as to glorification, and therefore it is said John 10:9, "He shall go in and go out, and shall find pastures," on which St. Augustine comments, "Going within he will find fruitful pasture in the divinity of the Savior, and going out he will find fruitful pasture in His humanity."

The ends of the soul are also twofold, namely the highest truth which is the goal of the intellect and the highest good which is the goal of the will. And of this Isaiah 58:11 says, "He will fill thy soul with brightness, and deliver thy bones." For as to its intellect the soul is filled with the splendor of truth and as to the strength of its will the soul is ordered to the highest good through the influx of which it will be delivered from every misery. Thus John 1:14 says, "We have seen his glory, the glory as it were of the only begotten of the Father, full of grace and truth," that is, of grace as to the good done by the will, and of truth as to the enlightenment of the intelligence.

The goal of beatitude is threefold...	In the truth of good which is beatitude
	In its universality
	In that it is infallible

Of the first it is said in Luke 18:19, "None is good but God alone." Second, of universality, it is said in Wisdom 7:11, "All good things came to me together with her," and Boethius says in his *The Consolation of Philosophy*, "Beatitude is a state that is perfected through the totality of all goods." And that beatitude is infallible it is said in Revelation 21:4, "Death shall be no more. Nor mourning, nor crying, nor sorrow shall be any more, for the former things are passed away."

The price [or reward] that is distant but regards the ultimate goals of life is threefold:

	Redemption
Reward…	Kingdom
	Crown

Of the price of Redemption Matthew 27:9-10 says, "And they took the thirty pieces of silver, the price of him that was prized, whom they prized of the children of Israel. And they gave them unto the potter's field, as the Lord appointed to me." The price of redemption is the reward of Judas who the sons of Israel bought to betray the Lord and it was the price for the purchase of the potter's field that is the human nature that God has shaped for us. And of this Zechariah 11:12-13 says, "Bring hither my wages, and if not, be quiet. And they weighed for my wages thirty pieces of silver. And the Lord said to me: Cast it into the house of the Lord to the statuary." The "sculptor" in the "statuary" making a beautiful image is the Lord and the "thirty pieces of silver" is the price of all things, namely, the Church, God's house. Thus we throw thirty silver coins into the house of the Lord for our redemption when the price of all things is offered to God in the Church for the redemption of the faithful, as Psalm 130:7 says, "Because with the Lord there is mercy, and with him plentiful redemption." And elsewhere in Psalm 111:5, "He hath sent redemption to his people; he hath commanded his covenant for ever."

The "price" [or reward] that is the Kingdom is the daily wage that was given to the laborers in the vineyard, as Jesus tells in Matthew 20:2, "And having agreed with the laborers for a penny a day, he sent them into his vineyard." And at the end of the day's labor, that is the merit of a lifetime, "they each received a single penny," that is, the kingdom of heaven, of which Psalm 127:2 says, "When he shall give sleep to his beloved," that is after death, "Behold the inheritance," price or reward "of the Lord are children," that is, the reward due to the Son, and this price is "the fruit of the womb," namely of the Virgin, who is Christ, our reward and beatitude.

Of the price [or reward] of the Crown, the Apostle says in I Corinthians, 9:24, "They that run in the race, all run indeed, but one receiveth the prize." The "prize" is the "crown" of the runners or contestants and so St. Paul advices, "So run that you may obtain. And every one that contesteth for the mastery refraineth himself from all things. And they indeed that they may receive a corruptible crown, but we an incorruptible one." Similarly Isaiah 28:5 says, "In that day the Lord of hosts shall be a crown of glory, and a garland of joy to the residue of his people," and in II Timothy 4:8 the Apostle says, "There is laid up for me a crown of justice which the Lord, the just judge, will render to me in that day, and not only to me, but to them also that love his coming."

OUTLINE OF CHAPTER II

"The heart of her husband trusteth in her, and he shall have no need of spoils" (v. 11)

§1. Acrostic Letter Beth ב signifies "daughter' or "house", Why Christ, her husband, trusts his wife, the Valiant Woman, the Church, regards two things
    1) She is a "daughter" or "measure," hence a Woman:
        1) She was prepared by God her Father to love Christ her husband.
        2) Her love for her husband is beyond measure
        3) Her chastity makes her Sister to Christ, fed with him at the breasts of Divine Wisdom;
            1) On milk from the breast of Truth
            2) Also from the other breast of Goodness
            3) This milk has two properties, it is
                1) White and undefiled
                2) It is nourishing
    2) She is with her husband, Christ, head of the "Household" of the Church and is trusted by Him:
        1) Because of her chaste love for him
            1) Why he trusts her: She contemplates Him
            2) She comes to meet him
            3) She desires only Him in his beauty
        2) What he trust her for
            1) Her fidelity
            2) She pays the marital debt
            3) She is fertile
            4) She cares for her family
            5) She cares for household goods
            6) She works for family support
    3) Who this Husband is, Christ. who trusts her in his heart
        1) Because of her virtue
        2) Because she is already virtuous
        3) Because he does not have to guard her feom infidelity
    4) Who this trusted Wife is, the Valiant Woman, the New Eve:
        1) She was created from the Man's side
        2) She was not taken from His feet
        3) She was taken from His rib, next to his heart; they are partners

§2) Because she cares for their household she gains riches by despoiling,
    1) Good spoils:
        1) From the devil from whom she takes two good spoils:
            1) Learning to discern spirits by conquering temptations
            2) Avoiding occasions of temptation by the world:
                1) Knowledge of this world
                2) Practice of virtue

3) Avoiding temptations of the flesh:
     1) Mortification of the flesh
     2) Vigor of chastity
  2) Rejecting bad spoils that would harm her household:
     1) Devil's pride & envy
     2) World's vanity and pleasure
     3) Self pride, since glory & dominion belongs to God alone.

CHAPTER II

The heart of her husband trusteth in her, and he shall have no need of spoils. (v. 11)

§ 1

BETH ב, the second letter of the Hebrew alphabet, marks this chapter. Beth is described in two ways, either through the *b* or the *th* at the end. In the first case it is interpreted either "daughter" or "measure"; in the second case as "house" or "dwelling."

As to the first interpretation three things should be noted: (a) the rule of a daughter by her father to prepare her for a loving husband, (b) the measure of her love for him and (c) her chastity.

As to the first we read in Psalm 45:11-12: "Hearken, O daughter, and see, and incline thy ear, and forget thy people and thy father's house. And the king shall greatly desire thy beauty."

As to the second Deuteronomy 6:5 commands, "Thou shalt love the Lord thy God with thy whole heart, and with thy whole soul, and with thy whole strength." From your whole heart in every way that your heart can desire so that nothing can equal or compare to it, since what incomparably exceeds everything else in the heart's love should not be compared to anything else. One loves with one's whole soul when the will's desire continually reaches out to the beloved so that one thinks in one's soul of nothing else and thus one's love is proven by the strength of this striving. Therefore it is obvious that the measure of love is that it has no measure.

The chastity of this love is noted by the fact that the bride is called the "daughter" of her father and therefore this bride wants also to call her husband "brother," thus speaking to him as does the bride in the Song of Songs, 8:1, "Who shall give thee to me for my brother, sucking the breasts of my mother, that I may find thee without, and kiss thee, and now no man may despise me?" For the mother of the bride is unborn Wisdom whose breasts, that is, of the spirit and savor of understanding, that Christ sucked by union to the Wisdom who is unborn and uncreated. He sucked the milk of understanding from the breast of truth and from the other breast, namely the savor of the Spirit, the milk of goodness by which he saved us. This is so, because by the intellect is manifested the shining whiteness of the milk of divinity and by love, as if by a nourishing drink, one is refreshed by the sweetness of goodness.

For in milk are two properties, namely whiteness and liquid nourishment. Therefore also the bridegroom in turn calls his bride "sister" as in the Song of Songs 5:2 he says, "Open to me, my sister, my love, my dove, my undefiled." He says "Open to me," that is, that the desiring heart be opened by the expansion of desire. And the bride is called "sister" because of her chaste embrace, and also "friend" because of her goodness, and "dove" because of her simplicity and freedom from any bitterness in taste, since, as Plato says, "appetite is in the liver and a dove's liver has no gall."

According to the other interpretation Beth means a house or dwelling and thus "house" implies family, as Psalm 134:19 says, "Bless the Lord, O house of Israel, bless the Lord, O house of Aaron," and in Exodus 1:21 it says, "Because the midwives feared God, he built them houses." And thus the Valiant Woman is said to be one in whom her husband is confident, both because of her chaste love that loves only him; but also because of her provident care of her family, since because of her they need no other householder, since she faithfully dispenses what is needed; and again because she is, as it were, the dwelling place of her husband's heart, as Deuteronomy 33:12 says, "As the best beloved of the Lord, Benjamin shall dwell confidently in him, as in a bride chamber shall he abide all the day long, and between his shoulders shall he rest." "Benjamin" is interpreted as "son of my right hand" and signifies the Valiant Woman in whom the heart of her husband confidently dwells because of the prudence with which she rules his whole household. He dwells in her as in a chamber because of the sweetness of her love. Indeed, he dwells in her arms, that is, he rests content in her endurance and patience, with which as in two arms she carries the burden of the day and the heat. And this is what is meant in what follows: "**The heart of her husband trusteth in her, and he shall have no need of spoils.**" In which verse two things are noted or considered, first the confidence of the husband in his wife and second, when it says, "he shall have no need of spoils," that is, of the abundance of riches, because of the woman's prudence.

Concerning the first of these phrases four things are to be noted, the man's confidence; second, what does this confidence in his heart concern; third , who is this husband who has this confidence in his heart; and four, in whom does he have this confidence, namely, in the Valiant Woman.

Now there is a threefold reason why a man trusts a woman:first because she loves no one but him; second because she thinks of no one but him as her husband; third because she takes delight in no love but his.

Of the first reason in the Song of Songs 7:10 the Bride says, "I to my beloved, and his turning is towards me." And Psalm 40:2 says, "With expectation I have waited for the Lord, and he was attentive to me." And this is also the meaning of that cry of desire in Isaiah 38:13, "Expect, expect again; a little there, a little there" to which the lover responds, "Command, command again; command, command again; expect, expect again; a little there, a little there," that is, a little in action and a little in contemplation.

Of the second reason we read in Judith 15:10, "And when she was come out to him, they all blessed her with one voice, saying: Thou art the glory of Jerusalem, thou art the joy of Israel, thou art the honor of our people: For thou hast done manfully, and thy heart has been strengthened, because thou hast loved chastity, and after thy husband hast not known any other, therefore also the hand of the Lord hath strengthened thee, and therefore thou shalt be blessed for ever"

Of the third the Bride in the Song of Songs 5:10 says, "My beloved is white and ruddy, chosen out of thousands." He is "white" because of the light of truth, and "ruddy" because of the fervor of charity, and hence is chosen from a thousand, as Psalm 73:25 says, "For what have I in heaven? and besides thee what do I desire upon earth?"

Second it must be noted that the man trusts his wife in important concerns and there are six such concerns that render this trust complete. The first is faithfulness to the bridal bed. The second is rendering of her marital obligations. The third is fertility in procreation. The fourth is family care. The fifth is care of family possessions. The sixth is contribution to family wealth by daily work.

The opposite of the first reason a man trusts his wife of these is mentioned in Isaiah 28:20, "For the bed is straitened, so that one must fall out, and a short covering cannot cover both." For the bed is the peace of heart, the covering is charity in which God cannot be united with the adulterous. And this is what is said in Hosea 2:16-17, "And it shall be in that day, saith the Lord: That she shall call me: My husband and she shall call me no more Baal. And I will take away the names of Baalim out of her mouth, and she shall no more remember their name." Baalim means "violent men" whom God does not permit his wife even to name when, because of the fidelity she has to her own man, she keeps faith with God and does not allow entrance to an adulterer, that is, to the devil or the world when they come prowling.

And the second reason a man trusts his wife is mentioned in Genesis 30:16 where it is said of Lia in regards to Jacob, "And when Jacob returned at evening from the field, Lia went out to meet him, and said: Thou shalt come in unto me, because I have hired thee for my son's mandrakes," because it is just that he should also pay to her the marital debt that she owes him. Mandrake is a kind of fruit and signifies the good works for which God is bound to embrace the worker in love. And this explains what is said in the Song of Songs 1:15-16, "Behold thou art fair, my beloved, and comely. Our bed is flourishing. The beams of our houses are of cedar, our rafters of cypress trees." The "bed" of the conscience or the body is at peace because it is flourishing through the payment of the marital debt through mutual love; for the "house" is the mind. The "beams" by which the house is bound together are the gifts of the Holy Spirit, and they are of "cedar," that is, have the incorruptibility of faithfulness. The "rafters" by which the roof is supported are good example and good intention. For a certain Gloss says "cypress has a strong and very pleasant odor, effective for bodily healing" and a good intention has a good odor in God's nostrils, since it heals he wounds of vanity that injure our relationships, as Jesus says in Matthew 6:22, "So let your light shine before men, that they may see your good works, and glorify your Father who is in heaven."

The third reason a man trusts his wife is her fertility in children of which it is said in Genesis 29:34, "And she [Lia] conceived the third time, and bore another son, and said: Now also my husband will be joined to me, because I have borne him three sons, and therefore she called his name Levi." "Levi" means "growing," namely in works of heart, mouth, and hand. To the contrary it is said in Job 24:21, "For he hath fed the barren that beareth not, and to the widow he hath done no good." For by the "barren" is meant the flesh which by worldly living produces nothing and by the "widow" is meant the soul which can produce many sons if married to the right husband.

The fourth reason a man trusts his wife is her care for the family of which it is said in Tobit 10:13 that Raguel and his wife Anna spoke urgently to their daughter [as she left them with her bridegroom], "Admonishing her to honor her father and mother in law, to love her husband, to take care of the family, to govern the house, and to behave blamelessly." And also in Ruth 4:11 [the elders say to Boaz who has just married Ruth]. "The Lord make this woman who cometh into thy house, like Rachel, and Lia, who built up the house of Israel, that she may be an example of virtue in Ephrata, and may have a famous name in Bethlehem." For Rachel built and ruled the "house" of contemplation, but Lia the "house" and family of action. And therefore Ruth is to be an "example of virtue in Ephratha," that is, in the fruitfulness of her good works, and also in "Bethlehem," which is interpreted as "house of bread," that is, in contemplation through which the family of the heart is nourished, as Sirach 15:3 says, "With the bread of life and understanding, she shall feed him, and give him the water of wholesome wisdom to drink."

The fifth reason a man trusts his wife is her care for their possessions, and this is mentioned later in the praise of the Valiant Woman, Proverbs 26:1, "She hath looked well on the paths of her house, and hath not eaten her bread idle." and also in Sirach 26:1, "Happy is the husband of a good wife, for the number of his years is double." A year is a circle of days and symbolizes the totality of the good works of this man's wife.

The sixth reason a man trusts his wife is that she increases their possessions, that is, performs good works. And this is exemplified by the wife Sarah of the younger Tobias through whom he, previously so poor, received a fortune. The same is said in Tobit 2:19 of the elder Tobit's' wife, Anna:"Now Anna his wife went daily to weaving work, and she brought home what she could get for their living by the labor of her hands." In weaving one thread is twined with another thread so that the warp of the cloth may be strengthened, and so it is in deeds when deed is connected to deed through charity so that a garment of virtue is woven. Hence further on in our text, verse 14, it is said in praise of the Valiant Woman, "She is like the merchant's ship, she bringeth her bread from afar." And again in verse 29, "Many daughters have gathered together riches, thou hast surpassed them all."

Next comes the reasons her husband trusts in her from his heart, for it says, "The heart of her husband trusteth in her." Note that some husbands trust their wives from the heart but others only in words and not in their hearts; and some neither in their hearts nor words, but only by external guardianship. It is in the first way in his heart, however, that her husband trusts in the Valiant Woman, for it says in Sirach 26:2, "A virtuous woman rejoiceth her husband, and shall fulfill the years of his life in peace" and further on in 26:16, "The grace of a diligent woman shall delight her husband, and shall fat his bones."

Someone trusts [in the second way] only in word when he has no reason because of his wife's works to trust her, but only when in the future she improves and therefore the man insists in words that she improve, as it says in Jeremiah 3:1, "It is commonly said: If a man put away his wife, and she go from him, and marry another man, shall he return to her any more? Shall not that woman be polluted, and defiled? But thou hast prostituted thyself to many lovers, nevertheless return to me, saith the Lord, and I will receive thee."

[In the third way] a man may trust his wife neither in his heart nor in his words but guards her, as we read in Hosea 2:6-7, "Wherefore, behold, I will hedge up thy way with thorns, and I will stop it up with a wall, and she shall not find her paths. And she shall follow after her lovers, and shall not overtake them, and she shall seek them, and shall not find, and she shall say: I will go, and return to my first husband, because it was better with me then than now." The "thorns" are troubles and the "wall" is poverty by which the wife is impeded if she goes out pursuing worldly desires. Then when she cannot get what she wants, she returns to her original commitments and begins to fear the Lord, so that the pleasure she could not have in the present, she at least hopes for in the future.

What follows in the text is the answer to who it is that has trust, namely, "her husband," and St. Gregory the Great says that, "A real man is one who fights against the twofold insults of fortune, fortified by steady constancy of mind." For the insults of fortune are both adversity and prosperity, so that "steady constancy of mind" is neither elated by prosperity, nor depressed by adversity. Such a real man is above all Jesus Christ of whom it is said in Psalm 1:1, "Blessed is the man who hath not walked in the counsel of the ungodly, nor stood in the way of sinners, nor sat in the chair of pestilence." For the "counsel of the wicked" is to break the law since the wicked deliberately do so. The "way of the wicked" is the works of sin in which any one "stands' by habitual sinful deeds. And the "chair of pestilence" is the teaching of evil through bad example and words, and the sinner "sits" in this chair when he praises evil and despises the good.

The next phrase in the text is "in her" which notes in whom it is that the husband Christ trusts, namely, in his wife, the Valiant Woman. As there are three things which were in the first description of the Valiant Woman three things are noted that confirm the husband's trust in his wife.

The first is that the woman was not taken from the man's head but from his side. In this phrase is expressed the reverential subjection of the woman to the man because just as long as she shows that due respect so does the man trust her in his heart. And this is what the Apostle in I Corinthians 11:3 says, "But I would have you know, that the head of every man is Christ; and the head of the woman is the man; and the head of Christ is God."

The second is that the Valiant Woman is not taken from her husband's feet, but from his side; in which is noted the manifestation of their mutual society, since as long as the woman manifests this companionship to the man, so long does the man trust her. And this [failure on Eve's part] is what the first man, Adam, claimed as his excuse, saying in Genesis 3:12, "The woman, whom thou gavest me to be my companion, gave me of the tree, and I did eat," as if to say "I had to have faith in my companion."

The third is that she was taken from his rib which is the part of the body next to the heart. And in this is noted the intimate love shown between the woman and the man, when Adam also says to his wife, Genesis 2:23-24, "This now is bone of my bones, and flesh of my flesh; she shall be called woman, because she was taken out of man. Wherefore a man shall leave father and mother, and shall cleave to his wife, and they shall be two in one flesh." Thus spiritually they are two in one heart, since as the Apostles says in I Corinthians 6:17, "He who is joined to the Lord, is one spirit" with him.

§ 2

What follows concerns the abundance of this woman's riches which is noted when it says Proverbs 31:11b "**and he shall have no need of spoils.**" This term "spoil" can be taken as in one sense good and in another bad. If it is taken as good then this means, "He shall not need spoils" because he is strong and despoils his enemies, but if taken as bad it means, "He does not need what belongs to others because he has enough of his own." If it is taken in the first sense it should be noted that the Valiant Woman despoils three enemies, the devil, the world, and the flesh. And from each of them she takes two spoils, through the experience of many temptations by the devil she learns discernment of spirits, but also she acquires caution in avoiding his temptations by frequent victory over them. And the first is mentioned by the Apostle in II Corinthians 2:10-11, "For, what I have pardoned, if I have pardoned any thing, for your sakes have I done it in the person of Christ. That we be not overreached by Satan. For we are not ignorant of his devices." And the second is noted in the Song of Songs 4:4, "Thy neck, is as the tower of David, which is built with bulwarks, a thousand bucklers hang upon it, all the armor of valiant men." For the "neck which joins the head to the body signifies the mind through which the soul is joined to God and which is like the "tower of David" fortified and founded on the mountain of the heights of the spirit, build with ramparts, that is, having the arts of spiritual vigilance by which the temptations of the demons are repelled. And on it are "hung a thousand shields," by which is signified the perfect guardianship of the Angels for a "thousand," as previously noted, is a perfect number. The "arms of valiant men" signify the examples of the Saints stored in the memory that can be used against the devil, and this is what is said in Psalm 144:1, "Blessed be the Lord my God, who teacheth my hands to fight, and my fingers to war." For a sign of the courage in the hands of a warrior is the care and skill of his fingers, as is said of the Saints in Isaiah 11:14, "They shall fly upon the shoulders of the Philistines by the sea, they together shall spoil the children of the east," in which "Philistines" is interpreted as "they who fall down drunk," and means the demons because after drinking the cup of God's wrath they fell into hell. Their "shoulders" are their evil plots on which they carry souls into sin. By these guilty shoulders the devils, who were once the holy Sons of the Dawn dwelling in the rising of eternal light, were dragged with the speed of a kind of spiritual effort into the pit of darkness.

Thus from the flesh are gained two trophies: the mortification of that flesh and the vigor of chastity of which it is said in Job 11:26, "Wilt thou fill nets with his [the Leviathan's] skin, and the buckets of fishes with his head?" as if to say, "You [Job] can not, but I [God] can." For the devil's "skin" is the lust of the flesh, while the "net" is the faith of Christ by which the flesh is freed and the "buckets" are the temperance of chastity which are filled with the serpent's head when his first motion [of temptation] is squelched. And this is what Isaiah 9:3 says, "They shall rejoice before thee, as they that rejoice in the harvest, as conquerors rejoice after taking a prey, when they divide the spoils." For two sorts of spoils are taken from the world: the knowledge of this world and the practice of virtue. This is indicated in Exodus 12:35-36, "And the children of Israel did as Moses had commanded, and they asked of the Egyptians vessels of silver and gold, and very much raiment. And the Lord gave favor to the people in the sight of the Egyptians, so that they lent unto them, and they stripped the Egyptians." Also Exodus 3:21-22 says, "And I will give favor to this people, in the sight of the Egyptians, and when you go forth, you shall not depart empty: But every woman shall ask of her neighbor, and of her that is in her house, vessels of silver and of gold, and raiment, and you shall put them on your sons and daughters, and shall spoil Egypt." "Egypt" is the world; the "sons" are the preachers of the Church doing manly work; the "daughters" are the penitent laity; the "vessels of silver" are the eloquent expression of knowledge; the "vessels of gold" are such wise knowledge as concerns worldly matters; the "raiment" are the practice of virtues which the Saints take back from the worldly wise who unjustly possess them. As it says in Genesis 31:1, "But after that he [Jacob] heard the words of the sons of Laban, saying: Jacob hath taken away all that was our father's and being enriched by his substance is become great." "Laban" is interpreted "white-robed" and signifies worldly brilliance in the sciences of the Philosophers and in the propriety of practiced virtue. The "sons" of Laban, however, are the sons of this world who complain because all the sciences and virtues that once were features of the pagan world now exist in the Church.

If, however, the spoils are evil then the husband of the Valiant Woman has no need of them since he has enough good spoils, giving to each, God, the world, and the devil what is his own; to God glory and dominion, to world vanity and pleasure; to the devils pride and envy. That the glory of God is to give to each what he deserves, Isaiah says, 42:8, "I will not give my glory to another," and 47:8, "I am, and there is none else besides me" and hence dominion is his. Also, Luke 2:14, "Glory to God in the highest; and on earth peace to men of good will," which show that the Angels distinguish between us and God, giving us peace, and God the glory. Thus the dominion is not divided among us, as Jesus says in Luke 22:26-27, "For which is greater, he that sitteth at table, or he that serveth? Is it not he that sitteth at table? But I am in the midst of you, as he that serveth."

Of the vanity and pleasure of this world Isaiah 5:18 says, "Woe to you that draw iniquity with cords of vanity, and sin as the rope of a cart." This "iniquity", namely pleasure, since it makes men unequal, causes the flesh to command and the spirit to obey, when it ought to be just the contrary. And therefore a little before in this chapter, verse 11, speaking of both [flesh and spirit, Isaiah] says, "Woe to you that rise up early in the morning to follow drunkenness, and to drink till the evening, to be inflamed with wine,." referring to pleasure, since by the heat of wine is meant lust. And the next verse 12 refers to vanity, "The harp, and the lyre, and the timbrel, and the pipe, and wine are in your feasts, and the work of the Lord you regard not, nor do you consider the works of his hands."

Of the devil's pride God says to the king of Tyre in Ezekiel 28:17-18, "And thy heart was lifted up with thy beauty, thou lost thy wisdom in thy beauty, I have cast thee to the ground: I have set thee before the face of kings, that they might behold thee. Thou hast defiled thy sanctuaries by the multitude of thy iniquities, etc." Here kings are called proud because they condemnably wish to reign in a worldly manner just as does Satan as ruler. Hence Job 41:25 says of the devil, "He beholdeth every high thing, he is king over all the children of pride."

Of the devil's envy it is said, Wisdom 2:23-24, "For God created man incorruptible, and to the image of his own likeness he made him. But by the envy of the devil, death came into the world: And they follow him that are of his side."

OUTLINE OF CHAPTER III

She will render him good, and not evil,
all the days of her life. (v. 12)

§1 Acrostic Letter Ghimel ג signifies the "full' or mutual "payment" that the Valiant Woman and Christ, her Husband should render each other
   1) That His payment is not evil, but even if it seems evil is really good
      1) Punishment for the remission of sins
      2) A test of virtue
      3) A manifestation of virtue through patience
      4) A manifestation of God's glory by a miracle.
      5) A manifestation of the sins of our forbearers
      6) A sign of an ancient curse
      7) To humble the proud
      8) Suffering for our redemption
      9) Proof of the truth of the Faith
   2) Or because it is simply good
      1) His good will toward her, predestination, which is unknown to us
      2) He has promised to do so; redemption, but not from all punishment
      3) She deserves it, glorification
      4) From the fullness of his generosity; a foretaste of beatitude
      5) From His matrimonial duty:
         1) Responsibility;
         2) The embrace of love;
         3) Fruitfulness in children;
         4) The needs of household & business administration;
         5) Kindness and intimacy of communication in the relief of weariness;
         6) The furnishing of clothing..

§2) Their mutual exchange of goods is perpetual
   1) Christ pays his wife, the Valiant Woman, the Church
      1) On the day of the Incarnation he has given the life of grace to souls
      2) On the day of the Resurrection he will give life to bodies
      3) One day of Eternity these gifts become perpetual
   2) The Valiant Woman during her life in time repays Christ her husband
      1) For the good of grace
         1) Advancement in virtue
         2) Thanksgiving
         3) Praise
      2) For what seems evil but is not:
         1) By humiliation
         2) By patience
         3) By her certitude of hope

CHAPTER III

She will render him good, and not evil, all the days of her life. (v. 12)

§ 1

GHIMEL ג . Ghimel is interpreted "plenitude" or "payment." When these two senses are combined Ghimel means the "full payment" that a man should render to the woman and vice versus the woman to the man. As it is said in Psalm 116:12-13, "What shall I render to the Lord, for all the things he hath rendered unto me? I will take the chalice of salvation; and I will call upon the name of the Lord." And this interpretation alludes to the sentiment of the following verse of the psalm ["Precious in the sight of the Lord is the death of his Saints"] that speaks of repayment.

The verse that heads this chapter, however, distinguishes two things, namely, the repayment of what is due and the perpetuity of this payment. The first is noted where it says "**She will render him good and not evil**" and the second "**all the days of her life.**"

If we consider the first two things that a man repays to a women of which one is good and the other is not, at least, to do her evil, then the two are distinguished in that "good" is the good as such, whether of nature, grace, or glory, while "not at least to do her evil" can refer to seven different cases:(1) If it refers to the evil of punishment but which is not really evil because the sufferer is being punished for the remission of his sins, as was the case with David when endured the suffering that Saul caused him [narrated at length in I Samuel 18:9 to 31-6], and that Absalom caused him [narrated in II Samuel 13:22-19:10] and that an Angel also caused him [when out of pride he attempted to take a census of his kingdom, II Samuel 24:1-17]. Or (2) if it is a test of virtue, as was Tobit's suffering and this is why the Angel Raphael said to him, as we read in Tobit 12:13, "And because thou wast acceptable to God, it was necessary that temptation should prove thee." Or (3) if it gives others an example of patience, as does blessed Job's. Or (4) if it manifests the glory of God, as does the suffering of the blind man in the account of John 9:1, "And Jesus passing by, saw a man, who was blind from his birth: And his disciples asked him: Rabbi, who hath sinned, this man, or his parents, that he should be born blind?", when Jesus said of him, "Neither hath this man sinned, nor his parents; but that the works of God should be made manifest in him." Or (5) if it manifests the sins of the forbears as did the sickness and death of David's son whom he bore from adultery with Bathsheba, as it is related in II Samuel 12:15-23. Or (6) if it is a sign of an ancient curse as are the pains we suffer as a sign of the curse on Adam's sin. (7) Or finally, suffering can also be to humble someone, as was the "sting" the Apostle Paul endured, of which he writes in II Corinthians 12:7-9, "And lest the greatness of the revelations should exalt me, there was given me a sting of my flesh, an angel of Satan, to buffet me. For which thing thrice I besought the Lord that it might depart from me. And he said to me: My grace is sufficient for thee; for power is made perfect in infirmity." (8) Suffering is for our redemption, just as was the passion of Jesus Christ [Matthew 26:36ff]. (9) It is also for the proving of the truth of faith, as was the passion of the martyrs and of those seven brothers of whom we read in II Maccabees 7:1-42; and later of Herod [Agrippa] who died consumed by worms, as is related in Acts 12:23. Thus a man renders good, not evil to his wife and she at the very least renders to him what is not evil.

First there are five ways that the Man [Christ] renders to his wife, the Valiant Woman [the Church] what is her due, thus he renders (a) some of what is due her from his good will toward to her; (b) some from what he has promised to do; (c) some from what she deserves; (d) some from the fullness of his generosity; (e) some from his matrimonial duty.

From his favor he renders her [the Church] the good of predestination, for it is by the good of creation that we exist, and also the good of grace by which we exist in goodness of which Psalm 110:3 says, "With thee is the principality in the day of thy strength, in the brightness of the Saints: from the womb before the day star I begot thee." In this verse "womb," means the generative power of the Father and the wisdom of the Son and of all the Saints who live in him in and his shining light. Hence Romans 1:4 says, "Who was predestinated the Son of God in power, according to the spirit of sanctification," that is, according to the Spirit as it sanctifies the Saints. For Romans 8:29-30 also says, "For whom he foreknew, he also predestinated to be made conformable to the image of his Son; that he might be the firstborn amongst many brethren. And whom he predestinated, them he also called. And whom he called, them he also justified. And whom he justified, them he also glorified." But in including in this good the fear of future risk he does not render his wife any evil, since no one is safe from possibly falling away from salvation as long as that one lives. Hence it says Revelation, 3:1, "Hold fast that which thou hast, that no man take thy crown," and in Ecclesiastes 9:1, "Yet man knoweth not whether he be worthy of love, or hatred," and in 8:10 of the same book, "I saw the wicked buried," that is, among the impious dead, "who also when they were yet living were in the holy place, and were praised in the city as men of just works," and in Jeremiah 18:9-10, "And I will suddenly speak of a nation and of a kingdom, to build up and plant it. If it shall do evil in my sight, that it obey not my voice: I will repent of the good that I have spoken to do unto it."

What he [Christ] renders his wife [the Church] because of his promise to her are the goods of redemption as Psalm 110:4-5 says, "The Lord hath sworn, and he will not repent: Thou art a priest for ever according to the order of Melchisedech. The Lord at thy right hand hath broken kings in the day of his wrath." I think that here it says "priest," because according to the rite of Melchisedech under the appearance of bread the body is offered as food, and under the appearance of wine it is offered as drink, while on the altar of the Cross the soul is offered as the price of redemption. The name "Melchisedech" here means "king of peace" or "king of justice" just as is says in Ephesians 2:14, "For he is our peace, who hath made both one, and breaking down the middle wall of partition, the enmities in his flesh," and in Hebrews 6:16-20, "For men swear by one greater than themselves, and an oath for confirmation is the end of all their controversy. Wherein God, intending more abundantly to shew to the heirs of the promise the immutability of his counsel, interposed an oath: That by two immutable things, in which it is impossible for God to lie we may have the strongest comfort, who have fled for refuge to hold fast the hope set before us. Which we have as an anchor of the soul, sure and firm, and which entereth in even within the veil; where the forerunner Jesus has entered for us, "made a high priest for ever according to the order of Melchisedech." Yet with this good the Man does not render the Woman the evil of punishment also, since that is due to the working of the sinful tendencies that may still remain even after the redemption mandated in baptism. And this is what is meant by the curse that Genesis 3:17-18 says the Lord left on the Sons of Israel that through them its lesson might be taught to others, "Cursed is the earth in thy work;

with labor and toil shalt thou eat thereof all the days of thy life. Thorns and thistles shall it bring forth to thee."

What the Man renders to the Woman because of her worthiness are the goods of glorification, but not the evil of the suffering through which she passes into glory. Of both these Luke 24:26 says, "Ought not Christ to have suffered these things, and so to enter into his glory?" and Romans 8:17-18 says, "And if sons, heirs also; heirs indeed of God, and joint heirs with Christ: yet so, if we suffer with him, that we may be also glorified with him. For I reckon that the sufferings of this time are not worthy to be compared with the glory to come, that shall be revealed in us," and Psalm 91:15 says, "I am with him in tribulation, I will deliver him, and I will glorify him," and II Corinthians 4:17 says, "For that which is at present momentary and light of our tribulation, worketh for us above measure exceedingly an eternal weight of glory."

What the Man renders to the Woman from the fullness of his generosity are goods that are only the foretaste of eternal goods, but not the evils of the necessary distractions of this life. Of the first of these Psalm 34:9 exclaims, "O taste, and see that the Lord is sweet: blessed is the man that hopeth in him" and I Peter 2:3 says, "If so you have tasted that the Lord is sweet." Concerning the evil that he does not render his wife, I Corinthians 5:6-7 says, "While we are in the body, we are absent from the Lord. For we walk by faith, and not by sight," as if to say, the needs of this body tend to draw us away form the foretaste of eternity. Also Wisdom 9:14-15 says, "The thoughts of mortal men are fearful, and our counsels uncertain. For the corruptible body is a load upon the soul, and the earthly habitation presseth down the mind that museth upon many things." Both of these possibilities, the good and the evil, are signified in Matthew 17:4 where Peter sees the transfigured Lord, because he first says, "Lord, it is good for us to be here: if thou wilt, let us make here three tabernacles, one for thee, and one for Moses, and one for Elias." but afterwards when it says in verse 6 "the disciples hearing that [the voice of God from the cloud] fell upon their face, and were very much afraid," it is evident that their bodily weakness prevailed.

What the Man renders the Woman from his matrimonial duty are six things:(1) responsibility; (2) the embrace of love; (3) fruitfulness in children; (4) the needs of administration; (5) kindness and intimacy of communication in the relief of weariness; (6) the furnishing of clothing.

Of the first, responsibility, in Genesis 3:16 God says to Eve, "Thou shalt be under thy husband's power, and he shall have dominion over thee," and I Corinthians 11:3, "The head of the woman is the man, " and "Let wives be subject to their husbands," and further on in verse 5-6 it also tells how, "After this manner heretofore the holy women also, who trusted in God, adorned themselves, being in subjection to their own husbands: As Sara obeyed Abraham, calling him lord: whose daughters you are, doing well, and not fearing any disturbance."

Of the second, the Husband's embrace of his Wife in love the Song of Songs 2:6:"His left hand is under my head, and his right hand shall embrace me" and in the same work, 1:1, "Let him kiss me with the kiss of his mouth." And this is what is meant in Genesis 24:67, where it says that Isaac took Rebecca "and brought her into the tent of Sara his mother, and took her to wife: and he loved her so much, that it moderated the sorrow which was occasioned by his mother's death." "Isaac" here is Christ and Rebecca is the Church or the faithful soul that the name "Rebecca" often signifies. The deceased "mother," however, is the Synagogue or Eve. The mother's "tent" is grace into which Christ leads the faithful soul or the Church and there finds her so loving that all the former grief of the ancient curse is tempered.

Third, the Husband renders his Wife fruitful in children, as Ephesians 5:25-27 says, "Husbands, love your wives, as Christ also loved the church, and delivered himself up for it, That he might sanctify it, cleansing it by the laver of water in the word of life: That he might present it to himself a glorious church, not having spot or wrinkle, or any; such thing; but that it should be holy, and without blemish," and in I Timothy 2:15, "Yet she shall be saved through childbearing." These "sons," however, are manly, meritorious works," and thus that advice goes on, " if she continue in faith, and love, and sanctification, with sobriety," which are the sons for whom Rachel in Genesis 30:1, implores her husband:"Give me children, otherwise I shall die."

Fourth as to the way the Husband entrusts the Woman with household administration it is said in Matthew 6:25-33, "Therefore I say to you, be not solicitous for your life, what you shall eat, nor for your body, what you shall put on. Is not the life more than the meat: and the body more than the raiment? Behold the birds of the air, for they neither sow, nor do they reap, nor gather into barns, and your heavenly Father feedeth them. Are not you of much more value than they? And which of you by taking thought, can add to his stature by one cubit? And for raiment why are you solicitous? Consider the lilies of the field, how they grow: they labor not, neither do they spin. But I say to you that not even Solomon in all his glory was arrayed as one of these. And if the grass of the field, which is today, and tomorrow is cast into the oven, God doth so clothe: how much more you, O ye of little faith? Be not solicitous therefore, saying, What shall we eat," that is, the animal necessities of this life, "or what shall we drink, or wherewith shall we be clothed? For after all these things do the heathens seek. For your Father knoweth that you have need of all these things. Seek ye therefore first the kingdom of God, and his justice, and all these things shall be added unto you." And in Psalm 37:25, " I have been young, and now am old; and I have not seen the just forsaken, nor his seed seeking bread" and II Corinthians 9:10-11 says, "And he that ministereth seed to the sower, will both give you bread to eat, and will multiply your seed, and increase the growth of the fruits of your justice: That being enriched in all things, you may abound unto all simplicity, which worketh through us thanksgiving to God."

Fifth, as to refreshment in intimate conversation between Husband and Wife it is written in Wisdom 8:16, "When I go into my house, I shall repose myself with her," that is with Wisdom who is Christ the Lord, "for her conversation hath no bitterness, nor her company any tediousness, but joy and gladness." Hence it is also the Wife who in the longing of the desire of her soul speaks to her spouse in the Song of Songs 2:14, "Shew me thy face, let thy voice sound in my ears: for thy voice is sweet, and thy face comely." and similarly in Psalm 45:3, "Thou art beautiful above the sons of men; grace is poured abroad in thy lips" and in I Samuel 3:10, "Speak, Lord, for thy servant heareth" and Luke 24:32 of the disciples on the way to Emmaus it is related, "And they said one to the other: Was not our heart burning within us, whilst he spoke in this way, and opened to us the Scriptures?"

Sixth it says in Revelation 21:2 "And I John saw the holy city, the new Jerusalem, coming down out of heaven from God, prepared as a bride adorned for her husband." Thus the Valiant Woman is adorned twofold, in the brilliance of her vestments, through which is meant the adornment of her virtues, and in precious jewels, which are a gift from her Husband. Of the first of these Psalm 45:10 says, "The queen stood on thy right hand, in gilded clothing; surrounded with variety," and so forth, and I Timothy 2:9-10 says, "In like manner women also in decent apparel: adorning themselves with modesty and sobriety, not with plaited hair, or gold, or pearls, or costly attire, But as it becometh women professing godliness, with good works." The gifts Christ gives to the Church are the precious Sacrament of his Body and Blood as it is related in Matthew 26:26-29; Mark 14:22-25; Luke 22:15-20 and in verse 19 of the latter citation, "Do this for a commemoration of me," and in I Corinthians 11:26 Jesus says, "For as often as you shall eat this bread, and drink the chalice, you shall show the death of the Lord, until he come."

Along with these six goods the Man Christ never renders the evil of absence to his wife, the Church. For he is always available to her for three purposes, namely, that she will more ardently desires his goodness, more diligently seek it, and more carefully preserve it. And of this absence Jesus in John 16:16 says, "A little while, and now you shall not see me; and again a little while, and you shall see me, because I go to the Father." This is also signified by the way Christ appeared after his Resurrection as a stranger to the women [John 20:14-19] and to his disciples [Luke 24:13-35]. The bride in Song of Songs 5:6 says, "I opened the bolt of my door to my beloved: but he had turned aside, and was gone." The "bolt of the door" stands for the consent of her will by which the Bride opens the door to the Lord, but the door of will is sometimes opened by the Bride, yet Christ deliberately hides Himself like a stranger and pretends to travel on and reject her embrace. He passes out of sight because the eyes of the Bride are kept shut and fail to recognize Him.

§ 2

What follows is:"**all the days of her life**," in which is noted the perseverance of this rendering [of good and not evil]. For three are the days in which the Valiant Woman, the Church, does good, not evil, to Christ, her husband.

The first is the day of the incarnation and this has a morning and evening because each day the sun rises and sets as it is says in Ecclesiastes 1:5 ["The sun riseth, and goeth down."]

The second day is the day of the Resurrection of which Psalm 118:24 sings:"This is the day which the Lord hath made: let us be glad and rejoice therein" and this day has a morning but not an evening.

The third day is the day of eternity of which it is said in Psalm 84:11, "For better is one day in thy courts above thousands." Of these three days taken together Hosea 6:3 says, "He will revive us after two days: on the third day he will raise us up, and we shall live in his sight." For in the first day he gives life to souls, on the second day he gives life to bodies, and on third day he will raise us up body and soul to be with him so that in the vision of him we will have eternal life.

Similarly life is threefold... | The life of grace
The life of resurrection
The life of eternity

And these lives and these days are lived in common by the Woman, the Church, and Christ, her Man.

Of the first life [of grace] Galatians 2:20 says, "And I live, now not I; but Christ liveth in me."

Of the second life [of resurrection] John 5:28-29 says, "Wonder not at this; for the hour cometh, wherein all that are in the graves shall hear the voice of the Son of God. And they that have done good things shall come forth unto the resurrection of life." Of the third life [of eternity], Psalm 36:10 says, "For with thee, [Lord], is the fountain of life; and in thy light we shall see light." The first life is in the Valiant Woman along with the weariness of venial sin; the second begins with the death of her body from which she will rise; and the third life flourishes with the full health of both former lives.

Since we have expounded this chapter truly as it speaks of the way a man renders good and not evil to his wife, let us also interpret it as regards the way the Valiant Woman conversely renders good, and not evil, to Christ, her Husband, for in that way also it is explained by the Church Fathers. It must be noted therefore, as has already been said, that the Wife has from the Husband, not the evil of suffering but the good of grace. In return for this first benefit she renders to him advancement, thanks, and praise; but for the second she endures humiliation, patience, and the certitude of hope.

Of advancement the Apostle says in I Corinthians 15:10, "By the grace of God, I am what I am; and his grace in me hath not been void, but I have labored more abundantly than all they: yet not I, but the grace of God with me," and in II Corinthians 6:1 again says, "And we helping do exhort you, that you receive not the grace of God in vain." The same is says also in II Timothy 1:6, "For which cause I admonish thee, that thou stir up the grace of God which is in thee" and in Hebrews 12:15, "Lest any man be wanting to the grace of God."

Of thanksgiving the Apostle in I Thessalonians 5:18 says, "In all things give thanks," and Ecclesiastes 1:7 says, "Unto the place from whence the rivers come, they return, to flow again." For waters of grace are flowing from God and they return to him through thanksgiving.

Of praise Psalm 49:23 says, "The sacrifice of praise shall glorify me: and there is the way by which I will shew him the salvation of God," and Hosea 14:3 says, "Take away all iniquity, and receive the good: and we will render the calves of our lips," for the "calves of the lips" are the jubilation of lively praises of God.

Or all three together Isaiah 51:3 says, "Joy and gladness shall be found therein [in Sion] thanksgiving, and the voice of praise." Joy and gladness pertain to advancement in grace, while the two others [thanksgiving and praise] are given their proper names in the biblical citation.

Of the humiliation as a troubling evil that the Valiant Woman, the Church, does not cause her husband, Christ, Jeremiah says, 31:18-19, "Thou hast chastised me, and I was instructed, as a young bullock unaccustomed to the yoke. Convert me, and I shall be converted, for thou art the Lord my God. For after thou didst convert me, I did penance: and after thou didst shew unto me, I struck my thigh," and Lamentations 3:1 says, "I am the man that see my poverty by the rod of his indignation," as if to say "The rod of his wrath, that is, of punishment not of death, makes me recognize my poverty."

Of patience Hebrews 10:36, "For patience is necessary for you; that, doing the will of God, you may receive the promise," and Lamentations 3:26 says, "It is good to wait with silence", that is, with patience, "for the salvation of God."

Of the certitude of hope Jesus in Matthew 5:11-12 says, "Blessed are ye when they," that is men, "shall revile you, and persecute you, and speak all that is evil against you, untruly, for my sake: Be glad and rejoice, for your reward," that is, the hope of mercy, "is very great in heaven," and Jeremiah 31:16-17 says, "Thus saith the Lord: Let thy voice cease from weeping, and thy eyes from tears: for there is a reward for thy work, saith the Lord: and they shall return out of the land of the enemy. And here is hope for thy last end, saith the

Lord:and the children shall return to their own borders." And this is what St. Gregory the Great says, "The thought of the reward, weakness, the force of the whip," and further on, "The higher rises the hope in God, the stronger one strives to reach him." What follows, namely "all the days of your life," is not changed by the foregoing exposition.

OUTLINE OF CHAPTER IV

She hath sought wool and flax,
and hath wrought by the counsel of her hands. (v. 13)

§ 1) Acrostic Letter Daleth ד signifies "door," "poverty, or "table" and indicates that the Valiant Woman seeks out the materials her family needs.
   1) They need wool and flax for clothing.
      1) What is wool? It is produced by shepherds
         1) It is sheared from Christ the Lamb in whose bosom she rests in heart & meditation
         2) Six kinds of wool of Christ's seamless tunic or warmth of charity:
            1) In origin
               1) We are in exile as Christ was born in Bethlehem
               2) In poverty as Christ was born in a manger
            2) In advancement in life, Christ's
               1) Meekness
               2) Humility in heart
            3) Exiting life
               1) Christ's obedience in suffering
               2) Christ's Death on the Cross
      2) What is flax? Produced by farmers from earth and made into white linen (virtue), it signifies the Saints
         1) Of the Old Testament:
            1) Moses the Lawgiver
               1) Meekness in ruling
               2) Zeal in punishing
            2) The Patriarchs
               1) Faith in words
               2) Hope in promises
            3) The Prophets
               1) Contemplation of Mysteries
                  1) God's throne of majesty and judgment is the Church Militant
                  2) The House of God is the Church Triumphant
                  3) Seraphim and Saints:
                     1) They are aflame with the fire of charity
                     2) They have six wings in pairs:
                        1) To fly to God in intellectual light
                        2) To fly to God by fervor of desire
                        3) To cover their feet of piety and good example
               2) Condemnation of vices
         2) New Testament; kinds of flax
            1) Apostles
               1) Works of supererogation
               2) Preaching

2) Martyrs
   1) Constancy in faith
   2) Mortification of flesh
3) Doctors
   1) Meditation on Scriptures
   2) Pastoral Care
4) Confessors
   1) Penitence
   2) Long suffering hope
5) Virgins
   1) Chastity
   2) Mortification of flesh
6) Widows
   1) Fidelity to husband
   2) Humility of dress
7) Faithful Married
   1) Mercy to the poor
   2) Governance of family

§2) The manner of the Valiant Woman's work
   1) Persistence of her work
      1) She is not idle because of the cold or weariness of this life,
      2) She is warm because she is clothed in hope
   2) Skill or counsel of her hands
      1) Taking counsel
         1) Because the task is difficult
         2) It cannot be done without foresight
      2) Two Hands; Right for neighbor; Left for herself but this left is not weak,
         1) Substance of hands
            1) Five fingers as instruments, three jointed for flexibility with a protective fingernail.
               1) Thumb: largest to war with senses, but short because it deals with
private matters: Honor your parents
                  1) First joint: reverence, as hiding form vanity of senses
                  2) Second joint: to receive discipline
                  3) Third to administer necessities
                  4) Fingernail: memory of labors our parents did for us and
               2) Second finger is longer: Obedience to superiors: work for a life time
                  1) First joint: Not seeking high places in world, abstinence
                  2) Second joint: Seeking humility; vigil
                  3) Third joint: Obeying at a nod; prayer
                  4) Fingernail: Not self-opinionated.
               3) Third finger as longest humbles shorter ones, humility contemplating God
                  1) First joint: Thinking self inferior to superiors, justice
                  2) Second joint: Thinking self inferior to equals; God's mercy
                  3) Third joint: Thinking oneself inferior to all; the Vision of God

4) Fingernail: One's emptiness; hope of reward, meditating Bible
   4) Fourth finger, shorter yet than thumb, is the society of those we love and foresight how we might err, how we might be purified
      1) First Joint: To will or reject same things as a friend does, with foresight
      2) Second Joint: Never to will any evil for a friend
      3) Third Joint: To work always for a friend's good
      4) Fingernail: love of virtue; confession of truth
   5) Fifth finger, still shorter, joins to thumb; loving enemies, we have more enemies than parents; its veins unite friends: confessions of sins
      1) First Joint: To forgive enemies & confess sins
      2) Second Joint: Greet kindly those who offend us, confess omissions
      3) Third Joint; Render them good for evil; confess laziness
      4) Fingernail: Remembering our own offenses against God
2) Skin
   1) White for innocent relations to each person:modesty; clean conscience
   2) Rosy for compassion for neighbor's faults: blush desires eternal things
   3) Bones: fortitude for bearing with feebleness of the infirm
   4) Muscles; sympathy with natural defects of neighbor
   5) Linkage of nerves & veins (charity & mercy);symbol of piety
3) Strength of hands:
   1) Ample strength in its members
   2) Supply of spirit (energy, warmth) coursing through the veins
3) Valiant Woman works with her own hands but not like hypocrites do.

CHAPTER IV

She hath sought wool and flax, and hath wrought by the counsel of her hands. (v. 13)

§ 1

DALETH ד. Daleth is interpreted "table," or "poor" or "door." And thus it has three meanings that the following verses express. First, the meaning "table" [*tabula*, account book] indicates that the Valiant Woman through the usefulness of what she earns is, as it were, the account book of her Husband, Christ, for their household in which he and her children escape the shipwreck of begging.

Hence further on in Proverbs 31:21 it says, "She shall not fear for her house in the cold of snow: for all her domestics are clothed with double garments."

Second Daleth taken in its sense of "poor' signifies the necessity of "seeking" and hence it is interpreted as "poor" since it is the poor who "seek" wool and flax [for clothing].

Third as "door" it signifies the possibility of gain, since a door is that through which one has access to the riches of a household. And thus Sirach 26:21 says, "As the sun when it riseth to the world in the high places of God, so is the beauty of a good wife for the ornament of her house."

In the verse that follows this acrostic letter two things are noted, first the material with which the woman works, second, that her work is "**wrought by the counsel of her hands**."

In the first of these two things are noted, namely, the way it which this material is sought:"**wrought by the counsel of her hands**", and what she seeks:"**wool and flax**." The way of seeking this material is twofold, namely by purchase and by work, for one buys wool and flax, but the wool is produced by raising sheep and the flax by farming. The former is referred to under another metaphor in Matthew 13:45-46, "Again the kingdom of heaven is like to a merchant seeking good pearls. Who when he had found one pearl of great price, went his way, and sold all that he had, and bought it." For in that text "pearl" means the same as "wool and flax" in this verse, namely, the beauty and honesty of virtue. And of both together it is said in II Samuel 12:3, "But the poor man had nothing at all but one little ewe lamb, which he had bought and nourished up, and which had grown up in his house together with his children, eating of his bread, and drinking of his cup, and sleeping in his bosom: and it was unto him as a daughter." For a poor person is like a woman who in seeking wool buys one little ewe lamb, that is, the humble Christ, at the price of all that pleases her in this life. Then afterwards nourishes it along with her children, that is with her intellect and will, by feeding it the food of action and contemplation and by letting it sleep in her bosom, so that it rests in her heart like a daughter, that is, as her very soul.

As to the working of the flax Isaiah 19:9 says, "They shall be confounded that wrought in flax, combing and weaving fine linen." Here linen signifies the dazzling white color of virtue and those who do such work in Egypt, that is, in this world where, [says Ecclesiastes 1:2], "All is vanity," because as the workers spin they are confused by the circumstances of their works and hence, as is customary, weave their deeds to gain human praise. And the explanation of all this is given in Exodus 9:31 where it is said [that during the ten plagues] because it was struck by hail "the flax was now boiled [ruined]." Here "hail" means the wrath of God which ruins all the pretended virtues of hypocrites, and "now boiled," because it is only in this time of growth that human rewards are sought. The Valiant Woman, however, does not seek flax [in this present world] but "in Jerusalem," that is, for the worship and honor of [the eternal] God.

Next it should be noted what "wool" and "flax" symbolize. Wool is sheared from a sheep, while "flax" grows from the earth, and then with much labor each is woven into cloth. The "sheep" is our Lord Jesus Christ of whom it is said, Isaiah 53:7, "He shall be dumb as a lamb before his shearer, and he shall not open his mouth." and John 1:29 says, "Behold the Lamb of God, behold him who taketh away the sin of the world." It is from that "sheep" that the woman shears six kinds of wool.

From Jesus' lowly birth the Valiant Woman understands two truths: first, recognition that we are in exile and secondly contempt for the world. For it was in exile that Christ was born, since although Bethlehem was his ancestral home town, yet as John 1:1 says, "He came unto his own, and his own received him not." Moreover Christ despised this world since he was not born of a queen but a poor woman, and not in a palace but in a stable. Nor was he clad in purple and fine linen, but in swaddling clothes, and he did not sleep in a cradle but in a manger, as Luke 2:7 relates, "And she brought forth her firstborn son, and wrapped him up in swaddling clothes, and laid him in a manger; because there was no room for them in the inn."

From Christ's growth in earthly life the woman takes two kinds of wool, namely, humility and meekness, as in Matthew 11:29 Jesus says, "Learn of me, because I am meek, and humble of heart: and you shall find rest to your souls."

From Christ's departure from earthly life she takes double wool, namely, the wool of obedience and the wool of patience. Of obedience Luke 22:42 says, "Not my will, but thine be done," while of patience I Peter 2:23 says, "Who, when he was reviled, did not revile: when he suffered, he threatened not." Of both these together Philippians 2:8 says, "He humbled himself, becoming obedient unto death, even to the death of the cross." And of that lamb's wool was made [what John 19:23] calls "the seamless tunic" of Christ by which the Church is clothed to retain the warmth of charity.

The flax that grows from the earth signifies the gleaming whiteness of human virtue and also signifies the Saints of both the Old and New Testaments from whose earth this flax grows. From [Moses], the Lawgiver, the woman accepts a twofold kind of flax, namely, meekness in ruling and zeal in punishing. Of the first it is said in Numbers 12:3, "For Moses was a man exceeding meek above all men that dwelt upon earth," and of the second Exodus 2:11-12 says, "In those days after Moses was grown up, he went out to his brethren, and saw their affliction and an Egyptian striking one of the Hebrews his brethren. And when he had looked about this way and that way, and saw no one there, he slew the Egyptian and hid him in the sand." "Hebrews" here means "transients" and signifies the Saints who by steps of meritorious deeds continually move toward the Promised Land. "Egyptians" signifies worldly men who strike the Saints and whom the Valiant Woman slays with "the sword of the Spirit," which, [as Hebrews 4:12 says,] is the word of God. Of both these kinds of flax, [virtue, and punishment of vice,] taken together II Samuel 23:8 relates, "David...[actually "Jesbaham" one of David's captains] was like the most tender little worm of the wood [who killed eight hundred men at one onset"], for a "worm" is very soft when touched and this signifies his meekness in governing, yet it stings when it touches and this signifies zeal in punishing.

Also a twofold flax is received from the patriarchs, namely, faith in words and hope in promises. Of the first Romans 4:3 says, "Abraham believed God, and it was reputed to him unto justice," and Hebrews 11:2 says, "For by this the ancients [the patriarchs] obtained a testimony."

Of the second kind of flax Romans 4:18 says, "[Abraham] against hope believed in hope," and further on in verses 20-21, "In the promise also of God he staggered not by distrust; but was strengthened in faith, giving glory to God: Most fully knowing, that whatsoever he has promised, he is able also to perform." Both these truths are the concern of the whole Chapter 11 of St. Paul's Epistle to the Hebrews.

From the prophets also is taken a twofold sort of flax, namely the contemplation of mysteries and the condemnation of vices. Of the first it is said in Isaiah 6:1, "I saw the Lord sitting upon a throne high and elevated and the house was filled by his majesty." Upon it stood the "seraphim" and so forth in what follows in that text. The "elevation" of God's throne is the exceeding majesty by which he judges the world. The "house" is the Church Triumphant from which shines forth the glory of God's majesty. His "throne" is the Church Militant which is upheld by what is under it, namely, the mirror of creation and also by the allegorical symbols of the Scriptures in which God is contemplated, as Romans 1:20 says, "For the invisible things of him, from the creation of the world, are clearly seen, being understood by the things that are made; his eternal power also, and divinity." The "seraphim" signify the Saints around God who burn with the fire of charity. The seraphim have six wings:two to fly to God, namely, the light of intelligence and the fervor of desire; two to cover and protect their faces, that is, contemplation, which is called "the face of God," because from their frequent insight into God and of God in themselves the light of God's face is signified and sealed on them. Hence they walk in the light of God and rejoice in his name all the day and exalt in his justice. Thus their faces shine as shone the face of Moses when he returned from the mountain, as it is related in Exodus 34:32-35 and following. The two other wings that protect them are the fervor of the spirit and the fragrance of God's face; and with these two they veil their "feet," that is, the deeds which they tread on the way of good morals, namely of examples to their neighbor and of piety in their attitude toward God. Of the second it is said in Sirach 48:1, "And Elias the prophet stood up as a fire, and his word burnt like a torch," namely, in the rejection and condemnation of vices.

The Saints of the New Testament are the apostles, martyrs, doctors, [confessors], virgins, widows, and the married faithful. From the apostles are derived a twofold flax, namely, of works of supererogation [doing more good than is required] and the exercise of preaching. Of the first in II Corinthians 12:14-15 the Apostle Paul says, "Behold now the third time I am ready to come to you; and I will not be burdensome unto you. For I seek not the things that are yours, but you. For neither ought the children to lay up for the parents, but the parents for the children. But I most gladly will spend and be spent myself for your souls," and in Acts 20:33-34 Paul says, "I have not coveted any man's silver, gold, or apparel, as you yourselves know: for such things as were needful for me and them that are with me, these hands have furnished." Also in I Samuel 12:2-3 Samuel says, "Having then conversed with you from my youth unto this day, behold here I am. Speak of me before the Lord, and before his anointed, whether I have taken any man's ox, or ass: If I have wronged any man, if I have oppressed any man, if I have taken a bribe at any man's hand: and I will despise it this day, and will restore it to you." Of the second kind of flax, namely preaching, Paul says in II Timothy 4:1-2, "I charge thee, before God and Jesus Christ, who shall judge the living and the dead, by his coming, and his kingdom. Preach the word: be instant in season, out of season: reprove, entreat, rebuke in all patience and doctrine."

From the martyrs, two kinds of linen are derived: constancy in faith and endurance in suffering. Of the first, constancy in faith, Romans 10:10 says, "For, with the heart, we believe unto justice; but, with the mouth, confession is made unto salvation," and Psalm 115:10 [Vulgate] says, "I have believed, therefore have I spoken," and in Matthew 10:32 Jesus says, "Every one therefore that shall confess me before men, I will also confess him before my Father." Of the second kind of linen, endurance of suffering, Hebrews 10:32-34 says, "Call to mind the former days, wherein, being illuminated, you endured a great fight of afflictions. And on the one hand indeed, by reproaches and tribulations, were made a gazingstock; and on the other, became companions of them that were used in such sort. For you both had compassion on them that were in bands, and took with joy the being stripped of your own goods, knowing that you have a better and a lasting substance," and Acts 27:24 relates [that angel of God said to the Apostle], "Fear not, Paul, thou must be brought before Caesar," and II Maccabees 6:19-20 relates how [Eleazer] "choosing rather a most glorious death than a hateful life, went forward voluntarily to the torment. And considering in what manner he was come to it, patiently bearing, he determined not to do any unlawful things for the love of life," and further on in verse 30, "Ready to die with the stripes, he groaned, and said: O Lord, who hast the holy knowledge, thou knowest manifestly that whereas I might be delivered from death, I suffer grievous pains in body: but in soul am well content to suffer these things because I fear thee."

From the doctors two kinds of flax are also taken, namely, meditation on the Scriptures and the solicitude of pastoral care. Of the first, meditation, Psalm 1:2 says, "His will is in the law of the Lord, and on his law he shall meditate day and night." And this is why the Lord commanded in the law that the law should be written down and fixed to the door-posts and even carried in the hand so that the Jews might meditate on yoke of the law. Thus Malachi 2:7 says, "For the lips of the priest shall keep knowledge, and they shall seek the law at his mouth: because he is the angel of the Lord of hosts." Of the second kind of flax, solicitude in pastoral care, Romans 12:8 says, "He that ruleth, with carefulness" meaning "Let that one rule," and the same passage further on in verse 11 says, "in carefulness not sloth," that is, you must not be slothful but careful. And this is also said in the Gospel According to John [21:15-19] where the Lord three times asks Peter whether he loves him more than do the other apostles, and when Peter replies, "Yes, I do," commissions him to feed his sheep. This is because a prelate ought to love God more than his own authority or his friends or even himself and should feed them by word and example and with the authority of the keys. The same is said in Acts 20:28, "Take heed to yourselves and to the whole flock, wherein the Holy Ghost hath placed you bishops, to rule the church of God, which he hath purchased with his own blood."

Of both meditation on the Scriptures and pastoral care taken together Sirach 44:5-6 says, "Such as by their skill sought out musical tunes, and published canticles of the scriptures. Rich men in virtue, studying beautifulness: living at peace in their house."

From the confessors also two kinds of flax are taken, namely the lamentation of penitence and the longsuffering expectation of the fulfillment of the promises. Of the first kind of flax, the lamentation of penance, Matthew 5:5 says, "Blessed are they that mourn: for they shall be comforted," and the Song of Songs 2:12 says, "The voice of the turtledove is heard in our land." And this is also what is meant in Joshua 15:19, where Axa, daughter of Caleb requests and receives, "Give me a blessing: thou hast given me a southern and dry land, give me also a land that is watered. And Caleb gave her the upper and the nether watery ground" which symbolizes a double lament: for the misery of her dwelling place and for the spread of her patrimony. Of the second sort of flax, the expectation of the promises, Genesis 49:18 says, "I will look for thy salvation, O Lord," and Hebrews 11:13 says, "All these died according to faith, not having received the promises, but beholding them afar off, and saluting them, and confessing that they are pilgrims and strangers on the earth."

From the virgins also are derived twofold kinds of flax, namely, the purity of chastity and the mortification of the flesh. Of the first, the purity of chastity, I Corinthians 7:34 says, "And the unmarried woman and the virgin thinketh on the things of the Lord, that she may be holy both in body and in spirit," and previously in verse 32 of the text [St. Paul] says, "He that is without a wife is solicitous for the things that belong to the Lord, how he may please God." The second kind of flax related to virgins is the mortification of the flesh and I Corinthians 9:27 says, "But I chastise my body, and bring it into subjection: lest perhaps, when I have preached to others, I myself should become a castaway." Again in Galatians 6:14 St. Paul says, "But God forbid that I should glory save in the cross of our Lord Jesus Christ; by whom the world is crucified to me, and I to the world," and in verse 17, "From henceforth let no man be troublesome to me; for I bear the marks of the Lord Jesus in my body."

From widows are taken two kinds of flax, namely, fidelity to their deceased husbands and the humility of their widows' weeds. Of the first, fidelity to their husbands, Luke 2:36-37 says of Anna, a prophetess, the daughter of Phanuel of the tribe of Asher; that she was "far advanced in years, and had lived with her husband seven years from her virginity. And she was a widow until fourscore and four years; who departed not from the temple, by fastings and prayers serving night and day." And the Apostle says of these [devout widows] in I Timothy 5:5, "But she that is a widow indeed, and desolate, let her trust in God, and continue in supplications and prayers night and day." Of the second kind of flax, humility, it is said in Judith 9:1 that Judith "went into her oratory: and putting on haircloth, laid ashes on her head: and falling down prostrate before the Lord, she cried to the Lord."

Of both of these kinds of flax taken together the Song of Songs 1:9 praises [the Beloved], "Thy cheeks are beautiful as the turtledove's," for it said that it is of nature of a turtledove never to mate a second time. Here also fidelity to marriage is signified by one cheek, while by the other cheek is signified the attainment of humility and maturity.

From the married faithful also two kinds of flax are taken, namely, mercy to the poor and governance of the family. Of the first sort, mercy to the poor, Jesus says in Matthew 5:7, "Blessed are the merciful: for they shall obtain mercy," and in 25:34, "Come, ye blessed of my Father, possess you the kingdom prepared for you from the foundation of the world." Of the second sort of flax, governance of the family, I Timothy 5:8 says, "But if any man have not care of his own, and especially of those of his house, he hath denied the faith, and is worse than an infidel." Sirach 1:1 speaks of "Simon the high priest, the son of Onias, who in his life propped up the house, and in his days fortified the temple," and Genesis 39:4 says, "Joseph found favor in the sight of his master, and ministered to him: and being set over all by him, he governed the house committed to him, and all things that were delivered to him."

§ 2

What follows [in the chapter text] is:"**And [she] hath wrought by the counsel of her hands,**" in which two things should be noted: the manner of the Valiant Woman's work and the "hands" by which she does this work. Concerning the first, the manner of her work, two things are to be noted: the persistence of her work indicated by the term "wrought," and its skillfulness indicated by the term "counsel."

Of the first, the persistence of her work, Ecclesiastes 9:10 says, "Whatsoever thy hand is able to do, do it earnestly: for neither work, nor reason, nor wisdom, nor knowledge shall be in the grave, whither thou art hastening." And in this comparison two kinds of persons are contrasted: the lazy and the idle. Of the first kind, the lazy, Proverbs 20:4 says, "Because of the cold the sluggard would not plough: he shall beg therefore in the summer, and it shall not be given him." Here by "cold" is meant the weariness of this life; through "summer" is to be understood the day of judgment when God will manifest in plain light the deliberations of hearts and by the warmth of each one's zeal render to each according to each one's works. Of the second kind of man, the idle, Matthew 20:6 says, "Why stand you here all the day idle?" and Proverbs 12:11 says, "He that pursueth idleness is very foolish."

Of both kinds together of lack of persistence in work Ecclesiastes 10:18 says, "By slothfulness a building shall be brought down, and through the weakness of hands, the roof of the house shall drop through." By "be brought down" is meant the hiding of the virtues which are acquired by persistent effort but which dissolve into slothfulness. By "the weakness of hands" is meant idleness; by "dissolve" is meant temptations to lust; by "roof" is meant charity, and by "house" is meant frequent activity.

The "counsel of her hands" through which is understood skillfulness or prudence, is called in Romans 12:1, "Your reasonable service [of God]." And it should be noted that two things are required to take counsel about a decision, namely, that it is difficult and that it is possible to act otherwise. And hence the Valiant Woman knows that they are blameworthy who without taking counsel from the Lord attempt to weave a "web," as Isaiah 30:1 declares, "Woe to you, apostate children, saith the Lord, that you would take counsel, and not of me: and would begin a web, and not by my spirit." Isaiah 19:9 also says, "They shall be confounded that wrought in flax, combing and weaving fine linen." And therefore without counsel wool and flax should not be woven, since the wise man says in Sirach 32:24, "My son, do thou nothing without counsel, and thou shalt not repent when thou hast done."

What instruments the Valiant Woman uses to do her work is indicated by the phrase "wrought by...her hands" in which is noted two things, namely, her two hands, and that they are The Valiant Woman's hands. Her hands, of course, are two, one that works for herself, the other that works for her neighbor, that is, her care of her family and her love of her neighbor. Again, for the shapeliness of her hands two things are required, first that they are long hands proportionate to her bodily size and second that they are of due color, that is, that they are white hands but with a rosy flush. To the substance of a human hand are required five things; namely, five fingers, skin, bones, muscle, and a due linkage of nerves and veins. For the strength of the hand two things are also required; namely ample strength in its members and a supply of spirit [energy] coursing through the veins. And all these qualities are found in both hands of the Valiant Woman; but in the hand that stands for the love of neighbor its length signifies love of all in the neighbor that is good; while the "whiteness" of the hand stands for innocence in relation to every person. The "rosy flush is compassion" for all the faults of the neighbor; but the "bones" stands for fortitude in bearing with the feebleness of the infirm; and the "muscles" stand for sympathy for the natural defects of the neighbor. The network of the "nerves" is a symbol of piety and in the "veins" is the warmth of divine charity. The spirituality of the Valiant Woman's hands is the energy that flows through all the joints, giving them vigorous life.

The Valiant Woman's right hand has five fingers and each finger requires fingernails for its protection and also needs three joints so as to be flexible for its work. The first finger is honor to parents and it has the first joint to show reverence, the second joint to receive discipline, the third to administer necessaries when necessary; and its fingernail is the memory of the labors our parents have sustained for us.

Its second finger is obedience to superiors, and has three joint of which the first is not to seek willingly what are considered the high places in this world; the second joint is to have of one's own will the desire for humility; and the third is being quick not to await orders but simply to obey at a nod. The fingernail protecting and preparing this whole finger signifies that one is not self-opinionated.

The third finger is humility before all others and has three joints for its bending, of which the first is to think one self inferior to one's superiors; second to subordinate oneself to one's equals, and third to subordinate oneself even to one's inferiors. The fingernail protecting this finger is the sense of our own emptiness.

The fourth finger is the society of those we love and it has three joints: first to will and reject the same things that a friend does; second, never to will any evil for a friend; third unceasingly to work for a friend's good. The fingernail protecting this finger is the love of virtue.

The fifth finger is the love of enemies and also has three joints. The first is to forgive injuries; the second is to greet those who offend one; the third is to render good for evil. The fingernail protecting this finger is the remembrance of injuries against God we have worked by sinning.

The first of these fingers is largest and most grasping but shortest, since it is extended only to be joined to the rest of our hand. The second is longer, yet still small. The third is the longest because extending beyond the other fingers it humbles them. The fourth is again shorter than the third and has the bodily vein that unites friends. The fifth is the least as it joins with the others yet is longer than the thumb, because we have more enemies than parents. Of the thumb it is said in Exodus 20:12, "Honor thy father and thy mother, that thou mayest be longlived upon the land which the Lord thy God will give thee." Of the second finger is said in Hebrews 13:7, "Remember your prelates who have spoken the word of God to you; whose faith follow, considering the end of their conversation." Of the third finger it is said Philippians 2:3, "Let nothing be done through contention, neither by vainglory: but in humility, let each esteem others better than themselves," and in I Peter 2:13, "Be ye subject therefore to every human creature for God's sake: whether it be to the king as excelling." Of the fourth finger it is said in Proverbs 27:9-10, "Ointment and perfumes rejoice the heart:and the good counsels of a friend are sweet to the soul. Thy own friend and thy father's friend forsake not." Of the fifth finger Jesus says in Matthew 5:44, "But I say to you, Love your enemies," and [St. Paul] says in Romans 12:20, "But if thy enemy be hungry, give him to eat; if he thirst, give him to drink."

The left hand is its own guardian and by it the Valiant Woman cares for herself. It has bones for strength and muscles that prevent any weakness. Its binding "nerves" are for distinguishing objects and its "veins" through which pulse spirit [energy] are the constant dominion of reason over sensuality and around which is spread the "skin" of modesty so as to be able to "handle" things, and this skin is colored with the whiteness of a clean conscience and the blush of the desire for eternal goods. It has five fingers with their joints and their fingernails.

The first finger of the Valiant Woman's left hand is her custody of the senses and it has three joints, namely, her hiding of vanity from the ears and eyes, of wantonness from smell and taste and of lingering over the softness of touch. And this finger is guarded by a fingernail signifying self-contempt.

The second finger is the exercise of work and its three joints are abstinence, vigil, and prayer. Its nail is the hope of reward.

The third finger is the contemplation of the future. The three joints by which it is bent are the consideration of justice in punishments, meditation on the mercy of the recompense, and vision of God. The whole finger is protected by a nail which is the understanding of the Scriptures.

The fourth finger is careful foresight of future actions and it has three joints, namely, that we should foreseen in what and how we might err and in what we might be purified. It has a protecting nail, namely, prudence that wisely chooses the better from the less good.

The fifth finger is the confession of sins and the three joints are confession of transgressions, omissions, and laziness. The protecting fingernail is confession of the truth itself.

The first finger [or thumb] of a hand is the largest because of the continual war [of the will] with the senses, but it is short because it concerns private matters. The second is longer and concerns our life in its whole length. The third, or longest, is the contemplation of Divinity. The fourth finger is shorter, yet longer than the first. Finally, the fifth is still shorter because it guards itself carefully so as to find the few sins that must be still confessed. Of the first it is said in Psalm 119:37, "Turn away my eyes that they may not behold vanity: quicken me in thy way" and Job 31:1, "I made a covenant with my eyes, that I would not so much as think upon a virgin." Of the second it is said in Daniel 9:3, "And I set my face to the Lord my God, to pray and make supplication with fasting, and sackcloth, and ashes" and Isaiah 21:5 says, "Prepare the table, behold in the watchtower them that eat and drink: arise, ye princes, take up the shield." A "table" is prepared when the mind is fixed on eternal truth. The "watchtower" is the height of intellectual contemplation. "Those that eat and drink" are the Saints rejoicing in the pasture of fulfillment. Of the fourth the Apostle says II Corinthians 8:21, "For we forecast what may be good not only before God, but also before men." Of the fifth it is said in Joshua 7:19, "My son, give glory to the Lord God of Israel, and confess, and tell me what thou hast done, hide it not."

And note that neither of these hands is a "left" one [in the sense of awkward]! Hence the Valiant Woman is represented by Aod of whom it is written in Judges 3:15 that he "used the left hand as well as the right," and hence it is said in the Song of Songs 5:14, "His hands are turned and as of gold, full of hyacinths." They are "turned" because of their flexibility in working, "gold" because of their intention of piety, and "full of hyacinths" because of the radiance of virtue according to the distinction of their joints.

The text [for this chapter] concludes with the phrase "**her hands**" in which it is noted that it is by her own hands and not those of another that the Valiant Woman works and this contrasts with those who do wonders through the hands of others yet who are unwilling to lift a hand of their own to relieve another's burden. Such persons do indeed commit themselves to praying to the Saints, but make themselves unworthy in their prayers by their depraved morals, as did Pharaoh in Exodus 8:28 and 9:28 when he asked the sons of Israel to pray for him often; and as did Antiochus, of whom it is said in II Maccabees 9:13, "Then this wicked man prayed to the Lord, of whom he was not like to obtain mercy." These are those enter on to the way of the Saints but not from its beginning, as it said of Balaam in Numbers 23:10, "Let my soul die the death of the just, and my last end be like to them."

OUTLINE OF CHAPTER V

She is like the merchant's ship,
she bringeth her bread from afar. (v. 14)

§1) Acrostic Letter He ה means "undertaking life" and the Valiant Woman is a merchant ship that is complete for this work:
    1) A ship has:
        1) A narrow prow is humiliation at how we were born into the world in original sin
        2) A narrow stern is the end of life and is narrowed by fear of death
        3) The broad sides of the boat where the rafts hang is the collection of the cardinal virtues, prudence, temperance, justice, and fortitude
        4) In the middle the belly or hold are the natural affections, namely, hope, despair, and joy
            1) The lookout is purgation of confession.
            2) The storeroom is the reminder through meditation
            3) The upper deck is confidence of security; the broad deck for walking is contemplation
            4) The cabin is the secrets of confession
            5) A suite for nobles
            6) Sailors' quarters
        5) Side boards: the powers of acting that God gives to body & soul and preserved with pitch of charity
            1) The five external senses
            2) The power of speech,
            3) Reason
            4) Memory
            5) Will
        6) The helm over the stern has two guy-wires; turned back by key of distinction of opinions
        7) The foremast is the height of faith; the rear mast is understanding
        8) The ropes spreading the sails are reason and study of faith known by the rings of metaphors and figures
        9) The cables draw the guy-wires
        10) The rudders are: authorities and revelations
        11) The sails hang from the masts: On the back masts are two guide-wires, namely:
            1) Counsel controls the ship in heavy seas
            2) Science controls it in smoother water
        12) The anchor by which it stops or sits immobile in the harbor.
            1) The anchor is hope holding the secret of beatitude certified by
            2) The grace and mercy of God,
            3) One's merits
            4) Christ passion
            5) The prayers of the Saints

2) Four kinds of ship
   1) Traveling ships: penance
      1) Its wood is the Cross
      2) The sea is the waves of life
   2) War ships are patience in temptations and in the perils one must fight.
      1) Perils at sea
         1) First peril is from pirates who are devils and the fires of lust and of hell
         2) Second peril is that the ship runs against a promontory of: ambition
         3) Third peril is Charybdis sucking down to hell through avarice
         4) Fourth peril is Syrtes, high sand dunes that are wrath to be met with 1) Patience in evil
              2) Prayer for one's enemies;
         5) Fifth peril is the Symplogades. colliding stones mocking and in sults
         6) Sixth peril is raging of the sea: the carnal appetites
         7) Seventh Peril is Scylla sharp rocks: empty popular glory
         8) Eighth peril is the song of the Sirens: the pleasures of this world
         9) Ninth peril is the conflict of warriors a sea; the persecution of the Saints
      2) Peril in the air:
         1) The tempest, which is the force of pride through impiety
            1) Cold dry, northern; the force of pride
            2) A mixed wind: cold through impiety and dry through cruelty and violent arrogant domination, yet warm from ambition
         2) No wind at all; laziness
      3) Peril in port; a divided port: fraud and deceit
      4) Against all these perils the protection is patience.
   3) A fishing boat is the boat of the ages
      1) Its nets are preaching the word of God
         1) Lowered on left side is preaching for money
         2) Lowered on right is preaching for souls without temporal gain
   4) Merchant ships make sales by bargaining.
      1) Ships that carry and sell temporal goods and finally sink
      2) Ships that carry and sell eternal goods and sail by fortitude like the Valiant Woman
         1) The sea is the instable flood and bitterness of this life.
         2) The shore is God's grace where the Saints engage in spiritual bargaining.
         3) The ships meet every three years, the circling of the Sun of Justice, Christ
         4) They exchange
            1) The gold of charity
            2) The silver of knowledge
            3) Ivory of chastity of mind and body
            4) Monkeys: the imitation of examples of the Saints
            5) Peacocks: the beauty of the holy virtues.
   5) No partnership with the wicked.

§2. The Valiant Woman brings bread from a distance
   1) Four kinds of distance
      1) Depth is hell that must be feared
      2) Height is charity
      3) Width is understanding beyond reason through revelation in Scripture
      4) Length is God's transcendence of his creation
   2) Four kinds of bread:
      1) Bread of sorrow: penitence
      2) Bread of consolation by hope of eternal beatitude
      3) Bread of life and understanding
      4) The Eucharist

CHAPTER V

She is like the merchant's ship, she bringeth her bread from afar. (v. 14)

§ 1

HE ה. HE is interpreted "life" or "undertaking" and these senses ought to be taken jointly as "the undertaking of life" so that they allude to the following sentence, because the "bread" taken from afar is the Valiant Woman's life, as it says in John 6:33, "For the bread of God is that which cometh down from heaven, and giveth life to the world" and further on in verse 52, "If any man eat of this bread, he shall live for ever."

Next "**She is like the merchant's ship, she bringeth her bread from afar.**" Here note three things: first, what a "ship" is; second, whose ship it is; third, what this ship is for, since it goes on to say that it "bringeth her bread from afar." Concerning the first it is be noted that here the Valiant Woman is compared to a ship in that everything is found literally in a great ship that is said of her morally.

Now a ship first has outside boards which are held together by strong nails before the prow, after the stern and also on the two sides and on the keel, as it is said in the verses:

> The prow comes first, next the ship and last its stern,
> Left and right the side-boards call, the belly the keel.

A ship also has a the helm over the stern to which are attached two guy-wires, one on the right one on the left, and it has a hold, a storeroom, a deck, a cabin, a suite for nobles, and a sailors' quarters. It also has a mast in front and behind, ropes that spread the sails, and cables that draw the guy-wires and the sails over the masts and it also has anchors by which it stops and sometimes sits immobilized in harbor. And all these parts exist mystically in the Valiant Woman. For the "boards" which are the foundation structures of the ship are the powers of acting which God gives to the body and the soul; namely, the five external senses, and the powers of speech, reason, memory, and will, to which boards are fixed as the planks of behavior by the "nails" of moral doctrine, as it says in Ecclesiastes 12:11, "The words of the wise are as goads, and as nails deeply fastened in, which by the counsel of masters are given from one shepherd." They are preserved with the pitch of charity, on the inside by the love of God and on the outside by love of neighbor, as it says of the Ark in Genesis 6:14, "Thou shalt pitch it within and without." This signifies the external protection of [the soul] by the covering of the most agreeable gentleness so that it more easily washes over the waves of this life.

The prow of the ship is the humiliations which arise from the consideration of how we are born into this world, for as the Apostles says in I Timothy 6:7, "For we brought nothing into this world:and certainly we can carry nothing out," and Job 14:1-2 says, "Man born of a woman, living for a short time, is filled with many miseries. Who cometh forth like a flower, and is destroyed, and fleeth as a shadow, and never continueth in the same state." Hence this prow of the ship is narrow because many are the confusions and humiliations of our origins by which are lives are limited, as is best expressed in Wisdom 7:1-4 where it says, "I myself also am a mortal man, like all others, and of the race of him (Adam from whom we derived original sin) that was first made of the earth, and in the womb of my mother I was fashioned to be flesh. In the time of ten months," (through which is noted our frailty because we are partially flesh). "I was compacted in blood, of the seed of man, and the pleasure of sleep concurring," (by which is meant the urgency of sexual desire and the heat of its fire). "And being born I drew in the common air" (which means the morality and brevity of life, since without breathing air we cannot live) "and fell upon the earth" which indicates that we are powerless to help ourselves), "that is made alike, and the first voice which I uttered was crying (which means the struggle in this world of misery) as all others do. I was nursed in swaddling clothes, and with great cares," (which means the warmth of our infirmity), yet in the following verse 5 it says, "For none of the kings had any other beginning of birth."

The stern of the ship is the last part of life, namely the thought of death and is narrowed by fear, Sirach 41:1-2, "O death, how bitter is the remembrance of thee" (to an unjust "man that hath peace in his possessions! To a man that is at rest, and whose ways are prosperous in all things, and that is yet able to take meat!" And this is also what is meant in Acts 27:41, "The forepart [of the ship] indeed, sticking fast, remained unmovable: but the hinder part was broken up by the violence of the sea," because when a man believes he is in the prime of life then by the fear of sickness he is dissolved in death.

The sides of the boat [where the rafts hang] is the collection of the cardinal virtues of prudence, temperance, justice, and fortitude listed in Wisdom, 8:7, "And if a man love justice: her labors have great virtues; for she teacheth temperance, and prudence, and justice, and fortitude, which are such things as men can have nothing more profitable in life."

The belly or hold of the ship is the natural affections, namely, hope, despair, and joy. The lookout of the ship is the purgation of confession; the storeroom is the reminder through meditation; the cabin the secrets of conscience; the upper deck the confidence of security; the broad deck for walking is the passing of contemplation; the foremast is the height of faith; the rear mast is understanding, since in divine matters understanding follows faith. The ropes that spread the sails are wonder at the ultimate truths of faith which are known, as it were, through certain rings of metaphors and figures. The rudders signify authorities and revelations, since as St. Augustine says, "What we believe ought to be based on authority." On the mast, which is understanding, are the ropes of reason by which the sails are connected to the mast through the rings and clasps of study and reading, and these sails are spread by the winds of disputation and teaching. On the back mast are two guy-wires of counsel and science of which one, namely counsel, controls the ship in heavy seas and the other, namely, science controls the ship in smoother water, which according to St. Augustine, "teaches one to converse well in the midst of a depraved and perverse nation." Of these guy-wires [Vulgate, *gubernacula*] it is said in Proverbs 1:5, "A wise man shall hear and shall be wiser: and he that understandeth, shall possess governments." These guy-wires are turned and turned back by the key of the distinction of opinions. Hence Solomon, Proverbs 23:34, as if rebuking a pilot, says, "And thou shalt be as one sleeping in the midst of the sea, and as a pilot fast asleep, when the stern is lost." The anchor of this ship is hope of which it is said in Hebrews 6:18-19, "That by two immutable things, in which it is impossible for God to lie, we may have the strongest comfort, who have fled for refuge to hold fast the hope set before us. Which we have as an anchor of the soul, sure and firm, and which entereth in even within the veil," that is, even to the veiled secret of beatitude. And it is noted in Acts 27:29 ["Then fearing lest we should fall upon rough places, they cast four anchors out of the stern, and wished for the day"] that those who sailed with St. Paul cast out four anchors through which can be understood the four certitudes of hope based on (a) the grace and mercy of God, (b) one's merits, (c) the patronage of Christ's passion, and (d) the prayers of the Saints, because by these hope is certified.

Next by "merchant" [Vulgate, *institor,* broker or dealer] in the text, is meant the ship's owner, for the Gloss says that "A merchant is called a dealer because he firmly insists on his bargaining," and it should noted that ships are of four kinds, traveling ships, war ships, fishing ships, and merchant ships.

A traveling ship signifies penance in which passage is made through the sea of this world, and of this Wisdom 14:5 speaks, "But that the works of thy wisdom might not be idle: therefore men also trust their lives even to a little wood, and passing over the sea by ship are saved." The "little wood" of penance is the cross of Christ to which penitents are configured. The "sea" is the floods of this evil world from which only penitents can survive. Matthew 9:1 says, "And entering into a boat, Jesus passed over the water and came into his own city." This must be referred, however, not to Jesus himself, since he never sinned, but to his members; for the Lord left this penitence to his own followers and arrived at the heavenly Jerusalem, his own city. This "boat" is also signified by the Ark in which righteous Noah was saved along with his family from the wrath of God. As II Peter 2:5 says, "God spared not the original world, but preserved Noah, the eighth person, the preacher of justice," that is, of penitence; and Wisdom 14:6-7 says, "And from the beginning also when the proud giants perished, the hope of the world fleeing to a vessel, which was governed by thy hand, left to the world seed of generation. For blessed is the wood, by which justice cometh." The "proud giants" are the great sinners who have much earthly influence. For the word "giant" is from Greek *ge* which in Latin means "earth," and these great sinners have much material substance. The "seed of generations" are the penitents who leave to the ages the seed of their spiritual rebirth which by the hand of God is governed in floods of the temptation suffered in this world, since Isaiah 1:9 says, "Except the Lord of hosts had left us seed, we had been as Sodom, and we should have been like to Gomorrha."

A "war ship" is patience in the temptations and tribulations that all suffer who wish to live piously in Christ, as the Apostles says, II Timothy 3:12, "And all that will live godly in Christ Jesus, shall suffer persecution." And note that there are five perils at sea which one must fight.

The first peril is from pirates who are named from Greek *pur* that is "fire" and "raft," because they throw fire on a raft and are carried on rafts and they signify the demons who carry with them the fire of hell and throw the fire of lust on us, as it says in Ephesians 6:12, "For our wrestling is not against flesh and blood; but against principalities and power, against the rulers of the world of this darkness, against the spirits of wickedness in the high places," that is, on the side of the heavenly powers against the spiritual wickedness of the devil.

The second peril is that the ship runs against a reef, called [in Latin] *acroceramina* from the Greek *akros* that means "mountain" and *keras* that means "horn" and *amnis* "water," because the mountains thrust into the sea and sometimes a ship runs against them and is broken up, and these symbolize worldly ambitions which sink the sailors, as is said in Psalm 107:26, "They [the sailors] mount up to the heavens, and they go down to the depths: their soul pined away with evils." Through ambition they ascend to the heavens and there strike the horned mountains, that is, strike against the dignity of those who wear "horns" or helmets [that is the nobility] and they go down to the depths of hell where their souls waste away forever.

The third peril is Charybdis. which is absorption into the jaws of the sea which is called, as it were, "the sucking down of the keel" [Latin *carina abdens*], which signifies avarice through which the ship of life is sucked down. From which can be understood what is said in Exodus 15:5, "They sunk to the bottom like a stone," and further on in verse 10, "The sea covered them: they sunk as lead in the mighty waters."

The fourth peril is Syrtes for *syrtes* are certain high sand dunes by which a ship is battered and they signify wrath, since in Proverbs 37:3 Solomon says, "A stone is heavy, and sand weighty: but the anger of a fool is heavier than them both." Concerning this peril Acts 27:17 says that those sailing with Paul were "undergirding the ship, and fearing lest they should fall into the quicksands." To "undergird a ship" signifies to arm oneself with patience against the injuries one suffers. One is thus armed through equanimity, endurance of evil, and prayer said for one's enemies; with these as with a sort of belt a ship is bound lest its own joints be loosened through such injuries.

The fifth peril is the running between the Symplegades which are moveable stones in the sea named from Greek *syn* which means "together," *cas*, "throw" and *pleso,* "fold" and this signifies mocking and insulting words that also must be resisted lest they break up the ship because we should bear up with such, as Psalm 69:10, "The reproaches of them that reproached thee are fallen upon me" and I Corinthians 4:13, "We are blasphemed, and we entreat; we are made as the refuse of this world, the offscouring of all even until now."

The sixth peril is the natural raging of the sea that raises a force that retards the progress of the boat to its destiny and it signifies the carnal appetites that retard the spirit, as Galatians 5:17 says, "For the flesh lusteth against the spirit: and the spirit against the flesh; for these are contrary one to another."

The seventh peril is Scylla (seizure) which is so named from [Latin *scopulus*, a rocky projection or a cavernous cliff sticking out under water through whose caverns water flows and then flows back. Whence such a cliff is also called by the poets "dogs' teeth," and is also named from Greek *skilleo-eis* which signifies "to move" [actually it is from *skyllo,* to tear to pieces] not that the cliffs move but that through its caverns the water flows back and forth. This signifies the empty popular glory that moves like water and of this it is said in John 5:44, "How can you believe, who receive glory one from another: and the glory which is from God alone, you do not seek?"

The eighth peril is the song of the Sirens, the sea maidens whose singing charms sailors and makes them dangerously retract their course and this signifies the pleasures of this world which those who journey through this world must resist, as Isaiah 13:22 says, "And sirens [shall dwell] in the temples of pleasure."

The ninth peril is the conflict of warriors in the deep and signifies the pressure which the Saints suffer in this world from evil men, as Psalm 104:25-26 says, "So in this great sea, which stretcheth wide its arms: there are creeping things without number: Creatures little and great. There the ships shall go." And note that all these perils take place in water. There are three other perils which are not in water but are in the air or in port.

A peril in the air is the tempest, that is, a wind that piles up the sea, and this stands for the force of pride which inflates the sea, that is the restlessness of the impious heart, for as Isaiah 57:20-21 says, "The wicked are like the raging sea, which cannot rest, and the waves thereof cast up dirt and mire. There is no peace to the wicked, saith the Lord God." And of this peril Acts 27:14-14 says, "But not long after, there arose against it a tempestuous wind, called Euroaquilo. And when the ship was caught, and could not bear up against the wind, giving up," that is, leaving "the ship to the winds, we were driven." The Euroaquilo is a mixed wind, for Aquilos is a cold, dry, very violent wind coming from the north. Thus it is said in Sirach 43:22, "The cold north wind bloweth, and the water is congealed into crystal; upon every gathering together of waters it shall rest, and shall clothe the waters as a breastplate." The Euros, on the other hand, is a warm, dry wind that rises from the southeast. Hence the Euroaquilo is a mixed wind and, so to speak, signifies pride which is cold through impiety, dry through cruelty, and violent and swollen through arrogant domination, yet warm from ambition. Hence, as quote from Acts says, the Euroaquilo blows over the plains as if from contrary directions, impeding the good ship of life.

Another aerial peril is that there may be no wind at all and such a calm signifies laziness which is always immobile. Solomon in Proverbs 6:9-11 asks of a man who is lazy in this way, "How long wilt thou sleep, O sluggard? when wilt thou rise out of thy sleep? Thou wilt sleep a little, thou wilt slumber a little, thou wilt fold thy hands a little to sleep: And want shall come upon thee, as a traveler, and poverty as a man armed."

A peril in port, however is provided by a divided port where the sea is divided by a tongue of land sticking into the sea and this signifies the peril of fraud and deceit in which a man hides and thinks he is secure. Acts 27:41 says of this peril, "And when we were fallen into a place where two seas met, they run the ship aground; and the forepart indeed, sticking fast, remained unmovable: but the hinder part was broken with the violence of the sea." Thus fraud puts on a innocent face but what we do not see is that it, like the sea, is shattering and breaking up the unseen stern of the ship.

Against all these perils a truly strong ship ought to be armed and fortified by patience, as Psalm 106:23-24 says, "They that go down to the sea in ships, doing business in the great waters: These have seen the works of the Lord, and his wonders in the deep." and in Sirach 43:26, "Let them that sail on the sea, tell the dangers thereof: and when we hear with our ears, we shall admire." It is not possible, however to escape all these perils except through constant prayer to the Lord so as to awake the Lord from his appearance of a guard who is asleep, as Matthew 8:23-26 narrates of Jesus, "When he entered into the boat, his disciples followed him: And behold a great tempest arose in the sea, so that the boat was covered with waves, but he was asleep. And they came to him, and awaked him, saying: Lord, save us, we perish. And Jesus saith to them: Why are you fearful, O ye of little faith? Then rising up he commanded the winds, and the sea, and there came a great calm."

Another kind of ship is a fishing boat and this is the boat of the ages. The net with which one fishes is the word of God which sometimes is lowered on the left side of the boat, that is, by the intention to make money through pastoral care and the word of God. And of this it is narrated in John 21:3, ["Simon Peter saith to them: I go a fishing. They say to him: We also come with thee."] where it said of Peter and the other disciples that they got into a fishing boat "but that night caught nothing." That "nothing" is temporal gain which is nothing and less than nothing because it is sin. And of this the Apostles says in I Corinthians 9:18, "What is my reward then? That preaching the Gospel, I may deliver the Gospel without charge, that I abuse not my power in the Gospel," since in Matthew 10:8 Christ said, "Freely have you received, freely give." Others, however let down the net on the right side of the boat as Christ commanded, John 21:6, "He saith to them: Cast the net on the right side of the ship, and you shall find." These are those who seek souls and not money. It was such fishers that the Lord made his disciples as it is written, Matthew 4:19 "And he saith to them: Come ye after me, and I will make you to be fishers of men."

Next is a consideration of merchant ships and this is a ship for of trading. There are, however, two kinds of bargaining, temporal and spiritual, and hence there are two kinds of merchant ships one that carries temporal and the other eternal goods.

Of the first kind of ship, namely of temporal bargaining, it is said in Wisdom 5:8-10, "What hath pride profited us? Or what advantage hath the boasting of riches brought us? All those things are passed away like a shadow, and like a post that runneth on, And as a ship that passeth through the waves: whereof when it is gone by, the trace cannot be found, nor the path of its keel in the waters."

Of the second kind of ship, that of spiritual bargaining, Genesis 49:13 says, "Zebulun shall dwell on the sea shore, and in the road of ships, reaching as far as Sidon." "Zebulun" is interpreted as the dwelling place of fortitude and signifies the Valiant Woman. The "sea" is this life which is a bitter, restless flood of events. The "shore" of this sea is stabilizing grace of God and on this restful shore the Saints live in a ship at anchor engaging in spiritual bargaining. The "port" is near Sidon which is interpreted "market" because in the turmoil of this world it is only through patience that eternal riches are gained, as it is said in Deuteronomy 33:19, "Who shall suck as milk the abundance of the sea, and the hidden treasures of the sands?" What these "treasures" are is described in I Kings 10:22 where it says that "Every three years the king's (Solomon's) navy went with the navy of Hiram by sea to Tharsis, and brought from thence gold, and silver, and elephants' teeth, and apes, and peacocks." Peaceful Solomon stands for the Valiant Woman, and Hiram is interpreted as "the Lord's olive tree" and stands for Christ whose ship meets the ship of the Valiant Woman, because this bargaining is that of like to like. "Tharsis" is interpreted "exploration of joy." The "meeting" of the ships takes place every "three years," because in one year the sun orbits one complete circle and thus the "sun of justice" who is Our Lord, the Christ, shines on that Valiant Woman to enable her to understand the Scriptures and contemplate eternity, as Sirach 43:4 says, "The sun three times as much [as a furnace], burneth the mountains [that is the high points of life], breathing out fiery vapors." The "gold" which the ship brings is charity; the "silver" is the knowledge of Scripture; the "ivory teeth" of elephants is chastity of mind and body by which the desires of the flesh are mortified. The "monkeys" are the imitation of the examples of the Saints because among animals monkeys best imitate man, who of all animals is the most discrete and rational. The "peacocks" signify the beauty of the holy virtues.

Once should note also that I Kings 22:49 tells how, "King Josaphat made navies on the sea, to sail into Ophir for gold: but they could not go, for the ships were broken in Asiongaber." Josaphat whose name signifies "the judgment of the Lord" signifies those who wish to reign someday with Christ, but who also seek for glory in this world. Hence Asiongaber is interpreted "chain" because such persons are chained to this world by love. Hence also II Chronicles 20:35-36 relates that, ["After these things Josaphat king of Judah made friendship with Ochozias king of Israel, whose works were very wicked, and became his partner in building ships to go to Tharsis: and they made the ships in Asiongaber."] Thus in building his ship Josaphat entered into partnership with Ochozias, King of Samaria, whose works were very evil, since "Samaria" stands for this world. Now the excessive love of this world devalues good works because the eternal reward of good works is thereby exchanged for this world's rewards. And this is what in II Chronicles 20:37 Eliezer, the prophet, says to Jehosaphat, "Because thou hast made a league with Ochozias, the Lord hath destroyed thy works, and the ships are broken, and they could not go to Tharsis."

§ 2

In the text follows: "**She bringeth her bread from afar.**" It should be noted first that "afar" is fourfold: according to depth, height, breadth, and length. According to "depth" "afar" refers to hell concerning which in fear the Valiant Woman bargains; according to "height" she bargains through charity, in "width" through understanding whose limits extend beyond his world and is bargained for by the study of Scripture; while bargaining in "length" refers to our distance from God who is the beginning of all creatures including man. In these four ways the Valiant Woman bargains through her faith and hope of redemption and through that "mediator between God and man, the man Christ Jesus," says the Apostle in I Timothy 2:5, ["For there is one God, and one mediator of God and men, the man Christ Jesus."] Of this fourfold "afar" [St. Paul in] Ephesians 3:16-18 prays, "That he would grant you, according to the riches of his glory, to be strengthened by his Spirit with might unto the inward man, That Christ may dwell by faith in your hearts; that being rooted and founded in charity, You may be able to comprehend, with all the Saints, what is the breadth, and length, and height, and depth."

Similarly there are four kinds of bread which the Valiant Woman is said to "bring from afar." First is the bread of sorrow of which we read in Psalm 80:6, "How long wilt thou feed us with the bread of tears: and give us for our drink tears in measure?" and in I Kings, 22:27, "And tell them: Thus saith the king: Put this man in prison, and feed him with bread of affliction, and water of distress, till I return in peace." The "prison' is the custody of the Church for those doing penance. The "bread of tears" is the bread of sorrow for sin and the "water of distress" is the water of repentant tears. This is signified in I Kings 19:3-4 where we read that Elias, fleeing from Jezebel, slept under a juniper tree and in verse 5 the Angel of the Lord awakens him, saying, "Arise and eat" and in the next verse he finds under his head "a hearth cake, and a vessel of water:and he ate and drank, and he fell asleep again." And again the Angel of the Lord roused him to eat and drink because he had a long way yet to travel, which he did, since it says in verse 8, "he arose, and ate, and drank, and walked in the strength of that food forty days and forty nights, unto the mount of God, Horeb." "Elias" is interpreted as "strong ruler" and signifies the penitent who controls himself. "Jezabel" is interpreted "dung" and signifies sin and hell, that is, one who avoids penance. The shade of the "juniper tree" signifies the protection and renewal of the keys of the Church under which a penitent sometimes rests from evil deeds. The "Angel" who aroused Elias is prevenient grace forgiving sins and stimulating the sinner to eat the bread of sorrow and drink the drink of tears by which he can travel the broad way even unto death. This bread is a "hearth cake" because of the instruments of penance which St. Augustine says are "ashes and hair-cloth." He sleeps again, however, because he rests after the regretting the noise of earthly love, but the Angel arouses him again and this signifies that the grace that follows on penance drives the penitent to bear with temptations. And that fact he "eats again" signifies that one should do penance and then again fight temptation as one travels the broad way to the secure of eternal life. He walks in the strength of that food through the performance of good works for forty days, that is, through the whole time of a life devoted to penance, because "forty" numbers the time of penance since it approaches the "fifty days of jubilee [Numbers 6:4] that stands for eternal joy. The mountain of God, Horeb, which is interpreted "fire" signifies the exaltation of the spirit burning with charity.

The second kind of "bread from afar" is the bread of consolation by eternal things, of which it is said in Genesis 49:20, "[The tribe of] Asher, his bread shall be fat, and he shall yield dainties to kings." Asher is interpreted as "blessed" and signifies those who are already blessed with the hope and foretaste of eternal rewards. This bread of consolation tastes good and hence is eaten among kings who are their own masters, as Isaiah 21:14-15 says, "Meeting the thirsty bring him water, you that inhabit the land of the south, meet with bread him that fleeth. For they are fled from before the swords, from the sword that hung over them, from the bent bow, from the face of a grievous battle." The "land of the South" is a place filled with light and warmth and signifies the heavenly fatherland. Its habitants are the "blessed" who meet us with prayers and enlightenment, bringing us the bread of consolation as we flee from the hands of swordsmen, that is from the devil's temptations and from the imminent face of the "sword," that is, from the temptations of the flesh which are always near us and from the face of the "bent bow," that is, also from the temptation of the devil who crouches in hiding to wound us. The "grievous battle" is the battle of the world in its vanities and pomps.

The third meaning of "bread from afar" concerns the bread of life and understanding of which Sirach 15:3 says, "With the bread of life and understanding, she shall feed him" and Amos 8:11 says, "Behold the days come, saith the Lord, and I will send forth a famine into the land:not a famine of bread, nor a thirst of water, but of hearing the word of the Lord."

The fourth meaning of "bread from afar" refers to the Sacrament of the Body of the Lord of which in John 6:48 Jesus says, "I am the bread of life," and Wisdom 16:20-21 says, "Of which things thou didst feed thy people with the food of angels, and gavest them bread from heaven . For thy sustenance shewed thy sweetness to thy children, and serving every man's will, it was turned to what every man liked." This means the Eucharist which by containing Christ contains the power of every grace and sweetness, which bread God gives to all of us, unworthy as we are, from his substantial and sweet goodness, because we find in all that we seek.

OUTLINE OF CHAPTER VI

And she hath risen in the night,
and given a prey to her household,
and victuals to her maidens. (v. 15)

§1 Acrostic letter Vau ו signifies "this" or "that" pointing out for praise the Strong Woman whose "rising" is considered both metaphorically and literally
  1) Who rises? Metaphorically there are three kinds of night
    1) Night of sin, especially of lust, but the Valiant Woman is not in sin
    2) Night of temptation. She is, however, subject to temptation
    3) Night of ignorance of true knowledge of God, but She has faith
  2) When does she rise? Literally, "in the night":metaphorically to praise God
    1) As Christ rose in the night to his eternal vision.
    2) As Samson broke the two gates of hell;
      1) Human pride
      2) Original sin
    3) Why does she rise? For two purposes
      1) To do lofty works of virtue
      2) To taste heavenly things

§2. What "prey" does the Valiant Woman "gives to her household"
  1) She delivers her household from the devil and hell and joins us to the household of the Angels
  2) She converts sinners and joins them to her household
  3) She delivers sinners from the two jaws of evil desires:
    1) Gluttony
    2) Lust

§3. With what foods and at what banquets does the Valiant Woman feed her household?
  1) Foods
    1) The seven virtues and grace and good works
    2) True doctrine
    3) Contemplation
    4) The Sacraments
    5) Eternal Beatitude
  2) Banquets
    1) Job's banquet; a lifetime during which every virtue is perfected and enjoyed
    2) Jacob's banquet:in the light of the full doctrine of Christ.
    3) Christ's Last Supper with the Twelve Apostles
    4) The Three Feasts of the Old Testament: Passover, Pentecost, Tabernacles
    5) The banquet of King Assuerus symbolizing God's Heavenly Banquet.

CHAPTER VI

**And she hath risen in the night,
and given a prey to her household,
and victuals to her maidens. (v. 15)**

§ 1

VAU: ו. Vau is interpreted "this'" or "that", both of which are demonstrative pronouns and through this letter is noted in the Valiant Woman something that is evidently to her praise. This is expressed in the following verse in which three things are noted: her "rising," the "prey" she gives her household and the kinds of that "prey." As to her "rising" three things are also noted, namely, who rises, when she rises, and why she rises.

As to the first, who rises, it should be noted that "**in the night**" can be understood metaphorically, but secondly it can be taken literally, and thirdly it can be understood as it is implied in the word "**risen.**" Concerning the first of these, "night" can be taken metaphorically as to that from which she rises in three ways: from the night of sin, from the night of temptation, and from the night of the ignorance of obscure knowledge.

Of the first sort of night, Wisdom 17:3 says, "And while they thought to lie hid in their obscure sins, they were scattered under a dark veil of forgetfulness, being horribly afraid and troubled with exceeding great astonishment." For all sin is "obscure" but especially the sin of lust hiddenly acted out. By this kind of sin men "forget" God and are troubled with extraordinary miseries, as it says further on in verse 5 of that passage, "And no power of fire could give them light, neither could the bright flames of the stars enlighten that horrible night." Here through "flames" is signified God's grace, as Hebrews 12:29 says, "Our God is a consuming fire." The "bright flame of the stars" signifies the example of the Saints that does not illuminate the night for those sinners since they prefer to remain always in the dark. Job 3:7 says, "Let that night be solitary, and not worthy of praise," that is, the sinner acts as if he had never done this before yet expects no one to know or approve what he is doing.

Of the night of temptation Job 30:17 says, "In the night my bone is pierced with sorrows: and they that feed upon me do not sleep." Through "bone" is signified the strength of virtue which is pierced by temptation. Through "feed upon me" is meant the devils setting the fire of temptation. Thus Psalm 119:55 says:"In the night I have remembered thy name, O Lord."

Of the third night Jesus says in John 11:10, "But if a man walk in the night, he stumbleth, because the light is not in him," and also Tobit 5:12 asks, "What manner of joy shall be to me, who sit in darkness, and see not the light of heaven? " that is, in the light of the knowledge of the truth of God of which Psalm 119:105 says, "Thy word is a lamp to my feet, and a light to my paths."

What follows is the answer to the question about *when* the Valiant Woman rises, literally, "in the night," but metaphorically to praise God as Psalm 134:2 says, "In the nights lift up your hands to the holy places, and bless ye the Lord," and also Psalm 119:62 says, "I rose at midnight to give praise to thee." And this signifies the Lord's Resurrection, because according to St. Gregory, "He rose in the night," and Judges 16:3 says that [in Gaza], "Samson slept till midnight, and then rising he took both the doors of the gate, with the posts thereof, and the bolt, and laying them on his shoulders, carried them up to the top of the hill, which looketh towards Hebron." "Samson" is interpreted as "strong sun" and signifies Christ, who slept in death, while "Gaza" signifies "strong" and refers to Limbo into which Christ descended when he lay asleep in death. First, the "doors" of these gates with their "posts are the devil's envy of God through which death entered into this world, as Wisdom 2:24 says, ["But by the envy of the devil, death came into the world."] Furthermore they are man's pride because of which he wishes "to be as God knowing good and evil." Second, these gates are the guilt of original sin, which Christ broke open in his blessed Resurrection when he arose to "eternal vision," since "Hebron" is interpreted "eternal vision." Of this same night Psalm 139:11-12 says, "Night shall be light as day."

What follows answers the question *for what?* she has risen, namely, for two purposes: first to do noble works and second to taste heavenly things Both of these purposes are noted in Colossians 3:1, "Therefore, if you be risen with Christ, seek [taste] the things that are above, not the things that are upon the earth," or, as the Gloss says, "in works of virtue," that is, taste only what is heavenly. But note that some rise with Christ, but others with Lazarus, that is, after rising, through sin they die again. Those, however, rise with Christ who persevere in a good life in Christ Jesus, our Lord, as Romans 6:9 says, "Knowing that Christ rising again from the dead, dieth now no more, death shall no more have dominion over him. For in that he died to sin, he died once; but in that he liveth, he liveth unto God."

§ 2

What follows concerns the "**prey**" which the Valiant Woman "**gives to her household**" and this is threefold: the prey of hell which she gives to the Angels, the prey of the world which she gives to her companions, and the prey of the flesh which she gives to the Saints.

The prey of hell the Valiant Woman gives through Christ who broke the doors of hell as Isaiah 8:3-4 says, "Call his name" that is, the name of Christ, " Hasten to take away the spoils: Make haste to take away the prey. For before the child know to call his father and his mother, the strength of Damascus, and the spoils of Samaria shall be taken away before the king of the Assyrians." Since "Samaria" means "guarded," this is to say that when God the Son became man, but was still an infant that already knew how to call on the name of God his Father and on the name of his Mother Mary, he had deprived hell of its spoils that had been so powerfully guarded by the devil, "Damascus," however, is interpreted as "drink of blood" and signifies the devils who drink up sin. Hence "before the king of the Assyrians," that is, before the spoils of Samaria, that is, of the devil "are taken away," means that when hell is broken open, as the Lord has promised his Saints, and as Isaiah 49:24-25 asks and answers, "Shall the prey be taken from the strong? Or can that which was taken by the mighty be delivered? For thus saith the Lord: Yea verily, even the captivity shall be taken away from the strong: and that which was taken by the mighty, shall be delivered."

Thus the prey the Valiant Woman gives "**to her household**" are the angels because, as Jesus declares in John 14:2, the angels dwell in the same house with us, "In my Father's house there are many mansions" and the Apostle in Ephesians 2:19 also says, "Now therefore you are no more strangers and foreigners; but you are fellow citizens with the Saints, and the domestics of God," that is dwellers with the angels in the house of God.

The prey which is taken away from this world is the multitude of converted souls and this is signified in Genesis 14:15-16, where Abraham conquers five kings and takes them captive along with Lot. The five kings signifies the five senses which by a life of concupiscence have "fallen" into sin but are brought back by conversion and this is also signified in I Samuel 30:19 by those who David saved from their captivity by Amalekites. And the same is true of the hundred foreskins of the Philistines which in I Samuel 18:27 David counts out before King Saul in order to be accepted as his son-in-law. For these foreskins signify excessive riches, which as [Ephesians 2:17] says, are circumcised by the "sword of the Spirit, which is the word of God." The heavenly King's "daughter:[whom David sought to marry] is the Church which is given in marriage to the doctors and preachers for the conversion of souls. Thus the "prey is given" to the Valiant Woman's household, that is, to the community that has been converted with us the baptized, as [the Apostle says] in I Timothy 5:8:"But if any man have not care of his own, and especially of those of his house, he hath denied the faith, and is worse than an infidel." This "house," the Church, in which we dwell with our fellow Christians is signified by the inn to which, as is told in Luke 10:29-37, the Good Samaritan brought the half-alive stranger.

The third kind of prey is taken from that flesh of which Isaiah 9:5 says, "For every violent taking of spoils, with tumult," since only with violent protest by the flesh can the prey of chastity be taken from the body, "and garment mingled with blood," that is, the body wounded by sin, "shall be burnt," and be fuel for the fire and similarly Job 29:17 says, "I broke the jaws of the wicked man, and out of his teeth I took away the prey." The wicked man is concupiscence and it has two jaws ["teeth"] namely, gluttony and lust which are broken by bodily mortification, since only thus can the prey of chastity be taken from the flesh. This prey is distributed to the household of the Saints, as is said in Sirach 32:25-26, "Lest thou set a stumbling-block to thy soul. And beware for thy own children, and take heed of them of thy household." For some through lust place a stumbling-block [scandal] for their own souls, when they ought to beware that they also are giving a bad example to their sons. Yet they ought to give good example to the Saints living with them in the same house of holiness, since as St. Gregory the Great says, "While we have time, do good to all, especially to one's household in the faith."

§ 3

The rest of the chapter text is: "**and victuals to her maidens.**" These are the various foods that are the virtues, namely: the food of doctrine, of contemplation, of the sacraments, and of eternal beatitude.

Of the foods that signify the virtues Isaiah 4:1 says, "And in that day seven women shall take hold of one man, saying: We will eat our own bread, and wear our own apparel: only let us be called by thy name, take away our reproach." The Gloss on this text says that "the seven women are the seven virtues and their bread is the refreshment of grace of which Psalm 104:15 says, 'That bread may strengthen man's heart.'" The "apparel" is the works. The "one man" is reason. The "reproach" is their infertility. The "taking away" signifies the removal of this reproach by fecundity.

Of the second kind of food that is doctrine, I Corinthians 3:1-2 says, "As unto little ones in Christ, I gave you milk to drink, not meat," that is, teaching about rudiments of the faith and the humanity of our Savior; and as Deuteronomy 8:3 says, "Not in bread alone doth man live, but in every word that proceedeth from the mouth of God" and Hebrews 5:12-14 says, "You are become such as have need of milk, and not of strong meat. For every one that is a partaker of milk is unskillful in the word of justice: for he is a little child. But strong meat is for the perfect; for them who by custom have their senses exercised to the discerning of good and evil."

Of the third kind of food, [the Sacraments] I Corinthians 10:16 says, "The chalice of benediction which we bless, is it not the communion of the blood of Christ? And the bread, which we break, is it not the partaking of the body of the Lord?" and in I Corinthians 5:7-8, "For Christ our Pasch is sacrificed. Therefore let us feast, not with the old leaven, nor with the leaven of malice and wickedness; but with the unleavened bread of sincerity and truth."

Of the fourth kind of food, that is contemplation, Proverbs 9:5 says, "Come, eat my bread, and drink the wine which I have mingled for you." Here "bread" is the efficacy of the substantial goods of God. "Wine" is the liquor of flowing and everlasting truth mixed with the water of saving Wisdom. Again the Song of Songs 5:1 invites us to "Eat O friends, and drink, and be inebriated, my dearly beloved." Friends eat and drink in contemplation and are inebriated by exaltation of mind.

Of the fifth kind of food that is eternal beatitude Jesus in Luke 22:29-30 says, "And I dispose to you, as my Father hath disposed to me, a kingdom; that you may eat and drink at my table, in my kingdom: and may sit upon thrones."

[There are also five kinds of such banquets]. The first is the banquet of Job's sons, of whom we read in Job 1:4 ["And his sons went, and made a feast by houses every one in his day. And sending they called their three sisters to eat and drink with them."] And the day of that banquet passes in a lifetime during which every virtue is perfected and enjoyed.

The second is the banquet of the sons of Jacob who ate with their brother Joseph at midday, [as Genesis 43:31-34 narrates,] "And when he [Joseph] had washed his face [of its tears], coming out again, he refrained himself, and said: Set bread on the table. And when it was set on, for Joseph apart, and for his brethren apart, for the Egyptians also that ate with him, apart, (for it is unlawful for the Egyptians to eat with the Hebrews, and they think such a feast profane):They sat before him, the firstborn according to his birthright, and the youngest according to his age. And they wondered very much: Taking the messes which they received of him: and the greater mess came to Benjamin, so that it exceeded by five parts. And they drank, and were merry with him.."] This is a banquet in the light of the full doctrine of Christ. Christ is inebriated before them because the banqueting sons perceive in his sayings the doctrine of truth that this Christ by his eternal birth from the Father has so abundantly received. This inebriation is not the vice of drunkenness, but signifies the abundance [of Christ's teaching].

The third kind of banquet is such as that ["Last Supper"] that the Apostles had with Jesus before his passion.

The fourth is a festive and rich banquet before the Lord, such as is celebrated three times during each year, namely, the Pasch, Pentecost, and the Feast of Tabernacles [Booths, a harvest feast], that recall the three themes of contemplation. For during the Paschal Season contemplatives meditate on the glory of the Resurrection and the work of salvation, while during Pentecost they ponder the power of the Holy Spirit flowing down from on high and inebriating the recipients with the love which they express in every tongue, namely, in the "tongues of men and of angels," breaking forth in remembrance of the abundance of God's sweetness and exalting in his justice. [The text does not interpret the Feast of Tabernacles, but as a harvest feast it perhaps stands for the eternal completion of salvation history].

The fifth kind of feast is the banquet of King Assuerus with his princes [Esther 1:3 and following]. His name is interpreted "blessed" and signifies God as he rules with his Saints, that is with the Saints of the people gathered with the God of Abraham "in his

[Abraham's] bosom," that is, in the rest where no one will be compelled to drink, as they are compelled, the laziness and weariness of this engender in us, which makes us unwilling to taste the wine of eternal happiness. Therefore we must be, and are, invited and driven by words and examples so that we may be persuaded not to leave these good things unconsumed. Then, however, our desire will be enkindled when we drink from the torrent of God's joy, so that there no one will need to urge his brother to drink avidly of the font of life and beatitude.

OUTLINE OF CHAPTER VII

She hath considered a field, and bought it:
with the fruit of her hands she hath planted a vineyard. (v. 16)

§1) Acrostic letter Zain ז means "olive" and relates to the Valiant Woman's who resembles and olive tree and the grape vine
  1) As regards the nature of an olive tree
    1) Bears fruit by sexual reproduction
      1) Without the heat of charity, a person is a wild olive cold through avarice
      2) Without the humidity of piety a person is wild olive through sterile lust
      3) If a wild olive is grafted into a good olive through grace and charity it bears good fruit
    2) Has foliage even in winter; Valiant Woman never says anything foolish about God but always speaks peace like the dove in the Ark after the Flood
    3) Olives have pits
      1) These signify that the liquid of her piety hardens into the strength of merit.
      2) While wanton women burn such pits and this signifies Pharisaic hypocrisy
  2) The utility of the olive tree is to produce oil that signifies mercy:
    1) Four kinds of mercy that are gates to Heaven:
      1) Mercy of redemption shown to all humanity
      2) Mercy of correction signified by Parable of Good Samaritan
      3) Mercy of forgiveness of venial sins
      4) Mercy in accepting our obedience
    2) Fourteen effects of the oil of mercy when used by us;
      1) Seven are corporeal works of mercy
        1) Feed the hungry
        2) Give drink to the thirsty
        3) Cloth the naked
        4) House pilgrims and wayfarers
        5) Visit the sick
        6) Visit the captives to redeem or comfort them
        7) Bury the dead
      2) Seven are spiritual works of mercy:
        1) Counsel those who need counseling
        2) Rebuke the delinquent
        3) Forgive those who sin against us
        4) Console the weak-hearted
        5) Lift and carry the weak
        6) Pray for the poor
        7) Teach the ignorant
    3) The olive tree is a symbol of peace
      1) Peace: as olive branches at Jesus' entrance to Jerusalem
      2) Peace as effect of mercy; Mount of Olives or heights of mercy,

3) Perpetually green in eternal life like those that feed the golden candlestick:Christ; body and soul

§2. The Valiant Woman has bought a field
   1) What is a field? Sixth things characterize it:
      1) The action of farming; plowing the field by perseverant obedience of commandments and counsels
      2) Viewing the field that flows with the honey of Wisdom
      3) The field of Scriptures read historically, allegorically, morally, & anagogically by revelation and study
      4) The field of human nature, the good with the bad
      5) The field of redemption; the Biblical salvation history
      6) The field of our hearts longing for the celestial fatherland.
   2) What must the Strong Women consider before buying it?
      1) Estimating its value; sin destroys all value
      2) Discretely not paying too much for it; worldly desire is waste; grace is beyond price
      3) Care lest it be reduced to sterility: without constancy goods deeds come to nothing.
   3) What price is to be paid for the field
      1) Price of an act of simple obedience performed:
         1) Simply,
         2) Quickly
         3) Prudently
      2) Price of the field of contemplation is purchased by a pure and clean heart, since
         1) The mind must be cleansed from the mire of sin
         2) The will must be cleansed from the fumes of concupiscence
         3) The reason must be cleansed from the darkness of error
      3) Field of Scripture at the price of study and mediation which we should do:
         1) For the enjoyment of knowing
         2) For the utility of guidance in acting
         3) For spiritually experiencing its sweetness
      4) Field of the world or our nature at the price of discipline by:
         1) Vigils
         2) Fasts
         3) Temptations and external troubles that impinge on us
      5) Field of redemption at the price of the action of grace by:
         1) Remembering my poverty and sin,
         2) Wormwood (martyrdom)
         3) Vinegar and gall (malicious accusations)
      6) Field of the hearts' heavenly desire can be bought at the price of devotion that cleanses
         1) Pious affection of the longing heart
         2) Readiness for prayer
         3) Raising of the heart to everlasting life

§3 Planting a vineyard in the field
   1) Who plants the vine:The Valiant Woman
      1) One hand cares for her own salvation

THE VALIANT WOMAN

1) The Wine of Sorrow in the field of one's own soul that is sinful
   1) Repentance for sin
   2) Pressed in the wine-press of contrition
   3) Bottled in the memory of misdeeds
   4) Poured out in confession
   5) Drunk by satisfying assigned penances
2) The Wine of Redemption
   1) Is drunk with honey and milk and bread
      1) Honey is divinity of Christ; the honeycomb his humanity
      2) Milk is Christ's teaching
      3) Bread (wheat) is strengthening grace
   2) Fruit of this vine is piety
      1) Grown on highest mountain of God's benefits
      2) Pressed out in press of thanksgiving
      3) Collected in vessel of the heart
      4) Leads to good works, unless wasted by ingratitude
3) The Wine of Rejoicing
   1) Blood of Christ facing the sun of a pure conscience
   2) Pressed out in mediation
   3) Collected in the vessel of longing, free of the dregs of sorrow
   4) Celebrated as on a feast.
4) The Wine of Inebriation
   1) Grows on mountain of charity
   2) Pressed out in warmest piety
   3) Freed from the dregs of self-love
   4) Drunk in the embrace of the Beloved, all the world forgotten.
   5) The Wine of Eternity
      1) Grows in the enclosure of Divine Wisdom
      2) Pressed out in eternal contemplation
      3) Received in vessel of the Celestial Kingdom of Christ and the Saints
2) The other hand of the Valiant Woman serves her neighbor and has five effects
   1) Stinging wine; severe rebuke of sin
   2) Spiced wine: doctrine that cools the heat of the vices,
   3) New wine bubbles with congratulation for good deeds
   4) Sorrowful wine of compassion
   5) Supportive wine that helps neighbor act well
2) How the vineyard, whether of our own soul or neighbor's, is planted
   1) Faces the sun and south wind; the light of grace
   2) On a high and rich place: mountain of the spirit and richness of devotion ?
   2) Cultivated with a hoe of fear and contrition
   3) Fertilized with abject humility
   4) Watered with penitent tears
   5) Walled in with the protection of Angels
   6) Built with a tower in the middle: Christ, the high hope of God's help
   7) With a winepress: Christ's passion
   8) Planted with the best seed: souls made to God's image and likeness.

CHAPTER VII

**She hath considered a field, and bought it:
with the fruit of her hands she hath planted a vineyard. (v. 16)**

§ 1

ZAIN ז, Two things are to be here considered: the interpretation of this letter and the whole sentence. Zain is interpreted "olive" and pertains to this particular verse because the verses is about the fruit of generous and productive hands that grow and press out olives [as well as grapes for wine], as Psalm 52:10 says, "But I, as a fruitful olive tree in the house of God, have hoped in the mercy of God for ever, yea for ever and ever."

The Valiant Woman is like this olive tree in three ways: first as regards the nature of the olive; second as regards its usefulness; and third as the olive tree is a symbol.

As to the first, three things are to be noted about the nature of an olive tree:that it bears bear fruit through sexual reproduction; that it has foliage not only in summer but in winter; and that its fruit has pits.

As the first, an olive tress is made fruitful by heat in some of parts, but the wetness of other parts supplies the matter for its reproduction. This "heat" is the fervor of charity; while the "wetness" is piety. Someone who lacks these virtues is not a domestic olive tree but a wild olive, cold with avarice and wet only with sterile lust, as is said in Romans 11:17, "And if some of the branches be broken, and thou, being a wild olive, art engrafted in them, and art made partaker of the root, and of the fatness of the olive tree." For a man is a wild olive through original and actual sin; but is grafted into a domesticated olive through grace and joined to it with the root of charity, because charity is the root of all that is good and shares in the richness of all good works.

The second thing about the nature of an olive tree is that it foliage is evergreen and this signifies what Ephesians 4:29 says, "Let no evil speech proceed from your mouth; but that which is good, to the edification of faith, that it may administer grace to the hearers." That it is evergreen in winter as well as in summer is because this Valiant Woman never says anything foolish against anyone either in prosperity or adversity, just as Genesis 8:11 tells how the dove brought an olive branch with green leaves, that is, the word of peace, into the Ark. This "Ark" is the Church and note also that according to Aristotle, *Posterior Analytics* II, [98b 1] "trees having broad, thin leaves shed them" which means that magniloquent speech and deceitful lips that utter lies and idle gossip speak evil abusively out of pride. Such speech is like a broad, thin leaf, since it is not thickened by wisdom and thus lacks weight. Note too that Aristotle also says [98b 37] "It is the juice that thickens the leaves where they contact each other that makes them flourish." The juice, however, is thickened by cold and it signifies the dissipation of pleasure in gluttony and lust. Cold signifies desires that resist what is divine and that is the cold that thickens the will and causes it to grow in the concupiscence of the flesh. Also these two vices are excused by many idle and meaningless excuses. And therefore Jesus says in Luke 16:19-31, ["There was a certain rich man, who was clothed in purple and fine linen; and feasted sumptuously every day...And the rich man also died: and he was buried in hell. And lifting up his eyes when he was in torments, he saw Abraham afar off, and Lazarus in his bosom: And he cried, and said: Father Abraham, have mercy on me, and send Lazarus, that he may dip the tip of his finger in water, to cool my tongue: for I am tormented in this flame,"] who for all his lamenting only received a greater torment because as St. Gregory the Great says, "To abound in idle talk is common at banquets," and therefore Proverbs 7:10 says, "And behold a woman meeteth him in harlot's attire prepared to deceive souls; talkative and wandering," that is, garrulous and aimless, because a vain young woman, as it says in verse 21, can "entangle" [a man] with many words and with the flattery of her lips." On the contrary Psalm 1:3 says of a just person, "And he shall be like a tree which is planted near the running waters, which shall bring forth its fruit, in due season. And his leaf shall not fall off:and all whatsoever he shall do shall prosper."

The third point about the olive three is that olives have oily pits, which signifies that in her work the Valiant Woman has the strength of merit which gains the eternal kingdom because she diffuses the liquid of her piety around her to her neighbors, while within she is strengthened by a secure conscience of deserving the everlasting reward of which Hosea 14:7 says, "His branches shall spread, and his glory shall be as the olive tree." On the contrary of those who only do good to be seen by others and thus lose the right to merit in exchange for temporal favor, Baruch 6:42-43 says, "The women also with cords about them sit in the ways, burning olive stones [like incense]. And when any one of them, drawn away by some passer by, lieth with him, she upbraideth her neighbor, that she was not thought as worthy as herself, nor had her cord broken." The ungirded woman is the vainly boastful soul who although girded with external observation of God's commandments is not internally girded since she loves to stand in the streets and pray and, as Matthew 6:2 says, when she gives alms, has, as it were, trumpets braying before her. Such women "sit" in the streets "burning olive stones" like incense before all the people, because whatever in their work ought to be of worth and merit is all burned up and turned to ashes in the fire of other's praises. Thus when such a woman goes on to engage in wantonness and hears herself flattered [by her lovers], she prizes herself all the more and despises other women who are not flattered as she is, as Jesus in Luke 18:11 says, "The Pharisee standing, prayed thus with himself: O God, I give thee thanks that I am not as the rest of men, extortioners, unjust, adulterers, as also is this publican." The "loosening of such a woman's cord" signifies that she distracted from the eternal goal to which she ought to be bound by the external practice of some particular precept for which she is emptily praised.

Next follows the utility of the olive tree, namely the usefulness of its oil which as Judges 9:9 says, is used by gods and men:["And the live tree answered:Can I leave my fatness, which both gods and men make use of, to come to be promoted among the trees?"] The "gods," according to the Hebrew manner of speech, are the Trinity who show us mercy. Men also use this "oil" of mercy since they should also be merciful as their Father in heaven as in Luke 6:36 Jesus teaches, ["Be ye therefore merciful, as your Father also is merciful."] The usefulness for us of this oil of mercy is shown in four ways: the mercy of redemption, the castigation of correction, the forgiveness of venial sins, and finally in the acceptance of our obedience.

Of the first of these mercies, it is said in the Song of Songs 1:2, "Thy name is as oil poured out" because this mercy of redemption has been shown to all humanity. Hence Psalm 130:7 says, "Because with the Lord there is mercy: and with him plentiful redemption."

Of the second kind of mercy in Luke 10:30-37 ["But a certain Samaritan being on his journey"], the guardian of our souls, ["came near him"] and seeing him wounded ["was moved with compassion. And going up to him, bound up his wounds"] that is, his violation of the commandments, ["pouring in oil and wine"] that is mercy in the forgiveness of sins ["and setting him upon his own beast, brought him to an inn"] of religion and virtuous life, and took care of him. And the next day he took out ["two pence",]the teaching of the two Testaments ["and gave to the host"] or inn-keeper, that is, a priest ["and said: Take care of him"] by continuing pastoral guidance.

Of the third kind of mercy Psalm 89:32 says, "If they profane my justices: and keep not my commandments: I will visit their iniquities with a rod: and their sins with stripes. But my mercy I will not take away from him," and II Maccabees 6:13 says, "For it is a token of great goodness when sinners are not suffered to go on in their ways for a long time, but are presently punished," and Psalm 118:18 says, "The Lord chastising hath chastised me: but he hath not delivered me over to death," as if to say, through punishment I have at least escaped death, and Job 5:18 says, "For he woundeth, and cureth: he striketh, and his hands shall heal." Whence it is said of David in Psalm 89:21, "I have found David my servant:with my holy oil" that is, the oil of mercy, "I have anointed him."

Of the fourth kind of mercy Titus 3:5 says, "Not by the works of justice, which we have done, but according to his mercy, he saved us," for as it says in Isaiah 64:6, "All our justices are as the rag of a menstruous woman," and therefore the mercy of God is great as regards what is—to speak humbly—acceptable in our works.

Similarly, however men also use the oil of mercy to produce fourteen effects or meanings of that word. Of these

Seven are corporal--	Feed the hungry Give drink to the thirsty Cloth the naked House the pilgrims and wayfarers Visit the sick Visit the captives to redeem or comfort them Bury the dead

Of these seven, Jesus in Matthew 25:35 mentions the first six together, "For I was hungry, and you gave me to eat; I was thirsty, and you gave me to drink; I was a stranger, and you took me in. Naked and you covered me: sick and you visited me: I was in prison, and you came to me," because the Lord, as the Judge, requires of those he will be judging in this life or after death all six of these. The seventh is to bury the dead for which in Tobit 12:12, Tobit is praised by the Angel Raphael, ["When thou didst pray with tears, and didst bury the dead, and didst leave thy dinner, and hide the dead by day in thy house, and bury them by night, I offered thy prayer to the Lord."]

The other seven are:

The seven spiritual acts of mercy---	Counsel those who need counseling Rebuke the delinquent Forgive those who sin against us Console the weak-hearted Lift and carry the weak Pray for the poor Teach the ignorant

Of these there is a verse:"Consult, correct, remit, console, bury, pray." But to this must be added "teach." When a man does these things he merciful like our Heavenly Father is merciful and thus has used the oil and the olive tree as a gate to the Kingdom of Heaven since it is through these deeds the Lord has to come to us and through them that we will gain entrance to return to him. As I Kings 6:31-32 says of Solomon, ["And in the entrance of the oracle he made little doors of olive tree, and posts of five corners, And two doors of olive tree"] one, namely, through which the mercy of the Lord reaches out to us and the other through which by the use of the olive tree of God's mercy man enters to meet God.

Thirdly it follows about the meaning of the olive, which signifies three things: first peace, second the effect of being merciful, third its perpetual greenness in eternal life.

Of the first of these Jeremiah 11:16 says, "The Lord called thy name, a plentiful olive tree, fair, fruitful, and beautiful," that is, rich in fruit, beautiful with the beauty of peace, fruitful in the wealth of a conscience at rest, and fair in the faith-filled tent of contemplation. As a sign of this peace the Hebrew boys, as it say in Matthew 21:8, "cut boughs from the trees, and strewed them in the way," that is, strewed olive branches before Jesus as he road into the Holy City announcing the peace that he brought.

Of the second it is said in Zechariah 14:4, "And his [the Lord's] feet shall stand in that day upon the mount of Olives, which is over against Jerusalem toward the east," that is on the heights of mercy which through merit looks over the heavenly fatherland. Thus also Mercy in the likeness of a virgin crowned with a garland of olive leaves appeared to the Blessed Joanna, standing by her side as she distributed alms.

Of the third it is said in Zechariah 4:2-3, "Behold a candlestick all of gold, and its lamp upon the top of it...And two olive trees over it:one upon the right side of the lamp, and the other upon the left side thereof." The gold candlestick is Christ shining from the heavens but principally within the soul and therefore on the right, but also in the body and therefore on the left.

§ 2

The chapter heading verse is "**She hath considered a field, and bought it: with the fruit of her hands she hath planted a vineyard**" and it has two parts: the buying of the field and the planting of the vineyard.

Concerning the **buying of the field** three things are to be noted: first, what this field is; second how it is to be considered; and third the planting of the field.

Concerning the buying of the field there are six things are to be noted concerning what the Valiant Woman must consider: first the action of farming; second, the viewing of the field, third the field of the Scriptures; four the field of our nature; fifth the field of redemption; sixth the field of our heart as it longs for the celestial fatherland.

The first of these is the action of plowing up the field by obedience to the commandments and counsels of which Jeremiah 32:7 says, "Buy thee my field, which is in Anathoth, for it is thy right to buy it, being akin." Thus to every Christian who has habitually promised obedience to the commandments belongs, by the right of this commitment, "the field which is in Anathoth," the name of which is interpreted as "obedience." Of this field is also understand what in Genesis 27:27 [the blind Isaac as he blesses his son Jacob says], "Behold the smell of my son is as the smell of a plentiful field, which the Lord hath blessed." This "smell" is the fragrance of good works done in obedience. A "plentiful field" is an active life of such works. The "blessing "of the Lord is the conserving of the same works in perseverance to the end.

Of the second, the viewing of the field to be purchased, Genesis 24:63 says of Isaac himself ["And he was gone forth to meditate in the field, the day being now well spent."] One "goes out into the field" of contemplation when the intellect goes beyond earthly things to meditate on eternal things. Isaac then sees in the distance Rebecca, which name is interpreted "she who has received much," coming to him. This is Wisdom, who is the Bridegroom as he waits to contemplate his Bride and by her beauty as she approaches is made her lover. Thus Solomon says in Wisdom 8:2, ["Her have I loved, and have sought her out from my youth, and have desired to take her for my spouse, and I became a lover of her beauty.."] This also is the field flowing with honey that is the honey of wisdom of which Jonathan ate, as I Samuel 14:27 relates, "Jonathan...put forth the end of the rod, which he had in his hand, and dipped it in a honeycomb: and he carried his hand to his mouth, and his eyes were enlightened."

Of the third field, that of the Scriptures, Ruth 2:2 relates how Ruth said to her [mother-in-law Naomi], "I will go into the field, and glean the ears of corn that escape the hands of the reapers, wheresoever I shall find grace with a householder." The ears of wheat are the Scriptures understood historically, allegorically, morally, and anagogically. In the field of the Scriptures the householder is the Holy Spirit and his grace is the grace both of revelation and of study.

Of the fourth field, that is, the world of our nature, of which Matthew 13:18-30 speaks in the Parable of the Sower. For the field of this world is the human heart or our nature in which among the good seed the devil has sown tares. II Samuel 23:11-12 also relates how one of David's soldiers named Shamma saved the people of Israel by standing in a field full of lentils and warding off the Philistines. The "lentils signify" the concupiscence in our members because "lentils" are reddish beans, like those that according to Genesis 25:29-33 the voracious Esau devoured and thereby lost the blessing due him as Isaac's first born son. ["And Jacob boiled pottage:to whom Esau, coming hungry out of the field, Said: Give me of this red pottage, for I am exceeding faint. And Jacob said to him: Sell me thy first birthright. He answered: Lo I die, what will the first birthright avail me? Jacob said: Swear therefore to me. Esau swore to him, and sold his first birthright" thus this hunger signifies the concupiscence of the flesh. But "Shamma' is interpreted "loudly heard renown" because he who conquers his flesh is worthily heard by God and Shamma was recognized by his battle in the lentil field where he struck the Philistines, that is, conquered his bodily urges. "Philistines" is interpreted, 'fallen down drunk," referring to the devils who have drunk the cup of God's wrath and fallen in to hell, as Proverbs 24:30-31says, "I passed by the field of the slothful man, and by the vineyard of the foolish man: And behold it was all filled with nettles, and thorns had covered the face thereof, and the stone wall was broken down." The "nettles" are the prurience of the flesh and the "thorns" are the pangs of guilt.

The fifth kind of field is that of redemption and this is related in all four Gospels in the Passion narratives and prophesied in Jeremiah 32:7, already cited. [In Matthew 27:7-8 we read that "And after they [the chief priests] had consulted together, they bought with them [Judas' thirty pieces of silver] the potter's field, to be a burying place for strangers. For this cause the field was called Haceldama, that is, the field of blood, even to this day. Then was fulfilled that which was spoken by Jeremiah the prophet, saying:["And they took the thirty pieces of silver, the price of him that was prized, whom they prized of the children of Israel. And they gave them unto the potter's field, as the Lord appointed to me"] [Note from New Jerusalem Bible, p. 1657, note d, "Actually this is a free quotation from Zechariah 11:12-13 combined with the idea of the purchase of a field, an idea suggested by Jeremiah 32:6-15. This plus the fact Jeremiah speaks of potters (12:2 seq.) who lived in Hakeldama district (Jeremiah 19:1ff.) explains how the whole text could by approximation be attributed to Jeremiah] and also in Acts 1:19. The "strangers" are the Saints who confess themselves to be strangers and foreigners on earth. Their "grave" is rest from the vexations of the devils that the Saints attain through the price of the Blood of Christ. This "field" is referred to in Genesis 23:11 as the field that Abraham bought from Ephron with four hundred [Albert's text said "two" or "two hundred"] sicles of silver with a double cave for a tomb for Sarah's burial. "Abraham," called the "Father of Many Nations" is Christ. "Ephron" is interpreted "vision of iniquity" and signifies the unfaithful Jews and the crowd of demons who impede the peace of the Saints. "Sarah" is interpreted as "Princess" and stands for the Saints. As for the "two caves" they are the twofold redemption in which the Saints rest, namely of, anticipation and of vision, or of expectation and comprehension.

The sixth meaning, namely the field of desire of the heavenly kingdom, is spoken of in Matthew 13:41, "The kingdom of heaven is like unto a treasure hidden in a field. which a man having found, hid it, and for joy thereof goeth, and selleth all that he hath, and buyeth that field." There the Gloss of St. Gregory the Great [Homily 12 on the Gospels], says, "The treasure stands for desire of heaven hidden in the heart, which when a man finds he counts all else as nothing until he can buy that field." Of this the Song of Songs 7:11 says,

"Come, my beloved, let us go forth into the field" that is, to seek the treasure, "let us abide in the villages," that is the dwellings of the Angels which we desire to enter.

What follows concerns how that field is to be considered if it is to bought, and there are three considerations: estimation, discretion, and provision; first careful pricing as to its value must be calculated and weighed; discretion must be taken lest too much be offered for it; and provision must be made so that it might not be soon reduced to sterility.

Some buyers estimate the value of the Kingdom of heaven at less than it is worth; whence Genesis 4:7 says of Cain, "Have you not sinned, if you have duly offered, but badly divided your offering?" or according to another translation, "If thou do well, shalt thou not receive? But if ill, shall not sin forthwith be present at the door?" For he duly offers who returns a creature to the Creator, but he badly divides who devotes what is better to concupiscence, but what is less good to God. Hence Malachi 1:14 says, "Cursed is the deceitful man that hath in his flock a male, and making a vow offereth in sacrifice that which is feeble to the Lord." This applies to those who by works that are themselves good wish to buy eternal beatitude yet nevertheless remain in sin; thus it is indeed clear they have not calculated correctly. For example, Simon Magus, Giezi, and Jason calculated badly; the first priced grace that is beyond price, the second did so as regards priceless virtue, and the third tried to price spiritual power and dignity that are precious beyond price. Thus Acts 8:18, says that "when Simon [Magus] saw, that by the imposition of the hands of the apostles, the Holy Ghost was given, he offered them money." In II Kings 5:20 [the Prophet Elisha curses his servant Gihazi for trying to extract money from Naaman in return for the miracle of his cleansing from leprosy by the prophet], and in II Maccabees 4:7-10, the Maccabee Jason sought to bribe King Antiochus to appoint him high priest, an office of spiritual power and dignity. Hence St. Augustine says that as a result of Jason's sin "the fire of the sacrifices was extinguished that until then had remained burning." This signifies that it is through those whose power and order of spiritual prayer are done only for payment that the manifest fire of devotion to the sacrifice of praise in the Church becomes extinct or loses all respect.

The second consideration regards discretion in paying for the field, for just as some badly calculate its value, so also some from indiscrete cupidity offer too high a price not attending to whether the seller is honest and is not demanding from us a price greater than the field's value or, if the quantity and price are really beyond its value, is taking advantage of our weakness. Thus there are some who price the field discretely but others who do not. Those who set a price discretely do so not just to please themselves but to meet some necessity of theirs. They make their payment not according to fleshly desires but entirely in Christ and out of love for Christ. They give themselves wholly to destroy sin and concupiscence and do not yield to sinful nature. In John 21:15-18 the Lord three time seeks this grace from Peter when he asks Peter, "Simon, son of John, do you love me more than these?" And three times repeats this same question. This is what is said in Deuteronomy 6:5, "Thou shalt love the Lord thy God with thy whole heart, and with thy whole soul, and with thy whole strength" more than your friends who have one heart with you; and "from you whole soul," that is, from you whole vitality, that is, more than the possessions that keep you alive; and 'with your whole strength," that is more than yourself so that you will do nothing against God. Some, however, there are who retain something from the price of the field for themselves both in friendship and possessions and they are signified by Ananias and Saphira who, as Acts 5:1-5 relates, fell dead at St. Peter's feet because of their fraud in pricing a field.

There are others who foolishly throw away the price which the Lord has rightly given them from the goods of this world, as Judges 11:30-40 tells how Jeptha did, who instead of offering an animal, instead slew his own daughter, that is, his own nature. And of this the Song of Songs says 1:2, "Therefore young maidens have loved thee," that is loved you too much, because crops that have such fervent, new vitality that they burn themselves up in the field, destroying their natural value for sale, are called "maidens."

Third, it should be considered whether the field may yield nothing as the Apostle says in Hebrews 6:7-8, "For the earth that drinketh in the rain which cometh often upon it, and bringeth forth herbs meet for them by whom it is tilled, receiveth blessing from God. But that which bringeth forth thorns and briers, is reprobate, and very near unto a curse, whose end is to be burnt." The cautious buyer who prudently measures and studies the field calculates especially how much work must be expended by the farmer to obtain a good yield, since that work needs to be constant and varied. Proverbs 14:4 says, "Where there are no oxen, the crib is empty:but where there is much corn, there the strength of the ox is manifest" and Isaiah 32:20 says, "Blessed are ye that sow upon all waters, sending thither the foot of the ox and the ass." "All waters" signifies the tears shed for our sins, for strangers, for the miserable, for compassion for the passion of Christ, for those acting out of ignorance, for slowness in progress, and for swiftness in failure. Above all it signifies that one should one sow seed that will multiply good works and bear the fruit of justice. The "foot of the ox" is set under its yoke to produce mature life in a crop of good deeds. Likewise the "foot of the ass," is a person, stupid in the things of this world, but who is wise before Jesus Christ, because he is simple in evil and wise in good, as the Apostle says in I Corinthians 3:18 ["Let no man deceive himself:if any man among you seem to be wise in this world, let him become a fool, that he may be wise], and Job 1:1 also says, "There was a man in the land of Hus, whose name was Job , and that man was simple and upright, and fearing God, and avoiding evil" and who like an ass fell into a dangerous pit in which he lay for some time. Similarly a man should premeditate on his degree of virtue lest he assume a task beyond his strength; for he ought to think of Jesus' words in Luke 9:62, "No man putting his hand to the plough, and looking back, is fit for the kingdom of God."

The third consideration is how this field is to be bought and what price is to be paid for it. Thus it can be bought at the price of an act of simple obedience, or the field of contemplation can be bought at the price of pure and clean heart, or the field of the Scriptures at the price of study and meditation, or the field of the world or of our nature at the price of discipline, or the field of redemption at the price of the action of grace, or finally the field of the hearts' heavenly desire can be bought at the price of devotion.

The price of obedience consists in three things, namely, that we obey simply, quickly, and prudently. Simply in Genesis 22:1-8, Abraham did in offering his son, and, as Hebrews 11:8 says, "By faith he that is called Abraham, obeyed to go out into a place which he was to receive for an inheritance." Thus Abraham did not act like Adam who was self-contradictory and was therefore ejected from Paradise, that is, Adam was inconsistent in that he demanded to know the reason for his obedience before he obeyed instead of yielding himself wholly to the will of God whom he ought to have obeyed without question. We should also obey quickly without delay, as Proverbs 22:29 says, "Hast thou seen a man swift in his work? He shall stand before kings, and shall not be before those that are obscure" and Ecclesiastes 9:10, "Whatsoever thy hand is able to do, do it earnestly: for neither work, nor reason, nor wisdom, nor knowledge shall be in the grave, whither thou art hastening." We should also obey prudently, since if, as St. Gregory the Great says, "If what is commanded is honorific and fitted to worldly success it should be obeyed not from our will but from obedience, but if it is something humble and lowly then we should obey it from our own will as well."

The price of purity by which the field of contemplation is purchased has three aspects, namely, that we should purge the mind of the filth of sin, the will from the fumes of concupiscence, and the reason from all temporal cares; because sin, "Sin is mire, concupiscence is fumes, and bodily phantasies are spiritual darkness", as St. Gregory the Great also says, The first, that sin is dirt, is exemplified in Luke 18:35-43 by the blind man sitting at the wayside who, when Jesus passed by, cried out "Son of David, have mercy on me; and when Jesus asked him, "What wilt thou that I do to thee?" said, "Lord, that I may see." And this also is what is meant in Matthew 5:8, "Blessed are the clean of heart for they will see God."

And the second, the fumes of concupiscence, are exemplified in Numbers 32:35 where the Lord says to Moses that if the Canaanites are allowed to remain in the land "they shall be unto you as nails in your eyes, and spears in your sides, and they shall be your adversaries in the land of your habitation." The "people of Canaan" signify the fumes rising from the fire of lust that penetrate the heart through the first motions of evil thoughts and also the spears in the eyes that are the spiritual blindness that blinds us from engaging in spiritual contemplation.

Concerning the third, spiritual darkness, Job 3:23 asks [how anyone can bear to live], "Whose way is hidden, and God hath surrounded in darkness?" "The way" is the eternal light hidden from us by the fact that the eyes of our intellect are clouded over with corporeal fantasies about the things of this world. As Tobit 5:12 laments, "What manner of joy shall be to me, who sit in darkness, and see not the light of heaven?"

The price of study and speculation by which the field of the Scripture is purchased has three parts:for we ought to study and meditate on the Bible for three purposes: to enjoy knowing it, for its usefulness in acting, and spirituality to experience its sweetness. Of the first it says in Daniel 12:3, "But they that are learned shall shine as the brightness of the firmament: and they that instruct many to justice, as stars for all eternity." Of the second it is said in Psalm 1:2,

"But his will is in the law of the Lord, and on his law he shall meditate day and night." And of the third Wisdom 13:1 says, "But all men are vain, in whom there is not the knowledge of God" because that is sweet and without it one perishes, as Wisdom says later on in 15:3, "For to know thee is perfect justice: and to know thy justice, and thy power, is the root of immortality" and also Jeremiah 9:4 says, "But let him that glorieth glory in this, that he understandeth and knoweth me, for I am the Lord that exercise mercy, and judgment, and justice in the earth." The first of these purposes builds up faith, the second instructs life in action; the third kindles desire and hope in the search for of beatitude, in hope now and in its future attainment. According to St. Augustine also there is a price for that field that is the study of the Holy Scriptures, since "we meditate on what is credible, intelligible, and open to various interpretations," Faith rests on revelation and the authority of the articles of faith and of the Scriptures. Intellection deals with the truths of reason. Opinion also helps us but, as regards truth it helps only superficially.

The price of discipline by which the field of our nature, which [as it says in Genesis 1:31,] God created and saw was "very good," but we which we must cultivate, is threefold, for as says, "The discipline of learning deals with difficult matters." There are three things which are difficult for us: vigils, fasts, and the endurance of temptations and external troubles that impinge on us.

Of the first of these Sirach 31:1 says, "Watching for honors consumeth the flesh, and the thought thereof driveth away sleep." and Psalm 63:2 says, "O God, my God, to thee do I watch at break of day." And the taming of the flesh follows, as the verse goes on to say, "For thee my soul hath thirsted; for thee my flesh, O how many ways!" For the flesh never thirsts for God, nor for virtue, until it is first tamed by vigils.

Of the second I Corinthians 9:27 says, "But I chastise my body, and bring it into subjection: lest perhaps, when I have preached to others, I myself should become a castaway" and in Psalm 35:13, "But as for me, when they were troublesome to me, I was clothed with haircloth. I humbled my soul with fasting; and my prayer shall be turned into my bosom."

Of the third Lamentations 1:13 says, "From above he hath sent fire into my bones" and Psalm 60:13 says, "Give us help from trouble: for vain is the salvation of man", which St. Basil expounds thus, "Our help from troubles causes us trouble, because when we have health of body we become vain." Also Hebrews 12:11 says, "Now all chastisement for the present indeed seemeth not to bring with it joy, but sorrow: but afterwards it will yield, to them that are exercised by it, the most peaceable fruit of justice."

Also the price of actions by which the field of redemption is purchased has three aspects, since first we ought always to remember so great a benefit; second we ought to extol it with magnificent praise and blessing, and third, we should take great care how we can value similar gifts.

Concerning the first of these, remembering its benefit, Lamentations 3:19 says, "Remember my poverty, and transgression, the wormwood, and the gall." We must recall Christ's "poverty" because he hung naked on the cross. We must also remember our "transgressions" because Christ did more than was necessary for our redemption. The "wormwood" signifies the bitterness of martyrdom and the "gall" the malice of his Christ's Jewish accusers. Or, to be more literal, they gave him wine mixed with vinegar [Matthew 27:34 and 48; Mark 15:36; Luke 23:36;], wormwood [hyssop, John 19:29], gall [Matthew 27:34], and myrrh [Mark 15:23]. Hence Jeremiah in Lamentations 3:20 says, "I will be mindful and remember, and my soul shall languish within me."

Of the second, praise, Psalm 146:2 says, "Praise the Lord, O my soul, in my life I will praise the Lord: I will sing to my God as long as I shall be," and again Psalm 103:1 says, "Bless the Lord, O my soul:and let all that is within me bless his holy name." And again as to both remembrance and praise the same Psalm, verses 2-5 says:"Bless the Lord, O my soul, and never forget all he hath done for thee. Who forgiveth all thy iniquities: who healeth all thy diseases. Who redeemeth thy life from destruction: who crowneth thee with mercy and compassion. Who satisfieth thy desire with good things: thy youth shall be renewed like the eagle's." All these are shown to us as benefits of redemption.

Of the third, care to value other gifts, Psalm 116:12 says, "What shall I render to the Lord, for all the things he hath rendered unto me? I will take the chalice of salvation; and I will call upon the name of the Lord," and Sirach 31:12, "Thou art set at a great table," know therefore how you should be prepared for it."

The price of devotion by which we buy the field of the heart's heavenly desires also has three parts: namely the pious affection of the longing heart, the readiness for prayer, and the raising of the heart to everlasting life.

Of the first, pious affection of the heart, the Apostle says in Philippians 3:13-14, "Forgetting the things that are behind, and stretching forth myself to those that are before, I press towards the mark, [to the prize of the supernal vocation of God in Christ Jesus,] and Isaiah, 26:8-9 says, "And in the way of thy judgments, O Lord, we have patiently waited for thee: thy name, and thy remembrance are the desire of the soul. My soul hath desired thee in the night."

Of the second, the readiness for prayer, Luke 18:1 says, "We ought always to pray, and not to faint," and the same Gospel, teaches this through two parables: one in 18:1-9 concerns the insistent widow beating on the door and praying for justice from a judge who "neither fears God nor man," and the other in Luke 11:5-10 concerning the man who asks for three loafs of bread for a guest who has just come from a journey.

Of the third, the raising of the heart, it is repeatedly said in the Holy Mass, "Lift up your hearts! We have lifted them up to the Lord!" and Psalm 63:7-8 [Vulgate] says, "Man shall come to a deep heart: And God shall be exalted."

§ 3

The second part of this verse follows:"**With the fruit of her hands she hath planted a vineyard,**" concerning which two things are to be considered, namely, who plants the vine and how it is planted. The first is noted when it says, "With the fruit of her hands" and since we have already said much of the meaning of "hands" here we will only say something about their "fruit." A hand has two fruits, care for oneself and care for one's neighbor; for one has care for the vine that is one's own soul and also love for that vine that is the Church in which one's neighbor is included.

In the care of one's own soul the vine of sorrow first bears fruit in a bad field; second the vine of devotion or redemption bears fruit on the mountain of blessings; third is the vine of joy in the horn of the son of oil, four the vine of inebriating love in the wine and the grape cluster; fifth, the wine of perfect joy in the vines of Engaddi.

Of the first, the vine of sorrow, it is said in Psalm 60:5, "Thou hast shewn thy people hard things; thou hast made us drink the wine of sorrow." That vine in a bad field of sins which are pressed in the wine-press of contrition and bottled in the memory of misdeeds and poured out through confession and drunk by the satisfaction of penance.

Of the second, the wine of redemption, it is said in the Song of Songs 5:1, "I have eaten the honeycomb with my honey, I have drunk my wine with my milk," and this commemorates the different benefits which excite one to devotion, for the "honey" is the sweetness of pure divinity which is given when God shares this divinity with us. The "honeycomb," however, is the wax of true humanity in which redemption takes place. The "vine" is the devotion thus conceived. The "milk" is pure and sweet and of a nature that agrees with the teaching of Christ, as Psalm 4:8 says, "By the fruit of their corn, their wine and oil, they are multiplied." The "fruit of the corn" is stability of solid and strengthening grace. The "fruit of the vine" is the fruit of piety that grows on the highest mountain of God's benefits and is pressed out in the wine press of thanksgiving and collected in the vessel of the heart. It is wasted by deceitful ingratitude but is well imbibed when the grace of God is not received on sterile ground but fills the good work for which it was given.

The third vine, that of joy, is that mentioned in Psalm 104:15, "And that wine may cheer the heart of men." and in Genesis 49:11, "He shall wash his robe in wine" [that is make the face of his soul to rejoice], "and his garment wrung out in the in the blood [Vulgate "son"] of the grape," that is, the state of the heart of Christ beating with sorrow through the wine of the grapevine of the Cross. [Isaiah 5:1 says, "My beloved had a vineyard on a hill in a fruitful place,"] that is, in a corner of the vineyard facing the sun of a pure conscience. "In the blood of the grape," that is, the blood of richness, eternal and internal, conceived by God through sweetness and security, but pressed out out in the wine-press of meditation on eternal joys and caught in a vessel of longing, free of the dregs of sorrow. It is then drunk in a man's thoughts as he confesses with the confession of praise to the Lord and in the rest of his thoughts celebrates for himself the feast day.

Of the fourth kind of vine that inebriates with love is it said in the Song of Songs 5:1, "Eat, O friends, and drink, and be inebriated, my dearly beloved." This vine grows in the mountains among the cypress that flourish in a very hot country where there is, as it were, a fire on Sion and a forge in Jerusalem, as Psalm 68:16-17 says, "The mountain of God is a fat mountain, a curdled mountain, a fat mountain. Why suspect, ye curdled mountains? A mountain in which God is well pleased to dwell," that is, on the mountain of the highest charity. This wine is pressed out in the press of warmest piety, freed from the dregs of vain self-love, and drunk down in the sweet embrace of the beloved even to full satisfaction and inebriation in which all that is earthly is forgotten.

Of the fifth vine, namely that of perfect grace, Proverbs 9:5 says, "Come, eat my bread, and drink the wine which I have mingled for you," which grows in the vineyards of Engaddi, because the Song of Songs 1:13 says, ["A cluster of cypress my love is to me, in the vineyards of Engaddi"] where this "wine" is the incorruptible balsam of eternity in the enclosure of the Divine Wisdom and is pressed out in the wine-press of contemplation. It is received, however, in the vessel of admiration of the glory of the celestial kingdom in which all the Saints rejoice with Christ. It is freed from the dregs of bad preparation lest anything worldly should be mixed with it, because, as it is say in I Corinthians 2:9, "That eye hath not seen, nor ear heard, neither hath it entered into the heart of man, what things God hath prepared for them that love him" [and Isaiah 64:4 says, "From the beginning of the world they have not heard, nor perceived with the ears: the eye hath not seen, O God, besides thee, what things thou hast prepared for them that wait for thee."] This wine is drunk in an elevation of mind in the rapture of the soul, as Psalm 89:19 says, "For our protection [Latin, *assumptio*, elevation] is of the Lord, and of our king the holy one of Israel." And the foregoing are the fruit of the hands of the Valiant Woman.

The hand that is the love of neighbor holds the fruit of the vine that is for the neighbor and this is first that wine of severe rebuke, the second is that according to doctrine, and the third that of congratulation for good deeds, the fourth of compassion, and the fifth of support. And these are taken from five effects of wine. For wine stings, but this shows that it gives off subtle spirits and hence should naturally be consumed moderately, when it often comforts.

Of the first sort of wine, that of rebuke, the Song of Songs 1:1 says, "Thy breasts are better than wine," about which the Gloss says that "A biting rebuke should be given to sins, as it says in I Timothy 5:20, 'Them that sin reprove before all: that the rest also may have fear."

Of the second kind, that of doctrine, it is said in the Song of Songs 8:2, "I will give thee a cup of spiced wine and new wine of my pomegranates." Spiced wine is doctrine that cools us off from the heat of the vices.

Of the third kind of wine, that of congratulation, it is said in Job 32:19, "Behold, my belly is as new wine which wanteth vent, which bursteth the new vessels.' For the spirit of congratulation bubbles in joy like new wine in a jar so that it is difficult to suppress or restrain joy. Hence it says in Luke 15:6, "And coming home, call together his friends and neighbors, saying to them: Rejoice with me, because I have found my sheep that was lost?"

Of the fourth kind, the wine of compassion Isaiah 16:9 says, "Therefore I will lament with the weeping of Jazer the vineyard of Sabama: I will water thee with my tears, O Hesebon, and Eleale: for the voice of the treaders hath rushed in upon thy vintage, and upon thy harvest." "Eleale" is interpreted as *descent* and signifies the immense evil that descends on the sorrowful; and it explains the cause of this evil, namely, that voice of the insulting, stamping demons comes down on the one to whom the vine of eternal joy and the refreshment of inebriating grace had before been given.

Of the last kind of wine, namely, that which gives support in helping our neighbor, it is said in III Esdras [Apocrypha] 3:18-19, "O ye men, how exceeding strong is wine! It causeth all men to err that drink it: It maketh the mind of the king and of the fatherless child to be all one; of the bondman and of the freeman, of the poor man and of the rich." This wine is one which strengthens the man who alone is unable to resist the devil but who is strengthen as by a drink of wine by another's aid and then draws his sword, and begins to fight, as Ecclesiastes 4:10-11 says, "If one fall he shall be supported by the other: woe to him that is alone, for when he falleth, he hath none to lift him up. And if two lie together, they shall warm one another: how shall one alone be warmed? "

The last point is how the vine is planted, and since the text speaks of the vineyard in the singular, in explaining how the Valiant Woman "hath planted a vineyard" we speak of one vineyard, the soul, either our own soul or our neighbor's soul.

This vineyard is planted toward the meridian where the sun is strongest and the wind is the Austro from the southwest and in a high rich place. It is plowed, then weeded with a hoe, and dunged, and watered, and the grapes are gathered. The vineyard is surrounded outside by a wall, and a wine-press is constructed in it, and a tower built in its center and it planted with vines of Soreth. The "meridian' is the hanging of the heart in the light of grace, as Job 38:24 says, "By what way is the light spread, and heat divided upon the earth?" It is planted in high and rich place, that is, on a mountain of the spirit and the richness of devotion as it is said in Genesis 27:39-40, "In the fat of the earth, and in the dew of heaven from above, shall thy blessing be." It is "plowed" with the plow of fear, "weeded" with the hoe of contrition, "dunged' with abject humility, and "watered" with penitent tears, as it says in Isaiah 26:19, "For thy dew is the dew of the light." The "walls" that enclose it outside are the guardianship of the Angels. The "tower" in the middle is the high hope of God's help, as Isaiah 16:1 says, "Sion the city of our strength a savior, a wall and a bulwark shall be set therein." This tower is the Savior since it says in Psalm 91:1, "He that dwelleth in the aid of the Most High, shall abide under the protection of the God of Jacob." While outside wall is the guardianship of the Angels, the inner wall is the human mutual guardianship of each other, as St. Augustine says, "Guard each others chastity, because the God who dwells among you guards you from yourselves." The "winepress" in middle of the vineyard in which the wine is pressed out is the memory of Christ's passion since to ponder that ought to extract from us all that is of use in good wine. This vine however is planted in the "vineyard of Soreth, that is, with seed of choice vines [Jeremiah 2:21 says, "Yet I planted thee a chosen vineyard, all true seed" and Isaiah 5:1 says, "My beloved had a vineyard on a hill in a fruitful place,] that is, of souls made to God's image and likeness.

OUTLINE OF CHAPTER VIII

She hath girded her loins with strength,
and hath strengthened her arm. (v. 17)

§1 Acrostic letter Heth signifies "fear" that leads to action against difficulties for which the Valiant Woman girds herself with fortitude
  1) Girding for what purpose?
    1) For running to confront the enemy;
    2) To meet friends, so as not to be impeded
    3) To serve others as Christ washed the Apostles feet
  2) Girding with what? With fortitude of which there are five kinds:
    1) The Valiant Woman has true fortitude that faces difficulties out of virtue and grace.
    2) Judas Maccabeus faced difficulties from fear of disgrace
    3) Joshua faced difficulties lest he be blamed by his superiors
    4) Mattathias the Maccabee faced difficulties because of his anger
    5) Judith faced difficulties without experience of dangers or full knowledge of them
  3) Which members of body are girded: the Valiant Woman's loins that have three traits:
    1) Seats of pleasure
      1) Eating
      2) Erotic pleasure
    2) Source of procreation
      1) The authority of preaching
      2) Sowing the seed of the Gospel
    3) Foundation of all bodily movements
      1) Austerity of penance is sorrowful
      2) Fillings of compassion are sorrowful and give birth

§2. "She has strengthened her arm."
  1) What is the Valiant Woman's arm?
    1) Her shoulders are her charity that carries the burden of the Law of God
    2) Her arm is the virtue of magnanimity that performs good works
    3) Her elbow on which her arm moves is the consideration of how to complete works of magnanimity
    4) Her hands have been discussed in Chapter VII
    5) The two bones of her lower arm
      1) Confidence of finishing what has to be done
      2) Patience in sustaining what has to be suffered in doing this work
        1) From the enemy, the devil who seeks to prevent the work being completed
        2) Raises obstacles to it being done rightly,
  6) Nerves connecting parts of the arm are perseverance and humility binding the action to its completion
  7) The vital spirit is the fervor of energy from the food we eat
  8) The muscles use this energy in action which is prudent from
    1) Memory of past experience

2) Foresight for the future
2) How her arm is strengthened for the struggle
  1) By the shield of equanimity
  2) By a bracelet of good works
  3) By a sword that is the Word of God
  4) By the spear of zealous anger

CHAPTER VIII

She hath girded her loins with strength, and hath strengthened her arm. (v. 17)

§ 1

HETH ח Heth is interpreted "fear" and alludes to the meaning of the above verse because fear is the cause of action as it is said in Song of Songs 3:7-8, "Threescore valiant ones of the most valiant of Israel, surrounded the bed of Solomon? All holding swords and most expert in war: every man's sword upon his thigh, because of fears in the night." The "bed" of Solomon signifies the soul of this Valiant Woman on which she reclines all day as on a couch. Sixty strong men surround this couch, that is, the perfect observance of the Ten Commandments. And these are the strongest in Israel because Israel is interpreted "most upright" because it is by the perfect observance of the commandments that the strength of virtue is acquired. All of them hold "swords" by which they are able to drive off temptation. And this is what is meant by "fears in the night," that is, because of the fear of arrows flying in the night, namely, demonic persuasions to hidden and obscure sins. Hence "fear" is the cause of what is said in the above verse.

Two things are noted in the chapter verse namely the "**girding of her loins with strength**" and the "**strengthening of her arms.**" Concerning the first of these three things are to be noted, namely, the mode of "girding" with strength or fortitude, and that the girded part or member of her body is "her loins."

Concerning the first of these it should be noted that to be girded for war (*accingimur*), differs from being girded for running (*succingimur*) and these differ from being girded to minister (*praecingimur*). Of the first we read in I Maccabees 3:58-59, "And Judas said: Gird yourselves, and be valiant men, and be ready against the morning, that you may fight with these nations that are assembled against us to destroy us and our sanctuary. For it is better for us to die in battle, than to see the evils of our nation, and of the holies," and in Psalm 45:4, "Gird thy sword upon thy thigh, O thou most mighty one," and in Genesis 49:19, "Gad, being girded, shall fight before him: and he himself shall snap at their heels."

Of the second it is said in John 21:7, "Simon Peter, when he heard that it was the Lord, girt his coat about him, (for he was naked,) and cast himself into the sea," because he was so eager to see the Lord. The "coat" is the business of living and this ought to be girt with the belt of justice lest by flowing on the ground it might impede the rapid motion of the feet, that is impede the affections. Thus Proverbs 30:31 calls a preacher, "A [crowing] cock girded about the loins." For a cock that arouses sleepers by his crowing that tells that it is morning is a preacher who arouses those who sleep in sin to penitential vigil and the hour of God's judgment that signifies the sweeping away of sin. And this is called "girding of the loins" because by the rectitude of justice the laxness of life's business is elevated.

Of the third, namely, the girding of the loins in the service of others Jesus says in Luke 12:37 says, "[Blessed are those servants, whom the Lord when he cometh, shall find watching. Amen I say to you, that] he will gird himself, and make them sit down to meat, and passing will minister unto them." Hence in order to signify that ministry which he will show in the fatherland, Jesus girded himself at the supper and showed his service of humility by washing his disciples feet.

Next in the chapter text is the consideration of that by which this girding was done, namely, "with strength". The Philosopher [Aristotle] uses strength or "fortitude" in the *Nicomachean Ethics*, III, Chapter 6, in five senses: The first is true fortitude that sustains terrible things and acts against such difficulties out of grace and virtue. The second, however, is that which sustains terrible and difficult things out of shame and blame if one yields. The third is that which sustains dangers and attacks difficulties because of the commands of authorities or the urging one's superiors; and this has also another form, namely, when one acts against difficulties to avoid some greater danger. The fourth is when one acts against difficulties out of fury, as from zealous anger. The fifth is when someone acts from the hope of some good, as the Philosopher says, and this kind of fortitude he calls confidence of victory, which also has a related kind of fortitude, namely, when some one attacks difficulties because he does not recognize the danger involved, as, for example, one inexperienced in such danger.

It is the first sort of fortitude or strength that this Valiant Woman possesses, as is said later on in verse 23 of our text, "Strength and beauty are her clothing, and she shall laugh in the latter day." For this "beauty" signifies that which is honorable as Cicero [Tully] says that "by his strength he arouses our admiration and by his worthiness he awes us" and what is admirable in this way is the grace of God and true virtue.

The second sort of fortitude is that which results from fear of disgrace if one fails and this was the strength of the Maccabees when Judas Maccabeus said,[I Maccabees 9:8-10, slightly different version] "Gird yourselves, and be valiant men, and be ready against the morning, that you may fight with these nations that are assembled against us to destroy us and our sanctuary. For it is better for us to die in battle, than to see the evils of our nation, and of the holies."

The third kind is that of Joshua of whom it is said in Sirach 46:1-2, "Valiant in war was Jesus [Joshua] the son of Nave, who was successor of Moses among the prophets, who was great according to his name, very great for the saving the elect of God, to overthrow the enemies that rose up against them, that he might get the inheritance for Israel," for Joshua, after Moses, made war because commanded by God and also by his name, which is interpreted "Savior," was strong and great in saving Israel and thus gave a model of why Jesus is called by that same title because he saved his people from their sins as it is said in Matthew 1:21, ["And she [Mary] shall bring forth a son: and thou shalt call his name Jesus, for he shall save his people from their sins.]

The fourth kind of fortitude was that of Mattathias of which it is written in I Maccabees 2:24-25 that when he saw someone sacrificing to idols at the order of the soldier whom King Antiochus had sent to force the Jews to commit idolatry, "And Mattathias saw and was grieved, and his reins trembled, and his wrath was kindled according to the judgment of the law, and running upon him he slew him upon the altar: Moreover the man whom king Antiochus had sent, who compelled them to sacrifice, he slew at the same time, and pulled down the altar." Also this was the fortitude of Phineas who cut down the Israelite who had been initiated into the cult of Beelphegor and was going to meet the Madian prostitute, as it is written in Numbers 24:6 and also that of Simon and Levi who slew the Sichemites out of zeal for the chastity of their sister, as is written in Genesis 34:25-26.

The fifth was the fortitude of the widow Judith who hoping for victory went to Holofernes and conquered and killed him as it is related in Judith 13:10 and following.

What follows concerns what member of the body of the Valiant Woman that is girded, namely, "her loins" and note that the loins of the body have three traits. The first is that, as St. Gregory the Great notes, they are the place of pleasure. The second is that they are the place from which flows the seed of reproduction. The third is that they are, as it were, the foundation of the whole body; for as St. Augustine says, "All the moveable parts of the body are moved by those that do not move and thus on the loins is founded the whole mobility of the bodily members both inferior and superior since they seem to be moved from the loins." The loins are the place of pleasure in two respects, both the pleasure of eating and of sex. Thus Job 40:11 says of Behemoth, that is, of the devil, "His strength is in his loins and his force in the navel of his belly," and Jesus in Luke 12:35 says, "Let your loins be girt, and lamps burning in your hands," on which St. Gregory the Great comments, "Our loins are girt when we restrain lust through continence...we hold burning torches in our hands when through good deeds to our neighbors we shown the light of a good example."

Also the loins from which flow the seed of reproduction are twofold, namely, the authority by which he who sows the Word is sent, since the Apostle says, Romans 10:1, "And how shall they preach unless they be sent?" And the loins are also the grace of preaching which is caused by learning and eloquence and the zeal for the good life of souls. Of these two senses of "loins" Job 40:2 says, "Gird up thy loins like a man: I will ask thee, and do thou tell me." For the work of males is to generate and produce semen. Thus a man girds his loins who with the grace of preaching and authority with which he has bound them and scatters everywhere seed to bring forth a harvest and thus is said to answer what the Lord "asks him," because the Lord questions him if he is a preacher who is simple and unprepared for preaching the truth. For as the Lord is fed and given drink, so is the Lord "answered" when he is answered only weakly and with little guidance in the Holy Spirit.

The loins that are the foundation and firmness of the body are two, namely, austerity and compassion, because life in us is strengthened by austerity and from the loins [feelings] of compassion within us is supported a good life in regards to our neighbor. On the loins taken in this sense Isaiah 21:3 says, "Therefore are my loins filled with pain, anguish hath taken hold of me, as the anguish of a woman in labor." For one loin, that of austerity, is filled with the sorrow of penitence, the other, that of compassion, is filled with the pains of giving birth, because the birthing of those who give birth in Christ, make us suffer for ourselves and also suffer the pains of others as our own.

§ 2

It follows: "**She has strengthened her arm.**" Here it must be considered what is her arm and what it is that strengthens it. For the arm of this Valiant Woman is her magnanimity, because, as Proverbs 30:30 says, "A lion, the strongest of beasts, who hath no fear of any thing [that is, of the devils] he meeteth."

And since previously we spoke of the Valiant Woman's "hand" now we will discuss the disposition of her "arm." For this arm has a shoulder from which it hangs and an elbow by which it is bent for motion and operation and by which it is joined to the shoulder but is divided below the elbow into two bones. Further it has nerves by which it has interconnections and the vital spirit through which it receives life from the heart which [according to Aristotle] is the seat of the soul, and it also has muscles in which the nourishment from digestion is worked out.

The shoulders of this Valiant Woman on which she bears burdens is her charity because every precept and burden of the law of God is carried and fulfilled through charity [Romans 13:10, " Love therefore is the fulfilling of the law."] These are the shoulders on which the Good Shepherd, Christ, carries the weak lamb [Luke 20:5]. Hence Isaiah 22:22 says, "And I will lay the key of the house of David upon his shoulder: and he shall open, and none shall shut: and he shall shut, and none shall open." The "key that opens" is redemption on the shoulders of charity and to do this in order to free those bound is done only out of charity. The key, however, closes on some as their just deserts because they have despised the offered redemption.

The elbow [*cubitus,* originally the length of the forearm from the elbow to end of the middle finger, about 17 to 22 inches] on which is bent and moved the arm is the consideration of the works which result from the arm of magnanimity, when commanded to Noah in Genesis 6:15, ["The length of the ark shall be three hundred cubits: the breadth of it fifty cubits, and the height of it thirty cubits:the breadth of it fifty cubits, and the height of it thirty cubits"] that in the building the Ark it should be finished as measured in cubits because our works, especially those made out of magnanimity, as St. Paul says to the Philippians 4:18, always require diligent consideration as to how they can be successfully completed. But two bones which hang from the elbow of consideration are the confidence of finishing what has to be done and patience in sustaining what has to be suffered in doing this. Thus the enemy [the devil] gains nothing against this Valiant Woman, since in carrying out any work she has confidence that patience in every trouble until she gains a successful conclusion, as God promises in Psalm 89:22-23, "For my hand shall help him: and my arm shall strengthen him. The enemy shall have no advantage over him: nor the son of iniquity have power to hurt him." Here by God's hand "my hand" is meant what he does and "my arm" signifies what he completes. The enemy impedes a person in two ways, namely, first by preventing something good being finished, and against this prevails confidence that a work once begun will be completed, and this is what is mean by "shall have no advantage over him." Second the enemy impedes good acts by raising obstacles, but against this patience prevails, and this what is meant by "nor the son of iniquity have power over him."

The "nerves" connecting the parts of the arm are the perseverance binding the action to its completion and this is humility that binds tightly. The "vital spirit" is the fervor of energy, as the Apostle says in Romans 12:11, "In spirit fervent; serving the Lord." The "muscles" through which the energy of food we digest is employed are the parts of prudence, namely memory of past experience, understanding of present circumstances, and foresight for the future, because prudence is employed in these deliberations must as physical energy is employed in moving our muscles. All this prudential thinking should be done before it is embodied in action, for as St. Augustine says, "Prudence sagaciously chooses those things by which a work is aided and rejects those by which it is impeded."

What follows pertains to how this arm is strengthened for the fight, and it is strengthened by a shield, bracelets, a sword, and a spear. The shield that nothing can pierce is equanimity as is said in Wisdom 5:20. ["He will take equity for an invincible shield"] and as the Apostle says, Ephesians 6:16, ["In all things taking the shield of faith, wherewith you may be able to extinguish all the fiery darts of the most wicked one,"] or as Psalm 5:13 says, "O Lord, thou hast crowned us, as with a shield of thy good will," where "shield" signifies the Saints.

A bracelet is the ornament of a good work as it says in Job 40:21, "Canst thou put a ring in his [Leviathan's] nose, or bore through his jaw with a buckle [*armilla*]?" because the efficacy of good works destroys the two jaws of the devil, namely, guilt and pain, that clamp down on the souls that the devil Leviathan attempts to devour.

The sword of the spirit is the Word of God as the Apostles says in Hebrews 4:12, "For the word of God is living and effectual, and more piercing than any two-edged sword."

The spear is zealous anger, so it says in Wisdom 5:21, "And he will sharpen his severe wrath for a spear" and it says "severe" to indicate that it cuts to pieces every vice and temptation of the devil.

THE VALIANT WOMAN

OUTLINE OF CHAPTER IX

She hath tasted and seen that her traffic is good: her lamp shall not be put out in the night. (v. 18)

§1. Acrostic letter Teth ט means "internal good" for the Valiant Woman's taste for good deeds and eternal life
  1) The interior joy of a good conscience as against the fear of a bad conscience
  2) The interior good of the experience and hope of the Kingdom of Heaven.
     1) The taste and sight of earthly life's marketing as such
        1) A bad taste, without salt, is sin to be spit out
        2) A good taste is the Lord
     2) The experience of sight has a fourfold vision by which we experience eternal truth.
        1) Or reason according to Faith known obscurely
           1) By the Creator's trace or image in his creatures
           2) By the allegorical sense of Scripture
        2) Of Faith according to the Gift of Understanding and full consent to God's authority but also to do penance in dust and ashes if we are slow to believe
        3) Understanding by the Beatitude of the Clean of Heart, free of worldly preoccupations
        4) According to the Gift that is called *Faith*
     3) Of taste and sight taken and also touch taken together and possessed by
        1) The faithful people and commonly by all of them
        2) The Doctors of the Church
        3) Contemplatives such as Moses on the mountain
        4) Persons in rapture, such as St. Paul
     4) Her business is thus seen, tasted, and touched because it is good:
        1) She engages in her business outside her country with her husband's money
           1) This money is for her own use but she also uses it for the poor
           2) Yet it is the good fortune of this world
        2) Also with the money of the community to which she and her husband belong
           1) This money is the Word of God
           2) It is used for sinners living in a foreign land
           3) This community money is the devotion of the heart and prayer for all living in this present world.

§2. Her lamp shall not be put out in the night
  1) What is this lamp? It is fivefold as in the Parable of the Lost Coin:
     1) The lamp of redemption by which a woman sweeps her house to find a lost coin
        1) The sweeper is Jesus Christ the Holy One.
        2) The house He sweeps is this world
        3) The candle in its holder is the light of divinity in the holder of our mortality.

  4) The search is all that we do for our own and others redemption, such as preaching and suffering.
  5) The searchers' friends are the holy Patriarchs.
   6) The neighbors who rejoice with the searcher are the Angels
 2) The lamp of the Word of God:"Thy word is a lamp to my feet, and a light to my paths."
  1) The feet or human affections that are guided are the ways of living this life
  2) The paths that are lighted are the various states of life and works done by persons in them
  3) The lamp of example
   1) The lamp is the light of good deeds in the fame and knowledge of one's fellows.
   2) The lamp stand is authority and eloquence in prelates or the radiance of charity in any subordinate.
   3) The lighted house is the Church of those who emend their lives by this light
   4) The lamp of right intention that is simple and single when free of evil
   5) The lamp of disputation is needed because by this lamp God disputes with us in judgment
2) What is the darkness of the night that threatens the lamp's light?
 1) The light that is threatened by darkness
  1) The light of redemption shines in the darkness of sin and original guilt
  2) The light of good example shines in the darkness of social intercourse
  3) The light of scrutiny shines in the hidden darknesses of the heart and conscience
 2) The fivefold darkness that threatens these lights:
  1) The darkness of sin and original guilt
  2) The darkness of ignorance
  3) The darkness of this world
  4) The darkness of conscience
  5) The darkness of the Last Judgment when the damned and Devils will be cast into Hell as the three lights of this world will be darkened:
   1) The sun is the light of worldly prosperity
   2) The moon is the mutability of temporal pleasures
   3) The stars are the power of the senses by which sinners live
3) Why in fact is the Valiant Woman's lamp not extinguished?
 1) It is protected by;
  1) The surrounding glass of the purity of bodily chastity
  2) Abundance of oil: the wise virgins' true piety, which the chaste but foolish virgins lacked.
  3) The shining fervor of the flame is the ardor of the most fervent charity that cannot be quenched by
   1) Carnal concupiscence
   2) Satan's pomps; worldly attractions and the vanity of shows
  4) The wick of the lamp
 2) The Valiant Woman carries her lamp with care and humility:
  1) Lest it be blown out by wind of vainglory
  2) Or knocked over by the crowd of pride

CHAPTER IX

She hath tasted and seen that her traffic is good: her lamp shall not be put out in the night. (v. 18)

§ 1

TET ט. Tet is interpreted "between" or "good" and taken together these mean "internal good" and this alludes to the verse that follows, which concerns the taste for the eternal and interior good. About this interior good a distinction must first be made, for there is the interior joy of a good conscience and an interior good of the experience of the Kingdom of Heaven.

Of the first of these I Corinthians 1:12 says, "For our glory is this, the testimony of our conscience," while Wisdom 17:10 says, "For whereas wickedness is fearful, it beareth witness of its condemnation: for a troubled conscience always forecasteth grievous things."

The second of these is included in the definition of hope as St. Augustine defines it, "The certain expectation of future beatitude arising from the consciousness of merit and the mercy of God." Hence later in our text, Proverbs 31:29 says, "Many daughters have gathered together riches: thou hast surpassed them all," and Psalm 45:14 says, "The glory of the king's daughter is within."

Of the third Jesus in Luke 17:21 says, "For lo, the kingdom of God is within you." the Apostles explains in Romans 14:17 what this kingdom is, "The kingdom of God is not meat and drink; but justice, and peace, and joy in the Holy Ghost," and St. Augustine says in *Confessions* X, c. 40, "Sometimes Thou admittest me to an affection, very unusual, in my inmost soul; rising to a strange sweetness, which if it were perfected in me, I know not what in it would not belong to the life to come. But through my miserable encumbrances I sink down again into these lower things, and am swept back by former custom, and am held, and greatly weep, but am greatly held. So much doth the burden of a bad custom weigh us down. Here I can stay, but would not; there I would, but cannot; both ways, miserable."[Pusey translation].

The chapter verse reads, "**She hath tasted and seen that her traffic is good:her lamp shall not be put out in the night**" and this has two parts, first the taste and sight of life's business as such, and second that her lamp shall not be in the night. Concerning the first of these three things are to be noted: the experience of taste, the experience of sight, and the experience of taste and sight taken together.

The experience of taste is twofold, namely, the experience of a bad taste to be avoided and this we experience as disgusting and to be spit out so as not to become part of us and thus sin is tasted by the Saints as Job 6:6 says, "Or can an unsavory thing be eaten, that is not seasoned with salt? Or can a man taste that which when tasted bringeth death?" Unsalted food is an imprudent act which is not flavored with the salt of divine wisdom and if tasted and consumed can bring eternal death; but if tasted and spit out leaves us alive and this is signified in the Lord's tasting of the wine on the Cross, Matthew 27:34 says, "And they gave him wine to drink mingled with gall. And when he had tasted, he would not drink" showing by this that all the bitterness of sin should be ejected from us.

There is also the experience of the taste of the sweetness of eternal things and of this pleasure I Peter 2:3 says, "You have tasted that the Lord is sweet," and Job 12:11 asks, "Doth not the ear discern words, and the palate of him that eateth, the taste? " namely, of heavenly and divine goodness. Of this taste as regards intellectual enlightenment we read in I Samuel 14:29 that Jonathan said...'You have seen yourselves that my eyes are enlightened, because I tasted a little of this honey.'" This "honey" is the heavenly sweetness whose taste enlightens the eyes to rightly know heavenly matters and reject what is worldly. Hence St. Gregory the Great says, "He, who has tasted what is spiritual, despises what is worldly," that is carnal pleasure.

Concerning the experience of sight there is a fourfold vision by which we experience eternal truth.

Vision---	Of reason according to Faith
	Of Faith according to the Gift of Understanding
	Of Understanding according to the beatitude of the Clean of Heart
	And according to the Fruit that is called *Faith*

In order that this diagram may be understood more clearly we can say that "reason" is given to us so that we may see and contemplate eternal truth but since we cannot perfectly do this of ourselves, therefore we are given the light of faith by which we can do this. II Corinthians 5:7 says of this vision, "For we walk by faith, and not by sight," that is by open vision. Also I Corinthians 13:12 says, "We see now through a glass in a dark manner; but then face to face." This "glass" signifies an image or a trace in a creature, while "in a dark manner" [an *aenigma*] means an obscure allegory in the Scriptures; and these two enlighten us in faith.

When, however, faith confirms in the heart of someone what that one thinks with admiration of all that is to be believed and with the firmest consent to this interior truth, then the light of understanding begins to shine in that one so as in that infused light to see with certitude that nothing is more reasonable than faith and its intellectual vision. Of this vision Job 42:5-6 says, "With the hearing of the ear, I have heard thee, but now my eye seeth thee. Therefore I reprehend myself, and do penance in dust and ashes." Thus we only believe with faith when through hearing we assent to the Scriptures and to the preaching of the truth of God, as Romans 10:17 says, "Faith then cometh by hearing; and hearing by the word of Christ." When, however, the light is infused in us so that faith seems to us reasonable and certain then also the gift of understanding is infused in us as St. Gregory the Great says, "God gives understanding when the mind is enlightened by what is heard." And then we see, as it were with the eyes of the Lord and correct ourselves because before were slow and lazy about believing and then we do penance in humility and this is signified by "dust and ashes."

But when we are enlightened by this light of interior truth we become eager that our heart should be cleansed from all worldly occupations and fancies so that in this light we can be beatified. This happens when already we begin to see like the blessed do and so much light is infused in us that rays shine out from the face of our soul, as Jesus says in Matthew 5:8 "Blessed are the clean of heart for they shall see God" and as we read in I John 3:2, "When he shall appear, we shall be like to him: because we shall see him as he is."

The vision of beatitude according to its fruits, that is, of the cleanness of heart and of that fruit [of the Holy Spirit] that is called in a special sense "faith," is generated in us when we have a clean heart and are blessed and enlightened in the divine light so that nothing seems more certain and more wonderful than the vision of God. We then begin to be refreshed and filled with a certain sweetness and this in Galatians 5:22 is called a "fruit of the Spirit," ["But the fruit of the Spirit is, charity, joy, peace, patience, benignity, goodness, longanimity, mildness, *faith*, modesty, continency, chastity."] which St. Ambrose explains is "the certitude of the invisible or eternal," and to this description ought to be added that this is the refreshment of fruition in that light so that then a person is perfect.

Of all these visions taken together Psalm 84:8 says, "They shall go from virtue to virtue [Hebrew:"through inner and outer wall"]:the God of gods shall be seen in Sion' and similarly the Apostle says in II Corinthians 3:18, "But we all beholding the glory of the Lord with open face, are transformed into the same image from glory to glory, as by the Spirit of the Lord."

The first sort of vision is that of the faithful people common to them all. The second is especially that of the Doctors of the Church. The third is that of contemplatives such as Moses on the mountain in Exodus 33:11, ["And the Lord spoke to Moses face to face, as a man is wont to speak to his friend."] The fourth is that of persons in a rapture, such as St. Paul, II Corinthians 12:2-4 says of himself ["I know a man in Christ above fourteen years ago (whether in the body, I know not, or out of the body, I know not; God knoweth), such a one caught up to the third heaven. And I know such a man (whether in the body, or out of the body, I know not: God knoweth), that he was caught up into paradise, and heard secret words, which it is not granted to man to utter. For such an one I will glory; but for myself I will glory nothing, but in my infirmities."

Next is the consideration of experiences of taste and sight taken together, but sight is also experienced along with touch in two ways, the choice of what is good and the sweetness of the Lord with whom it is exchanged. Of the first I Peter 2:4 says, ["If so be you have tasted that the Lord is sweet."] and this is understood of the exchange of the fruits of the field and the vine. Those of the field are exchanged as the bread of grace, as already said, and those of the vine are exchanged as the wine of joy. About the second Psalm 34:9 says, "O taste, and see that the Lord is sweet." Taste along with touch is experienced as the truth and glory of the resurrection, as the risen Lord says to Thomas in Luke, 24:39-43, "See my hands and feet, that it is I myself; handle, and see: for a spirit hath not flesh and bones, as you see me to have...But while they yet believed not, and wondered for joy, he said: Have you any thing to eat? And they offered him a piece of a broiled fish, and a honeycomb. And when he had eaten before them, taking the remains, he gave to them."

But there still is left another consideration about the business of this Valiant Woman, namely, that she sees and tastes because it is "good." This business is conducted therefore outside her native country with the money of her husband and is also conducted in her own country with the money of the community to which she and her husband belong. Her own money is for her own use and support and is the good fortune of this world, yet this money of her own she also uses for the poor of her country, since as Jesus in Matthew 25:14," For the poor you have always with you." Of this doing business for the poor the Lord also says [Luke 16:9], "Make unto you friends of the mammon of iniquity; that when you shall fail, they may receive you into everlasting dwellings" and of this business of the Valiant Woman Isaiah 23:18 says, "And her merchandise and her hire shall be sanctified to the Lord: they shall not be kept in store, nor laid up: for her merchandise shall be for them that shall dwell before the Lord."

The second kind of business is that in which the Valiant Woman engages with her husband's money, that is, the money of the Word, as the Lord says in Luke 19:12-13, "He said therefore: A certain nobleman went into a far country, to receive for himself a kingdom, and to return. And calling his ten servants, he gave them ten pounds, and said to them: Trade till I come." These goods are nothing other than money of the Word. It is traded outside its own country because it is done with sinners who are living faraway in a foreign land.

The third kind of business is with the common money, that is, the devotion of the heart and constant prayer by which is bought a taste of eternal life by those still living in this present world. And about this common money Jesus says in Matthew 13:45-46, "Again the kingdom of heaven is like to a merchant seeking good pearls. Who when he had found one pearl of great price, went his way, and sold all that he had, and bought it." Truly this one pearl is precious since none other has a comparable value; and this is the taste of divine goods in God's gifts that he gives to the devout soul who seeks and longs for them.

§ 2

Next is considered the second part of the chapter text that reads, "**her lamp shall not be put out in the night**," which concerns the safety of her lamp. Concerning this phrase three things are to be considered, namely, what the lamp is, what is the darkness of the night that threatens its light, and why in fact it is not extinguished.

The Valiant Woman's lamp is fivefold: it is a lamp of redemption, of the word, of example, of right intention, and disputation in judgment. Concerning the first of these Jesus says in Luke 15:8-9, "Or what woman having ten groats; if she lose one groat, doth not light a candle, and sweep the house, and seek diligently until she find it? And when she hath found it, call together her friends and neighbors, saying: Rejoice with me, because I have found the groat which I had lost." This "woman" is no other than Jesus Christ himself because of his fertile virtue. Her "house" is this world. Her "candle" in its "candlestick" is the light of divinity in the candlestick of our mortality. The searching for the "coin" is all that we do for our redemption, such as preaching and suffering. Her "friends" are the holy Patriarchs. Her "neighbors" are the Angels who rejoice at our redemption.

Concerning the light of the Word Psalm 119:105 says, "Thy word is a lamp to my feet, and a light to my paths." These feet are our affections that are guided by the light of the Word. The "paths" are the ways of living this life and doing the kinds of works in which we are guided by the Word of God.

Concerning the lamp of example Jesus says in Luke 11:33, "No man lighteth a candle, and putteth it in a hidden place, nor under a bushel; but upon a candlestick, that they that come in may see the light." The "candle" is the light of good deeds through its example and instruction. The "candlestick" is authority and eloquence in prelates or the radiance of charity in any subordinate. The "house" is the Church. "They that come in" are those who through the sacraments and form of life are received in the Catholic Church and who see the lamp so that they are corrected by this example of good works and emend their lives.

Concerning the lamp of intention Jesus also says in Luke 11:34-36, "The light of thy body is thy eye. If thy eye be single, thy whole body will be lightsome...and as a bright lamp, shall enlighten thee." The "eye," as the Gloss says, "is the intention that directs a work to the Lord and this eye is simple when it is without trace of evil." The term "body" here is the sum of all our works illumined by this lamp, that is, by its great brilliance,

Concerning the lamp of disputation in judgment Zephaniah 1:12 says, "I will search Jerusalem with lamps," that is, in disputation in judgment, since by this lamp God disputes with us in judgment. And in this lamp we need to be scrutinized so that in the future the Lord will not scrutinize us. As I Corinthians 12:31 says, "But if we would judge ourselves, we should not be judged."

What follow concerns the darknesses that cannot extinguish this light, which are five in number; for the light of redemption shines in the darkness of sin and original guilt, the light of the word of God shines in the darkness of ignorance, the light of good example shines in the darkness of social intercourse, [the light of intention], and the light of discussion ["scrutiny"] shine in the hidden darknesses of the heart and conscience.

Of the first of these darknesses, the darkness of sin and original guilt, John 1:5 says, "And the light shineth in darkness, and the darkness did not comprehend it." St. John Chrysostom in his original Greek explains that. "This light is the benefit and grace of redemption which shines into the darkness of sin and death and although 'the darkness did not comprehend it,' that is, it does not extinguish it, this light does dissipate the darkness of sin and death"

Of the darkness of ignorance into which the light of God's Word shines Job 3:20-23, says ["Why is light given to him that is in misery, and life to them that are in bitterness of soul? That look for death, and it cometh not....And they rejoice exceedingly when they have found the grave.] To a man whose way is hidden, and God hath surrounded him with darkness?" This St. Gregory the Great glosses as "the darkness of ignorance" and the Apostle in Acts 17:30 says, "And God indeed having winked at the times of this ignorance, now declareth unto men, that all should every where do penance."

Of the darkness of this world into which the lamp of good example shines, the Apostles in Ephesians 5:8 says, "For you were heretofore darkness, but now light in the Lord. Walk then as children of the light."

Of the darkness of conscience into which shines the light of intention, Matthew 6:23 says, "If then the light that is in thee, be darkness: the darkness itself how great shall it be!" that is, when to a bad intention is joined a bad action then the darkness rules without measure. So long, however, as the intention is good, so long as the sin is salted with fear; but when the intention is corrupt, then the sinner sins without hope of repentance. Of the darkness of judgment Joel 2:10-11 says, "Sun and moon are darkened, and the stars have withdrawn their shining. And the Lord hath uttered his voice before the face of his army: for his armies are exceeding great, for they are strong and execute his word." Here the "sun" is the light of worldly prosperity, the "moon" is the mutability of temporal pleasures and both these lights are eclipsed on the day of judgment. The "stars" are the power of the senses by which sinners now live, but by which they then can live no longer because, according to Matthew 25:41, then the Lord in a terrible voice will say, "Depart from me, you cursed, into everlasting fire which was prepared for the devil and his angels" This will take place before God's army when will be confronted by the Angels and Saints who with God will judge them. These are called his camp and shield because they will fight for him against the foolish when he revenges their sins and fulfills his word by casting them down to hell.

What follows concerns the third and last point, namely, the reason why these lamps are not put out by the darkness and there are five things protecting the lamps, namely the secure protection of the surrounding glass, the abundance of oil to feed the flame, the shining fervor of the flame, the wick of the lamp, and the care with which the lamp is carried.

The secure protection of the glass is the secure protection of purity of bodily chastity of which Job 28:17 says, "Gold or crystal cannot equal it," namely, divine [wisdom]." And St. Gregory the Great explains this "crystal" as meaning the purity of our bodies and this show what is the nature of glass, because it is made from sand but when melted becomes transparent, as our bodies are made from lowly dust but when they are not fouled by lust become transparent in purity.

The oil that feeds the light is the oil of piety which the wise virgins [Matthew 25:1-13] kept for themselves in vessels along with their lamps when they awaited the bridegroom in the middle of the night, while the oil of the foolish virgins failed because they had chastity but not piety and thus they only had the exterior appearance of piety but altogether lacked its interior virtue. Therefore their lamps went out before they could go in with the bridegroom and thus they remained in the dark outside, as Matthew 25:11-13 relates.

The shining fervor of the lamp is the flame of the ardor of the most fervent and indistinguishable charity of which the Song of Songs 8:7 says, "Many waters cannot quench charity, neither can the floods drown it." The "many waters" are the many lusts of carnal concupiscence which show themselves by breaking forth in many actions. The floods are the attractions of this world in the pomps of Satan and the vanity of shows. But no matter how wet are these waters with the humors of voluptuousness, nor how cold and slimy they are through the inconstancy of vanity, they never can extinguish charity from the ardent heart.

The most pure light of the lamp given off by that fire is the desire of the soul, for when the wick is made of earthly material it is not likely to emit a brilliant flame but only one that gives off stinking fumes. Thus also worldly desires, even when they are invited by some motive to charitable acts, do not burn cleanly but instead emit the fumes of carnal concupiscence. On the other hand a wick of matter can be such that it burns cleanly in the fire of charity and without stink. Such is a desire that has been cleansed of all that is worldly; it burns brightly in the fire of charity and the light of the Church. This is what the Lord says of John the Baptist in John 5:33, "He was a burning and a shining light: and you were willing for a time to rejoice in his light."

This lamp, however, is to be carried humbly with the greatest care lest as it is carried it may be extinguished by the wind of vainglory or knocked over by the crowd of pride, Job 18:5-6 says, "Shall not the light of the wicked be extinguished, and the flame of his fire not shine? The light shall be dark in his tabernacle, and the lamp that is over him, shall be put out."

OUTLINE OF CHAPTER X

She hath put out her hand to strong things, and her fingers have taken hold of the spindle. (v. 19)

§1) The Acrostic letter Jod ' means "Lady" and the Valiant Woman rules herself and evil forces
  1) What does "She puts out her hands to strong things" mean?
    1) What are the Valiant Woman's hands? They are for wrestling and contending.
      1) Wrestling with God: Jacob wrestles with an Angel by
        1) Tears of repentance
        2) Prayer
      2) Wrestling with the world: Jacob's struggle in servitude to his uncle Laban
        1) Deceived by Laban's promise of Rachel his daughter: worldly pleasures
        2) Struggle over sheep: worldly fortune; avarice which takes 10 forms
          1) Robbery:
          2) Theft,
          3) Usury
          4) Demanding interest that was not promised
          5) Fraud in sales
          6) Fraud in auction
          7) Fraud by patrons and teachers against the ignorant
          8) Storing up necessities till time of need when prices are high
          9) Loaning things to be delivered at a future date when prices rise
          10) Cruelly saving from the poor in time of famine
      3) Wrestling with the flesh, but often failing: Laban's pursues Jacob religiously fleeing the world
        1) Concupiscence: Valiant Woman battles to overcome it
        2) Weakness: she battles to endure it
          1) Rachel's idols were the pride falsely covered as humility
          2) By her excuses she began to admit her sin
        3) Moderation in conformance with nature: to discern good from bad
          1) Rachel's idols were the pride falsely covered as humility
          2) By her excuses she began to admit her sin
      4) Wrestling with the devil:
        1) The hand of humility restrains the proud will
        2) The hand of constancy in temptation foils the devil
  2) What strong deeds against ten vices that the Valiant Woman's hands, trusting in Wisdom, must battle.
    1) Seven capital sins' plus schism and heresy:
      1) Pride or vainglory
      2) Envy along with muttering, detraction, rising up against one's neighbor, sadness at his good fortune, etc.
        1) Sin of Cain
        2) Punished by tremors of the head
      3) Anger along with rancor, outcries, blasphemies, curses, enmities, etc.

THE VALIANT WOMAN

    1) The hardest battle: Saul and David
    2) Distorts whole body
    4) Sloth along with torpor, sluggishness, languor about the burden of penance worldly vanities, and so forth
        1) Venomed dragon of love of the world
        2) Venomless dragon; no generosity in serving God:Satan tempts Jesus & the Israelites in the desert
    5) Avarice along with fraud, robbery, demands for money, theft, hard heartedness to the poor and so forth. Absalom against his father David:
        1) Kills brother; our neighbor
        2) Drives out his father, David
        3) Deceives the people against David
        4) Steals his father's wives; symbol of Ten Commandments
        5) Yet he was sterile
        6) Like Judas. he died hanging by hair as misers hang by riches without truly living
    6) Lust of heart & body: lewd kisses & embraces, dirty talk, unclean touches sodomy, bestiality, masturbation, adultery, rape, seduction of virgins, incest
        1) Many, like Samson, have fallen
        2) Women like Judith, Jahel, Mary Magdalene, Virgin Mary have conquered lust
    7) Gluttony drunkenness, fondness for delicacies, orgies, drinking parties, etc. the strongest struggle
        1) Goliath was the body swollen in flux
        2) Like Goliath the addict falls to the ground
        3) David is pastor teaching abstinence with five stones in his sling
            1) Fast till meal time
            2) Diet
            3) Stop before filled
            4) Eat slowly
            5) Avoid fancy cooking
2) Two worst sins that separate from Church, as also vainglory tends to do
    1) Schism:despises authority, disobeys, ignores excommunication, violates confession ,etc.
        1) Tears Christ's seamless garment and kills charity
        2) Archangel Michael fights Satan's division of Church
    2) Heresy corrupts Scriptures, disbelieves Sacraments, obstinate in one's own opinion, pretence in believing the truth, confidence of victory in noisy disputes, andkills not only charity but faith.
        1) Worst of sins:Moses and the magicians:the Antichrist
        2) Three evil spirits from mouth of Dragon
            1) Blasphemy against eternal truth
            2) Blasphemy against God as if he were a liar
            3) Blasphemy against the Sacraments
2) How does the Valiant Woman put her hands to strong things?
    1) Prayer that God will aid her in victory
    2) Doing strong deeds to skillfully attack the enemy in foreseeing temptation.

3) Cautious to avoid tempting occasions & heal wounds so that they do not get infected.
   1) Avoid evil companions
   2) Bad celebrations and games
   3) Lewd Talk
   4) Idleness
   5) Venial sins like Lot's wife look back on the cities of sin and turns tot salt
3) Valiant Woman cares for her hands lest they lose their vigor for fighting

§2) What does the Valiant Woman take hold of? With what fingers does she hold the spindle?
1) With which fingers?
   1) Thumb: Gift of the Holy Spirit
   2) Index finger: Obedience to the Commandments written by God's finger on two tablets of stone
   3) Middle finger: Meditation on Christ's Passion
      1) Aaron dips fingers in blood, sprinkling the veil of the Tabernacle seven times
      2) Blood is Christ's
      3) Tabernacle is the heavens
      4) Seven sprinklings are seven Hours of the Liturgical Office.
2) What is the spindle? Wisdom spins out the thread of the garments of the Saints & twists the wool as by the rational circling of wisdom the essences of created things, confused as wool, are unified as thread
   1) Reading gathers the thread of thought
   2) Contemplation and meditation wind these threads together to make cloth
   3) Charity provides bands and borders that bind the cloth together.

CHAPTER X

She hath put out her hand to strong things, and her fingers have taken hold of the spindle. (v. 19)

§1

JOD ׳. Jod is interpreted "Lady" and refers to the sentence that follows since in this verse the Valiant Woman shows that she truly rules herself since a strong being is one that rules itself against the forces that battle it and she is said to put her fingers to the spindle by work for her family which is protected by her rule and of this rule Isaiah 26:13 says, "Other lords besides thee have had dominion over us, only in thee let us remember thy name," as if to say, "The rule of others is heavy and theirs is a yoke of iron, but your rule, O

Mother and Father, we freely bear for to be ruled by you is to reign for your rule is sweet and your burden light," as Jesus says in Matthew 11:30, "For my yoke is sweet and my burden light," and if somehow your yoke seems very heavy, so that it totally rots, losing the form of olive wood, we certainly ought to record your name.

Nor is this the rule of a woman over her husband that the Apostle forbids in I Corinthians 11:3, "But I would have you know, that the head of every man is Christ; and the head of the woman is the man; and the head of Christ is God." Rather she is the woman ruler over her enemies laying her hand on their necks, as well as the ruler of her family preparing plentifully for them so that as is said later in this chapter verse 21, her domestics "are clothed in double garments"...lest they "fear...in the cold of snow," and as it says in Genesis 27:15 of Rebecca that "She put on him (Jacob) very good garments of Esau, which she had at home with her."

Two things are to be noted in this chapter verse, namely, first what it means to say that the Valiant Woman "**put out her hand to strong things**," and second what did her fingers "**take hold of**."

As to the first of these, three things are to be noted: what are the Valiant Woman's hands, what does she take hold of, and third how does she take hold of that. And as to the first of these it should be noted that this is a hand for wrestling and contending and is fourfold: wrestling with God, with the world, with the flesh, and against the devil.

The first of these is the hand of Jacob wrestling with the Angel related in Genesis 33:24-30. Second is Jacob's hand sparring with his uncle Laban, Genesis 30:25-43. Third is the hand of a twin fighting with his brother in their mother's womb, Genesis 25:22. Fourth is the hand of Jacob fighting invisibly against all those who plotted against him.

The first battle has two arms, namely, tears and prayers, as Hosea 12:3-4 says, "In the womb he supplanted his brother: and by his strength he had success with an angel. And he prevailed over the angel, and was strengthened: he wept, and made supplication to him." For Jacob presented his hands to his father covered with the skin of a kid [Genesis 27:15-23] as he offered his father the cooked meat of a kid so that Jacob might bless him. For the hands, so to speak, are the hands raised in prayer with tears and with devout words. These hands, however, are covered with a kid's skin when sin is denounced and the pleasures of sin are boiled in the pot of contrition. The skin of sin, that is, the memory of it, covers the hands all over in payment so that no sin is remembered that is not covered by the required work of penance. The Heavenly Father willingly eats such food, since as it says in Luke 15:7, great is his joy when his prodigal son returns, and also of the Angels over one sinner doing penance. Then blessing in the grace of pardon follows. Afterwards, however, Jacob in wrestling with the Angel received the security of his blessing against temptation so that the blessing of his father refers to "prevenient" grace that enables one to will that a good act be completed as is done by a "sufficient" will. The second blessing on Jacob refers to "subsequent" grace against temptation lest one will the good in vain, which is called a "frustrated" will if by temptations it is easily taken away.

The hand of Jacob also battles with the world and this is signified in the struggle with Laban, which is threefold. For the first struggle was that of servitude to Laban for his daughters and then Laban deceived him by giving him not the daughter he had promised but the other older, blear-eyed daughter. The second struggle was for the sheep and then Jacob obtained for himself a greater reward that might be expected. The third battle [related in Genesis 31:21-55] was Laban's pursuit of Jacob when he confronted him on Mount Galaad [and tried in vain to make Jacob return].

The first of these struggles signifies the variety of worldly pleasures; the second the variety of the world in matters of fortune as regards the mammon of iniquity; the third its consequences in the vanity of the pride of life, as I John 2:16 says, "For all that is in the world, is the concupiscence of the flesh, and the concupiscence of the eyes, and the pride of life, which is not of the Father, but is of the world." This lust is twofold, one is the hunger for this world and the other is the hunger to clothe oneself in soft garments and this is reproached in the Rich Man, as he is described in Luke 16:19, "who was clothed in purple and fine linen; and feasted sumptuously every day." Jacob, however, wished out of necessity to choose a wife for pleasure, but that changed into lust since, she was not the one he supposed, just as the will to pleasure is not a man's proper partner.

But the varieties of avarice are ten forms of the same vice, since the world tempts just men to avarice in ten ways: first by robbery, second by theft, third by usury, fourth by demanding the return of money that at the time it was lent was lent without interest, fifth by fraud in the sale, sixth in an auction, seventh by clever trickery in which the ignorant permit themselves to be deceived by patrons and teachers, eighth by storing up necessities until a time of the year in which they will be higher priced, ninth by loaning things to be delivered at a future date so that they will be more costly, tenth and last by cruelly holding back from the poor in a famine so as to increase one's own wealth. Job 19:3 says of such a worldly deceiver, "Behold, these ten times you confound me, and are not ashamed to oppress me."

Similarly the varying nature of vain pride battled in Jacob, that is, with a struggling spiritual person, since as St. Augustine says, "Pride furiously rages against all the virtues and does not let go of Jacob when he flees [from Laban] but even on Mount Galaad embraces him." For every religious person is a fugitive from the world and rests on Mount Galaad, which is interpreted "heap of testimony," that is, a religious high place testified to by many holy fathers who were there sanctified, since from that high place the vanity of pride is seen. Yet [this view], which ought to make us humbler, often is the cause of making us more vain and subject to feelings of pride. This, as Genesis 31:31-35 relates, is why Jacob looked for the idols that Rachel had hidden. Pride is the first sin of the devil who wants to be worshipped and adored by all. But Rachel's idols, lest they be found, were hidden under her camel's covering, and hence she claimed that because she was suffering her feminine period, she could not get up. Thus she fooled Jacob's careful questioning. The "camel covering" by which we conceal the idol of our body is the various bodily necessities by which we ought to be humbled. Yet those who ponder the miseries of our mortality hide an idol, namely, the false humility of pride, lest it be recognized. Rachel by confessing that she was suffering from her feminine period did not get up, that is, although she confessed her sin of weakness, she through pride did not repent. Yet, when others found nothing on her, at least she began to admit some uncleanness in herself that needed somehow to be removed, as is signified by the pact Jacob made with Laban, related in Genesis 29 and 30, so that for Rachel in the new land [they were entering] the idols of her former life would be crucified. As the Apostle says in Galatians 5:24, "And they that are Christ's, have crucified their flesh, with the vices and concupiscences" and such persons no longer glory in this world. As [the Apostle also says] in Galatians 6:14, "But God forbid that I should glory, save in the cross of our Lord Jesus Christ; by whom the world is crucified to me, and I to the world."

Again the Valiant Woman has the hand of Jacob in struggling and warring with the flesh, and this war is conducted in three ways, first with the flesh of concupiscence, and second with the flesh of weakness, and third with the flesh of moderation and conformance to nature.

With concupiscence she battles to conquer it; with her weakness that she may endure and support it; with the moderation of nature and concupiscence by discerning what is to be forbidden and what is to be permitted. The first battle has many failures, the second much labor and sweat, the third has a heap of care and much subtlety. Of the first of these wars Galatians 5:17 says, "For the flesh lusteth against the spirit: and the spirit against the flesh; for these are contrary one to another: so that you do not the things that you would." Of the second I Timothy 5:23 says, "Do not still drink water, but use a little wine for thy stomach's sake, and thy frequent infirmities," and of the third the same Epistle 6:8 says, "But having food, and wherewith to be covered, with these we are content," and Proverbs 30:7-8 says, "Two things I have asked of thee, deny them not to me before I die. Remove far from me vanity, and lying words. Give me neither beggary, nor riches: give me only the necessaries of life."

Again the Valiant Woman has hands with which to battle the devil and this in two ways: the hand of humility by which she restrains a proud will, and the hand of constancy in temptation by which she foils the malice of the devil's trickery. The first hand is the hand of the Lord himself since by the humility of the Cross he conquered the pride of the flesh, as I Peter 4:6 says, "Be you humbled therefore under the mighty hand of God, that he may exalt you in the time of visitation." Isaiah 51:9 speaks of the arm to which that hand belonged and says, "Arise, arise, put on strength, O thou arm of the Lord, arise as in the days of old, in the ancient generations. Hast not thou struck the proud one, and wounded the dragon?" This same humility Isaiah seeks from the Lord so that he can fight against the devil. Thus that humility took possession of him as it was to do in Christ so that it might possess all the faithful. David in Psalm 144:7 says, "Put forth thy hand from on high, take me out, and deliver me from many waters: from the hand of strange children." In this prayer the hand of humility is sought against the proud demons that are called "strange children" because they were alienated from their original sonship to God with the loss of their inheritance and who raise many floods of trouble by their evil tempting.

Concerning the hand of constancy in battle, Genesis 49:8 says, "Thy hands shall be on the necks of thy enemies," and Psalm 144:2

says, "Blessed be the Lord my God, who teacheth my hands to fight, and my fingers to war," and this is said of the hand of battle or struggle which enables us to fight."

Next must considered to what strong deeds these hands of the Valiant Woman are put. They must battle the seven commanders and captains of all the vices which are called strong from the fact that they engage in the most violent wars, namely, pride, envy, anger, avarice, luxury and gluttony. Vainglory results in the eighth kind of war but is similar to pride. A ninth battle leads to schism and a tenth to infidelity. Of these commanders the Lord says to Job 39:25, speaking of the horse on which the king is mounted, that is, of the soul bearing and carrying Christ, "When he heareth the trumpet he saith: Ha, ha: he smelleth the battle afar off, the encouraging of the captains, and the shouting of the army." This battle is the difficulties to which the woman puts her hands and when she hears the trumpet, that is, senses the first motion by which the devil and vice invites her to battle, emits a sound of contempt, saying, "Ha!" because she enjoys the thought of the victory she already hopes for and by which she will win for herself a crown. The battle that is "smelled from afar off" is some temptation to vice that she subtly perceives is just beginning, as the Lord says in Genesis 3:15, "She shall crush thy head, and thou shalt lie in wait for her heel," which the Gloss says refers to the completed act. She hears and perceives the commanders' taunts, that is, how and by what acts they invite her to war against the enumerated ten vices, namely, the seven capital sins fought even by those not excommunicated from the Church, and the three others of which one impedes the faith, namely, vainglory, as the Lord says in John 5:44, "How can you believe, who receive glory one from another: and the glory which is from God alone, you do not seek?" One of the other two vices, schism, however, cuts through charity and unity and the second kills faith. The "shouting" of the army of the devil is the outcry of the companions of these ten vices, for example, under the flag of pride is ambition, presumption, hypocrisy, and so forth. Under the banner of envy is muttering, detraction, rising up against one's neighbor, sadness at his good fortune, and so forth. Under the banner of anger are rancors, outcries, blasphemies, curses, enmities, and so forth. Under the banner of sloth or boredom are, torpor, sluggishness, languor about taking on the burden of penances, the inclination to worldly vanities, and so forth. Under the banner of avarice are fraud, robbery, demands for money, theft, hard heartedness to the poor and so forth. Under luxury are lusts of heart and body, lewd kisses and embraces, dirty talk, unclean touching, sodomy, bestiality, masturbation, adultery, rape, seduction of virgins, incest. Under gluttony are drunkenness, fondness for delicacies, orgies, drinking parties, and so forth. Under schism are contempt of authority, disobedience, ignoring excommunication, the violation of confession and so forth. Under heresy are novel opinions, corruption of the Scriptures, disbelief in the Sacraments, obstinacy in one's own opinion, pretending one believes the truth when one does not really believe it, confidence of victory in noisy disputes, and so forth. All these vices the Valiant Woman, if their subjects are under her rule, begins to correct by exhortation. She sustains the great clamor of battle in her heart and thus, as she lays on her hand against them, strongly contests their advance because she knows that God will give her the strength to win. She also she knows that more powerful than all these foes is Wisdom, Christ our God, who is her spouse, as Wisdom 10:1 says concerning our ancestors, "She [Wisdom] preserved him, that was first formed by God, the father of the world, when he was created alone," and as St. Paul says in II Timothy 4:7, "I have fought a good fight, I have finished my course, I have kept the faith."

The first contest, that of pride, is the battle of the dragon in heaven against God, as it says in Revelation 12:7. ["And there was a great battle in heaven, Michael and his angels fought with the dragon, and the dragon fought and his angels"]. For the devil contended with God as with an equal as says Isaiah addressing Lucifer in 14:13-4 says, "And thou saidst in thy heart: I will ascend into heaven, I will exalt my throne above the stars of God, I will sit in the mountain of the covenant, in the sides of the north. I will ascend above the height of the clouds I will be like the most High." Here the "stars" are the choirs of the Angels. The "mountain of the covenant' here means the exaltation of the Witness, that is, of the Son, whom Lucifer seeks to equal. All those who are proud engage in this battle with God, as Psalm 73:23 says, "Forget not the voices of thy enemies: the pride of them that hate thee ascendeth continually" and Ezekiel, 28:16 says, "By the multitude of thy merchandise, thy inner parts were filled with iniquity, and thou hast sinned:and I cast thee out from the mountain of God, and destroyed thee, O covering cherub, out of the midst of the stones of fire. And thy heart was lifted up with thy beauty: thou best lost thy wisdom in thy beauty, I have cast thee to the ground: I have set thee before the face of kings, that they might behold thee. Thou hast defiled thy sanctuaries by the multitude of thy iniquities, and by the iniquity of thy traffic: therefore I will bring forth a fire from the midst of thee, to devour thee, and I will make thee as ashes upon the earth in the sight of all that see thee." The "cherub" here is the devil full of wisdom, among the "stones," formerly among the angels fiery with charity in heaven. He is called "covering" because he was superior to the other angels and ought to have protected them whom he had accepted to govern, but because of his pride he lost the splendor of his wisdom and was thrown out of the fiery stones into eternal fire from the mount of the blessedness of God down to earth as into prison where he continues to tempt humanity until the day of judgment, when he will be thrust down forever into hell. And this is what is meant by "have set thee before the face of kings", that is of those who seek the kingdom and glory of this world so that they may see that if the ambitious pride of a devil, who was an angel, is thus damned, how much more will miserable man be condemned who was formed from dust and dung, since in such a creature pride is more detestable because such a proud man is really more lowly and had less reason than the fallen angels to be swollen up.

The second contest is of envy with its accompanying vices and these are signified by the contest of Cain who out of envy slew his brother as Genesis 4:3-16 relates. And it is noteworthy that Cain envied his brother for no other cause than that his brother Abel was better than himself and more acceptable to God and this is what the envious do, namely, kill their brother. For they do not stalk an enemy, but seek to destroy a fraternal good which God gave someone, precisely because God loves the one to whom he gave this good, and this amounts to wanting to kill God himself, since as Matthew 27:28 says, "For he [Pilate] knew that for envy they [the Jewish leaders] had delivered him [Jesus]." The proper condemnation of this vice is the tremors of the head since envious persons see the good of others with tremors of mind. This vice also raised the strongest battle for the first man in paradise, whence it also drove him out of paradise, since Wisdom 2:24-25 says, "For God created man incorruptible, and to the image of his own likeness he made him. But by the envy of the devil, death came into the world: And they follow him that are of his side."

The third struggle is most difficult and is that of anger, as it says in James 1:20, "For the anger of man worketh not the justice of God." An example of this was the struggle between Saul and David, since it is said in I Samuel 16:14, "the spirit of the Lord departed from Saul, and an evil spirit from the Lord troubled him" and he seized a spear to pierce David. The Spirit of the Lord is one of meekness as Jesus says in Matthew 11:29, "Learn of me, because I am meek, and humble of heart." The evil and malicious spirit is the spirit of anger that agitated Saul and now agitates all the wrathful, since it literally bursts from the blood about the heart and from the fumes of the gall rising to higher organs, and from the expansion and multiplication of the vital spirits in the upper part of the body it begins to make the body shake, the lips to curl strangely, and the eyes to roll and redden, the nostrils to swell, when in some proverb it says that "the angry man has breath in his nostrils and a tongue sputtering out foolish words." And this is said of the agitation by some evil spirit though whom the angry man is agitated by [permission] of the Lord. Whence it is also said of Saul that he stood in the middle of his house and "prophesied" [I Kings 18:10] which is nothing other than God's permission that left him to constantly let himself go and work himself up to a revengeful fury sometimes promising revenge against the Philistines, sometimes against the men of Ceila and sometimes the men of Ziph. The spear by which he attempt to kill David signified his dire wrath as in says in Wisdom 5:21, "And he will sharpen his severe wrath for a spear."

The fourth struggle is also very difficult and this is the struggle against sloth related in the contest between Mardochai and Aman in Esther 10:7 and 11:6, for Mardochai saw in a dream two great dragons, one fighting for the Chosen People and another fighting against them. The first great dragon is the love of world which makes men slothful. The other dragon has no venom but is eager and generous in serving God. Consequently Mardochai suffered because Aman wanted for himself, a mere creature, that honor due the true God. Thus spiritual men, suffer from the world because others want to attribute to themselves the honor which they owe to God. Hence it is said that [Mardochai's dream, ended in Esther 11:11], "The light and the sun rose up, and the humble were exalted, and they devoured the glorious." For when knowledge of eternal things arises in their hearts, then persons, who before had a spirit that was honest and humble, will be exalted and those who with liveliness of spirit rejoice in the praise of God will devour those that in depths of their hearts, because they were adorned with the ornaments of the world, supposed that were the truly glorious. For such was the devil that tempted the Lord in the desert by raising doubts about the value of the austerity of fasting, the sanctity of life, and the desire for glory. Matthew 4 relates this about the austerity of fasting in verse 3 where the devil says, "If thou be the Son of God, command that these stones be made bread," and about the sanctity of life in verse 6 when on the pinnacle of the temple the devil says to Jesus, "If thou be the Son of God, cast thyself down," [for it is written: That he hath given his angels charge over thee, and in their hands shall they bear thee up, lest perhaps thou dash thy foot against a stone]. The desire for glory is referred to verse 8-9, "[Again the devil took him up into a very high mountain and shewed him all the kingdoms of the world, and the glory of them, and said to him: All these will I give thee, if falling down thou wilt adore me." Thus such questions arise from the sloth [boredom] that troubles spiritual men who are doing penance in the desert, because sometimes they wish to experience that God is in them through signs. This happens when they languish from long waiting for the fulfillment of God's promises, wishing to experience through some sign that they are sons of God; when also they begin out of boredom to doubt the efficacy of the rigors of religion, longing that "stones," that is, the hardness of penance, would be converted into the bread of temporal consolations, and when they even begin to hate their rejection of the world and begin to desire some excitement from the "pomps of Satan."

The people of Israel also experienced this worst of desires as it says in Numbers 11:4-6 "Who shall give us flesh to eat? We remember the fish that we ate in Egypt free of cost; the cucumbers come into our mind, and the melons, and the leeks, and the onions, and the garlic. Our soul is dry, our eyes behold nothing else but manna." Crying for the "meat" [fish] of carnal pleasures is in the heart of the slothful person. "Cucumbers and melons" are the longed for refreshments of the world. "Leeks, onions, and garlic" signify the bitter labors of this world that in fact weary us and turn us back to sloth. Our "soul" that seems so "dry" is our animality that suffers tedium and depression with regard to divine matters. Our "eyes" are the desire for praise in this world of vanities, because the slothful are beset with sadness since they see nothing in religion except manna, that is, the sign of grace and maturity.

The fifth struggle is avarice and this was the battle that Absalom had with his father David as is related in I Kings, 12 and following. Six facts are related about Absalom that notably contributed to make him avaricious. One is that he killed his brother. Second is that he drove his father out of his inheritance. Third that he deceitfully won the people to himself, kissing them in the gateway and praising their cause in detraction of the king by charging that David did not judge in their favor. The fourth is that he stole his father's wives sleeping with them on the roof of his father's house. The fifth if that he died suspended by his hair in a tree. The sixth and last is that he made of himself a triumphant and memorable harlot in that he had no son to succeed him in his inheritance.

The first of these facts shows the cruelty of the miser toward his brother, that is, his neighbor, because he deprives his neighbors of their lives, as Isaiah says 3:14, "The spoil of the poor is in your house." Second, because the miser attempts to deprive his father of his inheritance so that he can live alone on the land, against which Isaiah 5:8 laments, "Woe to you that join house to house and lay field to field, even to the end of the place: shall you alone dwell in the midst of the earth?" Third, because he distributes fraudulent kisses to deceive those whom he attracts, because although for a time he gives them freedom, yet he only does this to gain money from those he seduces and tricks. Fourth he again seeks to rival his father by defiling his father's ten wives, for that "father" is God and the "wife" by whom he begets worthy sons is obedience to his commandments. Thus the wives are the Ten Commandments which the avaricious person is always violating, as it says in Wisdom 15:12 that the avaricious have made idols [from worldly goods], "Yea and they have counted our life a pastime, and the business of life to be gain, and that we must be getting every way, even out of evil." Hence the Apostle says, Colossians 3:5,] "Mortify therefore your members which are upon the earth; fornication, uncleanness, lust, evil concupiscence, and covetousness, which is the service of idols], that is, that avarice is the worship of idols for some who think that to seek worldly goods is a kind of piety. The fifth fact, [that Absalom died suspended in a tree by his hair] signifies by the "hairs of the head" the affluence of encompassing riches by which the miser is impeded from really living because such riches prevent him from ever coming to eternal life as the Lord says in Luke 18:24, "How hardly shall they that have riches enter into the kingdom of God," and the Apostle says, I Timothy 6:9, "For they that will become rich, fall into temptation, and into the snare of the devil." This also was the rope by which was hung Judas the traitor who sold the Lord for money and also the "rope of hair" by which Absalom was hanged because the thousands of superfluous riches strangled him in the noose of eternal death. The sixth mark of a miser is that when they sees that they can take nothing away with them, they desire with their whole heart to leave after them under their name a great pile of famous wealth and inheritance, as it says in Psalm 49:18, "For when he shall die he shall take nothing away; nor shall his glory descend with him," and Job 27:19, "The rich man when he shall sleep shall take away nothing with him: he shall open his eyes and find nothing.' [Yet Absalom, since he left no sons, failed even in this respect.]

The sixth and strongest battle of all is the one involving the carnal vice of gluttony, for as the Apostle says, Philippians 3:18-19, "For many walk, of whom I have told you often (and now tell you weeping), that they are enemies of the cross of Christ; Whose end is destruction; whose God is their belly." And this is the battle of David with the Philistine Goliath [I Kings 17:40 and following,] and this is evident from three points: first, Goliath is interpreted as the "changing" because all that he took into his mouth when into his belly and was then flushed out, as the Lord said in Matthew 15:17, "Do you not understand, that whatsoever entereth into the mouth, goeth into the belly, and is cast out into the privy?" and thus his body was continually changing and never remained in the same state. "Philistine" is interpreted "falling down drunk" and so the glutton when he has had too much food and drink falls to the ground and is sickened by his bodily humors. "Giant" is from the Greek *ge* which is translated in Latin *"terra,* earth" because a giant is just a heap of earth and so the glutton swells with flesh on the head and has lard hanging from his earthly body. The third way in which this is noted is its mode of imperfection when in I Samuel 17:40, David chooses his shepherd's staff which signifies the pastoral life and a sling-shot which signifies eating not to for pleasure but for living and five very smooth stones from a brook. The "brook" signifies the tribulations and narrows of this life. The "smooth stones" are the five virtues of abstinence by which excessive appetite for food is quenched. The first is to fast until due meal time and the rumbling of the stomach and not before one is really hungry. The second is to satisfy oneself with the food of the poor, such as beans, other vegetables, and wheat or barley bread. The third is to eat sparingly and stop short of being entirely filled. The fourth is even when very hungry to feed oneself slowly so as not to push your knife down your throat and thus pour out your soul on your food, but to eat gradually with maturity and decency. The fifth is to devote little effort in the preparation of food, not caring how it is cooked, or chilled, or spiced, for concern for these differences produces gluttony. And there are five virtues contrary to five vices of gluttony which vices St. Gregory the Great enumerates and sums up in this verse:

Eagerly, splendidly, excessively, vigorously, officiously

One also should not eat too e*agerly*, because the children of Israel [in the desert] wanted to eat before the time of eating meat had come and therefore are dead in the tomb of desire as it says in Numbers 11:34, ["As yet the flesh was between their teeth, neither had that kind of meat failed: when behold the wrath of the Lord being provoked against the people, struck them with an exceeding great plague. And that place was called 'the grave of lust,' for there they buried the people that had lusted."]

Also one should not eat too *officiously* when it is not proper to do so [as it is said in I Samuel 2:12-15, "The sons of Heli wished the flesh of the sacrifice to be prepared in a way that was not customary, nor was it the office of the priests to the people: but whosoever had offered a sacrifice, the servant of the priest came, while the flesh was in boiling, with a fleshhook of three teeth in his hand, and thrust it into the kettle, or into the caldron, or into the pot, or into the pan, and all that the fleshhook brought up, the priest took to himself. Thus did they to all Israel that came to Shiloh. Also before they burnt the fat, the servant of the priest came, and said to the man that sacrificed: Give me flesh to boil for the priest: for I will not take of thee sodden flesh, but raw"] and therefore these priests died in the war with the Philistines, as is said in I Samuel 4:11, ["And the ark of God was taken: and the two sons of Heli, Ophni and Phinees, were slain].

To eat *excessively* is blamed in the god of the Babylonians who they conceived as possessing divinity only in that he ate and drank so much daily, as Daniel 14:5 says, " [And the king said to Daniel: Doth not Bel seem to thee to be a living god? Seest thou not how much he eateth and drinketh every day?"] Thus there are some gods of whom the divinity and omnipotence of their stomach and bowels are questioned unless they eat and drink much every day.

To eat too *vigorously* is exemplified in he way Esau sought and devoured the pot of lentils and therefore as a profane person lost through a single meal his inheritance as the older son, as Genesis 25:33 relates, "And Jacob said to him Esau, Sell me thy first birthright. He answered: Lo I die, what will the first birthright avail me? Jacob said: Swear therefore to me. Esau swore to him, and sold his first birthright. And so taking bread and the pottage of lentils, he ate, and drank, and went his way; making little account of having sold his first birthright."

To banquet too *brilliantly* in rich purple is reprehended by the Lord [in the Parable of the Poor Man and the Rich Man in, Luke 16:19-31, ["There was a certain rich man, who was clothed in purple and fine linen; and feasted sumptuously every day"] and therefore when he was buried and burning in hell he begged for a drop of cold water on his tongue. ["And he cried, and said: Father Abraham, have mercy on me, and send Lazarus, that he may dip the tip of his finger in water, to cool my tongue: for I am tormented in this flame]. This also was the conflict that moved Nabuchodonosor [who, as Daniel 4:30 relates, became mad and, "ate grass like an ox,"] to attack Jerusalem and thus this "King of Food" as St. Gregory calls him, "caused Jerusalem to be burnt," since the "king of food" signifies gluttony.

The seventh war is that made by lust, for it is exceedingly strong, but the Valiant Woman is stronger still. For in this respect she is, as Zorobabel, the wisest of the three young men guarding King Assuerus or Artaxerxes, indicated when he declared the courtesan Apame to be "stronger than wine, or than kings, and than all things but truth," when she slapped the king with her left hand, took the crown from his head, and with it crowned herself. Yet Assuerus was not angry [but only amused] as is related in [Apocryphal] III Esdras 4:29-30, [although the same book 4:35 concludes that, "Is he (God) not great that maketh these things? therefore great is the truth, and stronger than all things."] The same book also relates that man loves woman more than gold and out of love for her often murders, sails the seas and does many great deeds, which it lists.. Similarly we read in Judges 16:1-21 how Samson, although he was blessed from his mother's womb as the strongest of men was enslave and blinded through a woman. Solomon, wisest and strongest of kings, women also enslaved, and of him Sirach 47:21-22 says, "And thou didst bow thyself to women: and by thy body thou wast brought under subjection," that is, that you might satisfy your bodily lusts, "Thou hast stained thy glory, and defiled thy seed so as to bring wrath upon thy children, and to have thy folly kindled." This is the war that, as the strongest and the example and mirror of chastity, the Valiant Woman wages. Judith, also cut off of the head of Holofernes and defeated the reign of King Nabuchodonosor. She cut off his head with his own sword, that is, by "love." But [Judith did so out of love for her people] while his love for her was only shameful lust. The sword of true love has beauty and decorum as did Mary Magdalene who at first loved shamefully, but then switched that sword of love and cut off the head of lust, thus meriting to hear the Lord declare, "Wherefore I say to thee: many sins are forgiven her, because she has loved much." In this same battle against lust the Most Blessed Virgin Mary, Mother of God, completely cut off the dragon's head. So did Deborah in prophesying in Judges 4:2-10 and following. Likewise did Jahel, wife of Haber the Cinite, who was able to kill Sisara as related in Judges 4:18-23. She gave him a drink of cold milk and he slept, that is she cooled the heat that arouses lust and then with the uplifted tent peg of purity of heart and body she drove it through his temples, striking the power of lust so that he fainted away and lay dead at her feet.

The eighth very strong war but one different than the others is that which involves vainglory. This vainglory is not the same as pride which seeks excellence of worth, while vainglory only seeks the empty vanity of praise in certain spiritual or bodily matters. And this is the war which daily moved the wanton married woman who tried to seduce Joseph in Egypt as is related in Genesis 39:6-20. She daily said to him, "Sleep with me," and thus tormented the young man although he refused her seduction and said, "Behold, my master hath delivered all things to me, and knoweth not what he hath in his own house: Neither is there any thing which is not in my power, or that he hath not delivered to me, but thee, who art his wife: how then can I do this wicked thing, and sin against my God?" The name "Joseph" is interpreted "growing" and signifies those who engage in praiseworthy works. The "wife" of Joseph's master is glory which belongs only to God and his care for us as in Luke 2:14 it relates how the angels sang, "Glory to God in the highest; and on earth peace to men of good will" and as I Corinthians 11:7 also says, "Woman is the glory of her man" and as in Isaiah 42:8 God declares, "I will not give my glory to another, nor my praise to graven things." This facts requires of us growth in praiseworthy actions, especially when a man is young and full of lustful impulses. Immature men often and strongly daily experience this battle and as they advance in grace and good works nevertheless wish in the secret of their hearts to do only for vainglory what ought to be done for the sake of God alone. But a man rejects this defilement when he constantly throws it off and shakes its dust from his feet, as the Lord said to his apostles, in Luke 9:5, ["And whosoever will not receive you, when ye go out of that city, shake off even the dust of your feet, for a testimony against them." But also to be noted are the words which Joseph spoke when he rejected such glory and said, "My master," that is, Christ, my Lord and God, "has delivered all things to me," of salvation, good works, and natural life which suffice for my redemption, yet "knoweth not what he hath in his house," that is what is in my heart, and has committed to me the full power of possessing and sharing all grace except for you who are his wife, that is, his own proper glory [or honor] which he has won and reserved for himself. For my master alone has this glory in which glory nothing belongs to another. I am dust and what I have I have received. For if the axe by which the falling wood of a house is properly mended, that is, the native skill by which I perceive what is a fitting for this spiritual household, is a gift given me by God, how then can I glory as if I had not received it and sin against the Lord of all good deeds? As James 1:17 also says, "Every best gift, and every perfect gift, is from above, coming down from the Father of lights, with whom there is no change, nor shadow of alteration." Therefore the floods of grace return through glory into the sea, that is, to God, the fount of all good, to whom it returns so that it may flow forth again. Thus I do not attribute glory that I have accepted from elsewhere to myself. I do not think that what I have borrowed from God makes me equal to him that I may be myself glorious. As the Apostle says I Timothy 1:17, "Now to the king of ages, immortal, invisible, the only God, be honor and glory for ever and ever. Amen."

The ninth kind of battle has a strong tendency to result in schism. It causes the tunic of seamless charity to be divided and in this respect exceeds the sin of those who crucified Christ, who as it relates in John 19:24, "said then one to another: Let us not cut it [Jesus seamless tunic], but let us cast lots for it, whose it shall be; that the Scripture might be fulfilled [Psalm 22:19], saying: They have parted my garments among them, and upon my vesture they have cast lot." The "seamless tunic" is the authority of the keys and the unity of Christ's charity. The soldiers who crucified him are Christian "spirituals" [enthusiasts] who are public sinners but who still remain obedient to the keys and are numbered as still in the faith and practice of the Church, of whom the Apostle says in Hebrews 6:6, "[The baptized] who are fallen away: to be renewed again to penance, crucifying again to themselves the Son of God, and making him a mockery." Thus their sin has not risen to point that they reject the power of the keys and the unity of charity by which the whole mystical body of Christ, the Church, is held together but they have taken advantage of it and divided up among themselves the advantages that membership in the Church provides.

The sin of the schismatics, however, tears up the Church's seamless robe, since they reject obedience to the keys and wound the unity of charity with the teeth of detraction. This is the battle that the Archangel Michael wages in the air with Satan when the demons fought over the body of Moses as is described in Jude 1:9, ["When Michael the archangel, disputing with the devil, contended about the body of Moses, he durst not bring against him the judgment of railing speech, but said: The Lord command thee."] because Moses here stands for Christ. His body is the mystical body which is the church, which Satan wants to wound. Hence also under Zorobabel and Jesus the High Priest when they sought to free the body of Moses, that is, the Jewish people, Satan appeared as their adversary as Zechariah 3:1-2 relates, "And the Lord shewed me Jesus the high priest standing before the angel of the Lord: and Satan stood on his right hand to be his adversary. And the Lord said to Satan: The Lord rebuke thee, O Satan: and the Lord that chose Jerusalem rebuke thee: Is not this a brand plucked out of the fire?" As also Psalm 110:4 says, ["Jesus is our high priest according to the order of Melchisedech,"] who gives the power of the keys to prelates for the building up of the Church, not for its destruction. Satan, however, standing on God's "right hand to be his adversary" is the schismatic who enjoys temporal prosperity but who does not cease to be the adversary of the Lord, rebuking and rejecting him; because the Lord "chose Jerusalem," that is, the vision of peace which the schismatic hates.

And this is what we say of schismatics in relation to the whole Church, but it also holds for schismatics in communities of clerics or lay persons as it is the questioning voice of the quarrelsome as it says in the Song of Songs 1:5, "The sons of my mother have fought against me" and in Psalm 119:7, "With them that hate peace I was peaceable: when I spoke to them they fought against me without cause," and Psalm 109:4, "Instead of making me a return of love, they detracted me," and Psalm 55:13-15, "For if my enemy had reviled me...I would perhaps have hidden myself from him. But thou a man of one mind, my guide, and my familiar, Who didst take sweetmeats" [namely, the Word of God] "together with me in the house of God when we walked" [that is, we should have walked] "with consent."

The tenth battle that consists in infidelity and heresy surpasses all the foregoing in bitterness, because this is the most iniquitous battle and the most profound action against God. It is signified by the battle of Moses, [related in Exodus 7:8-14, and referred to with the names of the magicians in II Timothy, 3:8] in opposition to Jannes and Mambres before Pharaoh, the king of Egypt, that hardened the hearts of the Egyptians and liberated the sons of Israel. For Moses' "rod" signifies the authority of faith which is changed into a serpent of truth devouring the other serpents, that is, a sentence of excommunication binding in truth and handing over the heretic to Satan. But Pharaoh's magicians wanted to match what Moses had done but did not succeed in matching his third miracle, because the heretics resemble the Church but they fail in the grace of the Holy Spirit because in their sacraments the Holy Spirit does not confer grace, although as long as it follows the form of the Church it imprints the sacramental character, since, as it says in Wisdom 1:5, "For the Holy Spirit of discipline will flee from the deceitful." This is the "beast" pictured in Revelation 16:13, ["And I saw from the mouth of the dragon, and from the mouth of the beast, and from the mouth of the false prophet"], "three unclean spirits like frogs." The first spirit is blasphemy against the eternal truth of faith. The second spirit is blasphemy against God in that it attributes falsehoods to him. The third spirit is blasphemy against the power of God operating in the sacraments which the heretics reject. In this war are also engaged those who engage in simony, such as the Giezites [who are like Giezi in II Kings, Chapter 4:1ff, tried to delay a miracle that the prophet Eliseus worked for a poor widow] who attempt to draw back the Holy Spirit in his giving of gifts so that they can sell or buy them at a worldly price. For this war the Antichrist will wage against Christ, because the heretics are already messengers of the Antichrist as I John 4:3 says, "And every spirit that dissolveth Jesus, is not of God: and this is Antichrist, of whom you have heard that he cometh, and he is now already in the world." This spirit is the inspiration of the devil inspiring heretics to utter falsehoods. It dissolves faith and the presence of Jesus in the sacraments and corrupts Church office because its leaders bear the mark of the Antichrist who will come in the future but even now comes in his fellows and messengers. This is the "lying spirit" [that God permitted to deceive King Josaphat in I Kings 22:22, "And there came forth a spirit, and stood before the Lord, and said: I will deceive him. And the Lord said to him: By what means? And he said: I will go forth, and be a lying spirit in the mouth of all his prophets. And the Lord said: Thou shalt deceive him, and shalt prevail: a go forth, and do so."] Since when people will not believe the truth it is only just that they should be left [by God] to the spirit of error so that they believe lies.

Next the third question "How does the woman put her hands to strong things?" must be considered and there are four ways in which the Valiant Woman does this: first by praying that God will aid her to victory; second, by carefully and subtly striking the enemy; third by cautiously evading the attacks brought by the enemy; fourth by assiduously protecting and strengthening her hand lest it weaken in the battle.

Of the first, namely, how the Valiant Woman's hands are to be raised in prayer, Psalm 141:2 says, "Let my prayer be directed as incense in thy sight; the lifting up of my hands, as evening sacrifice," and in I Timothy 2:8 St. Paul says, "I will therefore that men pray in every place, lifting up pure hands, without anger and contention," and as Exodus 17:11 relates, "And when Moses lifted up his hands, Israel overcame: but if he let them down a little, Amalec overcame." Thus Moses on the mountain raised his hands in prayer while the armies of Israel repulsed Amalec, but when he lowered them Amalec's forces advanced. And this signifies that when any one on the mount of sanctity raises his hands in prayer then he conquers the foe, but when from weariness he lowers them, the devil begins to win.

Of the second, how the hands are to be applied to strong deeds in skillfully attacking the enemy, we must considered what is the virtue called "skill" in fighting spiritually to wound the enemy. It is a virtue of careful observance of the temptations that the enemy uses the most so that they will be most avoided and constantly opposed by us. Hence Job 29:20 says, "My glory shall always be renewed, and my bow in my hand shall be repaired," that is, the glory of victory is greatest when it renders the enemy powerless. To keep the bow in hand is the skillful way to pierce the enemy who is always about to attack because it constantly confuses and weakens the opponent. Such a hand is also referred to in Job 26:13 as "obstetric, "His [God's] spirit hath adorned the heavens, and his obstetric hand brought forth the winding serpent," that is, it is a "midwife's hand" because like a midwife it solicitously cares to exclude the bite of the serpent and the serpent itself from the heart, while the Saints by their virtues make the heavens shine.

The third use of the hand is when one cautiously knows when to avoid the occasions of temptation and to heal any wounds received so that they do not get infected. One avoids temptation who avoids evil companions and bad celebrations and games, lewd talk and laziness, as I Corinthians 15:33 says, "Evil communications corrupt good manners," and I Timothy 4:7 says, "But avoid foolish and old wives' fables: and exercise thyself unto godliness." It is also said of Lot in Genesis 19:17 that he escaped from Sodom and did not remain in its vicinity but for safety made to the mountains. Sodom signifies mortal sin and its environment is the multitude of venial sins which we inevitably pass through during this life, yet nevertheless ought not to stand still in them, but instead in order to save ourselves should strive through daily prayer and alms and making a general confession to go climb up the high mountain of the virtues. Also we ought not to look back on the sinners burning in sulphur in Sodom and Gomorrah, that is, to the stink of lust, because many have died because they gazed on lust and its trappings, as in Genesis 19:6 it relates how the wife of Lot, looking back in remembrance of the pleasures of Sodom, was turned into a pillar of salt, that is, hardness of heart, and remained in her sins so that she might be an example to others lest they act in the same way and suffer the same fate. Thus the salt of wisdom gives flavor for others, because, as the saying goes, "Happy are those who make others aware of dangers."

Of the fourth use of the hand, which is constantly to care for that hand lest it lose its vigor for fighting, Hebrews 12:12-13 says, "Wherefore lift up the hands which hang down, and the feeble knees, And make straight steps with your feet: that no one, halting, may go out of the way; but rather be healed," and earlier in this same chapter verses 1-3, "Laying aside every weight and sin which surrounds us, let us run by patience to the fight proposed to us: Looking on Jesus, the author and finisher of faith, who having joy set before him, endured the cross, despising the shame, and now sitteth on the right hand of the throne of God. For think diligently upon him that endured such opposition from sinners against himself; that you be not wearied, fainting in your minds."

§ 2

Next we consider the phrase of the chapter text that reads "**and her fingers have taken hold of the spindle**" in which is noted the assiduity and utility of the Valiant Woman's work by which she provides against the cold of the snow, which will be commented on later. There are three things here to be noted; first which and how many fingers take hold of the spindle, second what the spindle is, and third how it is taken hold of.

Concerning the first of these questions it is notable that women take hold of a spindle with three fingers, thumb, index finger, and middle finger. So this Valiant Woman has a thumb that is stronger than the other fingers of her hand, the gift of the Holy Spirit by which she is aided, for of this finger Exodus 8:19 says, "This is the finger of God," which the Gloss says means the manifestation of God" and therefore it says in the hymn, *Veni, Creator Spiritus... [dextrae] Dei tu digitus* ["Come Holy Spirit...finger of God,"] of which the Lord said in Luke 11:20, "If I by the finger of God cast out devils; doubtless the kingdom of God is come upon you."

The second or index finger is obedience to the commandments and of this Moses says, in Deuteronomy 9:10, "And the Lord gave me two tables of stone written with the finger of God," because it is by our obedience God that he writes his commandments in our hearts.

The third or middle finger is meditation on the passion of Christ of which Leviticus 4:17 says that God commanded that Aaron dip his finger in blood and sprinkle it seven times on the veil of the Tabernacle. This "blood' is the passion of Christ, the finger of compassion. The "veil" is the heavens which veil eternity from us. "To sprinkle seven times" is the seven daily hours of prayer chanting the praises of Christ's Passion.

Next is the question as to what is the Valiant Woman's "spindle" and since the Bible gives no explanation of what the spindle is, it is necessary that the authority of the Gloss should be followed, which says that "the spindle is divine wisdom." This is called a "spindle" because from it spins out the thread for the garments in which all the Saints are vested. And the wisdom of God is likened to a spindle because by its whirling motion it twists the wool into thread. Similarly by the rational circling of wisdom the essences of created things which are as confused as wool are unified and turned into threads from which are made the vestments of God's sanctity, for all the Saints are like vestments for God's glory. Of this wisdom the Apostle exclaims in Romans 11:33, "O the depth of the riches of the wisdom and of the knowledge of God! How incomprehensible are his judgments, and how unsearchable his ways!"

Thus I have said what the finger and the spindle signify, now it must be seen how they are to be understood in one of three ways: by reading, by contemplation, by meditation. Reading gathers the thread of thought, contemplation spins it, and meditation winds the finished thread by winding it together. Of reading, St. Paul advised Timothy, I Timothy 4:13, "Till I come, attend unto reading." Of contemplation it says in Habakkuk 2:1, "I will watch [*Contemplabor*], to see what will be said to me, and what I may answer to him that reproveth me." And of meditation, Psalm 119:47, "I meditated also on thy commandments, which I loved."

But it must especially be noted that this Valiant Woman who takes hold of the spindle and who has woolen and linen cloth also does not lack bands and borders to bond these cloths together. Hence St. Augustine says that "charity is nothing other than the bond by which the lover is bound to the beloved."

OUTLINE OF CHAPTER XI

She hath opened her hand to the needy,
and stretched out her hands to the poor. (v. 20)

§1) Acrostic letter Caph ⊃ means "stretching" and the Valiant Woman opens her hands to the needy,
   1) Inclining to them by two kinds of stretching
      1) Stretching to superiors out of humility
      2) Softening the heart out of compassion for others: Mary Magdalene at Christ's tomb
   2) Stretching out her hand to the poor
      1) Which hand? That of generosity with five fingers:.
         1) To the poor
         2) It gives gladly
         3) It gives generously
         4) To the truly indigent, not to actors, mimes, tricksters, or sinners
         5) For the sake of God
   2) Who are these needy ones?
      1) Orphans, widows, strangers, and aliens
      2) The helpless, the starving, the naked, cripples, etc.
      3) How is the hand opened to them? Abundantly
   2) How the Valiant Woman's had stretches out to the needy by three virtues opposed by three vices:
      1) Virtues:
         1) Charity gives what is due of its love of God.
         2) Generosity gives to the neighbor but not from sadness nor from necessity,
         3) Mercy gives to those to whom it ought to be given because of their needs.
      2) Opposed vices:
         1) Hatred desires evil for the neighbor.
         2) Avarice excludes the magnificence of generosity
         3) Hardness of heart vomits the slime of cruelly over the needy.

§2. How the Valiant Woman's hand is stretched out to the needy:
   1) What are the palms of her outstretched hands?
      1) The spirit of abundant piety pours itself forth in the outpouring of goodness; as Abraham &the three Angels
         1) He washed their feet
         2) He seated them under a tree for coolness
         3) He fed them
      2) The effect of the most gracious consolation by which all the needy are consoled.
   2) How the Valiant Woman's hands are outstretched.
      1) To give alms as explained above in section # 1
      2) The benefits the Valiant Woman reaches out her hands to supply so bountifully.
         1) Purging from sin, which frees a person from the punishment they deserve

2) Freeing men from slavery to what they were created to rule: The two winged women Zachariah's vision who carry a woman who is avarice in a vessel to hell
1) One woman has two wings of rape & violence and of hidden fraud and trickery.
2) The other has two wings of hardness of heart and delight in money.
3) Conforms us to God who from generosity created us
4) Social life is restored to us and sustained
5) Opens us to eternal riches
6) Increases for us a hundredfold merit simply gained through almsgiving.

CHAPTER XI

She hath opened her hand to the needy, and stretched out her hands to the poor. (v. 20)

§ 1

CAPH ‏כ‎, which is interpreted as "stooping." There is, however, a twofold stooping: one is owing to superiors out of humility, the other is softening of one's hardness of heart out of compassion.

Of the first Psalm 144:5 says, "Lord, bow down thy heavens and descend: touch the mountains and they shall smoke." The "heavens," that are high and proud because the very notion of pride is heavenly, yield through humility and descend toward earth where are the humble things that have descended there and there remain. These heavens touch the highest mountain tops through sorrow and emit the fire of contrition and the smoke of penance.

The other sort of stooping is referred to in John 20:11-12, "But Mary stood at the tomb outside, weeping. Now as she was weeping, she stooped down, and looked into the tomb, And she saw two angels in white, sitting, one at the head, and one at the feet, where the body of Jesus had been laid." The tomb of Jesus is the buried poor and afflicted laid with the Lord. He is their only consolation in this life, since the rich receive the consolation of material goods in their earthly lives, while Lazarus received evil, as it says in Luke 16:25, ["And Abraham said to him: Son, remember that thou didst receive good things in thy lifetime, and likewise Lazarus evil things, but now he is comforted; and thou art tormented."] And therefore the life of the poor man is compared to that of those who lie in the tombs of the dead, since he has no consolation except that of Christ laying in a poor tomb, lacking all consolation and having for clothing only the shroud in which Jesus was wrapped. Jesus, however, also had the company of angels, one at his head to comfort him mentally and one at his feet to sustain him in the necessities of this life. But why? As Mary Magdalene, steeped in the bitter sea (*mari*) of compassion and stooped from all hardness heart visited the tomb of Christ's poverty, the Valiant Woman. when she relieves the miseries of the very poor, weeps over them in the affection of piety and mercy. And thus it is evident how this agrees with the above verse, since both parts of that verse refer to compassion and mercy toward the poor and so that they stoop down to the poor, but do not despise them, as Tobit 4:7 says, "Turn not away thy face from any poor person [for so it shall come to pass that the face of the Lord shall not be turned from thee."] And the other stooping down, that of compassion, provides them with consolation.

The consideration of this verse concerns both its parts, namely, what it is for the Valiant Woman's hand to be "**open...to the poor**," and how it is "**stretched out**" to them. Concerning the first part three things are to be noted, first, which hand is open, second, who are these poor, and third, how the hand is opened to them. Concerning the first Jesus says in Luke 11:41, "From that [of your possessions] which remaineth, give alms; and behold, all things are clean unto you," and Proverbs 3:9 says, "Honor the Lord with thy substance, and give him of the first of all thy fruits," that is, for poor persons.

Of the second the Apostle says in II Corinthians 9:7, "Every one as he hath determined in his heart, not with sadness, or of necessity: for God loveth a cheerful giver," and in Hebrews 20:34, "For you both had compassion on them that were in bands, and took with joy the being stripped of your own goods, knowing that you have a better and a lasting substance."

Of the third it says in Tobit 4:9, "If thou have much, give abundantly: if thou have a little, take care even so to bestow willingly a little," for it is not right to have received many dollars from God and to give pennies to the poor, as Genesis 4:3-4 says of Cain; he inherited half the world but from it offered to others hardly a handful. As Malachi 1:14 says, "Cursed is the deceitful man that hath in his flock a male, and making a vow offereth in sacrifice that which is feeble to the Lord."

And as to the fourth, one ought not give to an actor, or a mimic, or a jester, or a sinner except for their living, but to the poor as Psalm 112:9 says, "He hath distributed, he hath given to the poor: his justice remaineth for ever and ever," for riches do not remain forever and ever, and Job 31:17-18 says, "If I have eaten my morsel alone, and the fatherless hath not eaten thereof: [For from my infancy mercy grew up with me: and it came out with me from my mother's womb."]

Fifthly the verse says that this giving must be for God and God alone, as Jesus says in Matthew 6:2-4, "Therefore when thou dost an alms deed, sound not a trumpet before thee, as the hypocrites do in the synagogues and in the streets, that they may be honored by men. Amen I say to you, they have received their reward. But when thou dost alms, let not thy left hand know what thy right hand doth. That thy alms may be in secret, and thy Father who seeth in secret will repay thee."

The next consideration is what in the chapter text "needy" (Latin *inops*) means. *Inops*, that is, not-power, is to be without power, and thus "to open the hand to the needy" indicates two things: the needs of orphans, widows, strangers, and foreigners and the solicitous care of these persons, such as the starving, the naked, etc. that lack the power themselves to meet their own needs. Of the first of these Psalm 9:10 according to the Hebrew, says, "And the Lord is become a refuge for the poor: a helper in due time in tribulation," and Lamentation 5:3 says, "We are become orphans without a father: our mothers are as widows." But some overpower the needy at the gate [before a judge] as it, Job 31:21-22 says, "If I have lifted up my hand against the fatherless, even when I saw myself superior in the gate: Let my shoulder fall from its joint, and let my arm with its bones be broken." For this is the proper punishment for those who oppress the poor, because the bones of the arm with its power of strength will be broken by this eternal punishment, as it says in Wisdom 6:7, "For to him that is little [such as the orphan and other needy persons] mercy is granted: but the mighty shall be mightily tormented." The shoulders on which a burden is sustained are nobility and wealth, because on these shoulders is carried the authority of secular power and the scepter of the kingdom of this world, but in the next life it will be broken because then there will be neither riches, nor honor, nor nobility, nor dignity.

As for the second kind of mercy of which the Scriptures speak in many places and as the Lord teaches in Matthew 19:21, "If thou wilt be perfect, go sell what thou hast, and give to the poor and thou shalt have treasure in heaven: and come follow me." This saying makes it clear that the perfection of our lives is constituted by alms to the poor. In Deuteronomy [for example, 14:4; 24:12] it often says that the Lord loves the poor and the pilgrim and gives him clothing and food, that is, makes us do so. And I John 3:17 says, "He that hath the substance of this world, and shall see his brother in need, and shall shut up his bowels from him: how doth the charity of God abide in him?"

Next it must be considered just how the Valiant Woman's hand must be stretched out to the needy and it is opened by three virtues;

A hand is opened by three virtues:	Charity Generosity Mercy

Charity opens the hand to any neighbor, generosity to a man of virtue, but mercy opens it because of the misery of the needy. Charity opens the hand because of God, generosity because of virtue, mercy arises from compassion for an other's misery, as Sirach 4:36 says, "Let not thy hand be stretched out to receive, and shut when thou shouldst give."

Of the stretching out of the hand through charity Hebrews 13:1-2 says, "Let the charity of the brotherhood abide in you; and hospitality do not forget; for by this some, being not aware of it, have entertained angels."

Of its stretching out through generosity I Chronicles 29:17-18 says, "[I] have joyfully offered all these things: and I have seen with great joy thy people, which are here present, offer thee their offerings."

Charity gives what is due because of God whom it loves. Generosity gives in the manner it should, not from sadness nor from necessity, but with joy because the giver loves God. But mercy gives to those to whom it ought to be given because of their needs.

Opposite to these virtues are three vices that close the hand, namely:

The hand is closed by:	Hardness of Heart Avarice Hate

THE VALIANT WOMAN

Hate breaks off the community of charity; avarice excludes the magnificence of generosity; and hardness of heart extinguishes all feeling of compassion and sympathy. Hatred simply desires evil for the neighbor. Avarice persuades itself that what the needy have is undeserved and hence nothing at all should be shared with them. But hardness of heart vomits the slime of cruelty over the needy.

Of hatred Wisdom 2:15 where it speaks of Christ in the person of the neighbor says, "He is grievous unto us, even to behold: for his life is not like other men's and his ways are very different."

Of avarice Sirach 10:9 says, "Nothing is more wicked than the covetous man."

O hardness of heart it says in Sirach 3:27, "A hard heart shall fear evil at the last: and he that loveth danger shall perish in it," because he has a heart that is hard to God in his poor. He is in danger that his hard heart will be judged by God because he loves his own possessions [more than his neighbor].

§ 2

The second part of the chapter text follows: and the Valiant Woman, "**stretched out her hands to the poor**" in which two things should noted, namely, what are the palms of her outstretched hands and how they are outstretched.

The palm of the hand, as the Philosopher says, "Is the measure of the whole hand, or quantitative dimension from the extreme of the thumb to the end of the jointed finger." [This seems to be from *Historia Animalium* Book I, c.15, 493b 26-494a4, but does not exactly correspond]. Thus the this woman has two palms, one of very abundant piety and the other the effect of her most gracious consolation, so that the one palm is measured in piety and the other palm in consolation, for this is what the word "palm" signifies, namely, the "measure" of the whole hand. If therefore this hand is the hand of generosity and the palm is the measure of the hand, the two palms each measuring a whole hand are the spirit of abundant piety and the effect of the most gracious consolation by which all the abandoned are consoled. The spirit of piety pours itself forth in the outpouring of goodness and the charm of this consolation encompasses the poverty of the abandoned with sweet company and assistance.

Of the first of these, piety, the Apostle in I Timothy 4:8 writes, "But godliness [piety] is profitable to all things, having promise of the life that now is, and of that which is to come." The patriarchs abounded in this spirit; they greeted strangers whom they met with the grace of piety and of goodness and were unwilling for them to pass by but spoke to them with kindly words as did Abraham [to the three strangers who were in fact angels] in Genesis 18:2, ["And when he had lifted up his eyes, there appeared to him three men standing near him: and as soon as he saw them he ran to meet them from the door of his tent, and adored down to the ground."] For when he saw the three men standing at the entrance of his tent who seemed to be transient, homeless paupers he invited them in and did this in the heat of the day when men are wont to seek greater shade and coolness. Thus it should be noted that the heat did not prevent Abraham from exposing himself to the sun knowing that at that time travelers are more accustomed to decline to stop when the sun's heat prevents their lingering. Instead he ran out to meet them lest perhaps someone else would do so before him and he bowed down to the ground so that his humility might prevent them from being unwilling to remain. As verse 3 to 4 goes on, Abraham called out to the Lord, ["And he said: Lord, if I have found favor in thy sight, pass not away from thy servant: but I will fetch a little water, and wash your feet, and rest ye under the tree."] He called out to the Lord so that by the reverence of his speech he might reassure these strangers, acting as if he were a worthy servant lest they think that he was not fit to serve them. Then he offered them the necessities: first to cool their feet in water since they had traveled far and so that he might at once free them from sweat, dust, and weariness. Then he invited them to rest under a tree from the heat of the sun. Next he brought food of which in the manner of good hosts he was not sparing but gave them plenty that was delicious and then, showing completely his pious intentions, ran (although he was an old man) to get the strangers very tender and nourishing meat. His wife cooked these delicate foods.

Similarly in Genesis 19:2 we read of Lot that he, sat at the gate of the city in the evening in order, as St. Jerome says, that he might greet travelers and when Lot saw Angels in the likeness of pilgrims coming there, he adored them and falling to the earth that he might conquer them by his reverence he said to them, " I beseech you, my lords, turn in to the house of your servant, and lodge there:wash your feet, and in the morning you shall go on your way." And when they refused he pressed them until they consented to enter his house.

And in Genesis 24:31 Laban says to the servant of Abraham, "Come in, thou blessed of the Lord: why standest thou without?" In Luke 24:29, when Jesus seems to be ready to travel on, Luke and Cleophas urge him to stop at the inn with them saying, "Stay with us, because it is towards evening, and the day is now far spent."

Concerning the effect of such exceedingly gracious consolations II Corinthians 1:3 says, "Blessed be the God and Father of our Lord Jesus Christ, the Father of mercies, and the God of all comfort. Who comforteth us in all our tribulation; that we also may be able to comfort them who are in all distress, by the exhortation wherewith we also are exhorted by God. For as the sufferings of Christ abound in us: so also by Christ doth our comfort abound." The grace of consolation is that which first speaks a word of compassion to the poor and does not blame or shout at them but provides help for their poverty.

On the contrary this consolation is burdensome when it provides help only with blame and not with the spirit of piety and mercy, as Job 16:2-3, "I have often heard such things as these: you are all troublesome comforters. Shall windy words have no end?" that is, "consolation" with harsh words proceeding from the arrogance of pride. To stretch out one's hands with one's whole strength to the poor is to multiply the effects of this work of piety and consolation. And since we have already discussed the various kinds of almsgiving in section §1, we wish here to speak of the causes that the Valiant Woman reaches out her hands so bountifully.

There are six goods which constitute alms for all who give them. The first is the most important, namely, that which frees the sinner from death. The second is that which does not permit a man to be oppressed by others whom he was created to rule. The third is that which especially conforms us to our heavenly Father. The fourth is the one that restores and sustains us in the society from which we have become excluded. The fifth is that which opens eternity to us. The sixth is that which increases for us a hundredfold the merit simply gained through almsgiving. We return therefore to proving by authority and reason that each of these is a true good.

The first of these goods of almsgiving is that by being purged from sin a person is freed from death and this is truly just since through God it raises to life those dying from starvation, hence as it says in Tobit 4:11, "For alms deliver from all sin, and from death, and will not suffer the soul to go into darkness," and Isaiah 58:7 says, "Deal thy bread to the hungry, and bring the needy and the harborless into thy house: when thou shalt see one naked, cover him, [and despise not thy own flesh,"] and further on in 10-11 of the same chapter, "When thou shalt pour out thy soul to the hungry, and shalt satisfy the afflicted soul then shall thy light rise up in darkness, and thy darkness shall be as the noonday. And the Lord will give thee rest continually, and will fill thy soul with brightness, and deliver thy bones, and thou shalt be like a watered garden, and like a fountain of water whose waters shall not fail."

The second good of almsgiving does not permit a man to be subject under those that he was created to rule. For the miser is the slave of money and yet was created to rule over all irrational things since, as Psalm 8:8 says, "Thou hast subjected all things under his [man's] feet, all sheep and oxen: moreover the beasts also of the fields." Since, therefore, almsgiving with stretched out palms scatters all temporal goods, it calls man from the stooping down of avarice to the upright stance of our first freedom when all the earth was subject to human rule. As Zechariah 5:5 says, "And the angel went forth that spoke in me, and he said to me: Lift up thy eyes, and see what this is, that goeth forth. And I said: What is it? And he said: This is a vessel going forth. And he said: This is their eye in all the earth. And behold a talent of lead was carried, and behold a woman sitting in the midst of the vessel. And he said: This is wickedness. And he cast her into the midst of the vessel, and cast the weight of lead upon the mouth thereof. And I lifted up my eyes and looked: and behold there came out two women, and wind was in their wings, and they had wings like the wings of a kite: and they lifted up the vessel between the earth and the heaven. And I said to the angel that spoke in me: Whither do these carry the vessel? And he said to me: That a house may be built for it in the land of Sennaar, and that it may be established and set there upon its own foundation."

This vision is to be understood and moralized as follows. The Angel who speaks to Zechariah is the Word of God that is God's messenger and he is called the "Angel of Understanding." Zechariah is interpreted as "remembering God" or as "the help of God," and signifies someone open to works of piety and to extending hands to the poor, who remembers how the Lord mercifully agreed and gave everything into his hands. The Lord showed by Zechariah by his word how the impiety of the miser dominates the miser who ought on the contrary to dominate his wealth. The "vessel" signifies our earthly human nature since it is a vessel made of lead. The "woman" in the vessel who is called "wickedness" [or impiety] is avarice as it is wickedness toward the poor and she sits in this vessel because she rests in an earth-bound heart. A heavy "leaden lid" closes the vessel over the woman because the heart of a miser is compressed by a very heavy concern about mere wind and is trampled under foot by it. Hence it is written in the history of the Philosophers that when Plato went to philosophize at Athens he carried a bag of gold in his bosom and as a result his heart turned from philosophy and, as it were, fled to the gold until finally grieved that his heart was too much occupied with gold, he threw the bag of gold into the sea and said, "It is better to lose gold than to lose one's soul and the damage of gold to the heart of a philosopher is heavier than the loss of this money." The Angel adds to the word of God that "this is the eye of misers in all the earth," as Ecclesiastes 10:19 says, "All things obey money," and in Philippians 2:21, "For all seek the things that are their own; not the things that are Jesus Christ's." The two women who have" two wings" like kites are the two servants of avarice, that is, of greed, which is to get possessions in every possible and even evil way and this woman has two kite-like wings of rapacity, one of open rape and violence and the other of hidden fraud and trickery. The other winged woman who serves avarice is a symbol of greedily holding and cherishing possessions already hoarded. She also has two wings like a bird of prey, namely, hardness of heart toward the poor and delight of the eyes in the contemplation of money. These two women lift the leaden vessel of their mistress Avarice and bear it to the land of Sennaar, which is interpreted "gnashing of teeth," that is, to hell, where for all eternity they are doomed to gnash their teeth with which they have eaten and consumed their poor victims. There is built for them a house of eternal habitation, founded on the unchangeable judgment of sin and malice and built on its own foundation. Thus the punishment of eternal fire is founded on guilt as its firm basis; hence it is evident why the miser is pressed down by a "talent of lead." But one who stretches out hands and puts down a full bundle [for the poor] is raised up to the freedom of our first dignity. As Isaiah 58:6 says, "Is not this rather the fast that I have chosen? Loose the bands of wickedness, undo the bundles that oppress, let them that are broken go free, and break asunder every burden." The bundles of impiety are the treasuries of money. And they are also the bundle that pressed the greedy down into hell. Thus it says in Sirach 31:8-9, "Blessed is the rich man that is found without blemish: and that hath not gone after gold, nor put his trust in money nor in treasures. Who is he, and we will praise him? For he hath done wonderful things in his life." This rightly says, "hath not gone after gold," since the good rich man has not departed from his primal dignity so as to be ruled by what was created to be ruled by him as his inferior. Nevertheless the rich, even though through the sin of avarice they have gone after gold, are to be praised if afterwards they are penitent and then stretch out their hands to the poor, thus recovering that pristine dignity.

The third benefit of almsgiving is that it conforms us to our Heavenly Father for out of his mercy he created us, redeemed us, and will glorify us. Hence Jesus says in Luke 6:36, says, "Be ye therefore merciful, as your Father also is merciful," and in Matthew 9:13 says of the mercy of God, "Go then and learn what this meaneth, I will have mercy and not sacrifice," and Lamentations 3:22 says, "The mercies of the Lord are not consumed: because his commiserations have not failed" and again in Luke 1:78 [Zachary, father of John the Baptist,] says, "Through the bowels of the mercy of our God, in which the Orient from on high hath visited us."

The fourth benefit of almsgiving is that social life of the poor perishing from famine is restored to us and sustained, because as the wise saying goes, "Feed those dying of hunger because, if you do not, you will worry that you killed them." Luke 19:8 shows that Zachaeus, the rich publican, when salvation [Jesus] came to his house and as a true son of Abraham, took care of the poor who out impiety he had previously neglected and of other poor also, saying, "Behold, Lord, the half of my goods I give to the poor; and if I have wronged any man of any thing, I restore him fourfold." And thus was verified in him what Job 20:15 says, "The riches which he hath swallowed; he shall vomit up, and God shall draw them out of his belly."

The fifth benefit of almsgiving is that through it the value of riches is made eternal, since temporal goods that are corruptible are made to survive as eternal beatitude. Hence Jesus says in Luke 16:9, "Make unto you friends of the mammon of iniquity; that when you shall fail, they may receive you into everlasting dwellings" and in Matthew 6:20-21, "Lay up to yourselves treasures in heaven: where neither the rust nor moth doth consume, and where thieves do not break through, nor steal. For where thy treasure is, there is thy heart also."

The sixth and last benefit of giving alms is that they are multiplied a hundredfold like good seed planted on good ground, as Genesis 26:12 says, "And Isaac sowed in that land, and he found that same year a hundredfold: and the Lord blessed him." This account tells how Isaac sowed his land in Gerara, a city of the Palestinians, and found that in that year it yielded this hundredfold. Gerara is interpreted "dwelling of the just," that is, the spiritual habitation of the poor. And Palestine is interpreted as "swollen mouth" and these are the poor who from poverty have swollen and closed mouths. "That same year" indicates the endless cycle of time. Hence Sirach 11:1 says, "Cast thy bread upon the running waters: for after a long time thou shalt find it again." And the Lord in Matthew 19:29 says, "Every one that hath left house, or brethren, or sisters, or father, or mother, or wife, or children, or lands for my name's sake, shall receive a hundredfold, and shall possess life everlasting." Thus almsgiving in this present life has a reward of repayment in our experience of its internal sweetness that the Lord grants and a hundredfold in merit and this justly, because he who gives others solace in exterior matters for the sake of God justly receives from God a good internal recompense.

OUTLINE OF CHAPTER XII

She shall not fear for her house in the cold of snow: for all her domestics are clothed with double garments. (v. 21)

§1) Acrostic letter Lamed ל signifies "doctrine of discipline" that the Valiant Woman provides her household, namely:
  1) To know our own weakness
  2) To cry to God and others out for help
  3) To confess our sins
  4) To despise this world and its worldly ways
  5) To long for heaven
  6) To renounce sin forever
2) Hence she does not fear for her house in time of snow.
  1) What is this house? Like Solomon's four palaces it has four features about which she need not fear
    1) An interior: the heart that is holy and cleansed of sin
      1) The ground floor of this house for widowhood and mourning,
      2) The upper house is a house of joy and jubilation and security and of every good,
    2) An exterior that is Holy Church adorned for a place of payer
    3) A roof that is heaven with many mansions, where dwells the God-Man Jesus Christ
    4) Its floor is the body, but it has no basement for that is Hell, where dwell only the Church's enemies
  2) In time of snow:
    1) What is snow? It is generated from warm vapor in the middle region of air and falls in winter.
    2) It has these properties that signify the attack of the enemy:
      1) The heat in the vapor of unnatural desires for pleasure ascends in a man and is empty gaiety
      2) The north wind is temptation by the devil.
      3) Crystal is the hardness of heart from cold of little devotion, all the more dangerous when the vapor of lust is hotter
      4) The whiter the snow the more it deceives, by transfiguring itself into an Angel of Light by promising future repentance, presuming mercy and impunity to punishment.
      5) In spring the Valiant Woman is called to her Beloved
  3) Four kinds of snow chill the house of the Church with four kinds of cold:
    1) God permits snow of sloth to attack the interior with the cold of lack of devotion,
    2) Snow of bad example from the world attacks the exterior with the cold of scandal
    3) Snow of lustful desire fights lower parts of the house, the flesh;
    4) Snow of pride coming from heights of anger and striking the roof the house with contempt of higher things, those of heaven that began with Satan's fall.
  4) All the house of the Valiant Woman is freed from snow that battles us all: the icy chill of hell from which we are freed only by penance:

  1) Red sins of the boiling blood of lust and gluttony
  2) Red sins that can lead to the shedding of blood of anger, envy, and greed

§ 2) The domestics, at least two for each of four parts of the house of the Church, are doubly clothed against the cold snow.
 1) Of the two domestics of the interior of the house of the Church
  1) One, the intellect, is vested with:
   1) Garment of light of divine truth. Light of Mount Tabor
   2) Garment of worldly communication; the rational science; Jacob's skins
  2) The other, the will, is vested with:
   1) Garment of charity, Christ's seamless garment, against the cold of the snow
   2) Garment of obedience of the Commandments and counsels
 2) The two domestics of the exterior of the house of the Church
  1) Active persons
   1) Garment of fervor of spirit
   2) Garment of perseverance
  2) Contemplative persons
   1) Garment of purity
   2) Garment of attention
 3) The two domestics of the lower house of the Church
  1) Chaste persons
   1) Garment of modesty
   2) Garment of holy purity
  2) Abstinent persons
   1) Garment of austerity
   2) Garment of discretion
 4) The two domestics of the upper part of the house
  1) Angels
   1) Garment of administration
   2) Garment of assistance
  2) Human persons
   1) Garment of soul
   2) Garment of body

CHAPTER XII

She shall not fear for her house in the cold of snow: for all her domestics are clothed with double garments. (v. 21)

§ 1

LAMED ל. To be first considered in this verse is the meaning of Lamed that is interpreted "doctrine of discipline" and alludes to the meaning of the chapter verse, namely that previous learning has taught the Valiant Woman to be cautious about the future, because discipline teaches six things. Before listing these, however, we should first accept the definition that St. Basil the Great in the beginning of his *Commentary on Proverbs,* [Probably not authentic] namely, that "Discipline is learning through what is difficult," as the Prophet Jeremiah 6:6 says, "Be thou instructed, O Jerusalem, lest my soul depart from thee, lest I make thee desolate, a land uninhabited."

Thus what discipline teaches us is the experience of our weakness. For a person sometimes believes himself to be strong, but when tribulation and discipline touches him, then he experiences what human weakness is. Thus in Job 4:3-7, Eliphaz says, "Behold thou hast taught many, and thou hast strengthened the weary hands: Thy words have confirmed them that were staggering, and thou hast strengthened the trembling knees: But now the scourge is come upon thee, and thou faintest: it hath touched thee, and thou art troubled. Where is thy fear, thy fortitude, thy patience, and the perfection of thy ways?" In this same sense Psalm 30:7 says, "And in my abundance I said: I shall never be moved" but then verse 8 says "O Lord, in thy favor, thou gavest strength to my beauty. Thou turnedst away thy face from me, and I became troubled," because when he did not feel weak the Psalmist claimed he was well off, forgetting the human condition of which Job 14:2 says that it, "Never continueth in the same state," that is, is not permanent but always changing. But then through troubles Job was brought to reflect on himself ["in his heart"] and to recognize that his appearance of strength was in fact only in the will of God and, when, thus disciplined, he faced that truth, yet remained troubled.

Similarly Antiochus to his misfortune and condemnation learned through discipline as we read of him in II Maccabees, 9:4, that "The judgment of heaven urging him forward, because he had spoken so proudly, that he would come to Jerusalem, and make it a common burying place of the Jews. But the Lord the God of Israel, that seeth all things, struck him with an incurable and an invisible plague. For as soon as he had ended these words, a dreadful pain in his bowels came upon him, and bitter torments of the inner parts," and further on in verses 8-12, "Now being cast down to the ground, [he] was carried in a litter"...but "worms swarmed out of the body of this man, and whilst he lived in sorrow and pain, his flesh fell off, and the filthiness of his smell was noisome to the army"...and "being brought from his great pride, he began to come to the knowledge of himself, being admonished by the scourge of God, his pains increasing every moment. And when he himself could not now abide his own stench, he spoke thus: 'It is just to be subject to God, and that a mortal man should not equal himself to God.'" So in Acts 12:21 the learned King Herod [Antipas] also was brought to extreme misery of which we read in Acts 12:21, "And upon a day appointed, Herod being arrayed in kingly apparel, sat in the judgment seat, and made an oration to them. And the people made acclamation, saying: It is the voice of a god, and not of a man. And forthwith an angel of the Lord struck him, because he had not given the honor to God: and being eaten up by worms, he gave up the ghost."

Second, what discipline teaches us is to cry out in prayer, for he who when still fortunate knows nothing about how to pray and expects to be given everything at a nod of his head, in the time of discipline and trouble begins to pray most eloquently as it says in Psalm 120:1, "In my trouble I cried to the Lord: and he heard me." Thus also king Josaphat learned to pray as it relates in II Chronicles 20:12 when against him gathered the great armies of the Idumeans, Moabites, and Ammonites and he began to pray to God, "O our God, wilt thou not then judge them? As for us we have not strength enough, to be able to resist this multitude, which cometh violently upon us. But as we know not what to do, we can only turn our eyes to thee." Thus also Judas Maccabeus was instructed and experienced that God was at his side when the Jews were gathered in Maspha and prayed to the Lord, as it says in I Maccabees 3:52-54, "Behold the nations are come together against us to destroy us: thou knowest what they intend against us. How shall we be able to stand before their face, unless thou, O God, help us? Then they sounded with trumpets," that is, with groans and prayers, "and they cried out with a loud voice." Nor is it surprising that weak man prays more devoutly and lengthily when he is under discipline, since he who is the mediator between God and man, the man Christ Jesus, as Luke 23:43 says, "being in an agony, prayed the longer."

The third thing that discipline teaches us is the confession of sins. Hence in the Canticle of Hezekiah in Isaiah 38:15, we read, "I will recount to thee all my years in the bitterness of my soul," and in this way he repented. Manasseh, a great sinner, but also a great penitent when disciplined said in his prayer [the apocryphal *Prayer of Manasses*, in an appendix to the Vulgate, based on the reference in II Chronicles 33:13-19] "I have sinned above the number of the sand of the sea. My transgressions are multiplied...I am bowed down by many iron bonds, so that I cannot uplift my head, and there is no release for me, because I have provoked thy anger, and have done evil before thee...I have sinned, Lord, I have sinned, and I acknowledge my transgressions: but I pray and beseech thee, release me, Lord, release me, and destroy me not with my transgressions; keep not evils for me in anger for ever...for me that am unworthy thou wilt save, according to thy great mercy: and I will praise thee continually all the days of my life: for all the hosts of the heavens sings to thee, and thine is the glory for ever and ever. Amen." Every man who is a sinner ought to know that prayer and say it as a disciplinary instruction.

The fourth thing that discipline teaches us is hatred of this life and this world, as St. Gregory the Great says, "This life flows with pleasures, yet they are to be fled. Since, however, it brings so many calamities on us, what else does it cry out than that it is not to be loved?" Hence the Lord taught Adam by casting him out of paradise not to love this life when he said in Genesis 3:17-18, "Because thou hast hearkened to the voice of thy wife, and hast eaten of the tree, whereof I commanded thee that thou shouldst not eat, cursed is the earth in thy work; with labour and toil shalt thou eat thereof all the days of thy life. Thorns and thistles shall it bring forth to thee; and thou shalt eat the herbs of the earth. In the sweat of thy face shalt thou eat bread till thou return to the earth, out of which thou wast taken: for dust thou art, and into dust thou shalt return." This curse is nothing more than the sufferings of his life [out of paradise]. "Thorns and thistles" are the major and minor exterior troubles of this life, and "sweat" is its interior troubles. The Lord willed that because of these pains this life should not be loved.

The fifth thing that discipline teaches is to desire heaven. Hence Baruch 3:14 says of those who accepted the discipline of the captivity [of the Jews in Babylon]: "Learn where is wisdom, where is strength, where is understanding: that thou mayst know also where is length of days and of life and food, where is the light of the eyes, and peace." "Wisdom" [Vulgate says "prudence"] is the virtue by which one lives rightly, understanding [intellect] is the virtue by which one knows what is eternal and divine, "length of days" signifies eternity, "life and food" signifies joy, "light" signifies the vision of God and "peace" signifies the concord of the mutual love of God and his creatures. St. Augustine in his *De Civitate Dei* says that "the peace of the celestial city is the most sweet concord in the enjoyment of God; for each saint enjoys the others Saints in God."

Sixth and finally discipline teaches the end of sin and the sons of Israel were taught in this way when, as related in Numbers 11:32-34, they murmured against the Lord [and "behold the wrath of the Lord being provoked against the people, struck them with an exceeding great plague. And that place was called, the graves of lust for there they buried the people that had lusted,"] as also Numbers 14:28-29 relates, ["As I live, saith the Lord: According as you have spoken in my hearing, so will I do to you. In the wilderness shall your carcasses lie."] Numbers 21:6-9 also tells how they perished from the bites of the fiery serpents, and in Numbers 26:9-10 how they rebelled against the Lord in the sedition of Core, "And the earth opening her mouth swallowed up Core, many others dying, when the fire burned two hundred and fifty men. And there was a great miracle wrought." And as in I Corinthians 10:6-12 St. Paul the Apostle says of those same Jews who died in the desert and were conquered. "Now these things were done in a figure of us, that we should not covet evil things as they also coveted. Neither become ye idolaters, as some of them, as it is written: The people sat down to eat and drink, and rose up to play. Neither let us commit fornication, as some of them committed fornication, and there fell in one day three and twenty thousand. Neither let us tempt Christ: as some of them tempted, and perished by the serpents. Neither do you murmur: as some of them murmured, and were destroyed by the destroyer. Now all these things happened to them in figure: and they are written for our correction, upon whom the ends of the world are come." And Psalm 95:8-9 says much the same thing, "Today if you shall hear his voice, harden not your hearts: As in the provocation, according to the day of temptation in the wilderness: where your fathers tempted me, they proved me, and saw my works." By these "works" God here means that because of the discipline he gave them they left off sinning. Thus, as is related in Numbers 12:1-15, Mary [Miriam], who for her murmuring had been struck with leprosy, then repented her sins and was cured by the prayers of her brother Moses.

As to the meaning of the chapter verse, the first part reads **"She shall not fear for her house in the time of snow"** in which two things are to be noted, first that she does not fear for her house in the time of snow" and second that the reason she need not fear is that **"for all her domestics are clothed with double garments."**

Concerning the first of these two phrases there are two things to be considered what about she not fear about her house and second what she need not fear in the time of snow.

Concerning the first of these it should be noted that a house has four things about which she need not fear, namely, an interior, an exterior, a roof, and a floor. The interior of the house is the heart, its exterior is Holy Church, its floor is the human body, and its roof is the heavenly fatherland in which dwells the man of the house who is Jesus the Christ. But is has no basement, that is hell; no free persons dwell there, since it is the prison of the inhabitants' enemies.

Of the heart of the house Wisdom 8:16 says, "When I go into my house, I shall repose myself with her [that is with Wisdom]:for her conversation hath no bitterness, nor her company any tediousness, but only joy and gladness."

Of the exterior of the house, the Church, Psalm 83:11 says, "For better is one day in thy courts above thousands. I have chosen to be an abject in the house of my God, rather than to dwell in the tabernacles of sinners," for in the house of God nothing is evil and thus all who live therein are there out of merit That is why sinners were excluded form the primitive Church and those who did not receive communion were excommunicated in order to signify that they were excluded from the community of the faithful until they did penance and recovered heir devotion.

Of the floor of the house Job 4:18-20 says, "Behold they that serve him are not steadfast, and in his angels he found wickedness: How much more shall they that dwell in houses of clay, who have an earthly foundation, be consumed as with the moth? From morning till evening they shall be cut down: and because no one understandeth, they shall perish for ever." Those "serving God" are the holy angels and good men, which company, however, was not always stable since the sin of angels caused their fall and the sin of man drove him from paradise, yet both were created in the grace that freely makes creatures holy. This is the teachings of the Saints, although some theologians have held the opinion that the angels were created in freely given grace only. Those who live in houses of clay, however, are men who in their condition of mortality are is not superior to the dust of the earth and because they will certainly die are no more than vessels of clay, for as Jeremiah sys in Lamentations 4:2, "The noble children of Sion," namely, Adam and Eve, "and they that were clothed with the best gold," that is in the grace of innocence in their primal state and the grace of immortality if they had wanted it, "how are they esteemed," because of sin, "as earthen vessels, the work of the potter's hands?" And these are consumed by the moth of corruption and original sin, because, just as a moth lurks in clothing and consumes it, so original sin is born in us and consumes our body through various illicit impulses. And these moths gnaw from morning, that is, from the rise of birth and youth, until evening, that is, even in old age; because they change and perish, for natural heat continually consumes a substance and turns it into something alien. And these weaknesses are in every human being. The phrase that follows, "no one understandeth, they shall perish forever," does not pertain to the Valiant Woman who understands what the ruin of her house would mean and therefore warns lest it fall on her and crush her. Sinners, however, because they are deceived, believe that in their bodies they have a place of security and happiness, are crushed by their flesh, as the Apostle says in Galatians 6:8, "For he that soweth in his flesh, of the flesh also shall reap corruption."

Of the roof the house it is written in John 14:2 that, "In my Father's house there are many mansions."

The interior of the house is the dwelling of holiness and cleanliness, as Psalm 93:5 declares, "Holiness becometh thy house, O Lord, unto length of days." For there the Lord rests because the house is his home and hence it should provide him with a most holy dwelling.

The exterior of the house, that is, the Church, is a house of adornment and of prayer as Psalm 26:8 says, "I have loved, O Lord, the beauty of thy house; and the place where thy glory dwelleth"' and Matthew 21:13 says, "My house shall be called the house of prayer." For the heavenly adornment of the Church is in the order of power which descends from heavens, "where Angels upon Angels ordered in adornment rule in power" as says Blessed [Pseudo-] Dionysius the Areopagite. And there is the place of the dwelling of the glory of the God that is the cause for different gifts of grace to shine out, whence I Corinthians 12:8-10 says, "To one indeed, by the Spirit, is given the word of wisdom: and to another, the word of knowledge, according to the same Spirit; To another, faith in the same spirit; to another, the grace of healing in one Spirit; To another, the working of miracles; to another, prophecy; to another, the discerning of spirits; to another, diverse kinds of tongues; to another, interpretation of speeches." For there in heaven the prayers and suffrages of the Saints are presented in vessels of devotion through the angels to God. Hence also the house of God is built from stones that by their consecration represent the beauty of the Church.

The ground floor of this house is the house of widowhood and mourning, as in Judith 8:5-6 it relates how Judith, wearing her widows weeds, dwelt in her home in which on an upper floor she had made for herself a secret chamber where, enclosed with her maidens, covering her limbs with sackcloth, she mourned and fasted all the days of her life except on the Sabbath, on the new moon, and the feasts of the house of Israel. This is also true of the Valiant Woman who does not dwell in the depths of the flesh in the filth of luxury but lives in the upper floor of honor and chastity, having sackcloth on her limbs, that is chastisement of the flesh as it is the seat of desire, and in constant abstinence from carnal pleasures except on feasts of God that are filled not with carnal but with spiritual banquets. She does so, because God consents only rarely to be received in the house of the flesh, though he sometimes does, as the Psalmist 84:3 says:"My heart and my flesh have rejoiced in the living God."

The upper house is a house of joy and jubilation and security and of every good, as the Psalmist says in 83:11, "For better is one day in thy courts above thousands," and as he has already said in verses 2 to 3, "How lovely are thy tabernacles, O Lord of hosts! My soul longeth and fainteth for the courts of the Lord." The Psalmist says that he "longs" for the courts of the Lord but here and now cannot yet enter them, although the time will come that he will no longer fail but will leave this world and ascend to house of the Lord and dwell in his holy place. [Psalm 24:3-4, "Who shall ascend into the mountain of the Lord: or who shall stand in his holy place? – the innocent in hands, and clean of heart, who hath not taken his soul in vain."]

These four houses are signified by the four houses that Solomon built as is related in I Kings 6 and 7 where it tells how he built a house for the Lord that is this is "upper house," and he also built a house for himself, and this is the "heart" of he house in which, as in says in 1 Kings 7:7, "he sat in judgment." He also built a house of passage in Libanon that is the "lower" house because it is a house of passage through a valley that is made of worldly matter which Plato called a "forest" or passage house [Note: Does this refer to the "ascent from the cave" in *The Republic* Bk VII?]. It is called "of Libanon" because of the whiteness of chastity since "Libanon" means "white." Solomon also built this as a house for his queen and it is the "exterior" of the house because the "queen" is the Church, as Solomon's father, David, said in Psalm 45:10, "The queen stood on thy right hand, in gilded clothing; surrounded with variety." The "gold" in her garments is the glory of divine grace. The "variety" of the garments encircling her is the variety of all the virtues.

What follows in the chapter verse is what she did not fear for her house, and this noted when the verse says, "from the cold of the snow" where two things are to be noted, what "snow" signifies and what "cold" signifies.

First to be noted, however, is the nature and origin of snow, as was explained by the philosophers of nature as is recorded [in Aristotle's] *Meterologica* Book II, c. 11. As to its matter snow is generated from warm vapor in the highly elevated middle region of the air, the significance of which is that it falls like carded wool and this happens to it because the warmth of the cloud is such that the cold changes not as a whole but only part by part through its greater parts so that the whole does not get hardened. Similarly as to its quality it is very cold because the law is that to the degree it was warm so much the colder it becomes when the heat is expelled. The sign of this is that warm water is more condensed and congealed than is water that is wholly cold. Snow is white in color because it is first changed from pure vapor through the heat of the cloud and then is congealed by the cold. For whiteness is caused by the cold itself and by the transparency and lucidity of the vapor. The place in which it is generated [when warm] is high up in the air, but with the cold of winter it falls. Similarly as to manner of its falling it penetrates obstacles very easily so that roofs that are effective against rain are less effective against snow.

These are the properties of snow that are common to its nature and here they signify the attacks of the enemy. For first of all the heat in the vapor of unnatural desires for pleasure ascends in a man and then chills with lack of devotion that does not permit the this vapor to dissolve into tearful rain but retains this vapor of vanity that maintains a certain gaiety of heart. Thus a man becomes "cold" in devotion, as it says in Sirach 43:22, "The cold north wind bloweth, and the water is congealed into crystal." The "north wind" from which all evil spreads out is temptation by the devil. "Crystal" is the hardness of heart caused by the cold of lack of devotion. There is danger that when the vapor of lust grows hotter so much greater grows the cold of the absence of devotion in the will. Similarly the "whiter" snow, the more it deceives, since it whitens itself by transfiguring itself into an angel of light by promising future repentance when in reality it is also promoting presumption of mercy and of impunity to punishment. The "time" also agrees with that of winter, since then snow is produced by the chilling of charity and not when spring is gentle and flowers appear in the land of the Valiant Woman. For in spring she is called by her Spouse, Christ, to the tender contemplation of eternal joys, as the Song of Songs 2:11 says, ["For winter is now past, the rain is over and gone. The flowers have appeared in our land, the time of pruning is come: the voice of the turtle is heard in our land: The fig tree hath put forth her green figs: the vines in flower yield their sweet smell. Arise, my love, my beautiful one, and come."] Nevertheless, the roof of the house, that is, joining of the walls of merit and prayer against the falling snow, is sometimes found to be less effective. And this is so because without the tar and cement of piety the timbers of the roof are more porous than when sealed by the unifying glue of piety.

We distinguish therefore four kinds of snow attacking the house with four kinds of cold: first the snow of sloth attacks the house with the cold of lack of devotion; second the snow of bad example disturbs the outside of the house, the Church, with the cold of scandal; third the snow of lustful desire fights against the lower parts of the house, that is, the flesh; and the fourth and final snow of pride comes from heights of anger and strikes the roof the house with contempt for higher things, those of heaven.

Of the first kind of snow Psalm 147:16-17 says, "Who giveth snow like wool: scattereth mists like ashes. He sendeth his crystals like morsels: who shall stand before the face of his cold?" This "sent snow" is sloth caused by temptation which is "sent" by God only in the sense that it is justly permitted by him. The "mist like ashes" that rises within the heart is when one is slow to practice devotion. The "crystals" are the cold consolations that it accepts in mouthfuls because a slothful person, since he has found little interior consolation, is poured out exteriorly in the joy of this world. But who can endure on his face the cold of the falling snow of lack of devotion? For then his heart is constricted and his feelings frozen and also all his limbs, and thus, I say, the interior of his soul will be frozen solid and rendered helpless as if paralyzed. Yet when it says in verse 18, "He shall send out his word, and shall melt them: his wind shall blow, and the waters shall run" consolation can follow, aiding him against that snow. The "wind that blows" is the word of Christ coming into the heart through the grace of devotion, thus immediately melting the snow. The "waters" that run are the warmth of charity and desire as the Holy Spirit of sanctity blows goodness and grace within the soul, so that the snow becomes a flow of water as tears of repentance flow from the eyes.

Concerning the snow of bad example that beats on the outside of the house with the cold of scandal Job 38:22-23 asks, "Hast thou entered into the storehouses of the snow, or has thou beheld the treasures of the hail: Which I have prepared for the time of the enemy, against the day of battle and war?" The "storehouse of the snow" is the abundance of bad example which, alas! abounds in the world. Yet God enters this world [of scandals] as one walking into a treasury of foresight and providence because he only permits evil example to lead to greater praise of the virtues of the good people and to the heavier condemnation of the impious. The abundance of this treasury signifies the abundance of the Church's persecutions which also abound in our times. Its riches are prepared for the "time of the enemy" that is of those acting in hostility against the Church and in the "day of battle," that is, of attacks on the Church and the wars of its persecution when it is involved in scandals. In Psalm 140:6 David laments, "The proud have hidden a net for me. And they have stretched out cords for a snare [*scandalum*]: they have laid for me a stumbling-block by the wayside." But the medicinal effect of the cold is also noted in Job 38:24, "By what way is the light spread, and heat divided upon the earth?" This way is the sign of divine mercies known only to God, and through that way "the light of a good example spreads" so that the cold north wind dissipates the scandal when all see the example of those [in the Church] who continue to seek what is good.

Concerning the snow of lustful pleasures which along with the cold of carnal filth battle the foundations of the house, that is, the body Exodus 4:6-8 says," [And the Lord said to Moses again: Put thy hand into thy bosom. And when he had put it into his bosom, he brought it forth leprous as snow. And he said:Put back thy hand into thy bosom. He put it back, and brought it out again, and it was like the other flesh. If they will not believe thee, saith he, nor hear the voice of the former sign, they will believe the word of the latter sign."] This hand signifies carnal deeds and the hand thrust into the bosom under the clothing is hidden lust and thus comes out white and leprous, that is, corrupted by carnal filth. But the medicine against that snow, mentioned in the last verse, namely, that the hand is again put into the bosom but into another [changed] bosom for it is impossible that the same as it is such can be the cause of an opposite effect, namely of cleanness and uncleanness. Therefore Moses reached into his hidden conscience considering what he had done and then took out his hand in an open confession and satisfaction. Then that hand was "like the other flesh," because penitence restores to health and immunity from sin. This is very well symbolized in II Samuel 23:20, "And Banaias, the son of Joiada, a most valiant man, of great deeds, of Cabseel: he slew the two lions of Moab, and he went down, and slew a lion in the midst of a pit [cistern], in the time of snow." For Banaias [Benaniah] is interpreted "building for the Lord" and signifies the Valiant Woman who builds for the Lord in the chastity of the house of her body as the Apostle says, I Corinthians, 6:20, "Glorify and bear God in your body." Banaias' father, Joida, moreover, is interpreted as "knowledge of the Lord," because Banaias strongly fulfilled what he had learned from the Lord about what is good. He killed the two lions of Moab which is interpreted "from the father," because these are the two vices that we are born with, gluttony and luxury, that arise from pleasures innate to us. And in the "days of snow," that is, in the time of carnal temptation, when charity is cold and lust burns as the winter solstice acts on our affections, Banaias descended into the "pit," that is, into carnal pleasure or concupiscence that is source of pleasure, but after drawing, dipping up, and retaining a little of the cistern's rain water, that is, the satisfaction and vanity of this world, by the work of bodily asceticism he slew the lion of lust which weakens. As St. Augustine says, "Do not kill the body so that it ceases to be, but so that it cannot injure us."

Concerning the snow of pride that battles against the walls of the upper part of the house which first begin to battle in the devil and then became the pride of all those who because of it hate God and that is always increasing, as it says in [Vulgate] Psalm 73:23, ["The pride of them that hate thee ascendeth continually," and Sirach 43:18-19 says, "The noise of his thunder shall strike the earth, so doth the northern storm, and the whirlwind: And as the birds lighting upon the earth, he scattereth snow, and the falling thereof, is as the coming down of locusts." Here the "north wind" is a symbol of the devil's proud will is always in the tempest he devil raises and this tempest scatters abroad the snow and cold pride which is the contempt of God and his commandments. It is said to scatter "like birds light upon the earth" because a bird coming down from on high and preparing prepares to settle, before it sits, folds its wings, pulling them in lest it fall over, flapping them harder than when it is actually flying. Just so the proud man in vanity flies aloft, but when he settles down to rest in some position of dignity from the very fact that he is seated increases his haughtiness and contempt Even when by bad fortune he descends and against his will is somewhat humiliated, still although his evil will is cut down, it still lifts him up and though he is no longer able to do much, he makes short hops on high, like locusts do, in words like those of his old arrogance that have the boldness ostentation of the great with whom he was once conversant. The medicine for this snow of arrogance is added further on in verse 20, "The eye admireth at the beauty of the whiteness thereof, and the heart is astonished at the shower thereof," that is, as Psalm 51:9 says, "Thou shalt sprinkle me with hyssop, and I shall be cleansed: thou shalt wash me, and I shall be made whiter than snow." For "hyssop" heals the sinner since it signifies that humility that cures the sin of the swelling of the heart [in pride]; it makes it clean in grace and causes it to pour out a flood of penitential tears, so that although the heart was terrified at seeing the evil that was within it, now it sees that the whiteness of virtue that surpasses the exterior whiteness of snow in all its beauty and worldly splendor.

There is, however, still a kind of snow from which all the houses of the Valiant Woman are equally freed. This kind of snow that battles all of us is the punishment and icy chill of Gehenna in which it is said in Job 6:16, "They that fear the hoary frost, the snow shall fall upon them." and this "hoar-frost" is, according to St. Gregory the Great, good for us since it is the tribulation of penance in this life. But the snow of eternal punishment mentioned in the chapter text falls on those who in this life avoid the trouble of penitence. Job 24:19 also says, "Let him pass from the snow waters to excessive heat, and his sin even to hell," and speaks of the damned who flee from the cold to heat and from the heat to the cold but cannot escape their torments. On the contrary, the snow that liberates is the snow of penance of which Job 9:30-31 says, "If I be washed as it were with snow waters, and my hands shall shine ever so clean: Yet thou shalt plunge me in filth, and my garments shall abhor me," that is, if I do penance for my sins and shed a watery flood of tears that are melted from the snow of sins and my hands that do deeds shine with the most clean virtues, nevertheless, if you wish to judge me strictly, you will sill find some spots, that is, evil tendencies that still show that all my justice is like the cloth of a menstruous woman, [as it says in Isaiah 54:6, "We are all become as one unclean, and all our justices are as the rag of a menstruous woman: and we have all fallen as a leaf, and our iniquities, like the wind, have taken us away."] And the vestments of my behavior seems abominable to me, that is, in strict justice they also seem abominable to you. Of this kind of snow Isaiah 1:18, says, "If your sins be as scarlet as oak berries, they shall be made as white as snow: and if they be red as crimson, they shall be white as wool." Red sins are sins of boiling blood or boiling in blood as sins of lust rising from the blood and sins of gluttony and carnal uncleanness; but sins of anger and envy and greed boil in blood because sometimes they lead to the shedding of blood, as in anger or envy, while others draw in the blood as if retaining it, as does greed. The sense of the text is therefore:If your sins, namely, of anger, envy, and greed are as "red as oak-berries" because colored by the blood of your fellow men, through penance they will be made white, that is, restored to the grace of pristine innocence. And if they be red as worms the blood of which has a purple color, like the sins that rise from the blood, such as gluttony and lust, they will be cleansed through temperance of the flesh and become white as the wool of a lamb, [that is, of Christ, who was called this by John he Baptist in John 1:29, "Behold the Lamb of God, behold him who takes away the sin of the world!"].

§ 2

Next comes the second part of this verse in which we look for the reason we should fear for this house, namely, "**for all her domestics are clothed with double garments**," from which two things are to be noted, namely who are these "domestics" and what are the double garments in which they are clothed."

The Valiant Woman has two kinds of domestics in her house, because in the interior house of her heart she has a reasoning power and a willing power and on the exterior of her house she is both active and contemplative. Likewise in the lower part of the house she has chastity and abstinence and in its upper part she lives with angels and blessed human persons.

As to the domestics living in the first part of the house, that is, in the heart of the Valiant Woman, Sirach 4:35 says, "Be not as a lion in thy house, terrifying them of thy household, and oppressing them that are under thee." Thus it should be noted that in their homes some women are like lionesses that are always proud and angry, which Sirach urges the Valiant Woman not to be, since by such behavior the domestics, that is, the reason and will are turned away from all that is good and true, and instead oppress those of the family subject to them, namely the powers of the soul, such as the five senses and the concupiscible and irascible appetites. They are oppressed because sin rules over them.

As to the domestics of the exterior house, in Matthew 10:24 the Lord says to all the faithful of the Church, active and contemplative, "The disciple is not above the master, nor the servant above his lord. It is enough for the disciple that he be as his master, and the servant as his lord. If they have called the master of the house Beelzebub," a wicked member of the devils, "how much more them of his household? Therefore, fear them not;" and St. Paul in Galatians 6:10 says, "Therefore, whilst we have time, let us work good to all men, but especially to those who are of the household of the faith," that is, both active and contemplative members living in the same house of the Church with Jesus their Lord.

Of the domestic of the lower house II Samuel 16:1-2 says, "And when David was a little past the top of the hill, behold Siba the servant of Miphiboseth came to meet him with two asses, laden with two hundred loaves of bread, and a hundred bunches of raisins, a hundred cakes of figs, and two jars of wine. And the king said to Siba: What mean these things? And Siba answered: The asses are for the king's household to sit on: and the loaves and the figs for thy servants to eat, [and the wine to drink if any man be faint in the desert]." Siba is interpreted as "lacking a father" and signifies a penitent who knows he is a prodigal son absent from his father [as in the parable of the Two Sons, Luke 15:11-32]. Miphiboseth is interpreted as "bone of shame" and signifies the lust of the flesh to which Siba was previously enslaved, but then he returned to David, that is, to Christ, who also was fleeing from his faithless son, [Absalom], who signifies a Christian driving Christ from Christ's own kingdom. Thus it is related how Siba, however, offered to David, that is, to Christ, two hundred loves of bread, that is, the perfect refreshment of the Ten Commandments fulfilled in the two precepts of charity to God and neighbor and also offered to him one hundred bunches of raisins, that is, pressed grapes. Pressed grapes signify Christ in his passion and those who are made perfect through that passion, since Christ says of himself [what St. Paul says of himself in Galatians 6:14], "God forbid that I should glory, save in the cross of our Lord Jesus Christ; by whom the world is crucified to me, and I to the world." And Siba offered David also no less than two jars of wine, that is, the two kinds of spiritual wine, that of compunction and that of devotion, and a hundred cakes of figs. Figs are pressed between two tables called *palae* and signify perfect suppression of all the sweetness of sin through works of penance, which Siba offers to Christ in his suffering, when Christ had cast off from himself everything of this world. This solace of sins also consoled Christ in his sufferings. Thus Siba offered two asses, namely, the nutritive and generative powers, which are called "asses" because, just as asses are solid but stupid animals prone to gluttony and lust, so more than any other powers these two are subject to bodily addictions with regard to food and sex; yet these animals are offered to the domestics of the king, namely of Christ, to ride on, because Christ dwells in our body. The two "domestics," chastity and abstinence, are mounted on these powers, and like soldiers guide these animals in their movement to a good goal. This also explains what I Timothy 5:8 says, "But if any man have not care of his own, and especially of those of his house, he hath denied the faith, and is worse than an infidel." For the servants of a human person are the virtues and powers that he possesses and he ought especially to practice abstinence and chastity lest they stray from his body because otherwise in his actions he will deny the faith and become worse than an unbeliever, wicked and good for nothing.

Concerning the domestics of the upper house Ephesians 2:19 says, "Now therefore you are no more strangers and foreigners; but you are fellow citizens with the Saints, and the domestics of God." This is very true of the Saints who already or in hope dwell in the house of God. In heaven are those who were in soul merely guests in this world and strangers to the body because what belongs to paradise is cast out from the world. But such persons are in hope or in fact citizens of the city of the Saints in the Kingdom and domestics of God dwelling in that house where [as Jesus says in John 14:2, "In my Father's house..."] there are many mansions.

Next, the chapter text speaks of the "double garments" in which the Valiant Woman clothes the domestics of her household. Therefore we assign to each domestic a double garment and since there are four kinds of houses [each with two domestics] and thus eight domestics, there must be provided sixteen garments. Thus the garments worn by the domestics of the inner house are "double" because they are clothed with both the science of worldly conversation to protect them against the snow and the light of divine truth to protect them against the cold. This is necessary because they are sometimes chilled by the cold of the snow of worldly conversation even if that snow does not actually touch them. Concerning the vestment of light Psalm 104:1-2 says, "Bless the Lord, O my soul: O Lord my God, thou art exceedingly great. Thou hast put on praise and beauty: And art clothed with light as with a garment." Concerning the knowledge needed for conversation in this world Wisdom 18:24 says, "For in the priestly robe which he [Aaron] wore, was the whole world: and in the four rows of the stones the glory of the fathers was graven, and thy majesty was written upon the diadem of his head." For on this priestly garment was pictured the whole earth's orb and the patriarchs' great deeds. Thus in the virtues of our hearts all the earth is depicted in scientific knowledge since we need to know what is good, bad, and indifferent and to know the great accomplishments of our forbears so that all our works may be improved. And this is what Psalm 104:6 says, "The deep like a garment is its [the earth's] clothing: above the mountains shall the waters stand." The "deep" or ocean is the profundity of scientific understanding. The mountains are the lofty meaning of Scripture over which the waters of doctrine are awash.

Yet the other domestic of this same house, namely the human will, is also doubly vested and this in charity against the cold of snow and obedience against the snow itself. Charity is symbolized by the seamless tunic [of Christ. John 19:23-24, "The soldiers therefore, when they had crucified him, took his garments, and they made four parts, for each soldier a part, and also his coat. Now the coat was without seam, woven from the top throughout. They said then one to another: Let us not cut it, but let us cast lots for it, whose it shall be; that the scripture might be fulfilled, saying: 'They have parted my garments among them, and upon my vesture they have cast lots' (Psalm 22:19)."] Obedience, however [is symbolized] by embroidery, Ezekiel 16:10, "I clothed thee [the Synagogue] with embroidery" because obedience is embroidered with all God's commandments and decrees.

The garments of the first sort of domestics, those of reason, are symbolized by the glory of the Lord's vestments when he was transfigured on Mount Tabor, the name of which mountain is interpreted "the rise of light." His garments are said [in Mark 9:2-8], to have become as "white as snow, so as no fuller upon earth can make white," because the light of truth exceeds human reason and similarly intelligence is vested in the plenitude and certitude of science. And by "fuller'" [bleacher] is meant the Philosopher [Aristotle] and all those who study the worldly sciences but whose researches cannot give that garment its perfect beauty.

The garments of the second kind of domestic are signified by the vestment of Jacob of whom Genesis 27:27 says, "And immediately as he [Isaac] smelled the fragrant smell of his [Jacob's] garments, blessing him, he said: Behold the smell of my son is as the smell of a plentiful field, which the Lord hath blessed." For charity produces all the good fruits of the field of the virtues.

The domestics of the exterior of the house are also doubly clothed and they are either active or contemplative and their house is the Church. The active ones are clothed with fervor of spirit against the cold of the snow; their perseverance against the snow itself. The contemplatives have a vestment of purity against the snow and also an admirable outer garment against the cold of the snow. Concerning the vestment of fervor of spirit it is said in Job, 37:17, "Are not thy garments hot, when the south wind blows upon the earth?" For the hot south wind signifies the warmth of the Holy Spirit that warms the vestments that are the fervor of spirit. As the Apostles says, Romans 12:11, "In spirit fervent, serving the Lord." Concerning the vestment of perseverance Isaiah 9:5 says, "Every... garment mingled with blood, shall be burnt, and be fuel for the fire." A vestment mingled with blood is a life without perseverance which is mingled with blood of sin and like fuel will be consumed in the eternal fire.

Concerning the vestment of purity of contemplation, Genesis 35:2-3 says, "Cast away the strange gods that are among you, and be cleansed and change your garments. Arise, and let us go up to Bethel," To "change your garments" is to acquire greater purity so that one's contemplation may be more luminous. To "arise" is to turn the attention of one's eyes to higher things. "Bethel" which is interpreted "house of God" is through meditation to penetrate truth to its depths. Thus the Song of Songs 4:11 says about this garment of contemplation, "The smell of thy garments is as the smell of frankincense." For this sort of wonder is not mere curiosity but is inspired by devotion and joy. Hence the smell is compared to that of incense that we customarily associate with the joy of devotion. All these double garments of action and contemplation are signified by the garments of the Valiant Woman, the "queen," who is praised in Psalm 45:10, "The queen stood on thy right hand, in gilded clothing; surrounded with variety."

The domestics of the lower house are also doubly clothed, some with the double garment of chastity: in modesty and holy purity; because chastity uses modesty against the snow and holy purity against the cold. Others are is clothed in the double garments of abstinence: austerity against the snow and discretion against its cold.

Of the double vestment of chastity Proverbs 6:27-29 says, "Can a man hide fire in his bosom, and his garments not burn? Or can he walk upon hot coals, and his feet not be burnt? So he that goeth in to his neighbor's wife shall not be clean when he shall touch her." The "fire in the bosom" is the heat in the heart of which Job 31:12, says, "It is a fire that devoureth even to destruction." The vestments that are thus "burned up" by this heat are modesty and the holiness of chastity. The "feet" are the affections that are scorched by the fire of lust. There is, however, also an ardent fire that does not burn the garments of chastity but illumines it so that chastity is not consumed but purified so that it shines and that is the fire of the love of God and of his divinity, as in Exodus 3:2 Moses sees a bush that burns but without burning up. And Moses wondered at this great sight, which by God's command he dared not approach without baring his feet because that place was holy ground; since such power of chastity is perfectly preserved in body and soul only when it is accompanied by the love of God and humility that provide an angelic holy dwelling place for God within the sanctity of our mortal bodies.

As to the garments of abstinence this is explained by what we read in Matthew 3:4 of the clothing of John the Baptist, "John had his garment of camels' hair," signifying his austerity, "and a leathern girdle about his loins," signifying his prudence because as a girdle tightens flowing garments so prudence reduces what is unsuitable and excessive to the limits of measure and decency. This also is shown by the garments of Elijah [IV Kings, 2:8 "And Elijah took his mantle and folded it together, and struck the waters, and they were divided hither and thither, and they –Elijah and Elisha – both passed over on dry ground].

Next it treats of the double garments of those who are in the upper part of the house. These are the angels and men and particularly the men who have as their two garments the body, which defends against the snow, and the soul. Similarly the angels have, as the Saints say, the double garment of the powers of administration and assistance, the first against snow and the second against the cold of the snow. These twofold human garments are signified by the change of the clothing of Joseph related in Genesis 41:14, "Joseph was brought out of the prison, and they shaved him, and changing his apparel, brought him in to Pharaoh [to interpret the king's dream]." For the "prison" is the world, and the shaving of Joseph signifies the cleansing of our mortality by the glorification of the body. The "change of clothing" signifies that faith is a passage into clear vision, hope into eternal possession, and the desire of charity into complete happiness.

The garment of the angels is signified as it says in Revelation 1:13 where John sees "One like to the Son of man, clothed with a garment down to the feet, and girt about the breast with a golden girdle." This "golden girdle" signifies the assisting virtues by which the angels are bound to God and the "lengthy vestment" signifies the ministry that the angels perform on our behalf. And therefore Daniel 7:10, says, "Thousands of thousands ministered to him, and ten thousand times a hundred thousand stood before him."

OUTLINE OF CHAPTER XIII

She hath made for herself clothing of tapestry: fine linen and purple is her covering. (v. 22)

§1 The Acrostic letter Mem מ signifies "entrails" for imperial purple derived from a mollusc and alludes to the Valiant Woman's tapestry garment, colored with Jacob's (Christ's) coat of many colors, and which is woven three ways:
1) It is tightly woven because Christ's passion had all that was necessary for our salvation
  1) Spitting
  2) Nails
  3) Lance
  4) Thorns
  5) Flagellation
  6) Mocking
  7) Blows
  8) Slaps
  9) Vinegar and gall
  10) Stripping naked
  11) The Cross and the earthquake and darkening of sun
  12) Hunger, thirst, rough clothing, exhausting work for thirty-years
  13) Stripping of Christ's soul from body for three days in death
2) How the Valiant Woman makes this garment
  1) She weaves the cloth (Chapter X) by meditation on Christ's passion and human mortality
  2) She cuts the cloth with the scissors of Wisdom
    1) One blade is the authority of Scriptures
    2) The other blade is the understanding of intelligence
    3) The two blades are united by the key of faith
  3) She sows with needle of fear of God: Hannah's little humble festal coat for Samuel for feasts of
    1) Passover
    2) Pentecost
    3) Feast of Booths

§2) What the garment of the Valiant Woman is like:
1) It is of fine linen:the justification of the Saints
2) Purple color for the Queen, Bride of the Lamb who like the Baptist and St. Paul gave three signs
  1) Chastity as a virgin
  2) Passion for justice as a teacher and preacher
  3) Martyrdom for the faith

CHAPTER XIII

She hath made for herself clothing of tapestry: fine linen and purple is her covering. (v. 22)

§ 1

MEM מ, This letter is the thirteenth letter of the Hebrew alphabet and is interpreted "entrails." It alludes to the chapter text because a tapestry-like garment is colored with the entrails and blood of certain kinds of fish [Tyrean purple dye extracted from a sea snail]. Thus also this garment of the Valiant Woman is colored with the blood of Christ after his resurrection appeared to the disciples standing on the shore and invited them to the breakfast he was preparing for them and [John 21:19], "As soon then as they came to land, they saw hot coals lying, and a fish laid thereon, and bread," flavored with the honey of his divinity. Whence in Isaiah 63:2-3 the angels ask the Lord, "Why then is thy apparel red, and thy garments like theirs that tread in the winepress?" and the Lord answers, "I have trodden the winepress alone, and of the Gentiles there is not a man with me." For Jesus through obedience to his Father has trodden the winepress of his passion alone treading out blood from the grapes of his body in which he has washed his stole and the mantle of his humanity, since as Genesis 49:1 says, ["He shall wash his robe in wine, and his garment in the blood of the grape."] So it is clear how the epigram fits the verse.

The "tapestry garment" is commonly expounded in two ways, for the Gloss says that "the tapestry garment is a garment tightly woven and diversely colored." And in this sense concerning the first part of the verse it should be noted that this tapestry garment is doubled and made in three ways.

According to this first sense the tapestry garment is the passion of our Lord Jesus Christ tightly woven because nothing of all the things that need to be done for our salvation has been left out. On it are colored pictures portraying the spitting, the nails, lance, thorns, wiping, insults, curses, mocking, blows, slaps, and finally the Cross, besides the hunger, thirst, exhaustion of carrying the Cross, the roughness of the garments and coverings that for thirty-three years he had continuously felt.

And this garment was signified by the coat of many colors which the Patriarch Jacob had made for his son Joseph, as Genesis [37:3-4, relates "Now Israel (Jacob) loved Joseph above all his sons, because he had him in his old age: and he made him a coat of divers colours. And his brethren seeing that he was loved by his father, more than all his sons, hated him, and could not speak peaceably to him,"] and further on in verses 31-33, "And they (Joseph's brothers) took his coat, and dipped it in the blood of a kid, which they had killed: Sending some to carry it to their father, and to say:This we have found: see whether it be thy son's coat, or not. And the father acknowledging it, said: It is my son's coat, an evil wild beast hath eaten him, a beast hath devoured Joseph." This "coat" is Christ's suffering body. The "stripping" of Jesus is the theft of his body through death; not that his body was ever separated from his divinity but that for three days that body was separated from Jesus' soul. The "many colors" of the garment signify the whole flood of the Passion that passed over Jesus when, as said before, his torturers sent Jesus, whom they claimed had blasphemed by saying he was God's son, back to his Heavenly Father, by this spitting, nails, lance, myrrh, vinegar with its taste of gall. With such words and blows they laid the garment of Christ's humanity in the Father's sight so that he might see if it was in fact his Son's, and the Father saw on it the marks of the worst and most violent hatred, because with claws and teeth they had torn that garment in tatters, back, head, hands, feet, and sides so that the Father immediately recognized that garment to be his Son's and wept over it with tears. For [as Matthew 27:51-54 relates]

"And behold the veil of the temple was rent in two from the top even to the bottom, and the earth quaked, and the rocks were rent. And the graves were opened: and many bodies of the Saints that had slept arose, and coming out of the tombs after his resurrection, came into the holy city, and appeared to many. Now the centurion and those who were with him watching Jesus, having seen the earthquake, and the things that were done, were sore afraid, saying: 'Indeed this was the Son of God.'] This tapestry garment therefore was "rent in two" and signifies the garment of mortality which is spread under us that we may be laid down upon it in humiliation so that we come down from our lofty pride.. This mortality is in the punishment and shame of our birth, of which King Solomon says in Wisdom 7:2-5 says, ["I myself also am a mortal man, like all others, and of the race of him, that was first made of the earth, and in the womb of my mother I was fashioned to be flesh. In the time of ten months] I was compacted in blood, of the seed of man, and the pleasure of sleep concurring. [And being born I drew in the common air, and fell upon the earth, that is made alike, and the first voice which I uttered was crying, as all others do. I was nursed in swaddling clothes, and with great cares; for none of the kings had any other beginning of birth."] And this is the punishment and shame of life which is verified through the experiencing of hunger, thirst, cold, heat and infirmity, of health and sickness, besides other matters that it is indecent even to mention. There is also the punishment and misery of death and ignorance of when death will come, whether at evening, the middle of night, cock-crow, or full daylight. This garment of the body of which II Kings 8:15 relates how Hazel "took a blanket, and poured water on it, and spread it upon his [the King of Syria's] face: and he died, and Hazel reigned in his stead." This signifies that the sons of this world, although they daily see the works of God that humble the proud, like Hazel whose name is interpreted as "seeing God," spread one over the other the blanket of death, pouring on it the cold water of mortality until it kills. Thus after one king of Syria (a name, which is interpreted "sublime") another heads the kingdom.

Next to be considered is how the Valiant Woman makes this garment and she does so in three ways, by weaving it, cutting it out, and sewing it up. How it is woven was explained in Chapter X. It is woven through thinking about all the sufferings of Christ and then on all the growing fears of one's own mortality that are turned over daily in one's heart. That this is a kind of weaving is evident through its opposite, because God reprehends evil thinking that distorts his counsels; as Isaiah 30:1 says, "Woe to you, apostate children, saith the Lord, that you would take counsel, and not of me: and would begin a web, and not by my spirit, that you might add sin upon sin."

The Valiant Woman cuts the cloth with the scissors of wisdom which has two blades that come together, namely, the authority of the Scriptures and intellectual understanding, which two are connected by the key of faith.

She sews with the very sharp fear of God because the fear of God penetrates and punctures. The thread holding the cloth together is the very long and very strong interrelation of the meritorious virtues and this structure is noted in I Samuel 2:19, where it says of Hannah and her son Samuel, "And his mother made him a little coat, which she brought to him on the appointed days, when she went up with her husband, to offer the solemn sacrifice," and thus fulfill her vows. Hannah is interpreted "grace" and signifies the Valiant Woman. Her son, the prophet Samuel, is the Spirit of Salvation for whom she made a little coat in these three ways: because she ascended to Jerusalem three times each year on the appointed days of the Passover, Pentecost, and the Feast of Booths. These three feasts are signified by the triple decoration of Samuel's little embroidered tunic. It is called "little" for the sake of humility. Hannah's sacrifices are the offering of praise and her vows are desires for eternal benefits that are offered to the Lord in Jerusalem, that is, "the vision of peace."

§ 2

The second part of the chapter text is: "**fine linen, and purple is her covering**" In which is noted the doubly lined garment of this Valiant Woman, namely, the justification of the Saints and its regal color as it says of the Bride of the Lamb in Revelation 19:8, "And it is granted to her that she should clothe herself with fine linen, glittering and white. For the fine linen are the justifications of Saints." This linen is of the kind that grows abundantly in Egypt, and "Egypt" signifies world in which the Saints achieve the merit of justification.

Of the purple color which is that a king's garment it is said in the Song of Songs 7:5, "The hairs of thy head [are] as the purple of the king bound in channels." Hence it is said in the Old Law that a purple garment is dyed purple with the blood of a sea-creature that lives in certain shells in the ocean. It may be used only by a prince and those whom he permits to use it, whence it is evident that purple is a sign of royalty. Our King, Jesus Christ, made himself known through three signs which he gave us while in the world, virginal chastity, a passion for justice, and the doctrine of truth, since he was a virgin, a teacher or preacher of the truth of the Gospel, and a martyr for the faith. These signs all were also found in Paul and John the Baptist both of whom personally possessed these three marks. Hence the hymn says of John the Baptist.

> Some they crown with flowers thrice ten;
> Lavishly others that number they double,
> But you, Holy One, with three hundred
> Fruit bearing garlands they gladly adorn.

OUTLINE OF CHAPTER XIV

*Her husband is honorable in the gates,
when he sitteth among the elders of the land. (v. 23)*

§1) The Acrostic letter Nun ב signifies "unique" and "eternal" as is the Valiant Woman's husband Christ
  1) She has loved chastity
  2) After her husband's death she has known no other, but in his resurrection is united with him forever.
  3) He is honorable in the gates" because;
    1) He is noble:
      1) With a nobility of nature: He is King and Mary, the Valiant Woman, is Queen
      2) With the nobility of Wisdom: He is Wisdom itself, she is Created Wisdom
      3) With the nobility of Virtue: He is God's image She is his image.
      4) With the nobility of Action: He had redeemed the world; She is the first of the redeemed
    2) He sits where? In the twelve gates of the heavenly Jerusalem where nobility is recognized
      1) North side gates look toward hell
        1) Gate Ruben opens when someone carefully observes evil and flies from it
        2) Gate of Judah opens when one has confessed and gained from his sins
        3) Gate of Levi opens when one satisfies for sin and grows daily in virtue.
      2) East side: Nativity
        1) Gate of Joseph opens as one: grows up through the Sacraments
        2) Gate of Benjamin opens by living rightly and no longer as a son of sorrow and wrath.
        3) Gate of Dan opens by humility, remembering our fallen nature
      3) South side: Eternal life
        1) Gate of Simeon opens by listening carefully to the Word of God
        2) Gate of Isaachar opens with hope for reward of good deeds
        3) Gate of Zebulun opens when one perseveres firmly in good deeds
      4) West side: Our death
        1) Gate of Gad opens if we work to be sure our conscience is clear at death
        2) Gate of Asher opens when we join the Saints according to our works
        3) Gate of Zebulun: opens joyfully in the vision of God, Angels, & Saints in perfect love
    3) When does he sit there?
      1) Some as judges: first Christ & his Mother and sister and wife: the Valiant Woman
      2) Some stand to be judged and are saved
      3) Some stand and are judged and condemned;
      4) Some are not judged but summarily condemned because they did not believe
  2) He sits among the seniors of the land.
    1) What land and who are these seniors?

1) We dwell in three lands.
   1) Our bodies:
   2) Our cell or prison which is this world
   3) Where all is well, the land of living
2) And each of these lands has seniors who are judges
   1) In the land of our bodies the seniors are mature and are:
      1) Our conscience judging subjective matters
      2) Our reason judging objective matters
   2) In the prison of this world; the seniors are aged and corrupt
   3) in the land of the living the seniors are the angels and Saints

CHAPTER XIV

Her husband is honorable in the gates, when he sitteth among the senators of the land. (v. 23)

§ 1

NUN ב. Nun is interpreted "unique" or "eternal" and alludes to the first part of this chapter verse because the Valiant Woman's husband is unique and eternal, just as she is unique because chaste, as Judith 15:11 says of Judith, ["Thou hast done manfully, and thy heart has been strengthened, because thou hast loved chastity, and after thy husband hast not known any other: therefore also the hand of the Lord hath strengthened thee, and therefore thou shalt be blessed for ever."] That the Valiant Woman has loved chastity and after her husband's death has received no other, persevering in the faith of her marriage bed is in contrast to the Samaritan woman to whom [in John 4:17-18] the Lord says] "Thou hast said well, 'I have no husband':For thou hast had five husbands: and he whom thou now hast, is not thy husband."]

The Valiant Woman's husband is also eternal because He is immortal. Hence the Valiant Woman is not like that woman who had seven husbands [all of whom died as is related in Matthew 22:25-29] that the Pharisees and Sadducees invented as an objection to the Lord, saying ["And last of all the woman died also. At the resurrection therefore whose wife of the seven shall she be? For they all had her. And Jesus answering, said to them: You err, not knowing the Scriptures, nor the power of God. For in the resurrection they shall neither marry nor be married; but shall be as the angels of God in heaven."] For the Valiant Woman has a husband who is unique and eternal who is the guide of her childhood and adolescence, who loves her chastely, embraces her cleanly, and accepts her as a spotless virgin and thus is united to her forever.

Concerning the phrase applied to her husband, that he "**is honorable in the gates**," four things are to be noted, namely his nobility, second where his nobility is recognized, that is, "in the gates" when he sits there, and by whom or before whom he is recognized as noble, that is, when he sits among the seniors of the land.

Concerning the first of these, the nobility of the man, four things should be noted:

Nobility---	of Nature
	of Wisdom
	of Virtue
	of Action

Nobility of nature is intrinsic to the Son of God and his Queen, his Virgin Mother, because something is called "noble" because it is that which in nature attains the highest principle and it is evident that Son of God in this sense has nobility of nature. Of this sense of nobility Jeremiah 39:6 says, "The king of Babylon slew all the nobles of Judah," for in that statement "noble" means those who had parents of high station. The meaning of "nobility" with respect to Christ, however, is that of Isaiah 11:1-2, although it is not to be understood literally, "And there shall come forth a rod out of the root of Jesse, and a flower shall rise up out of his root. And the spirit of the Lord shall rest upon him: the spirit of wisdom, and of understanding, the spirit of counsel, and of fortitude, the spirit of knowledge, and of godliness." For "Jesse" is interpreted "fire" and signifies the Father of the Lord. From God the Father as from a fire of love proceeds a Son born of him and consubstantial with him whom the Father wills should come to us in our world. Isaiah twice uses the term "out of his root" to note this double origin of Christ; one according to divine generation and one according to human generation. The dignity of grace is noted in this text when it says that the Spirit with all his gifts rests on the Lord with all his gifts.

Concerning the nobility of wisdom it is said explicitly in Deuteronomy 1:15, "And I took out of your tribes men wise and honorable, and appointed them rulers, tribunes, and centurions, and officers over fifties, and over tens, who might teach you all things." As Luke

2:52 says with this nobility Christ is also noble, "And Jesus advanced in wisdom, and age, and grace with God and men." And the Apostle says, Colossians 2:3 that "In whom [Jesus] are hid all the treasures of wisdom and knowledge," and similarly Jeremiah 31:22 says, "The Lord hath created a new thing upon the earth: a woman shall compass a man," that is, as the Gloss says, "perfect in grace and wisdom from the day of his conception."

Concerning the nobility of virtue Isaiah 3:5 also says literally, "The young shall rebel against the elder, and the ignoble against the noble." "Young" here means a young person: an "ancient" means someone with white-hair; and "noble" means a lover of virtue, and above all it refers to Christ, in contrast to whom the ignoble seem like the young, since no one rebels against him except someone who lives ignobly.

Concerning the nobility of action it must be understood that Christ is called noble because all the noble things he does he does like kings and priests are supposed to do, as the Saints says of him in Revelation 5:10, ["And hast made us to our God a kingdom and priests, and we shall reign on the earth."] And this is signified by the exultation of Saul who was elevated from the lowly family of Cis when he was herding asses and by the exaltation of David when he was herding sheep and through the exaltation of the Jew Mardochai in Persia, although he was foreign born. These examples confirm what Psalm 113:7-8 says, "Raising up the needy from the earth, and lifting up the poor out of the dunghill: That he may place him with princes," that is with the angels, "with the princes of his people," that is, with the Saints. Also what Hannah says, I Samuel 2:8, "He raiseth up the needy from the dust, and lifteth up the poor from the dunghill: that he may sit with princes, and hold the throne of glory."

The next consideration is the place of the noble one, namely, "in the gates," and note that it prescribe that judges sit in the gates of a city and there pass judgment. There are, however, twelve gates to the heavenly Jerusalem as we read in Ezekiel 48:31-34, "And the gates of the city according to the names of the tribes of Israel, three gates on the north side, the gate of Ruben one, the gate of Judah one, the gate of Levi one. And at the east side,...three gates, the gate of Joseph one, the gate of Benjamin one, the gate of Dan one. And at the south side,...three gates, the gate of Simeon one, the gate of Issachar one, the gate of Zebulun one. And at the west side,...three gates, the gate of Gad one, the gate of Asher one, the gate of Nephthali one."

Of these twelve gates there are three on the north in which Christ is noble through his deeds because standing in these gates he makes noble the Valiant Woman. One of these gates is that of Reuben, a second that of Judah, the third that of Levi. "Reuben" is interpreted "vision" and it opens when someone carefully observes some evil and flies from it as Jeremiah 1:14 says, "And the Lord said to me: from the north shall an evil break forth upon all the inhabitants of the land." Whence all three gates look out on the roads to hell. After another of these judges, namely Judah, which is interpreted "confessing' or "glorifying," has cautiously inspected these ways of sin, he turns back and sits at the second gate, because he needs to give glory to God for his liberation and sincerely to confess his sin, as Joshua 7:21 says, ["Joshua said to Achan: My son, give glory to the Lord God of Israel, and confess, and tell me what thou hast done, hide it not. And Achan answered Joshua, and said to him: Indeed I have sinned against the Lord the God of Israel, and thus and thus have I done. For I saw among the spoils a scarlet garment exceeding good, and two hundred shekels of silver, and a golden rule [ingot] of fifty shekels: and I coveted them, and I took them away, and hid them in the ground is the midst of my tent, and the silver I covered with the earth that I dug up."] The "golden rule' signifies the dignity of this world which shines in gold and rules man according to his vanity. The "scarlet garment" signifies the life of the body and blood in the luxury of banquets and luxuries. The "two hundred shekels of silver" are the riches of this world from which all sins originate. When anyone confesses honestly he must still grow daily through works of satisfaction and against sin must increase in virtue. He therefore must sit in the third gate, that of Levi, which is interpreted "growing."

Again on the east side of the heavenly Jerusalem there are three gates; the first of Joseph; the second of Benjamin; and the third of Dan. The east is our nativity and two of its three gates should be open. It must first be considered that from the prison of original sin in which our members are tightly bound, we are led out by Pharaoh, that is, by God, and exalted through the grace of the sacraments in this world, namely, through Baptism, Confirmation, the Eucharist, and the Anointing of the Sick and thus we sit in the gate of Joseph, which is interpreted "increasing," because he grew up there as previously related. Thus Psalm 105:17-22 says, "Joseph, who was sold for a slave. They humbled his feet in fetters: the iron pierced his soul, until his word came. The word of the Lord inflamed him. The king sent, and he released him: the ruler of the people, and he set him at liberty. He made him master of his house, and ruler of all his possession." The "fettered feet" and the "iron" in this text are the hardships of prison in which the tyranny and weariness of nature now detain us and they cannot be loosened unless the King coming through the gates of the sacramental graces loosens them. Thus Christ the Prince of the people releases us from that "prison" through the power of grace, It is the eloquence of the Lord that inflames us with charity and then makes us princes in his kingdom so that we enter into the joy of our Lord and are "set over all his goods" so that we can use them at a nod. Since, however, Christ makes us sit in that gate, we also daily sit in the second east gate that is the gate of Benjamin, whose mother died in bearing him, but whose name is interpreted "son of the right hand." As Ezekiel 16:3-5 says, "Thus saith the Lord God to Jerusalem: Thy root and thy nativity is of the land of Canaan, thy father was an Amorrhite and thy mother a Cethite. [And when thou wast born, in the day of thy nativity thy navel wast not cut, neither wast thou washed with water for thy health, nor salted with salt, nor swaddled with clouts. No eye had pity on thee to do any of these things for thee, out of compassion to thee: but thou wast cast out upon the face of the earth in the abjection of thy soul, in the day that thou wast born." This signifies our birth from the devil and lust, but this "mother" dies when we are spiritually reborn and through a good life we should cease to be sons of sorrow and of wrath. Then Christ leads us to the third eastern gate which is the gate of Dan which is interpreted "judgment" so that we will always consider the humility and misery of our fallen nature lest we become proud, because while we should not fear those of lofty wisdom, yet we should place ourselves with the humble.

There are also three gates on the south of the New Jerusalem: the gates of Simeon, of Issachar, and Zebulon. The south is the region of eternal life which rises over those who are in the grace of God. First, however, we must open the gate of Simeon which is interpreted "hearing" and there we should sit, carefully listening to hear the voice of the Lord and not hardening our hearts to receiving the grace of God in vain, as Psalm 85:9 says "I will hear what the Lord God will speak in me: for he will speak peace unto his people." This leads to the second southern gate, that of Issachar which is interpreted "wages" and signifies the hope of eternal goods, because hope expects wages, as a reward such as God promised Abram in

Genesis 15:1, "Fear not, Abram, I am thy protector, and thy reward is exceeding great," and which must also be patiently awaited, as Sirach 36:18 says, "Reward them that patiently wait for thee, that thy prophets may be found faithful: and hear the prayers of thy servants." Next the husband of the Valiant Woman sits in third gate on the south of the city, Zebulon's gate, and makes us sit with him. Zebulon is interpreted "dwelling of strength" because we must dwell firmly and perseveringly with ourselves [in our resolutions] that we may one of those of whom Jesus says in Luke 22:29-30, "And you are they who have continued with me in my temptations: And I dispose to you, as my Father hath disposed to me, a kingdom; That you may eat and drink at my table, in my kingdom." And as the Lord in verse 32 following also said to Simon Peter, "Simon, Simon, behold Satan hath desired to have you, that he may sift you as wheat: But I have prayed for thee, that thy faith fail not: and thou, being once converted, confirm thy brethren."

Finally there are three gates on the west of the City; the gates of Gad, Asher, and Nephthali. The west is "the third stroke that kills" in which Christ makes us sit thrice. First, because we ought to labor that at death our consciences will be clear, since it says Psalm 127:5 says, "Blessed is the man that hath filled the desire with them; he shall not be confounded when he shall speak to his enemies in the gate," that is, in the gate of death, and thus the gate to God is opened to us, because is the greatest happiness of this life is to be safe in death and thus able to sing with the Apostle in I Corinthians 4:55, "O death, where is thy victory? O death, where is thy sting?" recalling Hosea 13:14, "O death, I will be thy death; O hell, I will be thy bite: comfort is hidden from my eyes." And thus is opened up to us the gate of Gad which is interpreted "happiness" because this is the summing up of happiness in this life, namely, to be safe in death through a conscience that does not deprive us of hope. The second gate is that of Asher which is interpreted "blessed" because through death we at once join the company of the blessed Saints according to our works, for as Revelation 14:13 says, "Blessed are the dead, who die in the Lord. From henceforth now, saith the Spirit, that they may rest from their labors; for their works follow them." Third and last the Valiant Woman's husband sits is the gate of Nephthali which is interpreted "width" because through death is the passage from the difficulties of speculation to the breadth of the beatific vision and from the pressures of desire to the furnace of the dilation of the heart in the fire of love where we join the Seraphim in total adoration, the Cherubim in full knowledge, and the Thrones in the perfect quiet of peace.

Next is the question of when is the husband of the Valiant Woman recognized as noble, that is, "when he sits in the gate." Note that there are four orders in judgment some sit judging, some are judged, and of these, some are condemned, some are excused, and others are not judged but are condemned.

First, therefore we say that some sit as princes and among these sits Christ, the Valiant Woman's husband, who makes the other judges also sit. Of these judges Matthew 19:28 relates that "Jesus said to them: Amen, I say to you, that you, who have followed me, in the regeneration, when the Son of man shall sit on the seat of his majesty, you also shall sit on twelve seats judging the twelve tribes of Israel." By "twelve,' as the Gloss says is signified the totality of the perfect and by "seats of judgment" is meant the power they have from the Lord.

Second of those who are judged and saved, it says in Matthew 25:34-35, "Come, ye blessed of my Father, possess you the kingdom prepared for you from the foundation of the world. For I was hungry, and you gave me to eat; I was thirsty, and you gave me to drink; I was a stranger, and you took me in."

Third, of those who are judged and condemned Jesus says in the same chapter verses 41-45, "Then he shall say to them also that shall be on his left hand: Depart from me, you cursed, into everlasting fire which was prepared for the devil and his angels. For I was hungry, and you gave me not to eat: I was thirsty, and you gave me not to drink. I was a stranger, and you took me not in: naked, and you covered me not: sick and in prison, and you did not visit me."

Fourth, of those not judged yet condemned Jesus elsewhere in John 3:18 says, "He that doth not believe, is already judged: because he believeth not in the name of the only begotten Son of God."

From this it is evident that Lord makes the Valiant Woman sit with him in judgment as his beloved consort who, according to the Apostle, lives with him in his kingdom, and this is signified in I Kings 2:19, where we read that "Bathsheba came to king Solomon, to speak to him for Adonijah: and the king arose to meet her, and bowed to her, and sat down upon his throne: and a throne was set for the king's mother, and she sat on his right hand. And she said to him: I desire one small petition of thee; do not put me to confusion. And the king said to her: My mother, ask: for I must not turn away thy face." Thus Bathsheba came to King Solomon, her son, and spoke for Adonjah and the king arose to meet her and, reverencing her, had her to sit on the throne that was placed at his right hand for the queen-mother. For this woman is the Mother of Christ and also his sister and his wife by the different relations by which she is united to him, namely, that of conceiving him as mother in the Spirit of salvation, and as impregnated by him as wife in the works of grace, and finally she is his sister as co-heir of the celestial kingdom. Bathsheba came on a judgment day to speak for Adonijah, that is, to intercede for a sinner, so that Solomon might give Abisag to Adonijah for his wife, since "Abisag" signifies "charity," but Adonijah, who was a proud usurper of the crown, did not merit grace and therefore was slain. Nevertheless the Valiant Woman was honored, sitting at the right hand of King Solomon who in tranquil union with her judged all this matter, for he honored her, that is, he saluted his mother with the sign of peace and eternal life by placing her on his right and speaking words of peace to her in the very terms that Jesus uses in Matthew 25:34, "Come, ye blessed of my Father, possess you the kingdom prepared for you from the foundation of the world." And he places her on her throne that along with him she might judge. Thus when he sits in judgment it is evident that he is the noble husband of this Valiant Woman.

What follows concerns the other judges who sits along with this noble husband, namely, "the senators (elders) of the land" There is, however, a threefold land; namely, the land where we dwell [*gerimus*], the land that is our shell [*terimus*], and the land we seek where all is well [*quaerimus*],

The land where we dwell is our body of which Matthew 5: 4 Jesus says, "Blessed are the meek: for they shall possess the land" because we live in peaceful possession in it; and in Psalm 37:11 it says, "But the meek shall inherit the land, and shall delight in abundance of peace."

The land that is our cell or prison is this world of which Genesis 1:2 says, "The earth was void and empty." It is void because it has departed from its original goodness and is empty because it moves toward evil. Or it is void as to grace, and empty as to good works, as Job 9:24 says, "The earth is given into the hand of the wicked."

That land where all is well, the land of the living is that of which Psalm 26:13 says, "I believe to see the good things of the Lord in the land of the living." and God promises in Isaiah 58:14, "I will lift thee up above the high places of the earth."

In all these lands Christ sits with the elders. In the land in which we dwell Christ sits among the elders, namely, conscience and reason, whose judgment discerns all that is within us and of these elders, Isaiah 1:26, says, "I will restore thy judges as they were before, and thy counselors as of old." For the elders or judges are those who from their maturity of age have the rectitude and authority of judgment, as it is called, in the use of conscience and reason: conscience judging about subjective matters, reason judging about objective, public matters. These judges, in my opinion, are sometimes corrupt and so there judgment is dishonest. Between such wicked judges, Christ our God, the judge of truth, restores things as they were before they were corrupted. He does this by making someone his own true judge in confession, not making dishonest excuses for his sins or falling into malicious words as regards others. The "counselors" are our thoughts which are sometimes corrupt because they counsel us to do what is merely convenient and to put off confession in the presumption we will live longer. But Christ, the Word of God, restores the wholeness and expansion of the heart when he makes us think thoughts that are just and which judge, not in an earthly way, but in light of what is superior to us..

In the land that is our cell or prison sit aged judges from whom unjust judgments are issued. These unjust judges are pride and avarice which collaborate in every sin and of which Isaiah 3:14-15 says, "The Lord will enter into judgment with the ancients of his people [and its princes: for you have devoured the vineyard, and the spoil of the poor is in your house. Why do you consume my people, and grind the faces of the poor? saith the Lord the God of hosts."] According to a literal interpretation this means that God has come to judge contrary to the elders and condemn them because they have devoured the vineyards of the Lord, that is, the faithful people. Whence the Lord stands in the midst of these unjust judges and passes judgment on their decisions, as Daniel 13:5 so well says, "And there were two of the ancients of the people appointed judges that year, of whom the Lord said: Iniquity came out from Babylon from the ancient judges, that seemed to govern the people" and those judges lusted after Susanna whose name is interpreted "joy of grace" whom they sought to vilify and slander out of the pride and greed for this land that is our cell or prison. David who [frees Susanna and] condemns these wicked judges to be stoned is Christ, and thus these wicked elders justly perish according to Christ's severe judgments.

The elders of the land where all is well are of two kinds: angels and holy men who sit with Christ in judgment as nobler than all and ennobling all as it was said above and also as I Corinthians 6:2 says, "Know you not that the Saints shall judge this world? And if the world shall be judged by you, are you unworthy to judge the smallest matters?" that is, "Is it unworthy of you that concerning these temporal matters there should be judgment among you?"

THE VALIANT WOMAN

OUTLINE OF CHAPTER XV

**She made fine linen, and sold it,
and delivered a girdle to the Canaanite. (v. 24)**

§1) Acrostic Letter Samech ס signifies "help," or "raising" since the Valiant Woman raises her hand in business
  1) This business is of three kinds
    1) Hope that raises us from the despair of sin: Tabitha or Dorcas was dead through lack of hope
    2) Faith that raises us by liberating us from the devil, the stooped woman Jesus cured
    3) Contemplation which raises our eyes from lowly to supreme matters that needs:
      1) The beauty of the virtues
      2) The raising of intelligence to divine things
      3) The glory of an illumined face like that of Moses
      4) The loveliness of companionship which surrounds the contemplative like a garment.
  2) What the Valiant Woman did first:
    1) She made all four kinds of linen garments having different uses that the Scriptures mention:
      1) The garment of obedience that Samson promised the men of Ascalon if they solved his riddle.
      2) The garment of spotless chastity
      3) The garment of mercy and almsgiving
      4) The garment of preaching the Word of God: the preacher's good life.
    2) How she makes these garments
      1) The garment of obedience by keeping the commandments and counsels out of respect to God
      2) The garment of chastity is woven through custody of the flesh and the body
      3) The garment of mercy and almsgiving is woven through mercy and compassion to the needy
      4) The garment of preaching the Word of God is woven by;
        1) Exhorting to morality
        2) Announcing the faith
        3) Arguing against evil actions
        4) Rebuking the obdurate
        5) Abjuring the reverend
        6) Instructing the unlearned
    3) How the Valiant Woman sells these garments:
      1) They cast out devils, that is, convert sinners, but not by selling indulgences, etc.

2) They speak in tongues, that is, the truth of the Holy Spirit, not by lies
  3) They take up serpents, that is, do not take money for confessions or seduce women
  4) They reject temptations arising from hearing confessions
  5) By the sacraments they heal those sick in sin

§2. They deliver girdle to the Canaanite;
  1) This girdle is eightfold:
    1) Of justice
    2) Of fidelity
    3) Of humility
    4) Of mortality or mortification of the flesh
    5) Of tribulation which may be either
      1) Proportionate to merit, sometimes the just are tried more than they deserve
      2) Proportion to the utility which is achieved from it; in this they are always proportionate.
    6) Of the cleanness or continence of heart and body; because bodily chastity may not make the heart clean
    7) Of ministry (See Chapter VIII)
    8) Of glory: twice-dyed with the red of charity, and the white of wisdom
  2) Three kinds of Canaanites
    1) The accursed sons of Noah who lay bare their father, that is, the sins of the world by imitating them
    2) The deceitful in bargaining, like Canaanite hucksters
    3) The blessed are like the Canaanite woman who bargained with Jesus for healing

CHAPTER XV

She made fine linen, and sold it, and delivered a girdle to the Canaanite. (v. 24)

§1

SAMECH ס, Samech is interpreted "help," namely, hope or "raising," and alludes to the above verse since the Valiant Woman aids and raises herself by engaging in business.

To raise, however, can be done by three powers: hope which raises us from the despair of sin, faith which raises us by liberating us from the devil, and contemplation which raises our eyes from lowly to supreme matters.

Of the first sort of raising Job 5:11 says, "Who setteth up the humble on high, and comforteth with health those that mourn," and similarly Acts 9:36 and following relate how when a certain woman disciple named Tabitha or Dorcas, which is interpreted as "full of good works," St. Peter addressed her corpse, and taking her hand, raised her up to life again, entrusting her to the Saints and to other friendly widows. For she who was full of good works and almsgiving could not have been dead through sin but was dead from the failure of hope. Peter, that is, the knowledge of God, raised her again to life. And having seen Peter, that is having knowledge of the mercy of God, she sat up to live again and Peter gave her his hand, that is, trust in true merits, and raised her up to hope, and then entrusted her now alive with hope to continue living in goods works.

The second sort of raising is liberation from the devil and is exemplified by the raising related in Luke 13:11-16 ["And behold there was a woman, who had a spirit of infirmity eighteen years: and she was bowed together, neither could she look upwards at all. When Jesus saw her, he called her to himself and said to her: Woman, thou art delivered from thy infirmity. And he laid his hands upon her, and immediately she was made straight, and glorified God. And the ruler of the synagogue (being angry that Jesus had healed on the Sabbath) answering, said to the multitude:Six days there are wherein you ought to work. In them therefore come, and be healed; and not on the Sabbath day. And the Lord answering him, said: Ye hypocrites, doth not every one of you, on the Sabbath day, loose his ox or his ass from the manger, and lead them to water? And ought not this daughter of Abraham, whom Satan hath bound, lo, these eighteen years, be loosed from this bond on the Sabbath day?"] Here the daughter of Abraham is a soul who has informed faith but whom the devil, adversary of the salvation of humankind, has bent down through sin during many years, that is, in a circuit of eighteen vices, namely, the transgression of the Ten Commandments plus contempt for the eight Beatitudes enumerated by the Lord [Matthew 5:3-11]. And the Son of God through grace on the Sabbath day, that is, on a feast and cessation from servile work, that is, from sin, moved the Lord to pity and thus Luke 1:69 says, "And He hath raised up an horn of salvation to us, in the house of David his servant."

Of the third sort of raising, namely, by contemplation, Job 40:5, says, "Clothe thyself with beauty, and set thyself up on high and be glorious, and put on goodly garments,'" through which is to be understood four things which a contemplative should have; first the beauty of the virtues; second the raising of the intellect to divine things; third the glory of a face which is illumined as the face of Moses was made splendid [Exodus 3:29]; and fourth the loveliness of companionship which surrounds the contemplative like a garment.

The foregoing is the exposition of the letter Samech, and next we must consider the chapter verse, "**She made fine linen, and sold it and delivered a girdle to the Canaanite.**" In this is indicated two things that the Valiant Woman does: first, what the fine linen garment made by her is, and second, how she sells it. The Gloss says that the "fine linen" or *sindon* is "a garment finely woven from cotton." In Sacred Scripture, however, four kinds of such clothing are mentioned, having four sorts of uses: those of perfect obedience, those of spotless innocence and chastity, those of almsgiving, and those of teaching or preaching the Gospel. The Valiant Woman makes all four kinds of garments.

The garment of obedience is like those of Samson who it is said in Judges 14:14, promised thirty shirts to the men of Ascalon if they could solve a riddle that he would propose to them. Ascalon is interpreted "evil fire" and signifies those who burned with the fire of lust and also by greed by which they transgressed the commandment of God. Samson, whose name is interpreted "strong sun," that is, Christ's warning of eternal punishment for sinners, killed these men of Ascalon because they failed to solve the riddle or enigma whose right answer was, "the beauty of obedience to the Ten Commandments in the faith of the Trinity," since this would have been the sign of their will to keep these counsels and commands. The puzzle was "Out of the eater" that is, the devouring lion, "came forth meat, and out of the strong came forth sweetness." The eater or "lion" was the devil, who as St. Peter says, I Peter 5:8, "Be sober and watch: because your adversary the devil, as a roaring lion, goeth about seeking whom he may devour," who kills Christ in his members. Yet food comes out of the devil because his temptations actually serve to promote virtue, spiritual renewal, and the sweetness and strength of the spiritual life, since it is by the experience of struggle with the devil that spiritual men increasingly grow stronger.

A garment of spotless chastity is the garment of delicate women because delicate women are chaste virgins, widows, and wives, receiving only Christ. And of this Isaiah 3:17-24 says, ["Because the daughters of Sion are haughty, and have walked with stretched out necks, and wanton glances of their eyes, and made a noise as they walked with their feet and moved in a set pace: The Lord will make bald the crown of the head of the daughters of Sion, and the Lord will discover their hair. In that day the Lord will take away the ornaments of shoes, and little moons, And chains and necklaces, and bracelets, and bonnets, And bodkins, and ornaments of the legs, and tablets, and sweet balls, and earrings, And rings, and jewels hanging on the forehead, And changes of apparel, and short cloaks, and fine linen, and crisping pins, And looking-glasses, and lawns, and headbands, and fine veils. And instead of a sweet smell there shall be stench, and instead of a girdle, a cord, and instead of curled hair, baldness, and instead of a stomacher, haircloth."] Thus Isaiah prophesies that because of the people's sin the Lord will take from their women their spotless garments, although another prophet, Hosea 4:14, says, "I will not visit upon your daughters when they shall commit fornication and upon your spouses when they shall commit adultery: because you yourselves conversed with harlots."

The garment of mercy and almsgiving is the garment in which, according to Mark 14:32, Joseph [of Arimathea] wrapped the whole body of Jesus, that is, all his members, since as the Lord says in Matthew 25:40. "Amen I say to you, as long as you did it to one of these my least brethren, you did it to me."

The garment of preaching the Word of God is the garment John Mark was deprived of, as related in Mark 14:50-52, when Jesus' capturers came to force his followers to desert the faith, "Then his disciples leaving him, all fled away. And a certain young man followed him, having a linen cloth cast about his naked body; and they laid hold on him. But he, casting off the linen cloth, fled from them naked." Because a preacher if he does not have, as it were, the underwear of a good life between his bare body and his outer vestment, although he sometimes teaches Christ, will in time of persecution flee and even deny the Word.

Next follows consideration of how the Valiant Woman **makes** and **sells** these **fine garments**. She makes them in four ways and also sells them in four ways. The garments of obedience she makes by complying with the divine mandates and counsels by subjecting herself to all human creatures for the sake of God as St. Peter says in I Peter 2:13-15, "Be ye subject therefore to every human creature for God's sake: whether it be to the king as excelling, Or to governors as sent by him for the punishment of evildoers, and for the praise of the good: For so is the will of God, that by doing well you may put to silence the ignorance of foolish men" and as the Apostle says, Romans 13:1, "Let every soul be subject to higher powers: for there is no power but from God: and those that are, are ordained of God," and Hebrews 13:17, "Obey your prelates, and be subject to them. For they watch as being ready to render an account of your souls; that they may do this with joy, and not with grief." The Valiant Woman sells this garment by fulfilling her obligation to keep these precepts and through her vows to observe the counsels as it is commanded in the law: Deuteronomy 23:21, "When thou hast made a vow to the Lord thy God, thou shalt not delay to pay it: [because the Lord thy God will require it. And if thou delay, it shall be imputed to thee for a sin,"] and Psalm 66:13-14 says, "I will go into thy house with burnt offerings: I will pay thee my vows, which my lips have uttered, and my mouth hath spoken, [when I was in trouble,] and St. Augustine says that "to vow is a matter of the will, but to fulfill it is a matter of obligation." Likewise Psalm 76:12 says, "Vow ye, and pay to the Lord your God: all you that are round about him bring presents." The obligation to keep the commandments applies to all the Law's precepts beginning with Exodus 20:1, as it says in Isaiah 8:16, "Bind up the testimony, seal the law among my disciples." "Bind" through obligation and "seal the law," that is, confirm it with a vow.

The garment of cleanness and chastity is woven by custody of the flesh and the body, as Job 30:1 says, "I made a covenant with my eyes, that I would not so much as think upon a virgin." It says "of a virgin," since that class of woman is more likely to arouse desire, thus Job already knew what was long afterwards taught by the Lord in Matthew 13:8: "But I say to you, that whosoever shall look on a woman to lust after her, hath already committed adultery with her in his heart." The Valiant Woman sells this garment of purity by promising its fruit, as in Matthew 13:8 the Lord says, "And other seeds fell upon good ground: and they brought forth fruit, some an hundredfold, some sixtyfold, and some thirtyfold." The good ground is a clean heart and body; the seeds are the words of chastity by which married couples, bear thirtyfold of fruit, widows sixtyfold, and virgins a hundredfold.

The garment of almsgiving is woven by mercy and compassion toward all the needy, as in Hosea 6:6 the Lord says, "For I desire mercy, and not sacrifice: and the knowledge of God more than holocausts." The Valiant Woman sells this garment by showing the incertitude of riches, as in I Timothy 6:17 the Apostles writes, "Charge the rich of this world not to be high-minded nor to trust in the uncertainty of riches," and James 5:1-3, "Go to now, ye rich men, weep and howl in your miseries, which shall come upon you. Your riches are corrupted: and your garments are moth eaten. Your gold and silver is cankered: and the rust of them shall be for a testimony against you, and shall eat your flesh like fire."

The garment of preaching the Word of God is woven by exhorting to morality, announcing the faith, arguing against evil actions, rebuking the obdurate, abjuring the reverend, instructing the unlearned as the Apostle says in II Timothy 4:2-5, "Preach the word: be instant in season, out of season: reprove, entreat, rebuke in all patience and doctrine. For there shall be a time, when they will not endure sound doctrine; but, according to their own desires, they will heap to themselves teachers, having itching ears: And will indeed turn away their hearing from the truth, but will be turned unto fables." That time, alas! is now, because the people hear only according to their own sinful desires wandering preachers who deceitfully promise a hundred days indulgence for the donation of a small coin, and turn their hearers away from the truth by failing to preach penance. Or because they hear preached only trivialities by preachers who, seeking to gain temporal lucre, announce not Christ but lying fables and heresies. These preachers also preach vaguely because they have not studied and thus are silent about the Sacred Scriptures which all preachers are bound to know as the Word of God, as St. Augustine, commenting on the Epistle of St. Jude, declares. Because they teach what is not true (for they announce false indulgences) they are undoubtedly anathematized, if not by bishops whose letters of recommendation pass over their errors and accept these preachers as having great authority as preachers of the truth although this is to the confusion and damnation of their hearers. Nevertheless such preachers are certainly anathematized by the Apostle who says in Galatians 1:8, "If we, or an angel from heaven, preach a gospel to you besides that which we have preached to you, let him be anathema." and he confirms this sentence when he says again in verse 9, "As we said before, so now I say again: If any one preach to you a gospel, besides that which you have received, let him be anathema." Here St. Paul utters these anathemas to confound and refute these false views without considering them in detail.

We return, therefore, to showing how the Valiant Woman sold this garment, although it is not so much a garment as bunch of old dirty rags of deception that these false preachers sell. The Valiant Woman, however, sells the garment of the Word of God by persuasive deeds of living and by miracles. The Lord mentions these two arguments in Mark 16:17-18 when he says, "And these signs shall follow them that believe: In my name they shall cast out devils: they shall speak with new tongues. They shall take up serpents; and if they shall drink any deadly thing, it shall not hurt them: they shall lay their hands upon the sick, and they shall recover." And here the Lord touches on five things that a buyer should note about the true garment of God's Word.

The first is that preachers in the name of God cast out devils, that is, they convert sinners. But some do not do this in the name of God but of Mammon, the god of riches, who Isaiah 5:23 says, "justify the wicked for gifts," as do certain commoners, and archdeacons, and bishops, and their fund-raisers. But according to the Lord's own words in Mark 3:24, "How can Satan cast out Satan? And if a kingdom be divided against itself, that kingdom cannot stand. And if a house be divided against itself, that house cannot stand. And if Satan be risen up against himself, he is divided, and cannot stand, but hath an end." Thus devils agree with devils not in good but in evil; for example, if a pastor is greedy, his evil sheep will remain in sin.

The second sign is that they begin to speak with new tongues. The new tongue is the tongue of the Holy Spirit as the Apostle says in Romans 9:1, "I speak the truth in Christ, I lie not, my conscience bearing me witness in the Holy Ghost," since there are no lies in Jesus Christ, as Job 13:7 says, "Hath God any need of your lie, that you should speak deceitfully for him?" For lies are the ancient tongue of the devil by which he spoke to Adam and hence the Lord, speaking of his opponents, says in John 8:44, "You are of your father the devil, and the desires of your father you will do. He was a murderer from the beginning, and he stood not in the truth; because truth is not in him. When he speaketh a lie, he speaketh of his own: for he is a liar, and the father thereof." Thus it is evident that this ancient language is that of lying so that when a lie is told it is from the devil's own lips.

The third sign is that the preachers can take up serpents, not to put the poison drawn from these into their own bosoms, but to get rid of them, since Job 26:13 says, "His obstetric hand brought forth the winding serpent." But I do not know where these preachers come from; for they are not disciples of Christ if they in hearing confessions do not correct the poison of greed and what is even more shameful, the poison of lust, yet they even pollute young women in confession and are polluted by them. Whence, as I have said, they pour out poison into the bosom of their subjects, doubtlessly from the mouth of serpents, and in their own hearts construct a stable serpent's nest whence the fatal poison flows out over many.

The fourth sign is that if the preacher in hearing confessions drinks some deadly drink, they are not poisoned by it. On the contrary, these strive immediately to cast out of themselves all the evil they have heard, since there is no one who is lured by so many and such repeated crimes as are clerics; because they learn abut every evil and through desire may experience them all.

The fifth sign is that priests lay the hands of the sacraments over those sick in sin and heal them. And it should be noted that the sacraments are able to make us clean through the grace of God, since not man but God acts through them. That is why the sacraments have equally good and evil results, since they are not equally ministered and received devoutly. Yet what they can do they do. Thus in the sacraments are imitated Giezi, the servant of Eliseus, as is related in II Kings 5:20-27. [Giezi because he tried to profit from the healing of the leprosy of the Syrian Naaman was struck with the same leprosy], in the action of Simon [related in Acts 8:18-24 who tried to buy the office of an apostle], of Jason the Maccabee related in II Maccabees 4:7-20 [who tried to Hellenize the Jews]; and especially in the lust of the sons of the priest Eli, who [as related in I Samuel 2:12 and following] were wicked sons of Belial who drew men from the sacrifices to God.

§ 2

Next comes the phrase, "and **delivered a girdle to the Canaanite.**" The girdle made by the Valiant Woman is eightfold: first the girdle of justice, second of fidelity, third of humility, fourth of mortality, fifth of tribulation, sixth of cleanness of heart and body, seventh of ministry, and eighth of glory and dignity.

Of the first Sirach, 45:9 says, "He [Moses] girded him [Aaron] about with a glorious girdle, and clothed him with a robe of glory, and crowned him with majestic attire."

Of the first and second together Isaiah 41:5 says, "And justice shall be the girdle of his loins: and faith [this fidelity] the girdle of his reins."

Of the third, the girdle of humility Job 12:18 says, "He looseth the belt of kings, and girdeth their loins with a cord" and Isaiah 22:12 says, "And the Lord, the God of hosts, in that day shall call to weeping, and to mourning, to baldness, and to girding with sackcloth." This is done to "weep for sins, to "mourn for ingratitude and the pains of hell, to go "bald," that is, to cut one's hair for the wiping out of vanity and superfluity, and to "gird oneself with sack-cloth" in the humility of repentance.

Of the fourth, the girdle of mortality or mortification of the flesh Matthew 3:4 says, "And the same John [the Baptist] had his garment of camels' hair, and a leathern girdle about his loins," and II Kings 1:7-8, "And he said to them: What manner of man was he who met you, and spoke these words? But they said: A hairy man with a girdle of leather about his loins. And he said: It is Elias the Thesbite" because a hairy skin one made of the hide of a dead animal is the sign of the mortification of the flesh. Hence Genesis 4:21 relates that after the fall, "The Lord God made for Adam and his wife, garments of skins, and clothed them," to show them their mortality lest they become still more proud.

Of the fifth, the girdle of tribulation, Job 19:6 says, "At least now understand that God hath not afflicted me with an equal judgment, and compassed me with his scourges." And there are two senses in which this judgment might be "equal": first according to the proportion of merit and second according to the proportion of the utility which is achieved from it. According to the proportion of merit by which Job was judged there was not equal judgment and in that sense he objected to his friends who accused him of some crime, since God only punishes sinners, since they presumed falsely that Job was such, as did the Lord's disciples when in John 9:2-3 they asked of the man born blind: "Rabbi, who hath sinned, this man, or his parents, that he should be born blind?" Jesus answered, "Neither hath this man sinned, nor his parents; but that the works of God should be made manifest in him," that is, so that the miracle of his healing by Jesus might be performed. But according to the proportion of utility the judgments of God are always equal, [that is, just]. Yet it must be understood that it is possible to concede that sometimes God's judgments are not equal, yet in no sense can they wrong, because "unequal" [*iniquum*] sounds like a vicious corruption [iniquity] while "not equal" does not have that ambiguity and this is what is meant by John 21:18-19, where the Lord says to Peter, "Amen, amen I say to thee, when thou wast younger, thou didst gird thyself, and didst walk where thou wouldst. But when thou shalt be old, thou shalt stretch forth thy hands, and another shall gird thee, and lead thee whither thou wouldst not. And this he said, signifying by what death he should glorify God. And when he had said this, he saith to him: Follow me." This girdle is that of persecution which by his natural will Peter did not will [but by grace would accept], as St. Augustine explains in the Gloss on this text.

Of the sixth kind of girdle, that the girdle of cleanness or continence of heart and body the Lord says in Luke 12:35, "Let your loins be girt, and lamps burning in your hands." Hence St. Gregory the Great says in the Gloss, "We girt our loins when we restrict the desires of the flesh by continence," and in Revelation 1:13, the Apostle John says, "And in the midst of the seven golden candlesticks, [I saw] one like to the Son of man, clothed with a garment down to the feet, and girt about the breast with a golden girdle." Thus it should be noted that the beauty of chastity pertains even to the heart [since the girdle girts the breast,] lest one be like the foolish virgins who had no oil in the vessels of their hearts, but only the empty lamps of merely bodily chastity or lest one be like the barren fig tree in Luke 13:6, "A certain man had a fig tree planted in his vineyard, and he came seeking fruit on it, and found none," and thus exhibit the sweetness of continence in the covering of the body yet yielding no fruit in the internal chastity of the heart.

Of the seventh kind of girdle, that of ministry, the Lord himself says in Luke 12:37, "Blessed are those servants, whom the Lord when he cometh [in the kingdom of heaven], shall find watching. Amen I say to you, that he will gird himself, and make them sit down to meat, and passing will minister unto them," and of this 'girding of the loins" we have already said more in Chapter VIII, § 1.

Of the eighth and last kind of girdle, that of glory, it is said in Exodus 28:6-28 that the Lord commanded that a girdle or belt be made to honor and glorify the high priest and that it should be woven of four colors purple, hyacinth, scarlet twice dyed, and white, these four colors signify four things that we will enjoy in heaven. "Purple" is the glory of redemption. "Hyacinth" is the color of the sky that signifies glorification of our soul and body in the day of resurrection because then we will have totally the color of the heavens. "Scarlet twice dyed" is deep red and signifies the ardor of delight which we will have in God's divinity like that of Seraphim who are said to be pure flames. The "white color" signifies the candor of Wisdom within us of which Wisdom 7:25-26, says, "For she [Wisdom] is a vapor of the power of God, and a certain pure emanation of the glory of the almighty God: and therefore no defiled thing cometh into her; for she is the brightness of eternal light, the unspotted mirror of God's majesty, and the image of his goodness."

What follows "to the Canaanite" concerns those to whom the Valiant Woman sells this girdle that she has made and there are three kinds of the Canaanites, the accursed, the deceitful, and the blessed.

Of the accursed Canaanites it is said in Genesis 9:25, "He [Noah] said: Cursed be Canaan, a servant of servants shall he be unto his brethren." The Canaanites are descendants of this Canaan, son of Cham, son of Noah, who are cursed because of the ridicule Cham made of Noah, his father when he lay drunk in his tent, "Which when Cham the father of Canaan had seen, to wit, that his father's nakedness was uncovered, he told it to his two brethren without." Hence these Canaanites are doomed to servitude. "Canaan" is interpreted "negotiator" and indicates that the Canaanites were accursed because they were dishonest negotiators who do the devil's business, as are usurers, auctioneers, tax-collectors, profiteers, simoniacs, dealers, thieves, and such sort, who deride their fathers because they have seen them naked. Their "father" is this world whose nudity is laid bare when one imitates what is shameful and ought to be kept covered in oneself and others and since they ought not expose this they are cursed by the world with its curses, because the orb of the earth, that is, the world, fights against the foolish, as Wisdom 5:21, "And he [God] will sharpen his severe wrath for a spear, and the whole world shall fight with him against the unwise." They will be servants to the servants because they must obey the servants of Christ even if they are unwilling because when they precede they also follow and have no freedom, such as those servants experience who serve Christ, since to serve God is to reign.

The deceitful Canaanite is the negotiator who is occupied with his proper gain but nevertheless in actual buy and selling deceitfully circumvents his neighbor and deceives him, concerning which Hosea 12:7, says, "He is like Canaan, there is a deceitful balance in his hand." Against which the Lord says through Solomon, Proverbs 11:1 that "He is like Canaan, there is a deceitful balance in his hand." And the Lord forbids that there be diverse dry weights or liquid measures.

The blessed Canaanite is the negotiator of souls and especially of his own soul of whom Matthew 15:21-28 says, ["And Jesus went from thence, and retired into the coasts of Tyre and Sidon. And behold a woman of Canaan who came out of those coasts, crying out, said to him: 'Have mercy on me, O Lord, thou son of David: my daughter is grievously troubled by the devil.' Who answered her not a word. And his disciples came and besought him, saying: 'Send her away, for she crieth after us.' And he answering, said: 'I was not sent but to the sheep that are lost of the house of Israel.' But she came and adored him, saying: 'Lord, help me' Who answering, said: 'It is not good to take the bread of the children, and to cast it to the dogs'. But she said: 'Yea, Lord; for the whelps also eat of the crumbs that fall from the table of their masters.' Then Jesus answering, said to her: 'O woman, great is thy faith: be it done to thee as thou wilt' and her daughter was cured from that hour."] That Jesus "went out" from Israel signifies his going from the Father into the world although by this he did not leave the glory of the Father but, as it says in Philippians 2:7, "But he emptied himself, taking the form of a servant, being made in the likeness of men, and in habit found as a man." He "retired into the coasts of Tyre" which is interpreted "straits" since he did not assume all of these restrictions of the body but some that were not unfitting or contrary to grace, with which he was filled, but he did assume hunger, thirst, wandering, weariness cold, death, and other sufferings in the region of Tyre, that is, into the straits of this life in his passion and death, lessened only by the help of angels.

Jesus also entered into parts of Sidon which is interpreted "hunt,' but not all of this temporal world is the scene of hunting, since as it says in John 6:15, "Jesus therefore, when he knew that they would come to take him by force, and make him king, fled again into the mountain himself alone," yet nevertheless he did engage in the hunt for souls. Behold, then, a woman—and she is a woman to signify the flow of desire that women have monthly—who is said to have come from these same parts, that, is from the territory of Tyre and Sidon to which she had been confined, which signify, [as we have said], the regions of the anxieties of this world and the hunt for worldly happiness. She had left there and entered into the region of anxiety where the Lord was hunting for souls, She confronted the Lord boldly, begging him for her daughter, that is, for her soul, evil through sin and vexed by a demon. And when the son of God in order to test the woman's faith addressed her as a "dog," she confirmed the judgment of the Lord by the recognition of her own iniquity and said, "Yes, Lord," as if to say, "None of the Lord's words do me any injury because I am truly a dog as so is my daughter." And so she said, "Yea, Lord; for the whelps also eat of the crumbs" of salvation "that fall from the table of their masters," that is, of the Apostles. Thus she won health and praise from the Lord because of her faith and humility and alone among the Channanites was girded with the girdle of faith and humility and the word of God and all the other virtues. And it is evident from experience how she bought the girdle of prayer and conversion, since she went out of the lands of anxiety and the pursuit of temporal goods in which she had dwelt and by faith and humility attained to salvation from the Lord. And this suffices to explain the three kinds of girdles.

THE VALIANT WOMAN 209

OUTLINE OF CHAPTER XVI

Strength and beauty are her clothing,
And she shall laugh in the latter day. (v. 25)

§1) The letter Ain ע in "fountain" of Wisdom or "Eye" and the Valiant Woman contemplating looks to:
1) The Word of God
2) The fountain of life that produces fruit
3) How is the Valiant Woman clothed in strength and beauty?
    1) The act of fortitude is a mean between fearing and not fearing:
        1) By audacity in not fearing what is to be feared it excludes three kinds of wickedness
            1) Provoking God's justice
            2) Presuming on His mercy
            3) Putting God to a test
    2) Not fearing what should be feared that excludes three kinds of concerns
        1) Worldly anxiety about losing worldly goods
        2) Human but excessive anxiety about bodily health and Life
        3) Faintheartedness about shadow-dangers rather than real dangers
        4) But Fortitude does not exclude natural fears
    3) Fortitude is accompanied by three kinds of audacity:
        1) Not fearing to confess Christ before the powers of this world
        2) Bearing with great difficulties for God's sake
        3) The highest is to commit oneself not only on sense and reason, but to God in faith.
    4) What fears must be met with fortitude?
        1) Initial fear that fears to fall when tempted
        2) Filial fear: perfect fortitude that fears separation from God as Father
        3) Spousal fear, not of sin or punishment, but of separation from God
        4) Servile fear of punishment that precedes & accompanies holy fear

§2) What parts of the Valiant Woman are clothed in fortitude: Cicero names 1-4 and Bible 5-9
1) Magnificence, the undertaking and administration of great and excellent things with a breadth of mind and splendid purpose is fivefold:
    1) Thanksgiving
    2) Liberality or generosity
    3) Power
    4) Praise or glory
    5) Fortitude
2) Fearlessness, the soul puts a certain trust along with hope in matters that are great and honorable
    1) In word
    2) In internal consolation
    3) Species of fortitude proper
    4) Of support

3) Patience that causes honesty & utility of arduous, difficult & voluntary, long protracted suffering
   1) Patience of an ass, from dullness of senses
   2) Patience of hope, expectation of future good without dejection
   3) Patience of astuteness, which seems to ignore injuries to sustain them calmly for a time
   4) Patience that is a virtue which has three effects:
      1) Perfection of work
      2) Control of anger
      3) Propitiating of God and softening of his justice
4) Perseverance remaining permanently in the reason that is threefold:
   1) Determination to continue in a good action once it is begun
   2) Continuation of a good act clear to its end
   3) Under discipline, the learning through trials
5) Confidence (faithfulness) that looks to divine aid and thus is assured
   1) Confidence of faith
   2) Confidence of hope
   3) Confidence of fortitude
6) Assurance is also threefold:
   1) Assurance of faith
   2) Assurance of hope
   3) Assurance of fortitude
7) Longanimity
   1) Of mercy: defers punishment and conceals indignation to convert sinner
   2) Of hope: waits with equanimity for fulfillment of promises
   3) Of fortitude: tolerates adversity till victory is attained
8) Perseverance or confirmation in the Biblical sense
   1) Determination to continue in a good action once it is begun
   2) Continuation of a good act to its end: Pertinacity is continuation in evil
   3- Under discipline, the learning through trials
9) Constancy
   1) Of Maturity: A bad person hides this as calmness
   2) Of Fortitude: Continues in virtue no matter how long the trial lasts
   3) How the act of fortitude and its parts fit the Valiant Woman's clothing: Three things are necessary:
      1) Scissors to cut and shape the pieces
         1) One blade is faith
         2) Other blade is the authority of the Sacred Scriptures
         3) Key of intellectual understanding holds blades together
      2) The Needle to sew pieces together is Wisdom
      3) The Thread that joins the pieces is fortitude connecting the parts of its work in equanimity

§3) When is the Valiant Woman doubly clad in both strength and beauty, if "beauty is elegant measure of a thing parts"?
1) The Valiant Woman's personal beauty
   1) Natural beauty: the spirit controls the flesh and the will obeys reason
   2) Beauty is harmony of all the political virtues making the Valiant Woman beautiful in human sight

3) In God's sight the Valiant Woman is beautiful by the theological virtues of faith, hope, and charity
  2) The beauty of the Valiant Woman's work:
   1) It is licit in relation to God, not forbidden by any Commandment
   2) It is honest in itself: nothing in it would be called shameful by honest persons
   3) It is useful for the salvation of her neighbor
  3) It has glory, and not vainglory, that is threefold:
   1) Of a good conscience
   2) Of hope
   3) That is tested by trial

§4) Why the Valiant Woman when clothed in strength and beauty can "laugh in the latter day"?
 1) Her laughter is swelling (but not immoderate or worldly) joy of her heart and mind with the Saints
  1) She laughs at those she warns but who are unwilling to hear her voice and who therefore are condemned:
   1) For their contempt of her words
   2) For their contempt of her helping hands
   3) For their contempt of her counseling in conversation
   4) By anger of God through the ministry of demons
   5) By a threshing sledge that crushes and cuts up in punishment
   6) By the anxiety which like a worm eats at the heart of conscience
   7) By their despair of hearing an answer of pleas to God
  2) There is, however, a threefold laugh and a threefold scowl, although some do neither
   1) Some laugh and scowl like fools
   2) Some laugh and scowl deceitfully
   3) Some laugh and scowl in worldly consolation
 2) The four causes of her laughing
  1) For her part, she has four reasons for laughing
   1) She once was empty but now is filled with joy
   2) She has simple faith that she will be repaid by God for all her work
   3) She accepts the delay, because of her future satisfaction
   4) Her reward will exceed even what her faith, hope, and charity expect
  2) On God's part, He will repay all her for four causes
   1) He will be seen face-to-face
   2) The union with Him will be perfect
   3) His will be total fruition of all desires
   4) The union will resemble that of Man and God in Christ
  3) On society's part, the community of Saints gives four causes for laughing
   1) They will all enjoy God together
   2) All will share their joy with others
   3) This will be perfect friendship, the culmination of virtue
   4) This joy will be everlasting
 3) The latter or the latest day of her laughing, Why?
  1) Why is it called the day?
   1) It will be unexpected, "like a thief in the night"
   2) It will be night for sinners, eternal punishment in darkness

3) But it will be eternal day for the saved
2) Why is it called "latter" or latest? It will be eternal light which is called "lastest in three sense:
  1) In number he goes there will be no time following this day
  2) In joy only that no greater joy is possible
    1) All joys will be gathered into one; namely eternal peace
    2) Spiritual consolation is threefold
      1) As a child at its mother's breast
      2) We will be comforted with all the Saints
      3) There will be both exterior and interior vision
      4) The abundance of eternal, spiritual food
3) There is also a last day for punishment because it is the greatest and marked by:
  1) Mode of resurrection of the dead who are condemned
    1) The body will be in the fires of Hell
    2) Body and soul war against each other
      1) Principally of the body:
        1) Of the body as it is resurrected
        2) In the judgment
        3) In the prison of Hell
      2) Principally of the soul
        1) Worm of conscience
        2) Hatred against God & envy against Saints
        3) Perversion of intelligence; to know truth yet fight against it, as do all the devils
    3) The punishments on the part of the soul and its desire for eternal death without the possibility of ever dying are six:
      1) Insight of horrible judgment
      2) Exposure of all sins
      3) Hard reproach of judgment
      4) Sentence of condemnation
      5) Separation from society of all good and God
      6) Joining to the company of the reprobate
  2) Resurrection
  3) Judgment
  4) Prison in which the condemned are held: with ten major punishments
    1) The heat of interior and exterior fire
    2) The interior and consequent exterior cold
    3) The interior and exterior darkness
    4) The stink of the lake
    5) The horror of company in this place
    6) The perpetual face-to-face presence of the devils
    7) The chain of hissing, burning, and pressing bodies
    8) The grinding of teeth
    9) The captivity of the prison itself

CHAPTER XVI

Strength and beauty are her clothing, and she shall laugh in the latter day. (v. 25)

§ 1

AIN ע, is translated as "fountain" or as "eye." Now there is a twofold fountain to which this woman turns her eyes. One is the fountain of wisdom, to which she turns the eye of contemplation. Hence Ecclesiastes 1:5 says, "The word of God on high is the fountain of wisdom." This [as it says in Genesis 2:6] is the fountain that rose out of the earth on the day of his birth, watering all the surface of paradise, that is, of the Church, as is read in Genesis 2:10 and in Ecclesiastes 24:42, "I said, I will water my garden of plants, and I will water abundantly the fruit of my birth." The garden of plants is the Church in which are the plants of verdant virtues and the souls, which souls, I say, are the fruits of the birthings of the Church, as was said above in the first verse.

There is also the fountain of life in which is fixed the eye of fruition. This is dealt with in Psalm 36:10, "For with thee is the fountain of life; and in thy light we shall see light." In accord with this sense there is an epigram in the verse following that in which it is contained, both about the beauty of eternal strength and about the vision of the latter day, namely, when the eye will see light in light, will drink life in the fountain of life, will be inebriated with the plenty of the house of God, and will drink of the torrent of divine pleasure.

There follows in the chapter verse, "**Strength and beauty, etc.**" In this verse two things must be considered, namely how the Valiant Woman is clothed with strength and beauty, and what it is for her to laugh in the latter day.

As regards the first, three things must be noted. First, what is the clothing of strength, second what is the clothing of beauty, and third how and when she is clothed in both. With regard to the first of these three, the "clothing of strength," there are three things to be noted: first, according to what act the woman is vested with strength, second according to which species of this fortitude, and third how these species are made fit as clothing.

Note, then, that according to the wise of this world, the act of fortitude is in some determinate matter, and according to the exclusion of two kinds of wickedness in that matter. Now the matter of fortitude is adversity, whether suffering borne from the outside or else caused from within, such as from misfortune, fever, reproaches, persecutions, scourging, bearing with death, and other things of this sort. In these sufferings, fortitude is the moderator of the soul, so that it will fear what is to be feared, and not fear what is not to be feared; dare what is to be dared, and not dare what is not to be dared. It does all these things for the sake of the good, for the sake of virtue, and especially for the sake of God. Whence Tully [i.e. Cicero] says, "Fortitude is the deliberate confrontation of dangers and bearing with labor." Also Ecclesiastes 46:1 says, "Valiant in war was Jesus the son of Nave, who was successor of Moses among the prophets. The Apostle also in his letter to the Hebrews 11:33, says, "The Saints by faith conquered kingdoms, wrought justice, obtained promises" and in the following v. 34 that they became "valiant in battle". Therefore the proper matter of fortitude is the war of the passions which is waged in man that his soul might not succumb to adversities. Its act is a mean between two kinds of wickedness, namely audacity and fear.

Note that there are three kinds of wicked audacity which fortitude excludes through fearing what is to be feared. For first is an audacity which provokes God, as in Job 15:26, "He hath run against him, namely God, with his neck raised up and is armed with a fat neck." This was the audacity of Sennacherib who said, as related in Isaiah 36:20, "Who is there among all the gods of these lands that hath delivered his country out of my hand, that the Lord may deliver Jerusalem out of my hand?" He ran with a "raised neck," that is, with his mind raised haughtily against God, when he thus blasphemed the strength of God; and "with a fat neck," that is, with an exceedingly enlarged contempt for God, namely, when Sennacherib boasted that no one was able to free Jerusalem. Men of this sort can indeed be found in our days, who, when they act against God by oppressing the poor, blaspheme God saying that He will deal kindly with them, even while they are able to act this way with men. It is as if they said, "We do not fear God, nor do we forgive anything for his sake."

Second, there is the audacity of presumption, for the presumptuous dare to act against justice, while presuming upon mercy. Against this we read in I Samuel 2:25, "If one man shall sin against another, God may be appeased in his behalf: but if a man shall sin against the Lord, who shall pray for him?" And Susanna, at the end of Daniel 13:23 says, "It is better for me to fall into the hands of men than to sin in the sight of the Lord." Also the Apostle says Hebrews 10:28-29, "A man making void the law of Moses, dieth without any mercy under two or three witnesses: How much more, do you think he deserveth worse punishments, who hath trodden underfoot the Son of God, and hath esteemed the blood of the testament unclean, by which he was sanctified, and hath offered an affront to the Spirit of grace?" And, in the same chapter, verse 31, "It is a fearful thing to fall into the hands of the living God."

Third is the audacity of those who put God to the test, about which we read in Psalm 78:18, "And they tempted God in their hearts, by asking meat for their desires." And in the same, verse 19, "And they spoke ill of God: they said: Can God furnish a table in the wilderness?" Thus they dared to test whether God was in their midst to perform miracles for them. These three audacities exclude honest fortitude through its proper act, which is to fear what is to be feared, since these things are to be feared.

But also there is another sort of audacity which is not to fear what is not to be feared, as has been said, or to dare what is to be dared. And in this way it excludes three kinds of fear, namely worldly fear, human fear, and faintheartedness. It does not exclude however, a fourth kind of fear, namely, natural fear, but it binds it so that it does not lead reason astray. Fear is worldly when someone fears danger because of the loss of his possessions. Whence, he fears to be separated from the things of this world, just like the fear of that young man of whom it is related in Luke 28:22-23 that he had kept the commandments from his youth. Yet when he heard from the Lord that he lacked one thing to be perfect, namely, that he "go and sell all that he had and follow" Christ, "he went away sad, because he had many possessions." Also Psalm [Vulgate13:5] says, "They have trembled for fear, where there was no fear."

Human fear is when someone is exceedingly afraid for his own skin, since even according to the testimony of the devil in Job 2:4, "A man would dare to give skin for skin and all things for his life." Against such people the Lord says in Luke 12:4-5, "Be not afraid of them who kill the body, and after that have no more that they can do. But I will shew you whom you shall fear: fear ye him, who after he hath killed, hath power to cast into hell." And Hebrews 2:15 says, "[Who] through the fear of death were all their lifetime subject to servitude."

The fear of faintheartedness is of him who fears the shadow and not the truth. He is, in other words, so timid that he is fearful of anything, no matter how small, about whom we read in Job 15:21-23, "The sound of dread is always in his ears: and when there is peace, he always suspecteth treason. He believeth not that he may return from darkness to light, looking round about for the sword on every side. When he moveth himself to seek bread, he knoweth that the day of darkness is ready at hand." That is, when he "seeks bread," that is, the restoring of life, through certain good works, he knows, that is, he holds for certain, even though it is not true that "the day of darkness," that is, of sin, "is ready at his hand," that is, in his own work. A weakness of spirit and conscience causes this. Against this we read in Isaiah 35:3-4, "Strengthen ye the feeble hands, and confirm the weak knees. Say to the fainthearted: Take courage, and fear not:behold your God will bring revenge of recompense: God himself will come and will save you."

Fear is natural when someone is afraid of danger through nature, but nonetheless does not seek against God's will to avoid anything, just as the Lord was afraid in the Passion, when he said Matthew 26:38, "My soul is sorrowful even unto death," since, at verse 37 it says, "He began to grow sorrowful and to be sad." Similarly Matthew 14:30 relates that "Peter also, walking on the sea and seeing the strong wind, was sorely fearful." Again Matthew 8:25 tells how the disciples when their boat was covered with waves were afraid and "cried out, saying, Lord, save us, we perish." Now, this kind of fear, since it thus touches upon nature, such that it does not lead the reason astray into wicked fear, is called a pro-passion. However, when it does lead the mind astray, it is simply called a passion. Thus fortitude through its acts, by which it puts the soul virtuously between the extremes of vice, excludes certain audacities and certain fears, but at the same time permits certain natural audacities and fears along with its moderating virtuous acts.

Hence there are three kinds of audacity, of which the first is fearlessness in confessing Christ before the powers of this world. The second is the audacity of undergoing and bearing with dreadful things for the sake of God. The third and highest is the audacity of committing oneself with the help of God in those things which one holds neither by sight, nor hearing, nor understanding through reason, but by faith alone. The first of these is addressed in the Gospel according to Matthew 10:19, "When you stand before kings and governors, take no thought how or what to speak: for it shall be given you in that hour what to speak," and in Jeremiah 17:16, "I am not troubled, following thee for my pastor, and I have not desired the day of man, thou knowest. That which went out of my lips, hath been right in thy sight." This was the audacity of the apostles, and especially of Paul to whom the Lord said in Acts 9:15 "Go thy way; for this man is to me a vessel of election, to carry my name before the Gentiles, and kings, and the children of Israel." This was also the audacity of Mattathias in I Maccabees 2:19-22, who confessed the "good confession," of faith unto salvation [as it is called in 1 Timothy. 6:12,] saying "with a loud voice," that is, with a strong and brave voice, "Although all nations obey king Antiochus, so as to depart every man from the service of the law of his fathers, and consent to his commandments: I and my sons, and my brethren will obey the law of our fathers. God be merciful unto us: it is not profitable for us to forsake the law, and the justices of God: We will not hearken to the words of kind Antiochus, neither will we sacrifice, and transgress the commandments of our law, to got another way." By this audacity, the same Mattathias [as related in I Maccabees 2:23-25] also slew the man sacrificing to idols upon the altar, as well as the soldier whom Antiochus had sent.

That audacity by which one dares to undergo danger and undertake hardships for the sake of God is addressed in Judges 5:2, "O you of Israel, that have willingly offered your lives to danger, bless the Lord." And, in the same chapter, verses 9-11, "My heart loveth the princes of Israel: O you that of your own good will offered yourselves to danger, bless the Lord. Speak, you that ride upon fair asses, and you that sit in judgment, and walk in the way. Where the chariots were dashed together, and the army of the enemies was choked, there let the justices of the Lord be rehearsed, and his clemency towards the brave men of Israel." The martyrs are those "riding upon fair asses," that is, their bodies are configured to the Lord in his suffering; and the Lord is seated on high by subjecting these bodies to "judgment" by which those judged by tyrants nourish the tyrants, walking in the way of truth, teaching, and life. They speak to us where "the chariots are dashed together," because in their audacity, by not withdrawing from justice on account of death, the chariots of the wickedness of the world are dashed together. These chariots have two wheels, namely tyranny and the power of the world. The "horse" that pulls them is wrath. The "driver" who holds the horses [by the reins] is unfaithfulness. The "whip" is rage. The "bridle" which directs and bridles the horse are the laws and decrees of the world. The "scythes" sticking out from the chariot wheels are the torments striking down the martyrs. But here the army of the devil is choked, because the constancy of the martyrs entirely subdues the army of the world. In this the justice of the Lord has appeared to overcome death and show clemency towards the brave men of the Church, so that what they did not do while alive, they might accomplish by dying. This was the audacity of the seven brothers of the Maccabees who suffered for the Lord, as is read in the whole of II Maccabees 7:1-42. This was also the audacity of their very stern mother, who was borne up in praise above the world, and was worthy of the memory of those who are good. Implanting a manly soul in her womanly thoughts, and seeing her seven sons perish in the span of a single day, she bore it with a good spirit for the sake of the hope which she had in God.

The third kind of audacity, that by which one ought to commit himself to God, is addressed in Deuteronomy 33:9, "Who hath said to his father, and to his mother: I do not know you; and to his brethren: I know you not: and their own children they have not known. These have kept thy word, and observed thy covenant." This is because they have fulfilled what is in Psalm 55:23, Cast thy care upon the Lord, and he shall sustain thee," and in I Peter 5:7, "Casting all your care upon him, for he hath care of you." Also, Augustine writes, "Cast yourself upon God, for he is not so cruel as to withdraw from you and allow you to fall." These are the three audacities which acts of holy fortitude always have accompanying them.

There are also three fears which always accompany it, namely initial fear, filial fear, and spousal fear. The fourth does not accompany holy fortitude, but precedes it, and that is servile fear.

Fear is servile when it avoids sin more on account of eternal punishment than for the sake of God. Whence Gregory writes that "there lives in him the will to sin, and the deed would follow if he could hope to get away without punishment." This is spoken of in Psalm 111:10, "The fear of the Lord is the beginning of wisdom. A good understanding to all that do it: his praise continueth for ever and ever." Augustine says that "'The fear of the Lord is the beginning of wisdom' just as a bristle is the beginning of a thread through which skins are sewn. Now, the thread does not enter except through the bristle, yet the thread is with the bristle in the skin." Likewise, servile fear introduces a taste of love for eternal things, yet it is not in the heart of man along with the taste itself. Thus, this kind of fear leads one to draw back from the act of sinning, but not from the will to sin, and this is spoken about in I John 4:18, "Perfect charity casteth out fear, because fear hath pain" and St. Gregory writes, "Since he is a judge, he is feared, because no one lovest he face of his judge." Such fear is from fear, not from humility.

Fear is initial when it is accompanied with fortitude at its beginning. Now, this fear does not fear eternal punishments directly, because it is mindful of pardon, but it still fears guilt on account of the dangerous impulse of temptations, and consequently it also fears eternal punishment, namely, if one should yield to guilt. This is the fear of those beginning to do the works of fortitude in whom there is indeed no sin, but who are still worn out by the residue of sin acquired by long-standing habit. This fear is dealt with in Malachi 1:6, "If I be a master, where is my fear?" and Ecclesiastes 12:13, "Fear God, and keep his commandments: for this is all man."

Fear is filial when it is consistent with perfect fortitude, because filial fear is that which fears being separated from one's father through the demerit of disinheritance. Lest such a demerit be permitted to occur, one is fearful and returns to the father, taking special care not to commit any act which offends his father's eyes. This is spoken of in Psalm 19:10, "The fear of the Lord is holy, enduring for ever and ever," and Isaiah 11:3 says, "He shall be filled with the spirit of the fear of the Lord. But, in Christ there was no fear except to the extent he showed reverence for the Father."

Fear is spousal when it is concerned neither with sin nor with punishment, but flees being separated from love's embrace. What it fears especially is that, because her spouse's love cools, he will delay his embrace, or even draw back from it. Thus Isaiah 26:17-18 says, "As a woman with child...so are we become in thy presence, O Lord. We have conceived, and been as it were in labor, and have brought forth wind," that is, [spousal] fear itself lacks power to save; yet [because it leads to a search for the lover's embrace also leads] to conception, that is, salvation.

Fortitude is accompanied by these three fears, that is, those which fear what is to be feared; but still well worth noting is that in us fear is matter both of virtue and of vice, as the philosophers say. This fear is one of the four natural passions: fear, joy, hope, and sadness. We have spoken of these above. Now, fear, if it is rightly ordered among these, is matter for virtue, yet, if it not rightly ordered, is a vice.

Filial fear is perfected through fortitude since fear is filial when it fears some sort of separation from the father by some blame that entails disinheritance and therefore less it admit such blame, it fears and reveres the father, carefully avoiding lest one commit what might offend the father's eyes and of this Psalm 19:10 says, "The fear of the Lord is holy, enduring for ever and ever: the judgments of the Lord are true, justified in themselves" and Isaiah 11:3 prophesies, "And he shall be filled with the spirit of the fear of the Lord." But in Christ there was no such fear except the reverence he showed to his Father.

Spousal fear, however, does not relate to sin or punishment but flies separation from the marriage embrace, and it fears this especially that because of decline of love of the other spouse that one will put off such an embrace or even refuse it. And about this Isaiah 26:17-18 says, "As a woman with child…so are we become in thy presence, O Lord. We have conceived, and been as it were in labour, and have brought forth spirit." that is, the spirit of salvation. Thus fear that causes a conception is spousal fear and fortitude is compatible with these three fears, that is, those which fear what is to be feared.

§ 2

After seeing according to what acts of strength the Valiant Woman is clothed, it is necessary to see what and of what sort are her visible parts that are clothed.

Cicero gives fortitude four parts: magnificence, fearlessness, patience, and perseverance. From Sacred Scripture, however, five others are added to his four: namely, faithfulness, confidence, longanimity, confirmation, and constancy.

Cicero says that "magnificence is the undertaking and administration of great and excellent things with a certain breadth of mind and splendid purpose," and by "great things" he means very difficult things, while by "excellent" he means what is raised above the ordinary. By "mind" he means "mental force" and by it's "breadth" he means that it includes in itself what can be called a commendable daring. It is "splendid" because of the end it intends, since it is done for some honest good and for God. And he also says that it is an "undertaking" to show that it is done while foreseeing the dangers involved and also how the act is to be begun and aggressively completed. He says "administration" to indicate that such a work must be done perfectly.

Cicero also says that in this division of fortitude "fearlessness" is "that through which the soul puts a certain trust along with hope in itself in matters that are great and honorable." He says "great things" as already explained and "honorable," according to Cicero, means what "draws us by its own force and attracts us by its dignity," when, namely, it is not merely useful or some pleasure that arouses appetite in something, but because of the beauty and goodness and plenitude in the thing itself, such as virtue, grace, etc. And this description also notes that fearlessness implies confidence of victory in difficult matters. Whence it is also evident that "faithfulness, confidence, and confirmation" which according to some are called "parts of fortitude" are rather properties and differences or conditions of faithfulness and so Cicero does not list them but includes them under faithfulness.

Cicero also says that "patience is the cause of the honesty or utility of arduous, difficult, voluntary, and long protracted suffering." What "honesty" means is evident from the foregoing. "Utility" according to Cicero and to St. Augustine in his *De Doctrina Christiana* and *De Trinitate* is "that for which anything is sought and especially for what is honest." Something is called "arduous" by Cicero for the same reason that it is called "exalted," namely, that it transcends what is humanly possible. The difficult is that which stands far off from acting and doing, since to do it requires us to collect all our power and virtue. Voluntary acts are called laborious for the reason that St. Augustine says, "No one does very well unwillingly although sometimes what he does unwillingly is good." It should be understood of the will that it is right reason because according to St. John Damascene if is not reasonable it is not really voluntary. And even the Philosopher says that "all will is in the reason." It is said to be "long protracted" because it must be sustained until the difficulty is overcome, because a person is not strong unless he begins strongly, progresses still more subtly and strongly, and most strongly finishes. And therefore Cicero also includes protracted longanimity under patience and does not make it a part in itself. But Sacred Scripture, since it lists a species of virtue for every difference and condition of virtue, lists more than does Cicero who speaks philosophically and properly.

Likewise, says Cicero, perseverance "properly considered is in the reason and is stable and there remains permanently." He calls it "reason properly considered," that is, "deliberate thinking about the true good which should be stably sought through the work of fortitude." He says "stable'" because a virtue of the soul does not change or vary. And it is called perpetual up to the consummation of a glorious victory. And therefore again constancy as such is included under perseverance because constancy is nothing other than an unchanging virtue of the soul. Strength however is included as a species of magnificence because strength is that by which a person lifts himself to some great work out of hope of victory.

Given these definitions of the virtues, next are to be considered the authority of the Saints concerning the acts of the Valiant Woman, that is, of the faithful soul.

As to magnificence it should be noted that it is fivefold, namely, thanksgiving, liberality or generosity, power, praise or glory, ad fortitude.

Of the magnificence of thanksgiving we read in II Maccabees 1:11; "Having been delivered by God out of great dangers, we give him great thanks, forasmuch as we have been in war with such a king," that is, the devil, the king of pride, of whom it is said in Job 1:25 that "He is king over all the children of pride."

Of the magnificence of liberality or generosity we read in Exodus 15:11 where Moses praises God in his gifts, saying, "Who is like to thee, among the strong, O Lord? Who is like to thee, glorious in holiness, terrible and praiseworthy, doing wonders? "

Of the magnificence of power we read in I Kings 10:23-24, "And King Solomon exceeded all the kings of the earth in riches, and wisdom. And all the earth desired to see Solomon's face, to hear his wisdom, which God had given in his heart." And this pertains to Christ, the Valiant Woman's husband who in power is King of kings, and Lord of lords. His riches of grace are profusely distributed to all creatures. Similarly his wisdom transcends all counting and exceeds the whole earth, which is all those who desire to see the glory of his face in that all long for blessedness, although not all seek it where it is to be found. Likewise, concerning this II Chronicles 9:22-23 says, "And Solomon was magnified above all the kings of the earth for riches and glory. And all the kings of the earth desired to see the face of Solomon that they might hear the wisdom which God had given in his heart."

Of the magnificence of praise it is said in Psalm 8:2, "For thy [the Lord's] magnificence is elevated above the heavens," that is, thy majesty is to be extolled by the magnificence of praise and Zechariah 12:7 says, "In that day shall the Lord protect the inhabitants of Jerusalem, and he that hath offended among them in that day shall be as David," And note that the magnificence of glory does not differ from magnificence of praise as St. Augustine says in commentary on the Epistle to the Romans at the end, "Glory is nothing other than clear knowledge with praise."

Of the magnificence of fortitude it is said in Lamentations 1:15, "The Lord hath taken away all my mighty men out of the midst of me [Jerusalem,]" that is, the strong men, and Isaiah 10:13 says, "On that day...I [God] will visit the fruit of the proud heart of the king of Assyria, and the glory of the haughtiness of his eyes." For the heart of the king of the Assyrians is here called "proud" because out of the magnificence of his heart he dared to invade Jerusalem.

Similarly according to Cicero fearlessness is included under magnificence and is fourfold, namely fearlessness in word, in internal spiritual consolation, in fortitude, and in fearlessness of support, which, however, is included under the fearlessness of fortitude.

Of fearlessness in word Deuteronomy 3:28 relates how the Lord says to Moses, "Command Josue, and encourage and strengthen him: for he shall go before this people, and shall divide unto them the land which thou shalt see," and Job 4:4 says, "Thy words have confirmed them that were staggering, and thou hast strengthened the trembling knees."

Of fearlessness in internal consolation Psalm 104:15 says, "Bread may strengthen man's heart," and Genesis 18:5, "And I will set a morsel of bread, and strengthen ye your heart." In these quotations "bread" signifies the intrinsic grace as it strengthens and supports. Also in Acts 9:19 it says, "And when he [Saul] had taken meat, he was strengthened."

Of fearlessness that is a species of fortitude Judith in Judith 13:7 prays, "Strengthen me," or in another translation, "Make me fearless O Lord God of Israel, and in this hour look on the works of my hands, that as thou hast promised, thou mayest raise up Jerusalem thy city: and that I may bring to pass that which I have purposed, having a belief that it might be done by thee." She says this when drawing her sword from its scabbard she stands to cut off the head of Holofernes. And in II Samuel 2:5-7 David say to the men of Jabes-Galaad who were burying Saul, "David therefore sent messengers to the men of Jabes Galaad, and said to them: Blessed be you to the Lord, who have shewn this mercy to your master Saul, and have buried him. And now the Lord surely will render you mercy and truth, and I also will, requite you for this good turn, because you have done this thing. Let your hands be strengthened, and be ye men of valor: for although your master Saul be dead, yet the house of Judah hath anointed me to be their king."

Of the fearlessness of support it says in I Kings 2:12, "And Solomon sat upon the throne of his father David, and his kingdom was strengthened' or supported, "exceedingly," but he did this with the support of God and of the people that accepted him as king. Also it says in I Kings 3:1, "And the kingdom was established in the hand of Solomon."

Next to be considered is confidence under which are included two virtues: assurance and confidence. These slightly differ and only in this that confidence is proper to men and hence relates to difficult acts. Assurance, however, relates to the size of the difficulties which it believes it can overcome. Confidence looks to divine aid and through it is assured that it can overcome. Two kinds of confidence are found in Sacred Scriptures, namely, the confidence of faith and the confidence of fortitude.

Of he first of these, namely hope, it is said in II Corinthians 1:8-10, "For we would not have you ignorant, brethren, of our tribulation, which came to us in Asia, that we were pressed out of measure above our strength, so that we were weary even of life. But we had in ourselves the answer of death that we should not trust in ourselves, but in God who raiseth the dead. Who hath delivered and doth deliver us out of so great dangers: in whom we trust that he will yet also deliver us." Hence 'diffidence' or lack of faith is distrust about something as in Romans 4:20-21 it is said of Abraham, "In the promise also of God he staggered not by distrust," that is, despair, "but was strengthened in faith, giving glory to God: Most fully knowing, that whatsoever he has promised, he is able also to perform." And also Ephesians 2:1-5 says, "And you, when you were dead in your offences, and sins, Wherein in time past you walked according to the course of this world, according to the prince of the power of this air, of the spirit that now worketh on the children of unbelief...God hath quickened us together in Christ."

Of the confidence of fortitude Hebrews 2:13 says, "I will put my trust in him." that is, I will have confidence of victory in Christ's fortitude and strength because Christ is stronger in that he is in divinity the same with the Father.

Assurance, however, is threefold: the assurance of faith, of hope, and of fortitude. The assurance of faith is that which works strenuously because of the certainty of faith. Assurance of hope is that which is spoken of in Acts 4:28, "And now, Lord, behold their threatenings," that is, of the persecutors, "and grant unto thy servants, that with all confidence they may speak thy word, by stretching forth thy hand to cures, and signs, and wonders to be done by the name of thy holy Son Jesus." likewise in Acts 18:24-26 it relates, ["Now a certain Jew, named Apollo, born at Alexandria, an eloquent man, came to Ephesus, one mighty in the scriptures. This man was instructed in the way of the Lord; and being fervent in spirit, spoke, and taught diligently the things that are of Jesus, knowing only the baptism of John."] Apollo was learned in the Scriptures and instructed in the way of the Lord and spoke fervently those things that the Scriptures prophesy about Jesus, yet knew only of the baptism of John. And thus in verse 26 it goes on to related that "This man therefore began to speak with assurance in the synagogue," and thus showed assuredly the certitude of his faith through consistency of his teaching and the fervor of his good works.

Of the assurance of hope Tobit 4:12 says, "Alms shall be a great assurance before the Most High God, to all them that give it." Here assurance is taken for the security of hope that is produced by almsgiving, because as a man is conscious that he has been liberal toward the poor, so he takes to himself some security from God's liberality. Of the hope of the impious, however, it is said in Job 8:13-14, ["Even so are the ways of all that forget God, and the hope of the hypocrite shall perish]. His folly shall not please him, and his trust shall be like the spider's web." Of the assurance of fortitude in II Chronicles 14:11 it is related that Zara, King of Ethiopia marched against Asa, King of Judah having with him ten hundred thousand men with three hundred chariots and came as far as Maresa where Asa met them and ordered his own army to fight in valley of Saphatha near Maresa. "And he called upon the Lord God, and said, 'O Lord, there is no difference with thee, whether thou help with few, or with many: help us, O Lord our God: for with confidence in thee, and in thy name, we are come against this multitude,'" that is, the devil, who is the king of the Moors or noisome Ethiopians, namely, sinners and the devils from hell. The "ten hundred thousand men signify the infinite ways of temptation which the devils use and as David cries out in Psalm 3:2-3, "Why, O Lord, are they multiplied that afflict me? Many are they who rise up against me. Many say to my soul: There is no salvation for him in his God." Asa is interpreted "lifting up what is made" and signifies the strong man who is always lifting up by his powers what God has made. Here he orders his troops against the demonic hordes in the valley of humility near Maresa, which is interpreted "amputation" because in his first charge he drives back the devil. The valley is called Saphatha which is interpreted "judging them" because humility always judges itself lest it be judged by God. Asa, who stands for the Valiant Woman, prays, raising himself up in fearlessness to God, saying he has confidence of victory in the Lord and in His Name because in comparison to the divine aid it matters little if there are few or many opponents. Hence it is evident from the fact that assurance presumes to conquer such difficulties it is the strength of soul to acts vigorously.

Confidence is also threefold; of faith, hope, ad fortitude. Of the confidence of faith Ephesians 3:11-12 says, "Christ Jesus our Lord: In whom we have boldness and access with confidence by the faith of him," and in Matthew 27:43 [those who crucified Jesus mocked him] saying, "He trusted in God; let him now deliver him if he will have him; for he said: I am the Son of God."

Of the confidence of hope it says in Hebrews 6:9, "But, my dearly beloved, we trust better things of you, and nearer to salvation; though we speak thus," and in Romans 2:19, "Art confident that thou thyself art a guide of the blind, a light of them that are in darkness," and in the following verse 21, "Thou therefore that teachest another, teachest not thyself," and Hebrews 10:35-36, "Do not therefore lose your confidence, which hath a great reward. For patience is necessary for you; that, doing the will of God, you may receive the promise."

Of the confidence of fortitude it says in Jeremiah 2:36-37, "Thou shalt be ashamed of Egypt, as thou wast ashamed of Assyria. For from thence thou shalt go, and thy hand shall be upon thy head: for the Lord hath destroyed thy trust, and thou shalt have nothing prosperous therein," where the Lord is speaking of the Jews who had made a treaty with the Egyptians against the Assyrians and intended that as they had been oppressed by the Assyrians they would be mixed with the Egyptians, since otherwise they might not get their aid. Hence the Jews had trusted in them, but the Lord disdained that trust and impeded it by handing over the Egyptians to the Assyrians. When it says "Thy hand shall be upon thy head," it means "because of your great grief;" it means according to the literal sense that this confidence is a species of fortitude that presumes because of some source of aid it will conquer. Assyria which means "blessed" signifies the prosperity of this moral life in which evil men are frustrated because of their sins. "Egypt" which is interpreted "grief" or "anguish" signifies adversity in which we are depressed, since we are elevated by prosperity and dejected by adversity. Confidence, however, is worldly when it is the pleasures of life and youth, etc. because of which the Lord on the day of our death will inflict intolerable grief which is signified by that gesture of hands on head. Likewise Zephaniah 2:25, speaking of this world says, "This is the glorious city that dwelt in security: that said in her heart: I am, and there is none beside me: how is she become a desert, a place for beasts to lie down in? Every one that passeth by her, shall hiss, and wag his hand." For this world will be a desert on the day of judgment and is even now the habitation of beasts, that is of devils; and the Saints who pass through it, do not tarry in this world but laugh at it in derision and move their hands to push it aside lest anything of worldly business should stick to them.

Next patience is treated, which according to Cicero is the third kind of fortitude and this is threefold: first the patience of an ass, second of astuteness or cleverness, and third the patience of virtue, which is twofold; the patience of hope and the patience of fortitude.

The patience of hope is the expectation of something hoped for without dejection of soul Romans 8:24-25 says, "For we are saved by hope. But hope that is seen is not hope. For what a man seeth, why doth he hope for? But if we hope for that which we see not, we wait for it with patience," and Hebrews 10:36 says, "For patience is necessary for you; that, doing the will of God, you may receive the promise."

Asinine patience, however, is that which arise from the dullness of the senses when one does not know how to avoid injuries and therefore calmly tolerates them, and this is the patience of those who are drunk as they are described in Proverbs 23:35, "They have beaten me, but I was not sensible of pain: they drew me, and I felt not: when shall I awake, and find wine again?"

Of the patience of astuteness, namely, patience which seems to ignore injuries, not however in order to endure them, but to sustain them calmly for a time, as is show in II Maccabees 5:24-26, where it says that King Antiochus "sent that hateful prince Apollonius with an army of two and twenty thousand men, commanding him to kill all that were of perfect age, and to sell the women and the younger sort. Who when he was come to Jerusalem, pretending peace, rested till the holy day of the Sabbath: and then the Jews keeping holiday, he commanded his men to take arms. And he slew all that were come forth to see: and running through the city with armed men, he destroyed a very great multitude." Here it is evident that Apollonius was patient for a time out of deceit or astuteness. And the moral lesson of this is that because Apollonius signifies the devil, along with his satellites, namely lust, fornication, greed, and other vices of this kind. Jerusalem, however, not literally but spiritually, signifies the soul of the Jews who confess and glorify the Lord. They are not captured before the feast day but on it because as long as a good man is occupied with some work, the devil abide his time to tempt him and waits, but when he sees the man leave his house and become a target for worldly vanities and pomps and the attractions of worldly pleasures and spectacles, the devil takes with him the seven spirits more evil than himself, [as it says in Luke 11:27], "Then he [the devil that was cast out of a man] goeth and taketh with him seven other spirits more wicked than himself, and entering in they dwell there. And the last state of that man becomes worse than the first." And thus proceeding, the satellites of the devil first destroy men of mature age, that is, engaged in works of perfection, by involving them in pleasure with loose, women and then they sell the young ones, lusting in the desires of the flesh, to sin habitually. This was the astute patience by which Cain hid his anger against his mother and father and called Abel as a friend away from other men and then murdered him, [as it says in Genesis 4:8, "Cain said to Abel his brother: Let us go forth abroad. And when they were in the field, Cain rose up against his brother Abel, and slew him."

Of the patience that is properly a virtue, however, it is said in James 1:4, "Patience hath a perfect work; that you may be perfect and entire, failing in nothing," in Luke 21:19, "In your patience you shall possess your souls," and in Proverbs 25:15, and "By patience a prince shall be appeased, and a soft tongue shall break hardness," that is, by the words of patience. And in these three authoritative texts are mentioned the three effects of patience: first the perfection of work, second the immediate control of one's soul when anger stirs as contrasted to yielding to anger, and third the propitiating of God and the softening of his justice.

Longanimity, according to Cicero, is also contained under patience, but in the Sacred Scriptures is threefold: namely, of mercy, of hope, and of fortitude.

The longanimity of mercy is that which defers punishing the wrongdoer and conceals indignation so as in this way to draw the guilty to repentance and which is mentioned in Romans 2:4, "Or despisest thou the riches of his [God's] goodness, and patience, and longsuffering? Knowest thou not, that the benignity of God leadeth thee to penance?" and also in Psalm 103:8, "The Lord is compassionate and merciful: longsuffering and plenteous in mercy."

As to the longanimity of hope it should be noted that hope is said to be longanimous when with equanimity one waits for something promised that one hopes for oneself, as is mentioned in Hebrews 6:13-15, "For God making promise to Abraham, because he had no one greater by whom he might swear, swore by himself, saying: Unless blessing I shall bless thee, and multiplying I shall multiply thee. And so patiently enduring he obtained the promise."

The longanimity of fortitude by which someone tolerates adversity and is able to continue in danger until victory is attained is noted in II Corinthians 6:4-6, where the Apostle says, "Let us exhibit ourselves as the ministers of God, in much patience, in tribulation, in necessities, in distresses, In stripes, in prisons, in seditions, in labors, in watchings, in fastings, In chastity, in knowledge, in longsuffering, in sweetness, in the Holy Ghost, in charity unfeigned." This same longanimity the Apostle put among the gifts of the Holy Spirit in Galatians 5:22-23, ["But the fruit of the Spirit is, charity, joy, peace, patience, benignity, goodness, longanimity, mildness, faith, modesty, continency, chastity. Against such there is no law," and James 5:10-11 says the same, "Take, my brethren, for an example of suffering evil, of labour and patience, the prophets, who spoke in the name of the Lord. Behold, we account them blessed who have endured. You have heard of the patience of Job, and you have seen the end of the Lord, that the Lord is merciful and compassionate."

Finally we consider perseverance which is last part of fortitude and constancy is with and under it. It should be noted, however, that perseverance is threefold. First it is sometimes the determination to continue in any good action once it has been begun and is called perseverance; and St. Augustine writes in his book *De Bono Perseverantiae* that this is called the "gift of perseverance" that is given to a man as he begins a good work since without it no one begins such a work and continues it to life's end, for not until this work is finished can he be said to have persevered in it. Second, perseverance is said to be the actual continuation in the good until that end. Continuation in evil, however, as St. Augustine says, ought rather to be called "pertinacity." Third, it is called perseverance because by it the effort of the soul continues to work in spite of a difficulty up to its overcoming and this is a part or species of fortitude.

Of the first kind of perseverance which is nothing other than the determination to persevere in a good action once it is begun, Job 15:29-30 speaks of the hypocrite who does not have the intention of persevering in the good he has begun but only does this until he has done what follows what he really intends, "He shall not be enriched, neither shall his substance continue, neither shall he push his root in the earth. He shall not depart out of darkness: the flame shall dry up his branches, and he shall be taken away by the breath of his own month." He does not enrich himself in virtue because he does not persevere in the substance of his work, that is, he does not have the intention of persevering in it and therefore he does not plant the "root" of humility in the earth as a stable life, since as it says in Ecclesiastes 1:4, "The earth standeth for ever." And therefore he his heart does not withdraw from the "darkness" of sin and the "flame" of human praise consumes the "branches" of his work and "he shall be taken away' that is by God "by the breath of his own month," that is, he shall die since his head is the Antichrist.

Of the perseverance which is the continuation of the good clear to its end Matthew 10:22 says, "He that shall persevere unto the end, he shall be saved," and later 24:12-13 says, "And because iniquity hath abounded, the charity of many shall grow cold. But he that shall persevere to the end, he shall be saved."

Of the third species of perseverance that is a species of fortitude it says in Hebrews 12:7, "Persevere under discipline. God dealeth with you as with his sons; for what son is there, whom the father doth not correct?" Discipline, however, is the leaning of moral through trials, when it is the same to persevere in discipline as to persevere in trials.

Finally to be considered is constancy which can be reduced to perseverance. There is, however, a twofold constancy, namely of maturity and of fortitude. Constancy of maturity is when someone from the dissoluteness of debauchery regularly prefers a calm appearance and attitude. Constancy of fortitude, however, is when some out of the strength of a magnificent soul do not become dejected no matter how long they remain in adversity but persist in good works. When, however, a person shows themselves that way in evil works, it is only abusively called constancy, but should properly be called obstinacy.

The first kind of constancy is spoken of in Acts 4:13, "Now seeing the constancy of Peter and of John, understanding that they were illiterate and ignorant men, they wondered; and they knew them that they had been with Jesus," since the disciples of Jesus were known for their constancy in good works. Similarly in Acts 13:46 it is related how when the Jews were unwilling to hear the Word, "Then Paul and Barnabas said boldly: To you it behooved us first to speak the word of God: but because you reject it, and judge yourselves unworthy of eternal life, behold we turn to the Gentiles," for constancy is nothing other than this persevering in regular teaching and preaching.

Of the constancy of fortitude we read in Wisdom 5:1, "Then shall the just stand with great constancy against those that have afflicted them, and taken away their labors," and II Chronicles 20:17, according to the Septuagint states, "Be constant and you will see the help of the Lord over you"; although the version of St. Jerome has "Stand confidently and you will see the help of the Lord over you." Also I Maccabees 2:16, relates, ["Many of the people of Israel consented, and came to them: but Mattathias and his sons stood firm,"] says that many of the Jews, fearing Antiochus, departed from the law of God but afterwards Mattathias and his sons remained constant.

And the above are the nine parts of fortitude found by the Saints which we have explained as well as we are able.

Next follows a third division that deals with how the act of fortitude and its parts fit the clothing of the Valiant Woman. To do this three things are necessary: "scissors" to cut and shape the pieces, a "needle" to sew them, and "threads" joining and connecting all the pieces.

The scissors that shape these parts of the clothing is reason and it has two blades that come together, one is faith, the other the authority of Scripture and these two blades are connected by the key of the intellectual understanding of the truth as these two blades close together. Of this under another metaphor it is said in Hosea 6:5, "For this reason have I hewed [Latin *dolavi*, axed] them by the prophets, I have slain them by the words of my mouth: and thy judgments shall go forth as the light," in that here what is metaphorically called an "axe" I have called scissors. Again it says in Isaiah

41:7, "The coppersmith striking with the hammer encouraged him that forged at that time, saying: It is ready for soldering." For the Valiant Woman is a craftsman in brass who vigorously pounds the work of fortitude saying that it is good for the soldering that holds the whole work in one piece. We, however, use another metaphor because nothing more is said about bronze working in the Scriptures.

The needle is wisdom penetrating all the cloth and neatly disposing the garment to fit becomingly as it says in Wisdom 8:1, "She reacheth therefore from end to end mightily, and ordereth all things sweetly.

The thread of fortitude is all that connects the parts of its work, that is, equanimity; for equanimity is not part of fortitude nor its act but is all its parts and in all its acts connecting them all lest they fall apart, as the Angel says to Tobit 5:13, "Be of good courage, thy cure from God is at hand." The soul is not down cast by difficulties when in that soul equanimity is strong. And thus is fitted the Valiant Woman's clothing.

§ 3

The next consideration is about the "beauty of her clothing" and first we proceed by defining this beauty as to its appropriateness; for the Philosopher says that: "beauty is the elegant measure of the parts of thing;" when the color corresponds to the shape of the face, and the disposition of the hair sets off the face by their contrasting comparison. Thus the woman who is beautiful and becoming is praised in the Song of Songs 6:3, ["Thou art beautiful, O my love, sweet and comely as Jerusalem."] She is beautiful in disposition of the parts of her body and comely in their proportion. Therefore we accept that this woman has clothing of beautiful glory.

Natural beauty consists in the due proportion or commensuration of nature so that the flesh is under the control of the spirit and reason rules as the mistress and the will obeys it in all matters. Sensuality is restrained from excessive sensual desire as a handmaid or wanton daughter, and the concupiscible powers are subservient to reason in al things, and the irascible powers also are tempered easily, and thus the body as a whole is subject to the spirit and the spirit to reason, and reason also to God. And this beauty is the rectitude and honor of human nature, as is said in Psalm 49:13, "Man when he was in honor did not understand; he is compared to senseless beasts, and is become like to them," and in Ecclesiastes 7:30, "Only this I have found, that God made man right, and he hath entangled himself with an infinity of questions," that is, with questions of the devil that are still not answered, which the devil proposed in Paradise and which even to this day we are not able give their final perfect solution. Yet man is also sometimes called the "image" of God according to which he was made as it says in Genesis 1:27, "And God created man to his own image: to the image of God he created him: male and female he created them," and in Sirach 17:1, "God created man of the earth, and made him after his own image," and this image consists in this that man is governed by reason and his other powers also and his body is subject to his spirit and to the Spirit of God, as it says in Genesis 1:26, "And he [God] said: Let us make man to our image and likeness: and let him have dominion over the fishes of the sea, and the fowls of the air, and the beasts, and the whole earth, and every creeping creature that moveth upon the earth." The "fishes in the sea" that are nourished in the waters are our impulses for pleasure. The "birds of heaven" are impulses of pride and other spiritual sins. The "creeping creatures that move upon the earth" are our impulses of earthly animality, such as the tendency to greed, etc.

The beauty of virtue is in the harmony of all the virtues, so that temperance places its mode and measure in them all, fortitude its striving in them all, justice its decency and propriety in them all, and prudence its guidance and direction in them all. When temperance places a limit it produces meekness and gentleness. When it affects the manner of our exterior behavior it makes for moderation. When it measures pleasure in the power of procreation it makes for continence, virginal modesty, the chastity of widowhood, and conjugal restraint; of which the first always abstains in heart and body from all sex; the second abstains from all sex but not always, the third not from all sex nor always but does abstain after the death of the partner, and the fourth abstains sometimes, as in the time of prayer but after that resumes relations with its partner lest it be tempted by Satan to incontinence. Temperance also controls the pleasures which are involved in eating and makes for moderation.

Similarly fortitude furnishes strength in the difficulties raised for us by others even those which arise within ourselves such as sickness and it also makes us magnanimous in reason and in faith.

In suffering it makes us patient and strong to endure in perseverance.

Justice also in the same way makes us speak the truth, perform what is due in our works, obey and respect superiors, show piety, honor, and generosity to our neighbors and mercy to our inferiors in their miseries and by almsgiving, but also to show humility with regard to ourselves. Judges, vested with justice, act with clemency and humanity in passing judgment, fairness in their sentences, strictness in vindication, religious reverence to God and propriety in worship.

Prudence maintains order based on the memory of past experiences, examines and directs the present, and clarifies understanding, yet also carefully looks to the future so as to gain foresight for us and finally it operates with caution in dangers, takes counsel in doubtful matters, but in situations that are certain governs with certain understanding.

And again the beauty of these virtues is in how they relate to each other, for unless temperance is applied to situations prudence can not be effective and justice will be excessive and in dangers fortitude will become headlong. For unless fortitude gives force to every action, resolution will become weakened in every difficulty; and it is with difficulties that every virtue is concerned. Likewise unless justice determines what is proper and due, all action will be rejected, for [as Sirach 20:22 says, "A parable coming out, of a fool's mouth shall be rejected: for he doth not speak it in due season."] Again unless prudence governs every act, [as Matthew 15:14] says "the blind will fall into a ditch," and so will we fall into dangers we did not foresee.

Thus God has built the virtues so that there is no separation between them, whence they are respectful of each other so what one does not supply we get from another and what we have from the other quickly communicates with its companion so that the aid we did not get from one is quickly and mutually supplied by both.

This comeliness and beauty refers not only to the human body but also to the Church in which grace enables each member to communicate with the others and thus have all life in common, yet each part to have its proper function distributed to it as is said in Romans 12:4-6, where the Apostle says, "For as in one body we have many members, but all the members have not the same office: So we being many, are one body in Christ, and every one members one of another. And having different gifts, according to the grace that is given us," and also in I Corinthians 12:14-27, "For the body also is not one member, but many. If the foot should say, because I am not the hand, I am not of the body; is it therefore not of the body? And if the ear should say, because I am not the eye, I am not of the body; is it therefore not of the body? If the whole body were the eye, where would be the hearing? If the whole were hearing, where would be the smelling? But now God hath set the members every one of them in the body as it hath pleased him. And if they all were one member, where would be the body? But now there are many members indeed, yet one body. And the eye cannot say to the hand: I need not thy help; nor again the head to the feet: I have no need of you. Yea, much more those that seem to be the more feeble members of the body, are more necessary. And such as we think to be the less honorable members of the body, about these we put more abundant honor; and those that are our uncomely parts, have more abundant comeliness. But our comely parts have no need: but God hath tempered the body together, giving to that which wanted the more abundant honor, that there might be no schism in the body; but the members might be mutually careful one for another. And if one member suffer any thing, all the members suffer with it; or if one member glory, all the members rejoice with it. Now you are the body of Christ, and members of member." Similarly this is the case with all the virtues in the soul to which this quotation is easily adapted.

This Valiant Woman also has the beauty of the theological virtues, namely, faith, hope, and charity which three unite her to God making her beautiful in his sight. The four other virtues make her beautiful before men so that what is said in Wisdom 4:1 is true of her, "O how beautiful is the chaste generation with glory: for the memory thereof is immortal: because it is known both with God," through her beauty, "and with men," through her virtues. For faith joins us to the First Truth, hope unites us to eternal blessedness, love unites us to Goodness. Similarly these virtues have the beauty of harmony, since faith shows us God, hope reaches out to him, and charity embraces him. In the same way they are in harmony in building of the heart, as it says in II Corinthians 3:11, "For other foundation no man can lay, but that which is laid; which is Christ Jesus."

St. Ambrose in the Gloss explains that "Christ in the heart is the faith of Christ in the heart, as the Apostle says in Colossians 1:23, "in the faith, grounded." Hope, however, erects the walls and charity crowns the edifice." In the same way in a work they have beauty of preparation, for charity draws forth the work, hope leads to its reward, and faith directs its intention, as St. Augustine testify when he says that "the good intention causes the work, but faith directs that intention." These three are referred to in I Corinthians 13:13, "And now there remain faith, hope, and charity, these three: but the greatest of these is charity." These are the three men who [in Genesis 18:2] appeared to Abraham in the valley of Mambre and these are also the three young men in Daniel 3:13-97 and following. who came out unharmed from the fiery furnace, that is, from the wickedness of this world.

The beauty of all these things is noted in I Kings 10:4-5, "And when the queen of Saba saw all the wisdom of Solomon, and the house which he had built, and the meat of his table, and the apartments of his servants, and the order of his ministers, and their apparel, and the cupbearers, and the holocausts, which he offered in the house of the Lord: she had no longer any spirit in her." The Queen of Saba is worldly wisdom which consists in much eloquence, and she is interpreted by another interpretation as "captive" because she is captured in the service of Christ; but according to a third interpretation means "conversion" because she was converted to Christ. The "house" built by Solomon is the house of spiritual edification which was built by a peaceful man, that is, by Christ. "Wisdom" is the taste of eternity. The "meat of his table" is the refreshment and sweetness of all the virtues. "The apartments of his servants" are the powers of the soul, rational, irascible, and concupiscible in which the servants of Christ, namely the virtues, dwell. The "order of his ministers" is the order of the virtues as we have explained them. The "apparel", however, is the habitual works of the virtues and of grace. The "cupbearers' are those who pour out the wine of spiritual joy that gladdens the hearts of men who are disposed according to the beauty of virtue. The "holocausts" offered to the fire of devotion are three; namely, faith, hope and charity 'in the house of the Lord God," that is, in the heart. Seeing this, I say secular wisdom ceased to have its spirit of secularity but yielded to the Spirit of God.

These two sets of virtues, namely, the political and theological, are symbolized by Martha and Mary [Luke 10:38-42] For the theological virtues concern God, while the cardinal virtues satisfy the frequent service that are performed for men. They are signified through the arrangement of the Angels in heaven of which there are three choirs that serve God, some of whom perform one ministry while others perform other ministries. And this is enough to say about the beauty of the virtues of this most Valiant Woman.

Next comes a consideration of the beauty of her work and there are kinds of being in her work, namely, that it is licit, honest, and useful. For a licit work is beautiful in relation to God, honest in relation to herself, and useful for her neighbor.

According to St. Augustine something is licit if it is not prohibited by any commandment and the Valiant Woman attends to this first of all in her work. But granted that it is licit it is still must be considered whether it is honest. A work is honest that is worthy of praise in the light of the conscience of men or at least that nothing in it would be called shameful by honest persons. When, however, the Valiant Woman finds nothing shameful in a work, she still ponders whether it is really useful for her neighbor, for thus it fits what the Apostle says in Romans 12:17, "Providing good things, not only in the sight of God, but also in the sight of all men." For if all things that are licit should be done at once, the Apostle would not have said in I Corinthians 6:12, "Providing good things, not only in the sight of God, but also in the sight of all men," because some things that are in themselves licit are not helpful for the salvation of neighbors, of which the same Apostle says, I Corinthians 8:9. "But 8:10take heed lest perhaps this your liberty become a stumbling block to the weak," and he speaking of those who before weak persons eat meat offered before idols and therefore later in verse 13 he goes on to say, "Wherefore, if meat scandalize my brother, I will never eat flesh, lest I should scandalize my brother." Again if all that is licit was also honest, the Apostle would not have said, as he did in I Corinthians 6:12, "All things are lawful to me, but I will not be brought under the power of any," that is, I do not give others the occasion of judging me from my work even if it is not prohibited by a commandment, for what is judged by another has some appearance of indecency or shamefulness. Therefore the perfect beauty of a work is that it is licit, honest and useful for the salvation of my neighbors. Hence the Apostle in Philippians 4:8 says, "Whatsoever things are true, whatsoever modest," that is, honest,., whatsoever just," that is, licit, whatsoever holy, whatsoever lovely, whatsoever of good fame" that is, useful for the neighbor's good, "if there be any virtue, if any praise of discipline, think on these things." And also he says in I Timothy 2:12, "We should live soberly, and justly, and godly in this world' and here "justly," means licitly; "soberly" means lest we through an appearance of shame lose honesty; and "godly" means with usefulness to our neighbor because it is impious to do injury to our neighbor by scandalizing him.

This Valiant Woman also has beauty that is not vainglory but true glory.

This glory is threefold.... | of Conscience
| of Hope
| of Trial

The "glory" of conscience is the joy which rises from the peace and security of conscience. The Apostles says in II Corinthians 1:12, "For our glory is this, the testimony of our conscience, that in simplicity of heart and sincerity of God, and not in carnal wisdom, but in the grace of God, we have conversed in this world: " This glory arises particularity from three things existing in the conscience; first that it is not grieved by guilt and this is produced by purity from sin; second that is has security from an abundance of merit; and third because in its life and works it has the testimony of the Holy Spirit, because according to tradition of the Fathers of the Church and sacred eloquence the Valiant Woman is so gifted, as the Apostle says Romans 9:1, "I speak the truth in Christ, I lie not, my conscience bearing me witness in the Holy Ghost." Abel was also praised for his glory as Hebrews 11:4 says, "By faith Abel offered to God a sacrifice exceeding that of Cain, by which he obtained a testimony that he was just, God giving testimony to his gifts; and by it he being dead yet speaketh," as the Apostle says, Romans 14:23, "For all that is not of faith is sin," and the Gloss says that "all that is not from the faith of conscience instructs one about the way to hell."

Of the glory of trial or tribulation the Apostle in Galatians 6:14 says, "But God forbid that I should glory, save in the cross of our Lord Jesus Christ; by whom the world is crucified to me, and I to the world," and II Corinthians 11:30 says, "If I must needs glory, I will glory of the things that concern my infirmity and the same epistle 12:9-10 says, "Gladly therefore will I glory in my infirmities, that the power of Christ may dwell in me...For when I am weak, then am I powerful," and by "infirmity" the Apostle means the passion of trial.

Of the three kinds of glory taken together Isaiah 35:2 says, "The glory of Libanus is given to it: the beauty of Carmel, and Saron," that is, is given to the Valiant Woman. Libanus is interpreted "whiten", hence the "glory of Libanus" is glory in a white or clean conscience. Saron is interpreted "a mourning prince" and signifies lordship of glory in the mourning of trial. This is the threefold beautiful glory having nothing unfitting since it has nothing of vanity. For this Valiant Woman is not glorified as in this world many are glorified as it says in Psalm 52:3-5, "Why dost thou glory in malice, thou that art mighty in iniquity? All the day long thy tongue hath devised injustice: as a sharp razor, thou hast wrought deceit. Thou hast loved malice more than goodness: and iniquity rather than to speak righteousness." For some glory in mocking the dignity of others of whom the Apostle says in Romans 11:18, "Boast not against the branches. But if thou boast, thou bearest not the root, but the root thee." Others also glory in belittling the merits of others of whom I Corinthians 4:7 says, "For who distinguisheth thee? Or what hast thou that thou hast not received? And if thou hast received, why dost thou glory, as if thou hadst not received it?" Still others glory in wisdom for the sake of riches and its power against whom Jeremiah 9:23-24 says, "Let not the wise man glory in his wisdom, and let not the strong man glory in his strength, and let not the rich man glory in his riches: But let him that glorieth glory in this, that he understandeth and knoweth me," that is, through his secret conscience. But this Valiant Woman lest she glory in the power of her fortitude accepts it after the example of the most strong Samson [Judges 16:4-21] whom the little, weak harlot woman seduced by the temptation of a false love so that she might cut his hair and hand him over to the Philistines who blinded him and made him grind in the mill. "Samson" is interpreted "strong sun" and signifies one in whom shines the Son of justice, Christ our Lord. For such a one is very strong because his most strong support is Christ. The "little harlot" is lust which cuts of "hair" that is the beginning of thoughts of God and arouses thoughts of pleasure by which someone is so weakened and seduced that they are without resistance handed over to the "Philistines," that is he demons, who blind their victim with the sweetness of pleasure and make him "grind the mill," that is, circle around in the vanities of this world.

Lest the Valiant Woman glory in riches she takes as an example the Parable of Lazarus and the Rich Man dressed in purple who was buried in hell, related in Luke 16:19-31. Lest again she might glory vainly in wisdom, Solomon was a an example for her, since although the ends of the earth admired his wisdom, he fell through women so that he worship many idols [I Kings 11:1-9]. Lest the Valiant Woman glory in nobility of birth she had for example the shame as regards birth which no human being, not even kings, can escape that of which I Maccabees 2:62 says, "And fear not the words of sinful man, for his glory is dung, and worms," and worse than dung since it is polluted by such vileness that it is beyond words to describe. Likewise she accepts the medicine of grievous death lest she in death should glory as it says in Sirach 41:1, "O death, how bitter is the remembrance of thee to a man that hath peace in his possessions!" Lest the Valiant Woman should glory in life she takes an example from its incertitude which as I Maccabees 2:63 says, "Today he is lifted up, and tomorrow he shall not be found, because he is returned into his earth; and his thought is come to nothing," and Isaiah 40:67 says, "The voice of one, saying: Cry. And I said: What shall I cry? All flesh is grass, and all the glory thereof as the flower of the held. The grass is withered, and the dower is fallen, because the spirit of the Lord," that is, the judgment of God's wrath "hath blown upon it," namely, in death. In these ways, therefore, the Valiant Woman puts away glory, knowing such glory has no comeliness.

There is, however, a spiritual comeliness for this Valiant Woman in the victory of fortitude to which victory there are seven rewards that are enumerated in Revelation 1:11 and ascribed according to the order of seven churches ["which are in Asia, to Ephesus, and to Smyrna, and to Pergamus, and to Thyatira, and to Sardis, and to Philadelphia, and to Laodicea"] and some of these on the part of a warrior's body, some on the part of a warrior's soul, and some pertain to his body and soul taken together. For a fighting body often is killed through the exercise of fortitude and therefore will be made be made perfectly comely through immortality, it says in Revelation 2:7, "I will give to eat of the tree of life, which is in the paradise of my God," for the fruit of the tree of life is eaten as a remedy for death which it takes way through the taste of wisdom in the kingdom of Paradise and heavenly bliss. The soul of a warrior sometimes vacillates from weakness of will, for it can fall into sin, and therefore in Revelation 2:11, it is promised to a victor that he "shall not be hurt by the second death," because he will be confirmed in the good so that he can no longer slip into the death of hell through sin.

Yet in this life the soul of the warrior is afflicted by the fact that he still only possesses God in faith, while if he possessed him now in sight he would more easily sustain adversity. Hence in the third place Revelation 2:17 says, "To him that overcometh, I will give the hidden manna, and will give him a white counter, and in the counter, a new name written, which no man knoweth, but he that receiveth it." And in this verse are three things which the afflicted soul perfectly attributes to eternal joy. First is he sweetness of the taste of divinity that it even now attains and this is noted as the "hidden manna" which will not be "hidden" in eternity, but only here in this life during which we walk through faith and not through sight. Second he expects the most certain, clear and lucid vision of truth, which is noted through the "white counter" or stone[amulet], so that in that stone is noted solidity and in its whiteness the splendor of divine truth as even now we know it speculatively [in theology]. The third is that our God is enriched by the eternal name of honor and hereditary glory and this is noted in the "new name written, which no man knoweth, but he that receiveth it" since this is a name other than the worldly name by which God will calls his servant into the promised kingdom.

On the part of both body and soul, fortitude is decorated with a fourfold reward. The first is total defeat of those against whom he battles, as it says in Revelation 4:26-27, "And he that shall overcome, and keep my works unto the end, I will give him power over the nations. And he shall rule them with a rod of iron." The "nations" are the world and the tyrants who battle the Saints and who in hell are ruled with a "rod of iron" appropriate to their sins, when, as it says in Psalm 149:5-6, "The Saints shall rejoice in glory: they shall be joyful in their beds. The high praise of God shall be in their mouth: and two-edged swords in their hands," meaning by "two edged swords in their hands" that they will be victorious in body and soul.

The second reward of fortitude is in the signs of a young warrior, since a beginner who conquers is decorated with certain new medals as is noted in Revelation 3:5, "He that shall overcome, shall thus be clothed in white garments, and I will not blot out his name out of the book of life." For this "white garment" is the body and its "name will not be blotted out" since once resurrected it will survive in eternal life.

Fortitude has still a third reward, namely, because the house of God, the Church is sustained by fortitude in its weak members by preventing them from falling away from the faith and therefore in the kingdom of God it will be glorified, for this as is said in Revelation 3:12, "I will make him a pillar in the temple of my God; and he shall go out no more; and I will write upon him the name of my God, and the name of the city of my God, the new Jerusalem." The columns of a temple are what upholds the temple and since they continue to do so they never move further outside it as it says in Sirach 50:1-2, "Simon the high priest, the son of Onias, who in his life propped up the house, and in his days fortified the temple. By him also the height of the temple was founded, the double building and the high walls of the temple." Since, however, such a column is set for the sake of justice the name of God is inscribed on it as an everlasting memorial and since the wall supports the city of the Saints therefore the name of the city of Jerusalem is forever inscribed on it.

The fourth and ultimate reward of fortitude is a crown for the sake of which it is fought as the Apostle says II Timothy 4:7-8, "I have fought a good fight, I have finished my course, I have kept the faith. As to the rest, there is laid up for me a crown of justice, which the Lord the just judge will render to me in that day," and this is likewise noted in Revelation 3:21, "To him that shall overcome, I will give to sit with me in my throne: as I also have overcome, and am set down with my Father in his throne." For unless crowned to reign; no one sits on a throne.

What follows is the third thing that we said above must be considered namely how the Valiant Woman is clothed in these garments. To put it briefly she must be dressed as a married woman and dressed for the pleasure of her husband.

She is dressed as married woman by the same virtues alreay mentioned, for of a married woman it is said in Psalm 93:1, "The Lord hath reigned, he is clothed with beauty: the Lord is clothed with strength, and hath girded himself," that is with virtue. The Valiant Woman also is dressed with propriety and fortitude and thus is fulfilled concerning what Sirach 17:2 says of God that he "clothed him [Adam] with strength according to himself." But it is very important to note that in the clothing of the Valiant Woman, covering is first, and comeliness second, but the converse is the case in the garments of the Lord because for him comeliness precedes his strength, while wonderfully for the woman it is her strength with regard to suffering that gains her the comeliness of glory, as I Peter 1:11 says, "sufferings that are in Christ, and the glories that should follow" and in I Corinthians 4:17, "For that which is at present momentary and light of our tribulation, worketh for us above measure exceedingly an eternal weight of glory" and Romans 8:17-18, "If we suffer with him, that we may be also glorified with him. For I reckon that the sufferings of this time are not worthy to be compared with the glory to come, that shall be revealed in us." But the reverse is true of Christ since he comes from glory to the struggle of battle, as

Philippians 2:6-8 says, "Who being in the form of God, thought it not robbery to be equal with God: But emptied himself, taking the form of a servant, being made in the likeness of men, and in habit found as a man. He humbled himself, becoming obedient unto death, even to the death of the cross."

The Valiant Woman is dressed in garments to the delight of her husband so that he will take pleasure in her as Esther 5:1-2 reates, "And on the third day Esther put on her royal apparel, and stood in the inner court of the king's house, over against the king's hall:now he sat upon his throne in the hall of the palace, over against the door of the house. And when he saw Esther the queen standing, she pleased his eyes, and he held out toward her the golden scepter, which he held in his hand: and she drew near, and kissed the top of his scepter." "Esther" is interpreted "hidden" and signifies the Valiant Woman whose humanity hides her strength. Her "royal apparel" is the garment in which King Assuerus, who is interpreted "happy" himself clothed her and signifies being clothed in Christ and this is fortitude and comeliness of her clothing. She stood "in the inner court on the third day" and the first of these days is that of her birth, the second day of her maturing life, and the third day is that of her glorification when she stands in "the inner court." And then because of its freedom from any stain her garment of glory pleases the eyes of the king because he sees its loveliness. To "hold out toward her the golden scepter" of his clemency means simply show her the light and radiance of his face, since this is the true scepter, I think, of a king and leads all the blessed in the kingdom of eternal blessedness. To "kiss the top" of this scepter is full love to embrace that light and peace and to approach him with continual step of fulfillment, because the Saints enjoy without weariness what they forever thirst for.

§ 4

The second phrase of the chapter verse follows, which is "**and she shall laugh in the latter day**" On which the considerations are threefold: the Valiant Woman's laughter, the cause of her laughing, and the latter [better, "latest"] day of her laughing.

The laughter of this Valiant Woman is the swelling in joy of her heart, the jubilation of her mind, and a certain propriety and grace of the joviality of her mind that accompanies her laugh on her lips, but one that is not immoderate, as is said in Job 8:21, "Until thy mouth be filled with laughter, and thy lips with rejoicing." Jubilation," as Cassiodorus says, "is the joy of the heart that the heart neither can wholly contain, nor the tongue wholly express." And this is nothing other than that full joy of which the Lord in John 16:24 says, "Ask, and you shall receive; that your joy may be full." and of which it says in Matthew 25:21,23: "Well done, good and faithful servant, [because thou hast been faithful over a few things, I will place thee over many things:] enter thou into the joy of thy lord."

When the imperfect joy of this world enters man, his laugh is mixed with grief and his extreme joy overcomes his sorrow as Solomon says in Proverbs 14:13, "Laughter shall be mingled with sorrow, and mourning taketh hold of the end of joy." But that joy according to the Apostle I Corinthians 2:9, "That eye hath not seen, nor ear heard, neither hath it entered into the heart of man, what things God hath prepared for them that love him." For then according to Isaiah 35:10, "Everlasting joy shall be upon their heads: they shall obtain joy and gladness, and sorrow and mourning," which here occupy and impede joy, "shall flee away." Revelation 21:4, "God shall wipe away all tears from their eyes," that is, all cause for tears, "and death shall be no more, nor mourning, nor crying, nor sorrow shall be any more, for the former things are passed away." And therefore no wonder if the Valiant Woman's mouth and lips are filled with jubilation.

But it is very important to notice that this Valiant Woman not only laughs with joy over what the Saints laugh over but also laughs at those whom she here warns but who are unwilling to hear her voice, as it says in Proverbs 1:24-29, "Because I called, and you refused: I stretched out my hand, and there was none that regarded. You have despised all my counsel, and have neglected my reprehensions. I also will laugh in your destruction, and will mock when that shall come to you which you feared. When sudden calamity shall fall on you, and destruction, as a tempest, shall be at hand: when tribulation and distress shall come upon you: Then shall they call upon me, and I will not hear: they shall rise in the morning and shall not find me." And here should be noted those things which lead to the condemnation of those whom the Valiant Woman has reproved of which the first is their contempt in words of her call. The second is their contempt of her helping hand. The third is their contempt of their counseling in conversation. The fourth is the diversity of destroying punishment rushing down on them like a sudden tempest that is raised by the wind of the anger of God though the ministry of demons. The fifth is tribulation which is from a *tribula*, a threshing sledge that crushes and cuts up in punishment. The sixth is the anxiety which like a worm eats at the heart of conscience. The last is desperation as to hearing any answer to one's pleas to God, which as one reads [in the Parable of the Rich Man and Poor Man] in Luke 16:24-25 the rich man in hell prays to obtain a drop of cold water on the tip of his finger to refresh his tongue but cannot get it.

There is, however, a threefold laugh and a threefold mockery, for there are some things this Valiant Woman does not laugh about nor mock. For as Solomon says in Ecclesiastes 7:7, "For as the crackling of thorns burning under a pot, so is the laughter of a fool: now this also is vanity," and it is not in this way that they laugh "with" her. And there is a deceitful laugh as we read in Proverbs 10:23, "A fool worketh mischief, as it were, for sport," that is, such a one acts wickedly with a laugh. And there is a laugh of worldly consolation of which the Lord says in Luke 6:25, "Woe to you that now laugh: for you shall mourn and weep," and this is kind of derision of which Job 12:4-3 says, "He that is mocked by his friends as I, shall call upon God and he will hear him: for the simplicity of the just man is laughed to scorn. The lamp despised in the thoughts of the rich is ready for the time appointed," that is, although the simplicity of the just man is a lamp and light of life, nevertheless it is despised by the rich of this world and therefore he mocked by them. In these ways no man laughs at nor derides this Valiant Woman, but in foregoing ways a man does laugh or deride others.

Next are to be considered the causes for the Valiant Woman's laughing, and these are three in kind:

Causes for her laugh......	On her part
	On the part of God
	On the part of society

On her part she laughs for four reasons: The first is that the capacity of her nature is wholly filled with joy so that she who was once empty now has reason to rejoice. The second is because all her merits will be repaid whose repayment she could not have seen when she was living, but that in simple faith she believed would be repaid as servants are happy when they get their wages. The third is that because she will then have all that she could hope for, she accepts the delay that afflicts her soul in view of the reward of her patient endurance of this suspension and delay. The fourth is that because that reward will exceed all that her faith, hope, and love can comprehend. And these four causes are noted together by the Lord's authority in Luke 6:38, "Give, and it shall be given to you: good measure and pressed down and shaken together and running over shall they give into your bosom," where "good" means filling the capacity of nature. The measure is "pressed down and shaken together," so that the Valiant Woman can hold more and can be given a hundredfold reward. Yet this overflowing is infinite because God is the measure greater that anything created can hold and the Valiant Woman's reward is given to her only from God's goodness and liberality.

On the part of God there are also four reasons for laughing. The first is the open vision because the Saints according to Psalm 31:21, "Thou shalt hide them in the secret of thy face, from the disturbance of men." Second is perfect pleasure of God seen and possessed and this is Mary's best part "that will not be taken form her," as it says in Luke 10:42, ["The Lord answering, said to her: Martha, Martha, thou art careful, and art troubled about many things: But one thing is necessary. Mary hath chosen the best part, which shall not be taken away from her." Faith will be taken away, but possession will remain and charity will never be taken away but perfected [as it says in I Corinthians 13:8, "Charity never falleth away: whether prophecies shall be made void, or tongues shall cease, or knowledge shall be destroyed, for we know in part, and we prophesy in part. But when that which is perfect is come, that which is in part shall be done away."] The third cause is fruition itself for the blessed will continually taste the sweetness of the being of God and be inebriated by the breasts of his sweetness. The fourth cause is the fruition of God and man in the one person of Christ. And these last two are noted in Luke 22:29-30, [where Christ says to the apostles, "And I dispose to you, as my Father hath disposed to me, a kingdom; That you may eat and drink at my table, in my kingdom: and may sit upon thrones, judging the twelve tribes of Israel."] Thus he will make the Saints sit at his table in his kingdom that they may eat and drink. Eat, I say, the sweetness of his being and drink the nectar of fruition from the most limpid vein of his wisdom that is the very face of God openly shown.

On the part of the Saints there are also four causes for laughing of which the first and principal one is that the Saints will dwell as one and be in heart and soul united in enjoying God together, as St. Augustine says. Whence Psalm 133:1-2 says, "Behold how good and how pleasant it is for brethren to dwell in unity. Like the precious ointment on the head, that ran down upon the beard, the beard of Aaron, Which ran down to the skirt of his garment." This ointment is the unction of the sweetness of the Holy Spirit penetrating all and removing from them all that is contrary to the divine will. It flows down from God to his "beard," that is, to apostolic persons who by acting so courageously are so symbolized, and thence it flows down plentifully even to the last of the Saints who are signified by "the skirt of his garment." The second cause is the common possession of every good that belongs to each individual and it is the most perfect charity that which makes all individual goods common. Thus whatever good any individual person possesses will be possessed by all and then there will be fulfilled what is prophesied symbolically in Acts 14:32, "[And the multitude of believers had but one heart and one soul:] neither did any one say that aught of the things which he possessed, was his own; but all things were common unto them," and also unto God who is the generous dispenser of a share in his blessedness to each and every person in return for their good works. Since each joy causes laughter, considering how much and as many joys each has, individual by individual, who is not moved to laughter? A third cause for laughing is the social attitude that one shows to another, for, just as it is here in this life a virtue for friends to exchange signs of friendship, so also there in the future life it will be for one to show the others the affection of community and friendship. Thus Isaiah 32:18 says:"And my people shall sit in the beauty of peace, and in the tabernacles of confidence, and in wealthy rest." This says, "in the beauty of peace" as to unity of heart for this removes war and in this is noted the first cause; in "wealthy rest" as the common possession of the goods that each individual has and this notes the second cause; and in "tabernacles of confidence," because the faith one friend has in another, he also has for all. The fourth cause is the perpetual splendor of this society of which the Lord says in Matthew 13:43 that "Then shall the just shine as the sun, in the kingdom of their Father," and Wisdom 3:7-8, "The just shall shine, and shall run to and fro like sparks among the reeds. They shall judge nations, and rule over people, and their Lord shall reign for ever."

The time of laughter for this Valiant Woman is in the last days and two things are to be considered about this, namely why it is called a "day" and why it is the "last." Concerning the first what should be noted is, as I Thessalonians 5:2 says, that, "day of the Lord shall so come, as a thief in the night," that is, without the foresight of men and as the Lord says in Matthew 24:37, "as in the days of Noah, so shall also the coming of the Son of man be. For as in the days before the flood, they were eating and drinking, marrying and giving in marriage, even till that day in which Noah entered into the ark, and they knew not till the flood came, and took them all away; so also shall the coming of the Son of man be."

Second note that Day of Judgment is called a "night" [*nox*] and is fitted for "thieves" because it will injure [*nocebit*] and involve them in perpetual darkness. Hence in Joel 2:1-2 it is called, "A day of darkness, and of gloominess, a day of clouds and whirlwinds," which is said of inner "darkness" and exterior "gloominess." The "clouds" are punishments pouring sulphur and pitch which are part of the cup [from which they must drink]. The "whirlwinds" are the devils attacking and again attacking the damned. Whence it says in Joel 2:11, "The day of the Lord is great and very terrible: and who can stand it?"

Likewise it should be noted that for the just that will be a day of light; since it will be clothed with perpetual radiance, since as Isaiah 30:26 says, "The light of the moon shall be as the light of the sun, and the light of the sun shall be sevenfold, as the light of seven days," and again Isaiah 65:17-18 says, "For behold I create new heavens, and a new earth: and the former things shall not be in remembrance, and they shell not come upon the heart. But you shall be glad and rejoice for ever in these things, which I create."

These are said to be "latest" because they are

Latest in...	Number
	Joys
	Punishments

They are latest in number because there will be no further time to merit or to sin, when it says in Revelation 10:5, "And the angel, whom I saw standing upon the sea and upon the earth, lifted up his hand to heaven, And he swore by him that liveth for ever and ever, who created heaven, and the things which are therein; and the earth, and the things which are in it; and the sea, and the things which are therein: That time shall be no longer. But in the days of the voice of the seventh angel, when he shall begin to sound the trumpet, the mystery of God shall be finished, as he hath declared by his servants the prophets." That "Angel" is Christ who has put one of his feet, that of his humanity, on the sea of his passion, as it says in Psalm 77:20, "Thy way is in the sea, and thy paths in many waters: and thy footsteps shall not be known," that is, through the action of graces; while the other foot he has place on the earth, that is, on what is always stable and unmovable in the works of the Lord, as the Apostle says in Hebrews 6:13, ["For God making promise to Abraham, because he had no one greater by whom he might swear,] swore by himself" that is, declared forever. He also swore, however, by the glory of creatures and their even more glorious dwelling place, that is, by the heavens and things therein and through grace and the dwelling place of the most glorious dwelling place and its inhabitants, that earth and those who dwell there; and by the bitter waters, that is, the oceans and their inhabitants, because he created the elect in glory and grace but damned the others forever in the bitter waters of hell. Thus time will be no more but the seventh Angel whose trumpet will raise the dead will complete all things, as has been prophesized through the Prophets and preached through the Apostles.

They are said to be latest in joys, not in the sense that after them there be no further joy but because that joy will be incomparable to all other joys that have some share in it, as Isaiah says 66:10-11, "Rejoice with Jerusalem, and be glad with her, all you that love her: rejoice for joy with her, all you that mourn for her That you may suck, and be filled with the breasts of her consolations: that you may milk out, and flow with delights, from the abundance of her glory." In these words four singular joys concerning these good things are noted. The first is the gathering of all goods that are now scattered into one and his is noted when the prophet says "Rejoice with Jerusalem" and joy pertains to the heart, but exaltation to the body. Jerusalem, however, is a collection of all the goods pertaining to the vision of eternal peace. The second joy is the spiritual consolation of those who mourn for their peril [of losing heaven] for themselves and others who will then accept perfect consolation, as the Lord says in Matthew 5:5, "Blessed are they that mourn: for they shall be comforted," and this is noted when above it is said "rejoice for joy with her, all you that mourn for her." The third is the abundance of eternal food that is poured into to all the Saints to nourish them for eternal life sucked out of the maternal breasts of wisdom which is nothing other than presence of the goodness and truth of God. And this is noted when it says, "That you may milk out, and flow with delights, from the abundance of her glory." For "to milk out" is simply to draw forth new revelations.

Likewise Isaiah 66:12-13 says, "For thus saith the Lord: Behold I will bring upon her [Jerusalem] as it were a river of peace, and as an overflowing torrent the glory of the Gentiles, which you shall suck; you shall be carried at the breasts, and upon the knees they shall caress you. As one whom the mother caresseth, so will I comfort you, and you shall be comforted in Jerusalem."

Two things are to be noted in these words: what it is that gives joy to the Saints, and how it does so. As to the first, what they accept from the Lord is the abundance of peace that flows down over them and then is fulfilled what it says in Psalm 121:7, "Let peace be in thy strength: and abundance in thy towers." They accept, however, the "glory of the Gentiles" in the incomprehensible being of God whom they see, since this is the glory of all the Gentiles.

Secondly, how we will be consoled is threefold, namely, according what mode of likeness we will be consoled, and where we will be consoled, and what will consoled us. According to what mode of likeness, because it says, "you shall be carried at the breast" and this notes the likeness to a small, wandering child who is carried at the breast to keep it from crying. Just so God does for us, saying; "Let your voice be quiet from sleeping because you are carried at the breasts of the wisdom," that is, of truth and goodness, "of God from which you suck the milk of eternal happiness." Also it says "upon the knees they shall caress you" and note the simile, because a small child weeping is placed on its mother's lap and so God has knees on which he lifts us up to caress us, that is, the unchangingness and security of immortality and freedom from suffering.

Where are we comforted? It is in "Jerusalem," that is in company with all the blessed so that no consolation is so satisfying as it is when no one for whom we care is distant from us. Likewise that consolation will be more acceptable to us in so far as we are honored by God before all, because whoever ministers to Christ here, the Father who is in heaven will honor [as it says in John 12:26, "If any man minister to me, let him follow me; and where I am, there also shall my minister be. If any man minister to me, him will my Father honor"].

According to what is this consolation given? This must be asked because we see with both an interior and an exterior eye:an interior eye of our hearts that already tastes that glory of divinity and an exterior eye that when our dry bones first come alive from our graves will behold the glory of humanity through a glorious transformation like plants flourishing for all eternity. There is also a last day for punishments, not indeed such that there will be no future punishment but because they are the end and consummation of all punishments. These punishments are such that there is no greater punishment beyond them and they are fourfold, namely:

Punishments...	Mode of resurgence
	Resurgence
	Judgment
	Prison in which they are held

And these four are noted by Isaiah 24:17, "Fear, and the pit, and the snare are upon thee, O thou inhabitant of the earth." When the blessed are raised up to the clouds before Christ in the air thus to be with the Lord forever, [as the Apostles says in I Thessalonians 4:16,], this "inhabitant of the earth," that is, the impious person, will be left on the earth which he has so loved. Hence through these words is noted the punishment of some of the resurrected of which I will speak later. This "fear" is the dread of the judgment and the punishments which will then be pronounced. The "snare" is in the manner of rising, because while the pious dead will be raised in unchangeable glory, these impious dead will only rise bound in the snare of the eternal blame that they must forever bear. The "pit" is the prison of hell in which they are to be incarcerated.

In the this manner of rising from the tomb there are innumerable punishments; but there are some that are special and greater than the others, of which the first is that of the body receiving the flames and burning of the hell fire in which they were not previously tortured since they did not yet dwell in them. The second is the continual war of the body against the soul and of the soul against the body. The third is the desire for eternal death without the possibility of ever dying. Of the first the prophet Amos 4:2-3 says, "The Lord God hath sworn by his holiness, that lo, the days shall come upon you, when they shall lift you up on pikes, and what shall remain of you in boiling pots. And you shall go out at the breaches one over against the other, and you shall be cast forth into Armon, saith the Lord." God's oath is the unchangeable degree of judgment. Then the torturing devils will raise the damned on pikes. A "pike" is an instrument by which butchers lift cattle that have been skinned, stabbing the wood through the nerves of the rear limbs and thus lifting the beast and suspending it to be dissected. That wooden spear that they thus thrust through the nerves of the limbs is called a "pike" and signifies the fetters by which the damned are bound to be tortured. "What shall remain of you" are the bones which will be in the boiling pots. The whole body will rise and boil in itself as in a pot. "You shall go out at the breaches," indicates that one "breach" will be the opening of the grave and the body will come out, while the other opening will be that of hell and the soul will come out. "On over against the other" means the soul against the body. Jointly they will be "cast forth into the Arnon," which is interpreted "the damnation of grief" and signifies the hell where dwell those condemned by God in eternal grief.

Of the second punishment which is the continual war of the body against the soul and the soul against the body results from the body's resistance to the soul that ought to rule it for good deeds but directs it to evil, while the soul on the contrary, though seduced by corporal pleasures, is prone to this corporal evil because it was lazy and weak in controlling the body. This has its penalty as Job 30:16-20 says, "And now my soul fadeth within myself, and the days of affliction possess me. In the night my bone is pierced with sorrows: and they that feed upon me do not sleep. With the multitude of them my garment is consumed, and they have girded me about, as with the collar of my coat. I am compared to dirt, and am likened to embers and ashes." For the soul droops when weariness seizes the body and conversely and the person is in the possession of affliction when affliction dominates both body and soul. And it is said "possess" the body as if it were, so to speak, under the feet of its owner, since the two feet of affliction, confusion and grief, deeply and heavily take possession of the soul. Affliction "feeds upon me" signifies the strength of the body eaten through by the worm of conscience by which the soul kills the body. And again:"they that feed on me," that is, conversely the soul does not sleep but "with the multitude of the soul's miseries all the "garments' of virtue are consumed so that what remains is only naked confusion. Yet the ignominy of sin does not cover the beauty of virtue when in the Saints that sin is erased thorough penance. Worms, however, "have girded me about," that is, strangled my body and soul with what is foreign and unsuitable to them, engulfing them with vilest filth and the body in its own stink and the soul in is glowing ashes which is filled with eternal fire and both body and soul in these ashes in which fire rules.

The third punishment is the perpetual desire of death that is endured without dying as Revelation 9:6 says, "And in those days men shall seek death, and shall not find it: and they shall desire to die, and death shall fly from them." This is because there will be such discord between the soul and he body that they would be most willing to be separated if that could become possible, but through a most just judgment of God they are held together so that as they sinned together they will be punished together.

While those rising sinners will receive innumerable pains they will in their bodies receive four major ones, but three major ones in their souls. Those in the body are first the foul odor and sufferance of the body, second its heavy weight and ignobility. third its dark obscurity and opacity, fourth its animality and carnality.

Amos 4:10 speaks of the first of these when it says, "I made the stench of your camp to come up into your nostrils." Here the camp means the assembly of the damned who have armed themselves against God. And Isaiah 66:24 says, "And they shall go out, and see the carcasses of the men that have transgressed against me: their worm shall not die, and their fire shall not be quenched: and they shall be a loathsome sight to all flesh." The Saints will go out in the steps of their contemplation and see the beauty of the vindication of justice in these dead bodies, that is in the damned bodies sinking into the worms of stink and rottenness, as Isaiah 14:19 says, "But thou art cast out of thy grave, as an unprofitable branch defiled, and wrapped up among them that were slain by the sword, and art gone down to the bottom of the pit, as a rotten carcass," this prophecy will be verified in the last day when the wicked bodies are ejected from their graves with ugly speed as the useless hay of plants that bore no fruits useful in eternity. They will be forever polluted with a bloody smell and covered forever in a blood mess, because this foul blood is the uncleanness of the sin that that infects them.

The second punishment of the bodies of those rising from the tomb will be their weight as it says in Exodus 15:5, "The depths have covered them, they are sunk to the bottom like a stone" and further on in verse 10, "they sunk as lead in the mighty waters," since these mighty waters are the punishments roughly piling on them. This is what is meant in Revelation 18:21, "And a mighty angel took up a stone, as it were a great millstone, and cast it into the sea, saying: With such violence as this shall Babylon, that great city, [add "forever,"] be thrown down, and shall be found no more at all." The term "millstone" is well taken because in this world the sinner willed only to be occupied in the worldly works. And this stone is cast down into the sea because the sea is vast and bitter. Sinners are heavy in evil and therefore descend rapidly into the depths of hell but their weight is not that of matter but of sin which, as Isaac the Philosopher, says "weighs down and presses sinners under the sad orb of hell so that they are lost forever."

The third punishment of the bodies of the damned is their darkness and opacity. noted in the prophecy of Isaiah 13:8, "Their countenances shall be as faces burnt." And Lamentations 4:8 says, "Their face is now made blacker than coal, and they are not known in the streets: their skin hath stuck to their bones, it is withered, and is become like wood." They are blackened by the fumes of eternal fire and by the brands burning in a fire which is able to consume but not to illuminate since it does not give light but only burns and blackens. Where it says "they are not known in the streets" it means that they are changed to another color from the beauty they once had here on earth when they nourish and cultivated their flesh on delicious foods so that seen when seen they will no longer be recognizable, because then their appearance will have the deformity of a devil and no long a human color. Their skin will adhere to their bones with wrinkled ugliness since the fat of their former banquets and guzzling will be consumed and made like dried wood to feed the eternal fire.

The fourth punishment which is their animality and the carnality of their bodies will occur in the manner the Apostle describes in I Corinthians 15:52, "In a moment, in the twinkling of an eye, at the last trumpet: for the trumpet shall sound, and the dead shall rise again incorruptible: and we shall be changed."] Here the Apostle says that the trumpet will call forth the dead who will rise uncorrupt as to all their members, but only we if are among the Saints will be changed, so that it is evident that others will not be changed but gross animality and corporality will remain in their bodies, not, however, so that they will so that they will be no longer sustained by food as they once were but that they may be no longer spiritual but ignoble and able to be burned in the eternal fire. And this is what St. Augustine rightly says in *De Civitate Dei* that "ignobility will not be removed from the bodies of the damned."

Especially in regards to the soul there will be three punishments, of which the first is that for the sake of the divine vision the damned endure the worm of conscience, because in their hearts the thought of their past sins continuously gnaws with its sharp teeth that can never be dulled, as Isaiah 66:24 says, "Their worm shall not die, and their fire shall not be quenched: and they shall be a loathsome sight to all flesh." "Loathsome to all flesh" here refers to the elect who here are referred to as if they were all humanity because in them human flesh has its perfection as it was created by God; [but as regards the loathsome damned] as Isaiah 14:11 says, ["Thy pride is brought down to hell, thy carcass is fallen down:] under thee shall the moth be strewed, and worms shall be thy covering]. The "moth" is born from the expectations of the damned and is the worm of conscience and these are spiritual regrets for the loss of good and the survival of evil.

The second punishment is hatred, envy, and anger, by which the dammed are filled in place of the joy of the Saints. For themselves and each other they will have hatred, as well as anger against God their judge and envy against the Saints and the elect of God's kingdom, as Ezekiel 32:27 says the damned have, "laid their swords under their heads, and their iniquities were in their bones," for the arms of the angry are their anger and the hate and malice of their wills, and also their envy, which are sins which death does not remove but remain even in hell as the Gloss says. The swords with which they fight even against themselves are curses and blasphemies; whence it also follows the wickedness of their wills are as seals on their bones, that is, are in the core of their hearts. And so it says in Revelation 16:9, "And men were scorched with great heat, and they blasphemed the name of God, who hath power over these plagues,"

The third punishment is in the soul and is the perversion of intellect and reason since some know the true, such as do the devils, but nevertheless pervert and fight against it, and therefore Dionysius the Areopagite says that "the truth can be perverted." And concerning this it is said in Matthew 25:30, "And the unprofitable servant cast ye out into the exterior darkness. There shall be weeping and gnashing of teeth," and St. Augustine says, "That was before in the interior and the inner darknesses are the perversion of truth against truth and the ignorance of God of those who do not see." Therefore Amos 5:20 says, "Shall not the day of the Lord be darkness, and not light: and obscurity, and no brightness in it?" in which "darknesses" is exterior darknesses and "obscurity" is interior darkness. And on the part of the soul there are these kinds of punishment.

There are on the part of judgment six kinds of punishment...	Terrible insight of horrible judgment
	Exposure of all sins
	Hard reproach of judgment
	Sentence of condemnation
	Separation from society of all good and from God
	Joining to the company of the reprobate

The first kind of punishment is such that sinners would rather have mountains fall on them than see the Son in the form of a servant sitting in judgment over them and nevertheless they avoid the sight. Whence it says in Matthew 24:30, "And then shall appear the sign of the Son of Man in heaven: and then shall all tribes of the earth mourn: and they shall see the Son of Man coming in the clouds of heaven with much power and majesty," and Revelation 1:7 says, "Behold, he cometh with the clouds, and every eye shall see him, and they also that pierced him. And all the tribes of the earth shall bewail themselves because of him." And also Luke 23:28-30 says, "But Jesus turning to them, said: Daughters of Jerusalem, weep not over me; but weep for yourselves, and for your children. For behold, the days shall come, wherein they will say: Blessed are the barren, and the wombs that have not borne, and the paps that have not given suck. Then shall they begin to say to the mountains: Fall upon us; and to the hills: Cover us."

The second kind of punishment is exposure of all sins, when it is said in Daniel 7:9-10, "I beheld till thrones were placed, and the Ancient of days sat: his garment was white as snow, and the hair of his head like clean wool: his throne like flames of fire: the wheels of it like a burning fire. A swift stream of fire issued forth from before him: thousands of thousands ministered to him, and ten thousand times a hundred thousand stood before him: the judgment sat, and the books were opened." The "Ancient of Days" is God who created all time and is after all and above all, yet not old nor will he grow old, but "Ancient of days" is used of him because of his wisdom in governing and judging. In this citation he has a throne of flaming fire because the Lord will come to judge in fire as it says in Isaiah 66:15, ["For behold the Lord will come with fire, and his chariots are like a whirlwind, to render his wrath in indignation, and his rebuke with flames of fire." The "fiery river" in the text from Daniel above is, however, that fire which burns up the face the world and then whirling on itself will draw the damned into hell, and his "garments" are the Apostles of God who cling to Christ our head. The "ministers and assistants" are the Angels who will be with him in judgment. The "books" are the consciences of all which will then be opened as the Apostles says in Romans 2:16, "In the day when God shall judge the secrets of men by Jesus Christ according to my gospel," and I Corinthians 4:5, "Therefore judge not before the time; until the Lord come, who both will bring to light the hidden things of darkness, and will make manifest the counsels of the hearts; and then shall every man have praise from God."

The third punishment is the severest rebuke of Christ the judge narrated in a passage we have previously quoted, Matthew 25:42, "I was hungry, and you gave me not to eat: I was thirsty, and you gave me not to drink."

The fourth punishment is the sentence of condemnation in verse 41 that says, "Depart from me, you cursed, into everlasting fire which was prepared for the devil and his angels."

The fifth punishment is the separation from the society of all good persons by God cited in verse 33 of the same passage, "And he shall set the sheep on his right hand, but the goats on his left." The "sheep" are on the right because like Benjamin they are children of the right hand, as was explained in Chapter II, and which is the place of the Son as is said in Psalm 110:1, "The Lord said to my Lord:Sit thou at my right hand: Until I make thy enemies thy footstool." But the left hand is on the earth as it is perpetually dominated by its miserable condition whence also the Apostle says in I Thessalonians 4:16, ["Then we who are alive, who are left, shall be taken up together with them in the clouds to meet Christ, into the air, and so shall we be always with the Lord], so that the Saints will be raised in the air to Christ and thus will be always with the Lord while the impious will remain on the earth which they have too much loved.

The sixth punishment is that the condemned will be joined with the reprobate that have no love for each other, as Job 41:6 says of Leviathan, "His body is like molten shields, shut close up with scales pressing upon one another. One is joined to another, and not so much as any air can come between them: They stick one to another and they hold one another fast, and shall not be separated." For the "body of the devil" are all the damned who are like "molten shields" that no javelin of divine love can wound. This "body" is compact because the damned are not only joined together but are packed tight so that they are punished by this confinement. They are like scales which fight against God by obstinacy of will and one adheres to the other because they are alike in guilt and hence have the same punishment and thus cannot be separated. This sword that is "two-edged" and sharpened to cut both body and soul is the judge's sentence because as the damned were partners in sin so also they are in punishment.

There are ten major punishments in this prison...
1- The heat of interior and exterior fire
2- The interior and consequent exterior cold
3- The interior and exterior darkness
4- The stink of the lake
5- The horror of company in this place
6- The perpetual face-to face presence of the devils
7- The chain of hissing, burning, and pressing bodies
8- The grinding of teeth
9- The weeping of the eyes
10- The captivity of the prison itself

The heat of fire will be there literally but that fire is immensely hotter than any fire we know of here, nor is it light-giving but only fierce, nor does it burn the body only but both soul and body. Nor does it consume the human substance but forever persists along with sin and penetrates that substance. This is the explanation that St. Basil gives to Psalm 29:7 where it says, "The voice of the Lord divideth the flame of fire." "The voice of the Lord" is the command of the Lord, "dividing the flame" that is, the light, "of fire," that is from the strength of the fire: as light serves the Saints above, its heat pursues the unjust below. Hence it says in Deuteronomy 32:22, "A fire is kindled in my wrath, and shall burn even to the lowest hell: and shall devour the earth with her increase, and shall burn the foundations of the mountains." The "earth" signifies worldly persons, that is, sinners; the "mountains" are the proud; their "foundations" are sinners' sinful wills which the infernal fire will attack. And Isaiah 30:33 says, "For Topheth is prepared from yesterday, prepared by the king, deep, and wide. The nourishment thereof is fire and much wood: the breath of the Lord is as a torrent of brimstone kindling it." Tophet is a certain valley and it is named after hell which is "prepared from yesterday," that is, from the beginning of creatures, since along with the other works of the six days Gehenna was also created and prepared by the regal justice of God that in it might dwell whoever would obstinately stand against him. It is deep indeed in the heart of the earth, extensive enough for all the damned. The fuel on which its fires are fed give heat but not light, and the "wood' mentioned in the quotation is the damned lacking all the living sap of grace and they are many, since it says in Matthew 20:10, "For many are called, but few chosen." "The breath of the Lord" is his wrath and dominion and that dominion of vindictive justice follows them so that it burns them like a burning, foul-smelling "torrent of brimstone," because the damned feel the punishment of burning in which the foul-smelling life of sin has consumed them.

The second punishment is internal and external cold following on the fire but not mitigating its heat, as we see in feverish persons who have a high temperature and nevertheless feel intermittent chills as it says in Job 24:19, "Let him pass from the snow waters to excessive heat, and his sin even to hell" for, although such snow will not be there in the future, yet snow-like water will be poured out for it coldness, causing much injury and hence Exodus 9:24-25 says, that "The hail and fire mixed with it drove on together: and it was of so great bigness,[as never before was seen in the whole land of Egypt since that nation was founded. And the hail destroyed through all the land of Egypt all things that were in the fields,] and also in Wisdom 16:16-17, "For the wicked that denied to know thee, were scourged by the strength of thy arm, being persecuted by strange waters, and hail, and rain, and consumed by fire. And which was wonderful, in water, which extinguisheth all things, the fire had more force: for the world fighteth for the just." There is no hail or snow in hell, but through these names is signified the force of rushing cold on the damned which, punishing cold, I say is the result of the just decrees of God which the damned have transgressed as Wisdom 5:18-22, says "And his zeal will take armor, and he will arm the creature for the revenge of his enemies. He will put on justice as a breastplate, and will take true judgment instead of a helmet. He will take equity for an invincible shield: And he will sharpen his severe wrath for a spear, and the whole world shall fight with him against the unwise. Then shafts of lightning shall go directly from the clouds, as from a bow well bent, they shall be shot out, and shall fly to the mark." In this quotation are noted the modes of the condemnation of the damned; for the zeal of God's justice drives God to their condemnation. The instrument of their punishment are creatures created by him that he arms to punish his enemies when he gives them the power and force to injure and afflict, as to fire and to cold and darkness, etc. Nor can anyone blame God by denying the justice of his condemnation, because God is armored in justice and judges justly so that his sentence of judgment is altogether just and is a "shield" of equity against which the murmuring of blasphemies against his judgments will be extinguished, because these judgments only blame what is real guilt. God's "wrath" is not some mental disturbance on his part but the infliction of punishments that pierce and transfix the inner being of the sinner like a lance. The "whole world" fights with God against the condemned because whatever is ignoble in the elements of the world, such as heat, cold, darkness, etc. divide themselves from these elements [of nature] and serve in hell to torture the reprobate. "Shafts of lighting" rush down as sent by the wrath of God and deeply wound the vital powers of souls like "arrows" from the "well bent bow of the clouds, and strike at determined spots that are the sources of sin. For this divine bowman does not aim uncertainly but always hits the target because wisdom guides his arrow. Again Wisdom 5:23-24 says, "And thick hail shall be cast upon them from the stone casting wrath: the water of the sea shall rage against them, and the rivers shall run together in a terrible manner. A mighty wind shall stand up against them, and as a whirlwind shall divide them." Here God's "stone casting wrath" means hail stones and indicates that this punishment falls down on the sinner impetuously. "The sea will rage" means that the vast bitterness that is eternal yet which sometimes rests like the water of the sea to pour down on them, penetrating to their inner liver and heart like the rivers of Cocytus and Phlegeton, etc., that signify the continual succession of the punishments of hell as new punishments follow on previous ones and nevertheless the older never fail to flow on and therefore they are said to "run together,' that is, not smoothly but violently. The "mighty wind" is the spirit of power that feeds the fire. The 'whirlwind that divides them" comes from the winds beating on each other contrarily in that place in hell.

 The third punishment is the interior and exterior darkness mentioned in Matthew 25:30, ["And the unprofitable servant cast ye out into the exterior darkness. There shall be weeping and gnashing of teeth"], where God orders the wicked servant to be bound hand and foot and thrown into the exterior darkness. Lamentations 3:2 also says, "He hath led me, and brought me into darkness, and not into light," and Job 17:13 says, "If I wait hell is my house, and I have made my bed in darkness." And this darkness was signified by the darknesses of Egypt which was said to be palpable. Wisdom 17:5 says of them, "And no power of fire could give them light, neither could the bright flames of the stars enlighten that horrible night." for that fire did not illumine, as it says, but consumed. The stars, however, are limpid flames, since as Isaiah 48:13 says, ["My hand also hath founded the earth, and my right hand hath measured the heavens: I shall call them, and they shall stand together"], that is, they remain shining but do not light the damned.

The fourth punishment is the stink of the lake when Job 17:14 says, "If I have said to rottenness: Thou art my father; to worms, my mother and my sister." This smell should not be understood as the exhalation of something rotten because bodies in hell do not rot. But that filth that gathers in the lake is called "putrefaction' and the bites or punctures of punishment are called "worms." In Zechariah 9:11 we read, "Thou also by the blood of thy testament hast sent forth thy prisoners out of the pit, wherein is no water," and this refers to those redeemed from hell and refers to the water of cooling consolation that is entirely lacking there.

The fifth punishment is the horror of the company who are gathered in this place. That horror is generated by their hatred of each other of which we have already written. It says in Lamentations 5:10, where Jeremiah is speaking in person of the damned that "Our skin was burnt as an oven." Whence the damned are also bound together to mock and shout at each other, as Isaiah 14:9-10 says that when Nabuchodonosor came to hell they would receive him with shouting, "Hell below was in an uproar to meet thee at thy coming, it stirred up the giants," that is, the powerfully and violently punishing devils, "for thee. All the princes of the earth are risen up from their thrones, all the princes of nations. All shall answer, and say to thee: Thou also art wounded as well as we, thou art become like unto us. Thy pride is brought down to hell, thy carcass is fallen down: under thee shall the moth be strewed, and worms shall be thy covering." Hell here means the inhabitants of hell, putting the container for the contained, and these inhabitants of hell run to mock the damned and evil king and the "giants," that is, the stronger devils, have raised up in provocation of evil will against him because it pleases them to do so and demand that he be punished by harsher punishments. Furthermore also the kings and princes who have never received a throne in hell for the abuse of their dignity rise up in derision and the leaders of nations who are also often the first in receiving the punishments of hell, answer and say to him mockingly that his fortitude is wounded and destroyed and his body, so accustomed to many pleasures, has fallen like a fetid cadaver. Nor is it contrary to this that the rich buried in hell seem to be solicitous of the salvation of their brothers, as we read in the Parable of the Rich Man and the Poor Man in Luke 15:27-28, when he pleads with God "Then, father, I beseech thee, that thou wouldst send him to my father's house, for I have five brethren, That he may testify unto them, lest they also come into this place of torments." The damned rich man does not do this out of love for his brothers but that he himself would suffer less if his brothers were absolved from the crimes into which he had led them or so that he would not have to endure their reproaches that he had taught them vices and wounded them; or as St. Augustine still better explains, "This urging [by the Rich Man] was said for an example to the living that they should more believe the words of the Scripture that even the dead will rise again."

The sixth punishment is the perpetual sight of the faces of the devils. The Saints stand before the face of God but the damned see the faces of the devils that afflict them in punishment. And these faces are pictured in Job 41:9-14 [in the description of Leviathan], "His sneezing is like the shining of fire, and his eyes like the eyelids of the morning. Out of his mouth go forth lamps, like torches of lighted fire. Out of his nostrils goeth smoke, like that of a pot heated and boiling. His breath kindleth coals, and a flame cometh forth out of his mouth. In his neck strength shall dwell, and want goeth before his face. The members of his flesh cleave one to another: he shall send lightnings against him, and they shall not be carried to another place." This "sneezing" of the devil is the expelling of vapors multiplied in theirs skulls which are filled with the machinations of iniquity. This sneezing that goes out from such a skull is the worst thunder of malignity and it is the splendor of fire not from a torch but from sheer terror and arson and thus its malice is evident. Its eyes out of which it looks to do evil are huge and red as are the eyelids of the dawn that are red and signify anger in the mind of the demon because anger reddens the eyes. The "mouth" by which a devil speaks to souls emits fires which enkindle evil thoughts and that are like fuming pitch with fire succeeding fire. From a devil's "nose," that is from his head in which there should be discretion there proceeds demented lust and irrational fury. And the breath of his wicked will, that is, his spirit, makes froth turn to flame that lights the impious fires of hell. The column of his neck is his pillowed pride in which is strength because he dares a proud fearlessness greater than he can perform. And nothing good is left before his face because whatever is before his face is deprived of all good and implicated in all evil.

The seventh punishment is the chain of hissing, burning, and pressing bodies and these are said in II Peter 2:4, to be "For if God spared not the angels that sinned, but delivered them drawn down by infernal ropes to the lower hell, unto torments, to be reserved unto judgment." These chains are nothing other than spiritual bonds by which the impious are bound to punishments for their sins of which Jeremiah 27:2-3 says, "Thus saith the Lord to me: Make thee bands, and chains: and thou shalt put them on thy neck. And thou shalt send them to the king of Edom, and to the king of Moab, and to the king of the children of Ammon, and to the king of Tyre, and to the king of Sidon: by the hand of the messengers that are come to Jerusalem to Zedechiah the king of Judah." There are named six kinds of men who ought to be bound in hell. For Edom is interpreted 'bloody' and signifies those who in the world served the pleasures of the body. They are especially secular clerics who followed the pleasures of the flesh. Moab is interpreted "from the father" and signifies those evil religious who have their example of condemnation especially from the "father" because religious superiors, that is, "Fathers," before all others are buried in the grave of concupiscence in the desert of religion. Lot, who is interpreted "declining" begot Moab on that mountain from his fallen daughters. The "mountain" of religion is that in which religious superiors especially corrupt their daughters, that is, their carnal subjects, when by their bad example they beget from them works of perdition that they learn from their father. Ammon, however, is interpreted "useless people" and signifies secular men who fall into hell by fraud and trickery. Tyre is interpreted "narrow" and signifies evil married men of whom the Apostle says in I Corinthians 7:28, "They shall have tribulation of the flesh." Sidon is interpreted "hunting" and signifies the nobility of this world who are hearty hunters of poor people whence they are the same as the mighty hunter Nimrod [Genesis 10:8-10]and are bound with him in punishment. The King of Israel signifies the hypocrites openly in the uniform of the Lord who seem to be the sole kings and teachers in Israel but nevertheless, since in heart they are inwardly wolfish, are damned and bound together in punishment since. all these evil ones are bound together. Of this St. Bernard of Clairvaux says, "I am horrified at the deathless vermin that are bound hand and foot by fearful chains and at the weight of these bonds pressing, grinding, burning, yet never consumed."

The eighth punishment is the gnashing of teeth and the ninth of the weeping of the eyes of which Matthew 22:13 narrates that the king says concerning the man invited to the wedding feast who failed to wear the proper festive garments, "Bind his hands and feet, and cast him into the exterior darkness: there shall be weeping and gnashing of teeth." This should not be understand as if the eyes emitted real tears since there will be none there in hell but they will deplore even more bitterly, for the gnashing of teeth is the effect of cold.

The tenth punishment is the captivity in prison, whence Psalm 57:7 says, "They dug a pit before my face, and they are fallen into it." The pit of hell is dug by bad example and those who give bad example to the weak fall into hell themselves.

THE VALIANT WOMAN   265

OUTLINE OF CHAPTER XVII

She hath opened her mouth to wisdom,
And the law of clemency is on her tongue. (v. 26)

§1) The Acrostic Letter is Peh, פ, "exhorting" and the Valiant Woman to human hearts speaks Wisdom by the Holy Spirit
  1) Her mouth is twofold:
    1) The mouth of the heart, that is, of the soul, opens in five ways:
      1) Considering Wisdom
      2) Learning Wisdom
      3) Meditating Wisdom
      4) Tasting Wisdom
      5) Speaking Wisdom to others
    2) The mouth of the body opens in five ways:
      1) To confess one's sin
      2) To prayer
      3) To give thanks
      4) To praise
      5) To preach
    3) But to be opened in these ways the mouth must first be purged clean

§2) "The law of clemency is on her tongue."
  1) The tongue of her heart:
    1) Of devotion
    2) Of desire for God
  2) Her bodily tongue:
    1) Compares worldly truths to spiritual truths
    2) Speaks judiciously with discrete judgment not vainly
    3) Proposes as law only what is correctly understood
    4) What is preached is not refuted by the preacher's life
  3) The law spoken by bodily mouth is the law of clemency; don't out of hatred condemn too quickly

CHAPTER XVII

**She hath opened her mouth to wisdom,
and the law of clemency is on her tongue. (v. 26)**

§ 1

PEH פ, Peh is interpreted "exhorting" or "speaking forth" and thus alludes to the meaning of this chapter text, because in words of wisdom the heart speaks forth in good words, and the Valiant

Woman does this so that the words of her mouth are like pen of a scribe by which the Holy Spirit writes rapidly on the fleshly tables of hearts, because the word of this Woman more easily captures her hearers in that she proves it by her works, [as it says in Psalm 45:2, "My heart hath uttered a good word I speak my works to the king; My tongue is the pen of a scrivener that writeth swiftly."] And so she attributes her works to the king, that is, she recognizes that these works are not her own but are those of the Heavenly Father whom they glorify, as well as praise his wonders in his Saints.

The next consideration is about the chapter text itself which consists in two notions: the **opening of the Valiant Woman's mouth "to speak wisdom"** and "the law of clemency that is on her tongue."

"Mouth' is taken here in two senses: the mouth of the body and the mouth of the heart, concerning both of which the Lord says in Matthew 15:11, "Not that which goeth into the mouth defileth a man: but what cometh out of the mouth, this defileth a man," and he means that those which goes out of the mouth also comes out of the heart, such as thievery, blasphemy, etc. [And he also later says in Matthew 15:17-20. "Do you not understand that whatsoever entereth into the mouth, goeth into the belly, and is cast out into the privy? But the things which proceed out of the mouth, come forth from the heart, and those things defile a man. For from the heart come forth evil thoughts, murders, adulteries, fornications, thefts, false testimonies, blasphemies. These are the things that defile a man."] On which text St. Augustine says, "All sins go out from the mouth of the heart which defiles man. Food, on the other hand, enters from outside through the mouth and that does not make a man evil."

The mouth of the heart opens in five ways:

The Wisdom...	of Considering
	of Learning
	of Meditating
	of Digesting
	of Speaking

The considering of wisdom opens the mouth when through the intention of the heart we consider the beauty of wisdom as it says in Wisdom 7:8-9, "I preferred her before kingdoms and thrones, and esteemed riches nothing in comparison of her. Neither did I compare unto her any precious stone: for all gold in comparison of her, is as a little sand, and silver in respect to her shall be counted as clay," and later in verses 29-30, "For she is more beautiful than the sun, and above all the order of the stars: being compared with the light, she is found before it. For after this cometh night, but no evil can overcome wisdom." For those alone rightly estimate the value of wisdom who compare it to nothing else whether in heaven or on earth. For as the Psalmist says, 73:25, "For what have I in heaven? And besides thee what do I desire upon earth?" And this wisdom is the Son of God who is the sweetness of the heart and the rejoicing of the mind, the Word of the Father and knowledge of Him, as it says in Wisdom 7:28, "For God loveth none but him that dwelleth with wisdom."

Secondly the heart is opened by learning wisdom in thought and in work as it says in Sirach 24:30-31, "He that hearkeneth to me, shall not be confounded: and they that work by me, shall not sin. They that explain me shall have life everlasting." Those who hear in order to learn need not be confounded by sadness because wisdom reigns and directs their lives. Those who operate within themselves so that all their works are conformed to wisdom will never sin and those who explain wisdom that is, who exemplify wisdom to others as a light, such will gain eternal life. Hence it says in James 1:25, "But he that hath looked into the perfect law of liberty, and hath continued therein, not becoming a forgetful hearer, but a doer of the work; this man shall be blessed in his deeds," and in Wisdom 9:10 it says of wisdom, "Send her out of thy holy heaven, and from the throne of thy majesty, that she may be with me, and may labour with me, that I may know what is acceptable with thee." As if to say, send her that I may learn of her and thus knowing her testify according to her light, since it says in Psalm 119:105, "Thy word is a lamp to my feet, and a light to my path."

Thirdly, the mouth of wisdom is open to meditate. This means, however, to meditate often, turning over the thoughts of one's heart through frequent thinking and then to turn them in one's heart over and over again so that one's mind might be more sweetly and firmly imprinted by their truth, as Psalm 1:2 says a wise person does, "His will is in the law of the Lord, and on his law he shall meditate day and night," and also Psalm 19:15 says, "The meditation of my heart always [shall be] in thy sight, O Lord, my helper, and my redeemer," and Psalm 119:47-48, "I meditated also on thy commandments, which I loved. And I lifted up my hands [that is, my works] to thy commandments, which I loved: and I was exercised in thy justifications," and Wisdom 6:16, "To think therefore upon her, is perfect understanding," and Sirach 14:22: "Blessed is the man that shall continue in wisdom, and that shall meditate in his justice, and in his mind shall think of the all seeing eye of God."

Fourthly, the mouth of the heart opens to taste wisdom, and this is done when in spirit we perceive the savor of wisdom, as is said in Sirach 15:3, "With the bread of life and understanding, she shall feed him, and give him the water of wholesome wisdom to drink," and Psalm 81:17 says, "And he fed them with the fat of wheat, and filled them with honey out of the rock." This says "fat of wheat because it strengthens and expands the heart with regard to the taste for eternal things; and it says "honey out of the rock," that is, from Christ, [because it says in I Corinthians 10:4, "The Rock was Christ"], because to taste God never sates one's longing, as it says in Sirach 24:26-29, "Come over to me, all ye that desire me, and be filled with my fruits. For my spirit is sweet above honey, and my inheritance above honey and the honeycomb. My memory is unto everlasting generations. They that eat me shall yet hunger: and they that drink me shall yet thirst."

Fifthly, the mouth of wisdom is open to speak, and this is done when a man speaks to God in his heart so as to cast out the weariness of this life and take the road by which we travel to our fatherland [in heaven], as it says in Wisdom 8:9 of wisdom that, "I purposed therefore to take her to me to live with me: knowing that she will communicate to me of her good things, and will be a comfort in my cares and grief." And thus we read in Luke 24:15 and following of the Prodigal Son that "He went and cleaved to one of the citizens of that country. And he sent him into his farm to feed swine." So also the Incarnate Wisdom risen from the dead joins his disciples on the way and goes with them speaking of the Scriptures so that his speech also becomes for them, as it were, a companion on the way that keeps them moving on. Hence after his departure from them and their recognition of him, they said to each other in verse 32, "Was not our heart burning within us, whilst he spoke in this way, and opened to us the Scriptures?" for they had urged him to continue his sweet company with them further on their way.

The mouth of the bodily face also has no less than five way of opening to wisdom: namely in confession, in prayer, in thanksgiving, in praise, in preaching of doctrine.

The mouth opens in confession when someone from the counsel of wisdom and to its glory opens his mouth to denounce himself so that he may not put off humbling himself before God, lest God judge him before the Saints and God's Angels, and thus Psalm 32:5, "I said I will confess against myself my injustice to the Lord: and thou hast forgiven the wickedness of my sin," and Joshua 7:19 relates: "And Josue said to Achan: My son, give glory to the Lord God of Israel, and confess, and tell me what thou hast done, hide it not." Adam sinned and sinning hid himself and was thrown out of Paradise, as it says in Psalm 140:4 says, "Incline not my heart to evil words; to make excuses in sins with men that work iniquity," for, as it says in Proverbs 28:13, "He that hideth his sins," by excusing them, "shall not prosper," and Isaiah 43:25, "I am he that blots out thy iniquities for my own sake, and I will not remember thy sins," and further on in verse 26, "Tell if thou hast any thing to justify thyself," or as another translation has it "Confess your sins that you may be made just."

In prayer the mouth of wisdom is opened when we admit we are not wise so that we put ourselves down as regards what our conscience fears, and lay aside what our prayer does not presume to ask for, as Jesus says in Matthew 6:5, ["And when ye pray, you shall not be as the hypocrites, that love to stand and pray in the synagogues and corners of the streets, that they may be seen by men: Amen I say to you, they have received their reward"], and further on in verse 8-9, ["Be not you therefore like to them, for your Father knoweth what is needful for you, before you ask him. Thus therefore shall you pray: Our Father who art in heaven"], and Matthew 7:7, "Ask and it shall be given you. [Seek, and you shall find. Knock and it shall be opened to you]. Likewise in John 16:24 Jesus says, "Hitherto you have not asked any thing in my name. Ask and you shall receive; that your joy may be full"], and Luke 11:1 tells how "One of his disciples said to him: Lord, teach us to pray, as John also taught his disciples." Two parables also support the truth that one ought to pray always and never fail to do so, [as it says in the parable in Luke 11:5-8 where it relates of Jesus that, "he said to them: Which of you shall have a friend, and shall go to him at midnight, and shall say to him: Friend, lend me three loaves, Because a friend of mine is come off his journey to me, and I have not what to set before him. And he from within should answer, and say: Trouble me not, the door is now shut, and my children are with me in bed; I cannot rise and give thee. Yet if he shall continue knocking, I say to you, although he will not rise and give him, because he is his friend; yet, because of his importunity, he will rise, and give him as many as he needeth.] For although God has no authority superior to himself to fear, nevertheless constancy in prayer pleases him and therefore he hears constant prayer. Similarly the second parable in Luke 18:2-5 relates how "There was a judge in a certain city, who feared not God, nor regarded man. And there was a certain widow in that city, and she came to him, saying: Avenge me of my adversary. And he would not for a long time. But afterwards he said within himself: Although I fear not God, nor regard man, yet because this widow is troublesome to me, I will avenge her, lest continually coming she weary me."

We, however, are those that Christ comes to as a wayfarer on the road of mercy that the entire world must travel, yet we do not have a meal we have prepared in our hearts that we can place before him. Our "friend" [as in the former parable], however, is our Father who is in heaven who is in the house of eternal peace with his children, the elect Angels and Saints, and although when we first petition him, perhaps we think we are not heard, nevertheless we will be heard later if we persevere in knocking. The "three loaves" that we ask for and by which Christ is nourished in our hearts are the bread of God's Word, the bread of the Sacrament of the Eucharist, and the bread of the tears of our repentance.

Third, the mouth of wisdom is opened in thanksgiving, as the Apostle says I Thessalonians 5:18, "In all things give thanks," and I Corinthians 10:31, "Therefore, whether you eat or drink, or whatsoever else you do, do all to the glory of God." Hosea 14:3 likewise says, "Return to the Lord, and say to him: Take away all iniquity, and receive the good" that is our penitence "and we will render the calves of our lips." The calves of our lips are acts of gratitude which we ought to do for the gifts dispensed to us by God, and Ecclesiastes 1:7 says, "Unto the place from whence the rivers come, they return, to flow again." Here the floods are the floods of graces which flow out from God and flow back to him through thanksgiving and again flow down upon us through the increase of graces. Therefore we give thanks to the Lord our God who has give so many and such great graces to us by creating us, redeeming us, teaching us, converting us, thus multiplying graces and certifying to us through hope the promise of everlasting life and fulfillment of that promise by its realization.

Fourth the mouth of wisdom is opened in praise. We praise God in hymns and psalms, chanting and singing in our hearts to God and in vocal melodies as the Apostle in Ephesians 5:19 counsels us to do, "Speaking to yourselves in psalms, and hymns, and spiritual canticles, singing and making melody in your hearts to the Lord." Whence in Psalm 50:23 it says, "The sacrifice of praise shall glorify me: and there is the way by which I will shew him the salvation of God." On this St. Gregory says in his *Homilies on Ezekiel*, the first version, that "The praise of God petitions either repentance or prophecy." Likewise in Psalm 146:2, it says, "Praise the Lord, O my soul, in my life I will praise the Lord: I will sing to my God as long as I shall be," and Psalm 117:1, says, "O praise the Lord, all ye nations: praise him, all ye people," and Psalm 95:1 says, "Sing ye to the Lord a new canticle: sing to the Lord, all the earth," and many other Psalms say the same. St. Augustine in his *Confessions,* Book X, comments on this fact, "Thus I have delighted in the sweet sounding hymns and canticles of your Church and the truth has flooded into my heart and my tears have flowed and this was all to my benefit."

Fifth the mouth of wisdom is opened in preaching and doctrine and of this Matthew 5:1-2 tells how "Seeing the multitudes, he [Jesus] went up into a mountain, and when he was set down, his disciples came unto him and opening his mouth, he taught them," where the Gloss says, "He opened his mouth as a great orator," and Job 29:15, says, "I was an eye to the blind, and a foot to the lame," that is, through preaching," and Isaiah 2:3 says, "The law shall come forth from Sion, and the word of the Lord from Jerusalem." "Sion" indicates that the preacher as if standing before a mirror should be posed as in contemplation, while "Jerusalem" indicates that his actions should always respect peace. Thus it says in Job 29:21, "They that heard me, waited for my sentence, and being attentive held their peace at my counsel" and later in verse 23, "They waited for me as for rain, and they opened their mouth as for a later shower" and Wisdom 6:26, says, "Now the multitude of the wise." that is, of preachers and doctors, "is the welfare of the whole world."

It should be noted with regard to this last opening of the mouth, however, that this mouth must be purged clean, as in Isaiah 6:8 the Lord says, "Whom shall I send? And who shall go for us? And I (Isaiah] said: Lo, here am I, send me." But before he offered himself, he says in verses 6 and 7 how in a vision he was first purified, "One of the seraphim flew to me, and in his hand was a live coal, which he had taken with the tongs off the altar. And he touched my mouth, and said: Behold this hath touched thy lips, and thy iniquities shall be taken away, and thy sin shall be cleansed." That it was sin that had impeded his preaching is evident from what Isaiah says in v. 5 of his former self, "And I said: Woe is me, because I have held my peace; because I am a man of unclean lips, and I dwell in the midst of a people that hath unclean lips." This "man with unclean lips" is a sinful preacher standing in the midst of a people who have unclean lips as a symbol of their perversion, who, as St. Gregory the Great says, "As many as are guilty in soul, just so many others they lead on to hell by the example of their perdition." The Seraphim who are interpreted as "totally enflamed," are the fire of divine love which enkindles to cleanse and the "tongs" are the penance that touch the preacher's mouth and clear his lips of sin, that is, from false preaching, by cleansing his way of living.

§ 2

Next comes the second part of the chapter verse, "**and the law of clemency is on her tongue.**" By her tongue, however, is meant not only that of her body but also of her heart. That of her heart is either the tongue of devotion or that of desire, for St. Gregory the Great says in his commentary on Job that, "The tongue of the Saints with which they speak to God are their desires." When Psalm 38:10, says, "Lord, all my desire is before thee, and my groaning is not hidden from thee," as if to say, "My desires tell you about what is in my heart and Psalm 10:17 in Jerome's translation from the Hebrew says, "The Lord hears the desires of the poor, the preparation of their heart he has heard with your ears." If, therefore, desire is heard and then forms voices and words it is thus a "tongue' or language. St. Bernard therefore says, "Devotion is the language of the blessed and the Saints." and thus it says in Psalm 137:6, "Let my tongue cleave to my jaws, if I do not remember thee [Jerusalem]: If I make not Jerusalem the beginning of my joy." For all our devotion is the remembrance of heavenly peace and the security of heaven's eternal citizens.

Of the language of the bodily mouth it is said in Psalm 37:30-31, "The mouth of the just shall meditate wisdom: and his tongue shall speak judgment. The law of his God is in his heart, and his steps shall not be supplanted." This psalm touches on four points: the first is to propose wisdom with meditation so that wisdom is spoken among those perfect in wisdom and is spoken wisely so that spiritual truths are compare with spiritual truths; the second is that it be spoken judiciously in view of the fact that judicious speech must be understood with discrete judgment, since it can be wrongly taken one way by the proud, another rightly by the modest or by the continent and by others in this and that way. The third is that when a word is proposed as law it should be perfectly understood in the heart, because as the Gloss on the Epistle of St. James ["If any man offend not in word, the same is a perfect man," James 3:2] says "It is impossible that one who does not know the law will not offend in preaching or teaching." The fourth and last, however, is that success of the preacher's efforts should not be nullified by some vice.

In the language of the heart according to these twofold tongues one is the law of clemency, that is, the law inclining God himself to be clement. For these languages are signified by the tongues of fire that appear over the Apostles in the coming of the Holy Spirit [Acts 2:3]. And in this desire is a certain fiery law of charity which is a gentle yoke and not heavy burden but lightening the load of those obligations that without it might seem very heavy. Of this law Deuteronomy 33:2 says, "[The Lord came from Sinai, and from Seir he rose up to us: he hath appeared from mount Pharan, and with him thousands of Saints and in] his right hand a fiery law." And this is the law of Christ of which in Matthew 11:30 he says, "For my yoke is sweet and my burden light," which we ought to be able to bear.

In the language of devotion is the law of the commands of God since we should devote ourselves to his precepts and counsels of which it is said in Sirach 24:33, "Moses commanded a law in the precepts of justice," and in John 1:17, "For the law was given by Moses; grace and truth came by Jesus Christ."

In the language of the bodily mouth is the law of clemency that restrains the soul of which Cicero says in his First Rhetoric, "Clemency is the virtue through which souls are held back by fear of condemning someone too quickly out of hatred," and Proverbs 11:19 also says, "Clemency prepareth life: and the pursuing of evil things, death." And this is also "rod of clemency" which the Supreme King, although provoked by us by sin nevertheless extends to us sinners, symbolized by the scepter of clemency of Assuerus [who is interpreted "blessed') in Esther 5:2, "He held out toward her the golden scepter," of which we have spoke above.

OUTLINE OF CHAPTER XVIII

She hath looked well to the paths of her house,
And hath not eaten her bread idle. (v. 27)

§1) The Acrostic Letter Sade, **צ**, means "hunting" and is of four kinds:
  1) Hunting
    1) Bad hunting is threefold
      1) Lamech's hunting of revenge
      2) Nimrod's hunting of exploitation
      3) Sidon's hunting of avarice
    2) Useless hunting: Esau's hunting
    3) Good hunting Peter and the Apostles hunt for souls
  2) The Valiant Woman is a good hunter: "She hath looked well to the paths of her house."
    1) Her threefold discernment of what is good for her householder
      1) Discernment because paths go off in many directions
      2) Circumspection because from past experiences she sees perils
      3) Inspection of the goods she has gained is constant
    2) What are these "paths"?: sharing her wisdom about her Spouse's (Christ's) commands
      1) Precepts: Ten Commandments binding on all
      2) Counsels derived from the commandments the eight Beatitudes imitate Christ
      3) Challenges (supererogations) raised by Doctors of the Church or personal duties
        1) The Good Samaritan
        2) Challenge of labor like St. Paul's tent making
        3) Duties of Bishops of the Church
        4) Longing of the Saints for God of which there are many kinds
    3) What is this house? How is her house built (already discussed in Chapter X) but considered here in other terms
      1) Fortress set on highest mountain of virtues & protected by God and angels, grounded in humility, the house of Martha and Mary at Bethany
        1) Martha is the active life
        2) Mary is the contemplative life
      2) Enclosure is the virtue of obedience and has 16 rooms
        1) Oratory for prayer
        2) Library for reading
        3) Dormitory for quiet contemplation
        4) Privy for confession of sins
        5) Laundry for satisfaction of sins
        6) Infirmary of compassion with five porticos

THE VALIANT WOMAN 275

    1) Console the grieving
    2) Console the depressed
    3) Nurse the sick
    4) Sustain the impatient
    5) Help the feeble
    7) Cellar of memories and mediation
    8) Kitchen to prepare teaching and make it tasty
    9) Gate of charity open to all
    10) Guest room of mercy
    11) Auditorium for preaching
    12) Basement for penance
    13) School-room
    14) Exterior wall of religion
    15) Four-sided inner cloister whose 4 walls are the Cardinal Virtues
        1) Prudence side has 7 columns: wisdom. science, counsel, understanding, providence, memory and ingenuity
        2) Justice side has 7 columns: obedience, due cult of God, truth of judgment without respect to persons, companionship of equals, and mercy to inferiors, humility, and reverence to all according to their dignity
        3) Temperance side has 7 columns: continence, moderation in eating, modesty, moderation in talking and silence; graciousness, benevolence, piety yielding to all
        4) Fortitude has 7 columns, magnificence, patience, longanimity, steadfastness, confidence, fidelity, perseverance
    16) Christ is the Husband who heads the Valiant Woman's household
  3) Summer House
    1) Walk-way is worldly prosperity
    2) Garden is the support of friends
    3) Fountain is sacrament of confession and penance   4)
  4) Winter House: adversity brooding over loss of summerhouse

§2) Valiant Woman has not "eaten her bread idle." Bread is refreshment but can be idle in two ways
  1) Food of the lascivious, unclean food
  2) Food of the lazy
    1) The simply lazy who have no food
    2) Those who are ignorant and do not know how to work
    3) Those that celebrate festivals without grace but think they have grace

CHAPTER XVIII

She hath looked well to the paths of her house, and hath not eaten her bread idle. (v. 27)

§ 1

SADE צ. This letter is interpreted as "the hunt," but there is bad hunting, useless hunting, and good hunting.

Bad Hunting is threefold...	Lamech's Hunting Nimrod's Hunting Sidon's Hunting

Lamech's hunting [related in Genesis 4:23-24]: Lamech, the first polygamist, said to his wives Ada and Sella:"Hear my voice, ye wives of Lamech, hearken to my speech:for I have slain a man to the wounding of myself, and a stripling to my own bruising. Sevenfold vengeance shall be taken for Cain: but for Lamech seventy times sevenfold"], was in lust and anger. The first hunting, motivated by lust, was for bigamy, and what he hunted for was two wives, Ada and Sella, whose names signify gluttony and lust which those hunt who walk in the flesh. His hunting was also out anger because he killed a man to his own wounding and a stripling to his own bruising." Lamech was angered by two events, the killing of his father Cain although God had commended Cain not be killed [Genesis 4:15] and by [some action of] a "stripling," that is, of some strong person who had murdered in fury, that is through hate and envy, because hate and envy are like a deadly bow from whose curve fly the arrows of cursing and reproach and contempt of our worldly state of affairs.

Nimrod's hunting narrated in Genesis 10:8-9, ["Now Chus begot Nimrod: he began to be mighty on the earth. And he was a stout hunter before the Lord. Hence came a proverb: 'Even as Nimrod the stout hunter before the Lord.' And the beginning of his kingdom was Babylon, and Arach, and Achad, and Chalanne in the land of Sennaar:], was representing the power of this world which is attained by oppression, rape, and plunder, and such deeds. And this is power had not through asking but through force of which Sirach 13:23

says, "The wild ass is the lion's prey in the desert: so also the poor are devoured by the rich."

Sidon's hunting [Genesis 10:15, after who whom the great commercial city of Sidon was named,] was that of the avaricious who are filled with fraud, cheating each other in business and with tricks of deception and theft and usury and so on. And this is a hunt for cobwebs which like a spider eviscerates itself of its natural juices to catch flies, the temporal goods of this world.

The hunting of the careless is like Esau's hunting because of which he lost the blessing of his father since he gave it such little attention as we have already seen is related in Genesis 27:3-46. And this is to hunt in vain in which are occupied those who are weary of God and divine matters because they are engrossed in hunting deer and fowl and such things of which it is written in Baruch 3:16-19, "Where are the princes of the nations, and they that rule over the beasts that are upon the earth? That take their diversion with the birds of the air. That hoard up silver and gold, wherein men trust, and there is no end of their getting? Who work in silver and are solicitous, and their works are unsearchable. They are cut off, and are gone down to hell, and others are risen up in their place."

Good hunting is such as that of St. Peter and the Apostles who by the Lord were made fishers of men as was promised them by the Lord in Matthew 4:19, "And he saith to them: Come ye after me, and I will make you to be fishers of men." And this interpretation fits the chapter verse when it is translated as follows: "That woman by going round the roads has cared for her household and by fleeing laziness has sought out an abundance of food" in which verse are contained both thoughts. "She hath looked well to the paths of her house: " two things, as already noted, are implied in this verse; her care of her household and the merit of her supplying it with bread, since we gets that bread by her labor. Concerning the first of these, three things are noteworthy: first the concern she has for her household, second the nature of these "ways," and third how her house is built.

Consideration is threefold...	Discernment Circumspection Inspection

It is discernment because all its ways and paths go off in different directions, as Jeremiah 6:16 teaches; "Thus saith the Lord: Stand ye on the ways, and see and ask for the old paths which is the good way, and walk ye in it: and you shall find refreshment for your souls." For the Valiant Woman stands searching among the paths seeking which of these was the example given by the ancestors, because the way which seems right and newest to many may in fact lead to their death [as it says in Proverbs 14:12, "There is a way which seemeth just to a man: but the ends thereof lead to death."] Thus by discernment she knows how to choose the good and reject the evil.

She also considers by circumspection, that is, by turning over in her mind all future perils, taking care from the consideration of past experiences and secure in the present by reviewing all her works, because she has done everything with counsel and therefore does not need to regret what she has done, [as it says in Sirach 32:24, "My son, do thou nothing without counsel, and thou shalt not repent when thou hast done."] Hence the Valiant Woman is symbolized in Job 39:5-8, "Who hath sent out the wild ass free, and who hath loosed his bonds? To whom I have given a house in the wilderness and his dwellings in the barren land. He scorneth the multitude of the city; he heareth not the cry of the driver. He looketh round about the mountains of his pasture, and seeketh for every green thing." She is free of the cares of the flesh and therefore "heareth not the cry of the driver" such as an ass ordinarily must obey, but "looketh round about the mountains" for pasture, seeking "for every green thing." The mountain pastures are the lofty counsels of God on which she feeds herself and is satisfied. The green things are whatever helps her in her good works, such as good conversation, good society, and so forth and she seeks all these with providence and circumspection.

She constantly inspects her goods like a shining light since as it also says in Proverbs 4:18, "The path of the just, as a shining light, goeth forwards and increaseth even to perfect day"; but she does not inspect her goods as did the Pharisee spoken of in Luke 18:11-12, who said, "O God, I give thee thanks that I am not as the rest of men, extortioners, unjust, adulterers, as also is this publican." For the Valiant Woman inspects so that she might increase her goods and give thanks for them and preserve them, as it says in Sirach 27:12, "A holy man continueth in wisdom as the sun: but a fool is changed as the moon."

The next question is: "What are these ways?" that the Valiant Woman has [of sharing her wisdom about God's commands].

The Ways of the will of the Valiant Woman's Spouse...	Precepts Counsels Challenge (Supererogations) Of the Longing of the Saints for God

These ways of precept are the Ten Commandments as it relates in Exodus 20:1-17, of which three relate God and of which the First Commandment is; "You are the Lord God," that is, "God is One," and "There is no other God but You," and in this first precept is contained the whole faith of the Trinity and its unity.

The Second Commandment (v. 7) is "Thou shalt not take the name of the Lord thy God in vain," that is in false and perverse perjury and in this precept every perjurer is condemned, as it says in Zechariah 5:4 concerning the vision of the Flying Scroll, "One that sweareth in like manner shall be judged by it. I will bring it forth, saith the Lord of hosts: and it shall come to the house of the thief, and to the house of him that sweareth falsely by my name: and it shall remain in the midst of his house, and shall consume it, with the timber thereof, and the stones thereof," that is, a Flying Scroll covered with written curses will fall on the house of the thief and those swearing falsely in God's name.

The Third Commandment in Exodus 20:8 is "Remember that thou keep holy the Sabbath day". The Sabbath is the day of rest and our hearts can rest only in God, that is, in nothing that is contrary to God, since if we do we defile the Sabbath that God left to his people. Hence also in the Church there are assigned feast days in which the people, resting from the works that serve the weaknesses of this life and uplifting our hearts to rest in God and sing to him to answer us, and we delight in the Lord that he may grant the petitions of our hearts.

The seven other precepts pertain to our neighbor of which only one, the Fourth Commandment, is affirmative, Exodus 20:12, "Honor thy father and thy mother, that thou mayest be long-lived upon the land which the Lord thy God will give thee" in which we are commanded not to neglect to give all honor and aid which we can to help our neighbor, who is included in the name of our parents, as it says in Romans 12:7-9, "ministry, in ministering; or he that teacheth, in doctrine; He that exhorteth, in exhorting; he that giveth, with simplicity; he that ruleth, with carefulness; he that sheweth mercy, with cheerfulness. Let love be without dissimulation." We should show honor and obedience to our superiors, share social life and agreeableness with our social equals and mercy to our inferiors.

The Fifth Commandment in Exodus 20:13, is "Thou shalt not kill" in which is prohibited to us that through anger or hatred are we to strike or injure any person, neither in deed or word

The Sixth Commandment in v. 14, is "Thou shalt not commit adultery" in which all illicit intercourse and sins against nature are forbidden us.

The Seven Commandment is "Thou shalt not steal" in which is forbidden all illicit seizure of property, robbery, usury in all it species, unjust fees, and deceitful contrasts.

The Eighth Commandment in Exodus 20:16, is "Thou shalt not bear false witness against thy neighbor" in which is forbidden lying and speaking as if from the heart but really contrary to the heart, and all deceit which one can do in words to one's neighbor; for one's words ought to be a testimony to the truth in one's heart.

The Ninth Commandment Exodus 20:17, is "Thou shalt not covet thy neighbor's house: neither shalt thou desire his wife, nor his servant, nor his handmaid, nor his ox, nor his ass, nor any thing that is his," in which is forbidden uncleanness of heart because of what is contained in the body but not in the heart.

And the Tenth Commandment in the same verse 17, is "You shalt not covet thy neighbor's house, etc." in which is forbidden the avarice of the heart that is not expressed in external acts.

Of these ways Isaiah 2:3, says, "Come and let us go up to the mountain of the Lord, and to the house of the God of Jacob, and he will teach us his ways, and we will walk in his paths" and Psalm 25:4 says, "Show, O Lord, thy ways to me, and teach me thy paths."

The ways of God's Counsels are derived from the Commandments and are eight in number. Matthew 5:3-12 and following relates them and places the First Counsel in verse 3 as, "Blessed are the poor in spirit: for theirs is the kingdom of heaven," for the precept given before this counsel is in Psalm 62:11, "If riches abound, set not your heart upon them," and this precept is in regard to the subjection to riches, as Peter says in praising Christ, Matthew 19:27, "Behold we have left all things, and have followed thee," that is, they are poor in spirit, spiritually poor in act and will, followers of the Poor Man, Christ, poor pilgrims following a Pilgrim.

The Second Counsel in verse 4 is, "Blessed are the meek: for they shall possess the land." Those are meek who are not irritated or provoked by injuries from others nor irritate or provoke others, and this corresponds to the older Fifth Commandment that we should not kill or wound another.

The Third Counsel, verse 5, is "Blessed are they that mourn: for they shall be comforted" and this is understood of two kinds of mourning, namely, for one's own sins and those of others.

The Fourth Counsel, verse 6, is "Blessed are they that hunger and thirst after justice: for they shall have their fill" and is to be understood as putting all in decent debt to provide the body with what is proper to it and the soul with what is proper in turn to it, and also that we render our superiors what is due them, as is verified by what the Lord says in Matthew 22:2, "Render therefore to Caesar the things that are Caesar's; and to God, the things that are God's."

The Fifth Counsel in verse 7 is "Blessed are the merciful: for they shall obtain mercy" and is to be understood of mercy to the poor when this is devoutly exercised to them, even if it cannot be done in works, at least in the sympathy of heart.

The Sixth Counsel in verse 8 is "Blessed are the clean of heart: for they shall see God" and it teaches us here that we must purge our hearts of their vices and the occupations and cares of this world so that we can keep the Sabbath of God in which God is seen through a taste of eternal peace.

The Seventh Counsel in verse 9 is "Blessed are the peacemakers: for they shall be called children of God" and is understood of those who make peace between themselves and their neighbor, between their conscience and their desires, and between themselves and God. For this is he peace of time, the peace of the breast, and peace of eternity.

The Eighth counsel in verse 10 is "Blessed are they that suffer persecution for justice' sake: for theirs is the kingdom of heaven." By this precept it is granted to all Christians that they should confess the Name of Christ when this is required, although it applies differently to those who avoid the occasion and those who offer themselves to the danger of persecution, as is intended in this verse.

Of these paths it is said in Proverbs 4:26, "Make straight the path for thy feet, and all thy ways shall be established," and in Isaiah 26:7, "The way of the just is right, the path of the just is right to walk in," in which the term "the just" is of neuter gender or if anyone wants to take it in the masculine gender, it refers to Christ who in the way of life he took is our exemplar.

The path of Supererogations (challenges) is divided into three because the teaching of the Doctors of the Church raises such greater challenges, or they are raised due to matters that are put under one's care. The Word raises greater challenges in the views of the Saints about matters of truth that support the Faith and by reflection about good morals that has been further thought out [by theologians], as is signified in Luke 10:34-35, where it is related how the Good Samaritan after carrying the wounded man to the inn gave the innkeeper two pence, that is Christ, the true caretaker of our souls, gave the Two Testaments to the pastors in the Church, saying that if anything more was needed when he returned at the Judgment he will pay it. Likewise in Luke 19:23 in the Parable of the Hard Master, the Master says to his negligent servant, "Why then didst thou not give my money into the bank, that at my coming, I might have exacted it with usury?" For this is the Lord's own money which he lends us but demands back with interest and he condemns a servant who has not invested it in a bank that will pay that interest.

The challenges of labor or of work are noted in Acts 20:33-34, [when St. Paul said to the elders of Ephesus "I have not coveted any man's silver, gold, or apparel, as you yourselves know: for such things as were needful for me and them that are with me, these hands have furnished." For those who serve at the altar have a right to live from the altar and those who announce the Gospel to live by the Gospel [as the Apostles also says in I Corinthians 9:13-15, "Know you not, that they who work in the holy place, eat the things that are of the holy place; and they that serve the altar, partake with the altar? So also the Lord ordained that they who preach the Gospel should live by the Gospel. But I have used none of these things." St. Paul did not make a living by his preaching lest this should give the impression among the greedy that he preached the Gospel of Christ out of greed. Much the same is true of Samuel, as related in I Samuel 12:3, who when the people asked him to anoint a king in his stead, said "Speak of me before the Lord, and before his anointed, whether I have taken any man's ox, or ass: If I have wronged any man, if I have oppressed any man, if I have taken a bribe at any man's hand: and I will despise it this day, and will restore it to you." Moses also says of himself in Numbers 16:15, "Moses therefore being very angry, said to the Lord: Respect not their sacrifices: thou knowest that I have not taken of them so much as a young ass at any time, nor have injured any of them."

The challenge of care is understood of the office and title of Bishop, for this title is interpreted "superintendent or overseer" since beyond what is his strict duty he ought to aid and oversee the flock entrusted to him, as the Lord says in Micah 6:3-4, "O my people, what have I done to thee, or in what have I molested thee? Answer thou me. For I brought thee up out of the land of Egypt, and delivered thee out of the house of slaves: and I sent before thy face Moses, and Aaron, and Mary." "My people" means the Lord's people for whom the pastor, beyond supplying the sacraments and the preaching of faith and morals, must also meet three challenges. For just as by the sacraments he leads his people from the Egypt of their sins and through preaching of faith and morals he leads them from the house of slavery, that is, from servile works to the free practice of the virtues, so the challenges of his pastoral office are threefold, namely, good example, prayer with sacrifice, and bitter penance for the sins of his sheep. A good example of this is found in Moses who was the leader and chariot of the people of God in those matters that pertain to God. Through Aaron, however, is signified prayer and sacrifice for the people, because he was consecrated a priest to offer gifts and sacrifices for those who were ignorant and erring. Mary, their sister, however, is interpreted "bitter sea" because [as it says in Hebrews 4:15, "For we have not a high priest who can not have compassion on our infirmities: but one tempted in all things like as we are, without sin" for a bishop should weep and mourn over the sins of his people as if they were his own. For the bishops are a royal priesthood in reigning by authority and example as it says in I Peter 2:9, "You are a chosen generation, a kingly priesthood, a holy nation, a purchased people: that you may declare his virtues, who hath called you out of darkness into his marvelous light." For the bishops are a royal priesthood in offering most holy sacrifices and they purchase their people by their groans and tears through which they win over sinners, and they are a gate through which the elect enter, not taking the honor themselves, but as first chosen by others for the burden of office.

Of these paths it is said in Job 28:7, where it says of bad prelates, "The bird hath not known the path, neither hath the eye of the vulture beheld it," where the bird is Christ who flies through the heavens and is also called a vulture because he sees so far, for this is said to be a trait special to vultures. But a bishop who does not pasture the flock entrusted to him is like a bird blind to the way. In his case the vulture's eyes see nothing, since they fail to foresee the perils of the people of God and the temptations to which they are liable.

The paths of desire are the ways of the heart striving for God and there are may such paths. For we ascend to God through as many desires as there are kinds of such pathways as is said in Isaiah 26:8, "The way of the just is right, the path of the just is right to walk in. And in the way of thy judgments, O Lord, we have patiently waited for thee: thy name and thy remembrance are the desire of the soul."

Next is the question of what is this "house" in the chapter text. Because above in Chapter X, §1, we distinguished four parts of a house: its upper floors, its basement, its interior, and its exterior. Lest we seem to repeat this, here we will use four other terms:

House...	Fortress
	Enclosure
	Summer House
	Winter House

A fortress is a house for security and is set on the highest mount of virtue as is said in Psalm 24:3-4, "Who shall ascend into the mountain of the Lord: or who shall stand in his holy place? The innocent in hands, and clean of heart, who hath not taken his soul in vain, nor sworn deceitfully to his neighbor." This is the mountain of the Lord, the holy mountain, Tabor the mountain of God. which is interpreted "rising light" in which the Lord was seen transfigured as if he were another man [Matthew 17:1-9]. This house is fortified by the moat of our mortality; for the mortality of our misery helps the Saints not to delight in this world, whence it says in Job 3:22, "They rejoice exceedingly when they have found the grave," and this speaks of holy persons who enjoy having a fortress against the devil, the tomb of the morality of this life, because they are confident that the certitude of death saves them from pride and fills them with the fear of God. Thus a fortress is the wall of God's protection as in says in Psalm 91:1, "He that dwelleth in the aid of the Most High, shall abide under the protection of the God of Jacob."

The outer wall of this fortress is the custody of the Angels as it says in Psalm 91:11, "For he hath given his angels charge over thee; to keep thee in all thy ways." It has a tower of humility and this is the Tower of David of which we read in the Song of Songs 4:4, "Thy neck, is as the tower of David, which is built with bulwarks: a thousand bucklers hang upon it, all the armor of valiant men." The bucklers of true humility are four which are noted in two verses of poetry;

> To spurn the world, spurn none, yet spurn thyself
> And thus be spurned, these four are good indeed.

Humility is called a "tower" because it has deep foundations and the Philosopher says, "the height and the depth are identical." The thousand bucklers are the infinite examples of the humility of the Saints. The "armor of valiant" is the battles of the Saints by which they destroy their pride.

This fortress is also symbolized in Luke 10:38, "Now it came to pass as they went that he entered into a certain town [Latin *castellum*] and a certain woman named Martha, received him into her house. And she had a sister called Mary." Martha stands for the active life and Mary for the contemplative life and they received Christ into their house. He entered it as if it were a fortress since he was safe under the tower of their humility. In this house the Valiant Woman keeps vigil protected by bucklers, guards on the towers, soldiers on the walls. For vigils are watch-keeping that is kept in foreseeing dangers as St. Peter commands in I Peter 5:8-9, "Be sober and watch: because your adversary the devil, as a roaring lion, goeth about seeking whom he may devour, whom resist ye, strong in faith." The guardians are two: fear and love. For fear makes us flee evil and love strengthens us in good. Fear is a good guardian in that it excludes, namely enemies; love, however, is a good guardian in that nourishes friends within; and of these Isaiah 62:6, says, "Upon thy wails, O Jerusalem, I have appointed watchmen all the day, and all the night, they shall never hold their peace. You that are mindful of the Lord, hold not your peace," that is be not silent in praising the Name of the Lord, for fear praises only in the daytime when it is light. The "guardians" signify the struggles against temptation as it says in Job 7:1, "The life of man upon earth is a warfare." Of this so strongly guarded fortress Isaiah 26:1 says, "Sion the city of our strength a savior, a wall and a bulwark shall be set therein.'

The enclosure of the house is the second part to be built and this therefore is the obedience which is Bethany that is interpreted as "house of obedience " in which Jesus so often dwelt with his friends, Lazarus, Mary, and Martha, as in an oratory of prayer, as it says in

Isaiah 56:7, "Their holocausts, and their victims shall please me upon my altar: for my house shall be called the house of prayer, for all nations" and in Matthew 21:13 Jesus says, "It is written, My house shall be called the house of prayer," and Augustine says in his *Rule* c. 2, 2 (Russell translation): "In the Oratory [place of prayer] no one should do anything other than that for which was intended and from which it also takes its name," and much the same is said in the Gloss on the Gospel of John.

This enclosure also has a second room for reading, where St. Augustine also says in his *Rule*, c. 3, 2, "Let not your mouths alone take nourishment but let your hearts too hunger for the words of God," and Amos 8:11, says, "Behold the days come, saith the Lord, and I will send forth a famine into the land: not a famine of bread, nor a thirst of water, but of hearing the word of the Lord."

The enclosure has thirdly a dormitory of contemplation and quiet, as when Job 3:13 complains and curses the daylight of sin because it deprives him of the contemplation of eternal things, saying, "For now I should have been asleep and still, and should have rest in my sleep. With kings and consuls of the earth, who build themselves solitudes, or with princes, that possess gold and all their houses with silver," because he was silent and sleeping in contemplation from the rumors of this world, and was quiet in sleep dreaming of eternal things. He rested from the labor of a dweller in misery together with kings who are their own rulers and the counselors of the earth who give counsel of perfection to others which they draw out of their contemplation and with princes who desire eternal things which are of first importance and therefore possess gold, that is, the splendor of divine wisdom and fill the house of their hearts with the silver of eloquence in the sound of preaching and build for themselves solitudes in the secret of conscience. In this place of dreaming the Lord cast a deep sleep on Adam and took out his rib and made out of it a woman [Genesis 2:21-22]. "Adam" is interpreted as "man." His "rib" which is next to the heart, is hard and signifies the endurance of this life which is rooted in the heart of man. Out of it was built the woman who when she is engaged in contemplation is fruitful in the joys of eternal goods although in the labors of this life she is found to be sterile.

Fourth in the house is the chapter hall [*capitulum*] of confession where the perverse are charged and emended, as Isaiah 38:15 says, "What shall I say, or what shall he answer for me, whereas he himself hath done it? I will recount to thee all my years in the bitterness of my soul," and Psalm 32:5 says, "I have acknowledged my sin to thee, and my injustice I have not concealed. I said I will confess against myself my injustice to the Lord: and thou hast forgiven the wickedness of my sin."

Fifth in the house is the washroom of satisfaction of which it speaks in Isaiah 1:16-17, "Wash yourselves, be clean, take away the evil of your devices from my eyes: cease to do perversely, Learn to do well" and John 9:7 relates how Jesus said to a blind man, "Go, wash in the pool of Siloe, which is interpreted, Sent. He went therefore, and washed, and he came seeing", since he was sent to a priest who imposed a penance on him. Again the prophet told Naaman that he should wash seven times in the Jordan and he would received health in his flesh and be clean of leprosy [II Kings 5:10], for a "leper" is one who in the state of mortal sin and "washing in the Jordan" is satisfaction for sin, since Jordan is interpreted "humble descent". Naaman washed seven times by shame for his sins, and made satisfaction by tears, fasts, prayer, alms-giving, vigils, and scourgings. For these were his seven washings.

The sixth room in the house is the infirmary of compassion, as it says in Romans 14:1, "Now him that is weak in faith, take unto you: not in disputes about thoughts" and in Hebrews 13:3, "Remember them that are in bands, as if you were bound with them; and them that labour, as being yourselves also in the body." This infirmary is signified in John 5:3 by the portico of the Probatica pool [Bethesda] around which lay a multitude of languishing invalids.

And there are five porticos of compassion and five of affects...	Console the grieving Console the sad Care of the sick Sustain those laboring under impatience Help the feeble

The seventh part of the house is the storehouse or cellar of memories and of meditation and hence it says in Psalm 144:13, "Their storehouses are full, flowing out of this into that," since out of memory and meditation all that is demanded by reason should be prepared to bear on what is of faith and hope in that meditation [as it says in I Peter 3:15, "But sanctify the Lord Christ in your hearts, being ready always to satisfy every one that asketh you a reason of that hope which is in you."]

The eighth part of the house is the kitchen of study and doctrine because in study and doctrine are cut up into parts and boiled and flavored so as to have a sweet and agreeable taste. Hence in Ezekiel's last vision 46:23-24 [among the other rooms of the house he also sees that "There was a wall round about compassing the four little courts, and there were kitchens built under the rows round about. And he – the Angel – said to me: This is the house of the kitchens wherein the ministers of the house of the Lord shall boil the victims of the people"], and this kitchen is also signified by those chambers [*pastaphoria*] which were built in the in courts of he house of the Lord as it says in I Maccabees 4:47, "They adorned the front of the temple with crowns of gold, and escutcheons, and they renewed the gates, and the chambers, and hanged doors upon them."

The ninth part f the house is the gate of charity which is open to all that is good and gives it entrance. Whence in Genesis 24:31 it is said of charity how [Laban greeted Abraham's messenger], "Come in, thou blessed of the Lord: why standest thou without? I have prepared the house, and a place for your camels." Hence also in Genesis 28:17 Jacob says, "This is none other but the house of God, and the gate of heaven." And so it still is where charity is found in the gate of cloisters.

The tenth part of the house of mercy, as the Apostle says in Philemon 1:7, "For I have had great joy and consolation in thy charity, because the hearts of the Saints have been refreshed by thee, brother," and later in verse 22, "Prepare me also a lodging," and in Hebrews 13:2, "And hospitality do not forget; for by this some, being not aware of it, have entertained angels."

The eleventh part of the house is auditorium for preaching, as it says in the Song of Songs 2:14, "Let thy voice sound in my ears: for thy voice is sweet, and thy face comely," and in Psalm 45:3, "Thou art beautiful above the sons of men: grace is poured abroad in thy lips; therefore hath God blessed thee for ever."

The twelfth part of the house is the basement of penance into which we pile all in us that is corrupt, as it says in Micah 7:19 of God, "He will put away our iniquities: and he will cast all our sins into the bottom of the sea."

The thirteenth part of the house is the schoolroom as the Apostle says in Hebrews 12:11, "Now all chastisement for the present indeed seemeth not to bring with it joy, but sorrow: but afterwards it will yield, to them that are exercised by it, the most peaceable fruit of justice."

The fourteenth part of the house has the exterior wall of religion, as St. Augustine says in *Rule* c. 4, 3, "In your walk, deportment, and in all actions, let nothing occur to give offense to anyone who sees you, but only what becomes your holy state of life." [Russell translation] and the Bride in Song of Songs 5:10 says, "My beloved is white and ruddy, chosen out of thousands" for whiteness signifies chastity and ruddiness signifies charity but someone is chosen out of thousands by interior and exterior religion whence it also says of the Beloved in verse 16 that he is "wholly desirable."

The fifteenth part of the house is the interior cloister built with the four sides that are the four cardinal virtues; of which one wall is the virtue of prudence which has seven columns, namely wisdom, science, counsel, understanding, providence, memory, and ingenuity. Wisdom is the taste of divine things; science of the ordering of world, counsel of what is pleasing to God, understanding of the eloquence of the Saints, providence of future perils, memory of the past, and ingenuity of human cunning, and these seven virtues are like columns, of which prudence is the first, uphold the first wall of the cloister.

The second interior wall of the cloister that is justice is also upheld by seven columns carved by the hand of wisdom itself. The first column is obedience to a superior's precepts; the second is worship of God, which is the due cult of God, also named *latria*; the third is rectitude or truth of judgment without respect to persons; the fourth is companionship for equals; the fifth is mercy to inferiors; the sixth is humility; and the seventh is reverence to all who are ranked according to their dignity.

The third wall of the cloister is built to uphold the house as does the virtue of temperance having also seven columns by which it is supported, of which the first is continence; the second is moderation in eating, the third is modesty of deportment both interior and exterior; the fourth is moderation as regards [talking and] silence; the fifth is graciousness of manner; the sixth is benevolence or benignity; and the seventh and last is the affect of piety yielding to all.

The fourth wall of the cloister extends like the virtue of fortitude supported by seven columns, namely, patience in adversity, long-suffering in endurance, magnificence in the expansion of a heart that seeks great deeds, steadfastness in resolution, confidence in arduous undertakings, faith in God's help and perseverance in tribulation to the very end.

And this is the house that wisdom built carving seven columns for it on every side as is said in Proverbs 9:1, "Wisdom hath built herself a house, she hath hewn her out seven pillars," and in Revelation 21:16 when it says that the heavenly Jerusalem is built "foursquare, ["And the city lieth in a foursquare, and the length thereof is as great as the breadth."]

The husband of the Valiant Woman is Christ who houses his whole family in the house called that of Bethany, [as related in Luke 10:38-42] where Mary contemplates and Martha serves them as they contemplate, herself troubled and solicitous about many things. This house is also where Christ's disciples as students hear him teaching. As he sits teaching, Simon [Peter] and Lazarus recline so that they may happily refresh themselves on this banquet of inner consolation. Here also Judas stole from the apostles' purse and thus through him is signified lovers of wealth while through Simon [Peter), since "Simon is interpreted "obedient,' is signified those who murmur against obedience. In this house also the Lord as the dispenser of the family goods of the Valiant Woman shows himself by all his works as a very generous family-man and father. Here also he cured Mary of seven devils, that is, the soul of a sinner from the seven capital sins and he also, according to St. Ambrose, cured Martha from a flow of blood, that is, controlled the flow of the flesh through continence. Jesus also cured Simon [the Pharisee] of leprosy, which is a disease that is humanly incurable, although curable only by God, which corrupts and defiles the whole body, that is, from sin that is habitual and impenitent. Jesus also reprehended the Pharisee who was indignant because Jesus cures a sinful woman [as is related in Luke 7:36-39]. Thus here Jesus confounded the pharisaical who are always judging others and are full of indignation of soul at others' behavior.

Here also, [as is related in John 11:33-44] Jesus raised Lazarus, that is those desperately fouled by sin after four days in the grave. On the first day Lazarus as a sinner lies dead when he consents to sin. On the second day he completes that sin. On the third, he continues in that sinning, till on the fourth day at last he stinks in despair, so that even the Lord weeps over him and groans in spirit, making known by this the difficulty of bringing a sinner back to life. Here also Jesus spoke to the crowds and the voice of his Father confirming him was heard [as is related in John 12:28-30, "Father, glorify thy name. A voice therefore came from heaven: I have both glorified it, and will glorify it again. The multitude therefore that stood and heard, said that it thundered. Others said: An angel spoke to him. Jesus answered, and said: This voice came not because of me, but for your sakes." This voce to the crowds was heard as praise by which the crowds in the cloister were struck with awe and, as the voice of the Father glorifying his Son, it is the fame of the liturgical celebrations that rise from cloisters.

Here also feet are anointed, that is, the dispensing of mercy and truth by which every heart walks the way of the ointment of penance. And the head of Christ's divinity whence all good descends is here anointed with the ointment of devotion and acts of thanksgiving. It should be noted that according to the Gospels [Matthew 26:7; Luke 7:37; John 12:3] these all were completed in Bethany, which is interpreted "house of obedience' and signifies the cloister of the Valiant Woman's house, as we have said.

Next is the consideration of the summer house. This house has a walk-way and garden in which the Valiant Woman cools off from the summer's heat. It also has a fountain in the garden. Of this garden and fountain there is reference in Daniel 14:4 where we read that Joachim, husband of Susanna, was very rich and had an orchard joined to his house and further on in verse 5 it says that Susanna had entered the orchard the day before noon and wanted to bathe in the orchard because it was so warm. This summer house is simply the prosperity of this world which sometimes mocked this woman; hence she did not live there but walked through it. That walkway is a kind of expansion of the heart in the prosperity of this world. Thus, as it is related in Judges 3:15-30, how Eglon, [the King of Moab who tyrannized Israel] sat in this summer house enjoying its comforts and feeding on its delights until he was slain by a messenger of the Lord named Aod. For Eglon was sitting in his summer parlor [when Aod, concealing his sword in his left hand, thrust it into the king's exceedingly fat belly and killed him and then, escaping, became a judge over the chosen people of God, Israel that he had thus freed. A garden adjoining a house in which coolness is maintained signifies powerful and flourishing friends, such that they join one's children in games, as also are nephews and neighbors who are like trees in a forest. A fountain in which one washes off the sweat contracted working in the house signifies the fount of the sacraments of penance and confession. Hence in the garden of her house Susanna was accused of crime but was freed by the efforts of Daniel. But hardly any of this world who prosper are able to live without sin or taint of sin, since unless a Daniel, that is the divine Word, defends them, they will be stoned by the very harsh words of Job 21:13 who said. "They spend their days in wealth, and in a moment they go down to hell."

The next consideration concerns the winter house, and this is the adversity of one who, having unwillingly had to leave his summer house, is continually consumed in the furnace of the fire of anger at having undergone that injury. Thus it was in his winter house that Joachim, King of Judah, cut up the book of the words of the Lord [in the prophecy of Baruch] and burnt them in the fire. Thus it is written in Jeremiah 36:22-23, that the king sat in his winter house in the ninth month and there was placed before him a bowl filled with burning coals and it was there that he burnt the Word of the Lord. The winter house, as already noted, is the house of adversity. The ninth month is the recent injury he had suffered, because the more recent an injury the greater the anger it arouses. The words of the Lord are those by which we are commanded that we should repay our debts to him, patiently tolerating the injury this does us. But the words of the Lord are torn up when someone listens carefully to them but does not obey them, for such persons tear the word from its effects they ought to have.

The Valiant Woman owns these two summer and winter houses to prove them but not to live there herself, since she knows what the Prophet Amos 3:15 says, "And I will strike the winter house with the summer house: and the houses of ivory shall perish, and many houses shall be destroyed, saith the Lord."

§ 2

Next comes the second phrase of the chapter verse, "**and hath not eaten her bread idle.**" Here it should be noted that "bread' signifies refreshment, and this can be twofold: idleness, whether this is lascivious, laziness, or ignorance or it can be the celebration of a feast. The first has bread but it is unclean, as Ezekiel 4:13 says, "So shall the children of Israel beat their bread all filthy among the nations whither I will cast them out," that is, when they are converted to the evil ways of the Gentiles. The second, the lazy, have no bread and don't deserve any. The third have no bread but believe they have it. The Valiant Woman does not lack bread in any of these ways.

Of the first kind of idleness, that which is lascivious, II Thessalonians 3:7-10 says, "For yourselves know how you ought to imitate us: for we were not disorderly among you; Neither did we eat any man's bread for nothing, but in labour and in toil we worked night and day, lest we should be chargeable to any of you," and then in verses 11-12, says, "For also when we were with you, this we declared to you: that, if any man will not work, neither let him eat. For we have heard there are some among you who walk disorderly, working not at all, but curiously meddling. Now we charge them that are such, and beseech them by the Lord Jesus Christ, that, working with silence, they would eat their own bread."

As to the idleness of the lazy who have no bread, there is no reason they should have it, as Proverbs 6:6-11 advises, "Go to the ant, O sluggard, and consider her ways, and learn wisdom" [that is foresight] "Which, although she hath no guide, nor master, nor captain, provideth her meat for herself in the summer, and gathereth her food in the harvest. How long wilt thou sleep, O sluggard? When wilt thou rise out of thy sleep? Thou wilt sleep a little, thou wilt slumber a little. Thou wilt fold thy hands a little to sleep: And want shall come upon thee, as a traveler, and poverty as a man armed. But if thou be diligent, thy harvest shall come as a fountain, and want shall flee far from thee." And Proverbs 13:4 also says, "The sluggard willeth and willeth not: but the soul of them that work, shall be made fat" and Proverbs 19:15 adds, "Slothfulness casteth into a deep sleep, and an idle soul shall suffer hunger." These last two authoritative texts touch on both sorts of idleness, namely that of lasciviousness and of laziness, but of laziness in particular we read in Proverbs 20:4, "Because of the cold the sluggard would not plough: he shall beg therefore in the summer, and it shall not be given him," and Proverbs 21:5, "The thoughts of the industrious always bring forth abundance: but every sluggard is always in want," and Proverbs 22:13, "The slothful man saith: There is a lion without, I shall be slain in the midst of the streets."

Of the idleness of the ignorant and the bread they ought to have but do not because although they have the tools for work they do not known how to apply them to work, in Matthew 20:6 the master says to workmen, "Why do why stand you here all the day idle?" for they were not lazy since they went out to work with their tools but did not know how to use them and this explains what it says in Proverbs 28:19, "He that tilleth his ground, shall be filled with bread: but he that followeth idleness shall be filled with poverty," and in Sirach 33:29-30, "For idleness hath taught much evil. Set him to work: for so it is fit for him."

Concerning the idleness of keeping festivals thinking one has the bread of grace when one does not, in Isaiah 1:14, [the Lord says through the prophet], "My soul hateth your new moons, and your solemnities: they are become troublesome to me, I am weary of bearing them." These new moons are feasts and signify the idleness of those who pretend to contemplate, who always want to be idle and never to work, [daring to say] as it says in John 6:27, "Labor not for the meat which perisheth, but for that which endureth unto life everlasting" but of these Lamentations 1:7 says, "Her enemies have seen her, and have mocked at her sabbaths" and Amos 5:23, "Take away from me the tumult of thy songs: and I will not hear the canticles of thy harp." Hence this is also signified in I Maccabees 2:38 and 40, "So they gave them battle on the Sabbath: and they were slain with their wives, and their children, and their cattle, to the number of a thousand persons...And every man said to his neighbor: 'If we shall all do as our brethren have done, and not fight against the heathens for our lives, and our justifications: they will now quickly root us out of the earth,'" where it is read that ten thousand Jews who were keeping a festival were killed because, obedient to the Ten Commandments, they we would not fight on the Sabbath, until Mattathias ordered that they should fight manfully against all who were waging war against them, even on the Sabbath.

THE VALIANT WOMAN 295

OUTLINE OF CHAPTER XIX

Her children rose up, and called her blessed:
Her husband, and he praised her. (v.28)

§1) The letter Coph, ק, means "conclusion" and this chapter begins the last part of the treatise in four chapters in which the Valiant Woman is praised. XIX gives her husband and children's' praises, XX praises her wealth, XXI her figure and beauty, XXII her works.
 How do her children stand up to praise her? She has four fruitful powers and bears Christ twelve sons who pass on to her the blessing given them by Jacob and by Moses.
 1) Christ has four powers in the Valiant Woman's soul by which she bears twelve sons, as Jacob's wives Leah and Rachel and his concubines Bilhah and Zilpah did for Jacob
  1) Leah whom Jacob mistakenly first married is the active life which is:
   1) Blear-eyed because it is the will not the intellect
   2) Yet some meritorious works must precede contemplation
  2) Before Jacob embraced Rachel Leah bore:
   1) Reuben who signifies prudence about what is to be done
   2) Simon who signifies obedience to the Commandment not to sin in one's actions
   3) Levi who signifies taking vows to carry out the counsels of perfection
   4) Judah who signifies thanksgiving to God for help in action
  3) Then Leah who had become infertile gave Jacob her servant as concubine who then bore
   1) Dan who signifies knowledge of God thorugh the analogies of creatures
   2) Nephthali who signifies wonder at God's transcendence of creatures
  4) Leah then gave Jacob her servant Zilpha who bore:
   1) Gad who signifies the height of contemplation
   2) Asher who signifies the zeal for the conversion of souls
  5) Leah then by eating mandrakes (Scripture study) became fertile again and bore:
   1) Issachar who signifies the preacher who converts souls
   2) Zebulon who signifies a Doctor who defends the Church
   3) A daughter, Dina, who signifies the lusts of the flesh that opposes contemplation
  6) Rachel who signifies the contemplative life bore:
   1) Joseph who signifies the illumination of the contemplative
   2) As Jacob returned to the Holy Land, Rachel, clinging to her idols, bore Benjamin who signifies the total transcendence of God and then she died.

§2) How did the Valiant Woman's children "Stand up and praise her"? By passing on to her the blessing given to the twelve sons Jacob by Jacob and Moses:
 1) Reuben
  1) He was not blessed by Jacob because he sinned by lust and by treachery

  2) Moses blessed him out of mercy, because he repented but souls have few descendents
 2 & 3) Simeon and Levi
  1) Jacob did not bless them because they signify religious intolerance
  2) Yet Moses blesses them at least for their
   1) Obedience to the Law
   2) Fidelity to the covenant
   3) Fidelity to prayer
   4) Chastity
   5) They fight the devil
 4) Judah signifies one gifted in grace:
  1) Jacob blesses Judah in six ways:
   1) His brothers will praise him
   2) He overcomes his enemies
   3) His brothers admire and imitate him
   4) He receives graces by the force of his piety
   5) He washes his robes in wine which signify Christ's Passion
   6) He is beautiful in purity of intention and efficacy of his preaching of praise
  2) Moses praises him for his endurance through trials
 5) Dan signifies the first steps of contemplation
  1) For Jacob, Dan is a serpent, cautious about not confusing creatures with God
  2) For Moses, Dan is a lion, because he contradicts the wise of the world by faith
 6) Nephthali signifies the second grade of contemplation
  1) For Jacob he is a beautiful deer, the wonder of the Incarnation and the Sacraments
  2) For Moses he possesses land and sea, the abundance of divine wisdom
 7) Gad signifies ultimate virtue in a will that finds perfection in God's will
  1) For Jacob Gad is girded in front battling for his people and in back against the devil
  2) For Moses he is a lion who has like Christ conquered all of his enemies
 8) Asher signifies zeal for conversion of souls
  1) For Jacob Asher has the rich food of the Divine Word
  2) For Moses Asher's feet are dipped in the oil of mercy and clad in the armor of war against heresy
 9) Isaachar, as a son of Leah signifies the active life
  1) For Jacob he is strong as an ass not in stupidity but in the tasks of the preacher
  2) For Moses his tent is the Church
 10) Zebulon, last son of Lia, signifies the courage of Doctor and Bishop
  1) For Jacob he is the width of the sea, that is, rules over all
  2) For Moses he is the one who visits the flock
 11) Joseph signifies the third grade of contemplation
  1) From Jacob he has a fourfold blessing all relating ot the illumination for the intellect
  2) Joseph's praise
   1) Many children, sons of illumination, especially Manassas and Ephraim
    1) Manassas signifies forgetting this life in light of heaven
    2) Ephraim signifies the fruit of good works

THE VALIANT WOMAN

3) Jacob crossed hands and blessed Ephraim first; we worship God for the short time we live, but are reward eternally
2) Beauty from walking always in God's light in contemplation
3) Patience in trials when his hated him because of his dreams
   1) One dream sun, moon and stars worship him
      1) Sun is knowledge of Sacred Scripture
      2) Moon is secular knowledge
      3) Stars are grammar, rhetoric, dialectics, geometry, arithmetic, music, physics, metaphysics, ethics, and the sciences of positive and natural law
      4) Manner of liberation from prison: he came forth as shepherd & rock of truth
   2) Blessing of the multiplication of his graces
   3) Confirmation by the patriarchs whose example must guide us
   4) Prophecy of sanctity for Joseph's progeny and of the Nazarites
2) Moses the Lawgiver, however, when he blessed Joseph said,
   1) Of the fruits of the earth and their fullness:
      1) The "fruits of heaven", that is, the fruit of eternal beatitude
      2) The "dew of heaven", that is, the dew of graces
      3) "The deep that lieth beneath"; eternal punishment
      4) "The fruits of sun & moon": Sacraments of Church and pre-Sacraments of Synagogue
      5) "The Tops of the ancient mountains", that is, eminence of the ancient patriarchs
      6) The "fruit of the everlasting hills", that is, the ranks of angels
      7) The fruits of the earth, that is, the common contemplation of all that is good by all the Saints,
      8) Christ the fire of God in the use of the Virgin Mother of God
   2) The beauty of Joseph's face (previously explained) that displays a young bullock's favor
   3) The strength of the perception of truth like the two "horns of rhinoceros"
      1) One that reveals faith
      2) One that reveals morals as against the worldly
         1) Ambition for honor
         2) Desire for pleasure
         3) Greed for riches
12) Benjamin
   1) For Jacob he is a wolf whose eyes glow in the dark, the highest grace of contemplation
   2) For Moses he is the blessed of the lord, the highest grade of sanctity

§2) Why is the Valiant Woman blessed?
1) She is blessed in three ways:
   1) She only seeks and finds the Kingdom of God and its justice
   2) She wishes only virtue and never anything evil
   3) She loves only the good
2) Her husband, Christ, praises her for three things:
   1) Her usefulness as Ever-Virgin, conceiving & bearing God, yet remaining ever Virgin Mother of God
   2) Her dignity found especially in her humility

3) The mystery of her election to heal all the wounds caused by Mother Eve

CHAPTER XIX

Her children rose up, and called her blessed: her husband, and he praised her. (v.28)

§ 1

COPH, ק, Here first should be noted how this letter corresponds to the chapter verse. It is interpreted "conclusion" and thus by this letter it is noted that we have come to the concluding part of this treatise on the Valiant Woman. For all that has been said of her is concluded in the fourfold of her praises, which [praise she receives in the four verses that now remain]. In this verse are mentioned the praises of which she is worthy, in the second of these four chapters she is praised for her wealth, in the third for her figure and beauty, and in the ultimate verse for her works and thus this work is concluded with her four praises. To the other verse, however, this epigrammatic verse is added because principal and special praise is in the mouths of her sons and husband who know her most familiarly and extol her most affectionately.

In the first phrase "**Her children rose up,**" three things should be noted: who are children, how they "stood up," and how they praised their most blessed mother. Concerning the first question it should be noted that just as Jacob had two free wives, Lia and Rachel and two concubines, Bilhah and Zilpah [Genesis 29:21-35 and 30:1-5] so Christ in the soul of one faithful wife, the Valiant Woman, has four fruitful powers by which she bears twelve sons from their father's blessed seed. Thus, Leah whose name is interpreted "hard-working," who, [it says in Genesis 29:17] was "blear-eyed" but fertile, less delicate, but first to mate with her husband; not promised to him, yet given him; is the active life which is totally founded in that part of the soul which is called the free will. She is blear-eyed in her action since she does not know what child is to be the result of her work; nevertheless she is fertile in all good works. She is, however, lest loved [by Jacob] since he did not desire her since our whole desire is rather to attain the eternal quiet of contemplation for which Jacob, a great struggler, slaved for seven years, that is, through the perfect cycle of the virtues. Yet he first had intercourse with Leah, since unless Christ is joined to us so that through meritorious works we are made comely, we are not able to obtain some degree of contemplation. So it was fitting that Jacob for some time had intercourse with Leah before he could enjoy what Rachel alone could offer him. Thus Leah was not the one promised him because in her, that is in free will, is not the reward of our labors, but rather that through her, [that is, by acts of free will] we come to the reward of contemplation, because in our place, that is, in this life, it is not customary that the younger daughter, such as Rachel, be the first to marry, but rather the eldest, that is, that active labor should be done by us before we attain the solace of contemplation.

Rachel is interpreted "seeing the beginning," and signifies contemplation of the eternal God who is beginning of all created beings, as it says in John 1:2-3, "The Word was in the beginning with God. All things were made by him: and without him was made nothing that was made." This contemplation, however, is primarily in the intelligence of the faithful soul [not in the free will] who is joined to Christ in marriage.

Laban, Leah and Rachel's father, assigned the concubine Bilhah to Leah as her handmaid and her name is interpreted "absorbed'" and signifies our imagination or imaginary power which according to St. Augustine is "the mental power of the inferior reason in which is implanted the images of sensible things created by God," and thus Bilhah served Rachel because the human intellect frequently draws the truth of eternal things from images of sensible things that bear traces and reflections of their Creator as it says in Psalm 19:2, "The heavens shew forth the glory of God, and the firmament declareth the work of his hands." the more excellent creatures indicate uncreated truth to the human intelligence, as Job 9:7-10 says, "Who commandeth the sun and it riseth not: and shutteth up the stars as it were under a seal: Who alone spreadeth out the heavens, and walketh upon the waves of the sea. Who maketh Arcturus, and Orion, and Hyades, and the inner parts of the south. Who doth things great and incomprehensible, and wonderful, of which there is no number," so also Job 12:7-10 cites the feebler creatures to manifest man's Creator, saying, "But ask now the beasts, and they shall teach thee: and the birds of the air, and they shall tell thee. Speak to the earth, and it shall answer thee: and the fishes of the sea shall tell. Who is ignorant that the hand of the Lord hath made all these things? In whose hand is the soul of every living thing, and the spirit of all flesh of man." So also Bilhah was joined to her man, as indicated in Genesis 41:18-22 where it relates that [Pharaoh asked Joseph to interpret] the following dream "And seven kine came up out of the river exceeding beautiful and full of flesh: and they grazed on green places in a marshy pasture. And behold, there followed these, other seven kine, so very ill-favored and lean, that I never saw the like in the land of Egypt: And they devoured and consumed the former, And yet gave no mark of their being full: but were as lean and ill-favored as before. I awoke, and then fell asleep again and dreamed a dream: Seven ears of corn grew upon one stalk, full and very fair." Thus as Joseph conjectured the clear truth in images that served his intellect when that was coupled to the spirit of prophecy, so Bilhah served Rachel. The same was the case for Nabuchodonosor's dream of the statue, [related in Daniel 2:31], for which image Daniel gave an intellectual interpretation and also of the handwriting on the wall shown externally to the king. Thus Daniel through his intellect expressed in his own words this meaning of eternal truth. He himself, as it relates in Daniel 7:2-28, saw within his soul in a dream saw through the power of his imagination four beasts and four winds fighting in the sea and then by his intelligence interpreted these images as meaning four kings and four kingdoms. Similarly to Jeremiah 1:13-14 future punishments appeared to his external eyes as the image of a boiling caldron, ["And the word of the Lord came to me a second time, saying: What seest thou? I see a boiling caldron and the face thereof from the face of the north. And the Lord said to me: from the north shall an evil break forth upon all the inhabitants of the land."] Thus Jeremiah, interpreting this vision clearly in his intellect, preached its truth about the future conquest and burning of Jerusalem. Likewise Bilhah served Rachel, because the imagination serves the intellect which discovers truth in what has previously been proposed to it in images of physical objects.

The active life is that is truly within the power of the free will. Hence Rachel also had from her father a servant, Zilpah, who names is interpreted "open mouth" and signifies the operation of the free will, because whatever a free person chooses the will opens itself like a mouth to carry out. For this mouth opens to command all the effective members of the body so that they obey her, that is the free soul, as their mistress in all things. This is also evident in the handmaid of the widow Judith 10:2 when Judith, accompanied only by that handmaid and prayer to God, walked through the city gates to slay Holofernes, that is, the devil. Those gates are the senses through which free act of choice, accompanied only by its handmaid, the free will, strengthened by virtue, steadily progresses to kill the devil and cut off his head, that is, as Judith did in her first completed act. Hence in Judith 13:11 it goes on to say, "After a while she [Judith] went out, and delivered the head of Holofernes to her maid, and bade her put it into her wallet," since when free choice by its free dissent from sin cuts off the devil's head, it afterwards escapes the occasion of temptation. Yet if again the first motion of the serpent in the bag of memory excites the will, just as Judith reported to the elders of the city, the free will should lead us to report to the priests of the Church in confession any such reviving temptations, since even the first motions of the will are not passed over by the Saints when they confess.

These four powers of the Valiant Woman from the seed of Jacob conceived and bore the sons of God, grateful in their praise of their mother. The first she bore when she was first married to Jacob, namely, free choice in the active life, thus the firstborn was named Reuben, a name interpreted "vision," and Genesis 29:32 relates that his mother said as she birthed him, "The Lord saw my affliction: now my husband will love me." This son signifies knowledge and prudence about what is to be done, which in the active life is what is first required, since unless one knows how carefully to choice the good and reject the evil no one is able to do the good well. In giving her this son the Lord saw the contempt and humiliation of her blear-eyed condition; because before she became prudent she was so blear-eyed about what was to be done that even in the eyes of her husband she was despised, namely, when she was imprudent and hasty in her actions.

Then Leah again gave birth this time to Simon, whose name is interpreted "hearing," saying in childbirth, according to Genesis 39:33, "Because the Lord heard that I was despised, he hath given this child also to me." This "hearing' signifies the hearing of obedience as it says in Psalm 45:11, "Hearken, O daughter, and see, and incline thy ear," since even if one has prudence about what is to be done, one is still despised unless one bears the son of prudence, which is obedience to the Commandments.

According to Genesis 29:34, "Leah conceived the third time, and bore another son: and said: Now also my husband will be joined to me, because I have borne him three sons: and therefore she called his name Levi," a name that is interpreted "given" or "increase," because after obedience to the Commandments which is necessary for salvation, a voluntary vow may be added to carrying out of the Counsels which it is not necessary for salvation but is done in pursuit of perfection, as in Matthew 19:21, "Jesus saith to him [the rich young man]: If thou wilt be perfect, go sell what thou hast, and give to the poor, and thou shalt have treasure in heaven: and come follow me." And therefore Leah, as a wife now secure in the love of her husband, as she give birth rejoiced that henceforth her husband would be happy to mate with her, since he had born him three sons.

Then, according to Genesis 29:35, "The fourth time she conceived and bore a son, and said: now will I praise the Lord: and for this she called him Judah," a name which is interpreted as "trusting" or "glorifying," and signifies thanksgiving concerning all good precepts, because after Leah saw that she had become prudent in action, obedient to the Commandments, and willing to keep the Counsels, she returns thanks to God, but she does not know that these thanks will in fact be sterile because when these thanks are returned to God she no longer accepts the duty of conception. And this is noted in the word she speaks in her childbirth when she says, "Now I will praise the Lord," that is by the action of the soul's power of confession of thanksgiving to God from whose seed comes whatever joy I have in my sons, I praise and magnify him in praise which pleases God [as it says in Psalm 69:32] "better than a young calf, that bringeth forth horns and hoofs," that is, more than joy of a new child, when she was already made pregnant and first produced the horn of the virtues by which she threw the devil to the winds and the hoofs of the rigor of discipline by which she trampled under foot the concupiscence of this world.

After this the Leah, wife who represents active life, ceased bearing, and in her place Jacob embraced Rachel, the contemplative life, who had rightly envied the young sons of her sister's great fertility as they grew up, said to Jacob her husband, as Genesis 30:1 relates, "Give me children, otherwise I shall die," as if to say, I am rich with so many sons in action that I experience a great and urgent desire for sons of joy in contemplation, especially since you can no longer object to me that it is vain to hope for the peace of contemplation since I have not labored in the field of action, because she who is in the active life has already born you four sons.

But it is very important to note that before Leah bore before her handmaid, since it is necessary to be engaged in the active life before the desire of the will is achieved, which will we have said is the handmaid of Leah, that is, in the service of the active life. But in no way is the intellect enlightened in contemplation unless one first collects the images of things as figures and enigmas in the imagination, which above we have symbolized by Rachel's handmaid. Therefore Rachel offered her handmaid Bilhah to her husband Jacob, as Genesis 30:1, "When her husband had relations with her [Bilhah], she conceived and bore a son. And Rachel said: The Lord hath judged for me, and hath heard my voice, giving me a son, and therefore she called his name Dan," which name is interpreted "judgment of reason" which we have from God through the traces and images of creatures. Through which judgment God judges, that is, discerns us, that is, hears our voice, not as if we were horses or mules in which there is no intelligence, that is, lest we be compared to brutes of which the Apostles says in Romans 1:21, "When they knew God, they have not glorified him as God, or given thanks; but became vain in their thoughts, and their foolish heart was darkened," and in verse 20, "For the invisible things of him, from the creation of the world, are clearly seen, being understood by the things that are made," and Wisdom 13:5, "For by the greatness of the beauty, and of the creature, the creator of them may be seen, so as to be known thereby," and Sirach 42:19, "For the Lord knoweth all knowledge, and hath beheld the signs of the world, he declareth the things that are past, and the things that are to come, and revealeth the traces of hidden things."

Again Bilhah conceived a son, and [as Genesis 30:8 relates] of whom "Rachel said: God hath compared me with my sister [Leah], and I have prevailed and she called him Nephthali" which is interpreted "width" and signifies the wideness of admiration in the heights of wisdom in which hidden things are revealed to men, concerning which the Apostles exclaims Romans 11:33, "O the depth of the riches of the wisdom and of the knowledge of God! How incomprehensible are his judgments, and how unsearchable his ways!" Whence Rachel, although this son was hiddenly born of her handmaid, thought of him as her own son so that she compared herself to her sister Leah and boasted, because of the joy of this contemplative wonder as compared to the usefulness of activity, thus sensing her expansion in wonder so that she consider all men vain in whom there is no knowledge of God, as it says in Wisdom 13:1, ["But all men are vain, in whom there is not the knowledge of God: and who by these good things that are seen, could not understand him that is, neither by attending to the works have acknowledged who was the workman."] Bilhah is the active life, as it says in Genesis 30:9, "perceiving that she had left off bearing, that is, finding herself sterile in works because her husband was too much occupied with embracing Zilpah, who stands for the will, because of the sweetness of the wonder of contemplation. Zilpah, the handmaid of Rachel who had given him to her husband, conceived and brought forth a son and cried out: "Happily! and therefore called his name Gad," which is interpreted as "happiness" or "happy." This signifies the highest and most perfect state of virtue by which someone when he knows and perceives the sweetness of contemplation in mental admiration; then comprehends it even in action, for according to the Philosophers happiness is the state of perfect virtue in the soul.

But "Zilpah also bore another son and said: This is for my happiness: for all women will call me blessed. Therefore she called him Asher," which is interpreted "blessed" and signifies the zeal for the conversion of souls and is properly born after his next older brother, Gad, because after the state of perfect virtue as such one ought to burn with zeal to the advantage of others, as the Lord says, John 2:17, "The zeal of thy house hath eaten me up" and it is well said, "This is for my happiness" since none of all possible works so pleases God as the zeal for souls, since the Lord seeks and works that souls may be converted, but this task he has left to his disciples since he says, Matthew 9:37-38, "The harvest indeed is great, but the laborers are few. Pray ye therefore the Lord of the harvest, that he send forth laborers into his harvest." Also in James 5:20 it is said, "He must know that he who causeth a sinner to be converted from the error of his way, shall save his soul from death, and shall cover a multitude of sins." When Zilpah said that "all women will call me blessed," she spoke well, since all converted souls preach that soul to be blessed who is liberated from sins and hell.

[As it then says in Genesis 30:14-16 about Jacob's first son: "And Ruben, going out in the time of the wheat harvest into the field, found mandrakes: which he brought to his mother. And Rachel said: Give me part of thy son's mandrakes. She [Leah] answered: Dost thou think it a small matter that thou hast taken my husband from me, unless thou take also my son's mandrakes? Rachel said: He shall sleep with thee this night, for thy son's mandrakes. And when Jacob returned at even from the field, went out to meet him, and said: Thou shalt come in unto me, because I have hired thee for my son's mandrakes. And he slept with her that night." Thus again of her own accord Leah accepted fertility, because Ruben, going out into the field of the Scriptures, that is the knowledge of truth, found mandrakes which he brought home to his mother, who stands for prudence, retaining through memory what had been poured out by others in preaching. Then Rachel, that is, contemplation, seeing these mandrakes was aroused to desire, as always contemplatives are accustomed to go to the truth of Scriptures, and when she had the tasted the mandrakes, she permitted Jacob her husband to mate with her. It followed [verse 18] that "God heard her [Leah's] prayers: and she conceived and bore the fifth son, and said: God hath given me a reward, because I [formerly] gave my handmaid [Zilpah] to my husband. And she called his name Issachar," which name is interpreted "trade" or "salesman" which signifies the office of preacher in the care of souls. For the term "handmaid" (*ancilla*) is from *an*, around, and *cilleo*, I move [actually it is from *an* and *ancus*, servant] because her will is moved to obey each of the Commandments of God according to the state within one's soul of perfect virtue and the zeal for the souls of one's neighbors. And therefore a salesman accepts the office and care of preaching that shows that he thinks this care will be repaid and rewarded by God in the conversion of sinners. For the labor of preaching is in fact paid by of the conversion of sinners and therefore the preacher is called "a salesman" or a "merchant" because it is twofold in merit because he merits both in himself and in others, as the Apostle says of those that he himself converted which were his joy and crown in the Lord, [as it says in Philippians 4:1, "My dearly beloved brethren, and most desired, my joy and my crown; so stand fast in the Lord, my dearly beloved." Hence a son was obtained from tasting the mandrake, that is, the truths collected in Sacred Scripture, since through these teaching the souls of sinners are redeemed from the power of the world and the devil.

After this [v. 19-20] "And Leah conceived again, and bore the sixth son, And said: God hath endowed me with a good dowry: this turn also my husband will be with me, because I have borne him six sons: and therefore she called his name Zebulun" which name is interpreted "home of fortitude," and signifies fortitude of the Doctor who constantly offers himself as a wall for the house of Israel and this is constancy in one's feelings for the flock committed to one. And this mother rightly says, "God hath endowed me with a good dowry," because this is the ultimate grade of perfection in the active life and her husband, that is, Christ, was now so pleased with her that he was himself willing to die for his sheep and to submit to bodily death that he might redeem us spiritually from death.

[As it goes on to say in Genesis 30:21: "After whom [Zebulun] she [Leash] bore a daughter, named Dina," whose birth the Lord did not bless, since she signifies the lust of the flesh that sometimes seduces Church leaders, since the name Dinah is interpreted "judgment," because by judgment bodily things of themselves judge themselves. This daughter is a wandering woman, impatient of quiet, moving through the fields of license that she might see other women of this region of the world and thus exposed be made the torch and fire of lust and [as it says in Genesis 34:1-2, "And Dina the daughter of went out to see the women of that country. And when Sichem the son of Hamor the Hivite, the prince of that land, saw her, he was in love with her: and took her away, and lay with her, ravishing the virgin." Thus she became the occasion of death of Sichemites and the cause of malediction of his brothers, as will be explained later.

Finally it is recorded in Genesis 30:22-24, "The Lord also remembering Rachel, heard her, and opened her womb. And she conceived, and bore a son, saying: God hath taken away my reproach. And she called his name Joseph, saying: The Lord gave me also another son." Joseph, however, is interpreted "growing' and signifies the illumination of the intellect, which is always growing until the perfect day of eternity, since also in him the reproach of the intellect that it had lost its vision through sin was at last lifted. After Joseph was born Jacob immediately wanted to return to his homeland, but he was delayed for a time by until it could warn some sheep. Thus, although we human persons, once our intellect has been illumined concerning God and celestial things, desire to be dissolved and to be with Christ; yet sometimes we find it necessary to remain in the flesh for the sake of our brothers and in order to gain greater merit, as Jacob had to wait until he had gained some sheep. Yet finally, even without Laban's approval, he departed and then Rachel by secretly carrying away her father's idols with her endured her husband's reproach; because when one is asked by contemplation to leave this world, Rachel, that is, contemplation, is so attached to her idols, the images of this world, that she is not able to leave them behind. And when these idols are sought by Jacob she has them hidden under her camel's covering that signifies nothing other than the weaknesses of this life in which we are not able to see anything of eternal truth without idols and copies. Rachel excuses herself from rising but saying is suffering from her monthly period. This is because since she still carries the images of earthly things in her contemplation, because she was created with that defect as if with a menstrual flow.

Next it is related in Genesis 35:16-19 that once Rachel was living in the Promised Land she bore another son, but died in her travail. "She called the name of her son Benoni, that is, The son of my pain: but his father called him Benjamin, that is, The son of the right hand." By this event is signified the transcendent illumination of the mind in the light that streams not from this world but from beyond this world because no man can see God in this human life and live, as it says in Exodus 33:20 that [God said to Moses], "Thou canst not see my face: for man shall not see me and live." Thus, Rachel, the mother of contemplation died in giving birth because human contemplation becomes destitute of its powers not knowing by what virtue and reason of the intellect it is rapt in infinite light. And the child was called by his mother "son of my pain" because contemplation comes forth to such a state only with much suffering and quickly recedes; but the boy is called by his father "son of my right hand" because without doubt such a change is from the right hand of God, since a human person is raised up to the vision of the angels in the third heaven with St. Paul and [as the Apostle says of himself in II Corinthians 12:4, "And I know such a man (whether in the body, or out of the body, I know not: God knoweth), That he was caught up into paradise, and heard secret words, which it is not granted to man to utter," that is, hears the hidden truths of the revelation of God of which human beings may not speak, Whence it says in Psalm 68:28, "There [in the procession to the Jerusalem Temple] is Benjamin a youth, in ecstasy of mind."

Next is the consideration of how these "children rose up and blessed her." They rose up with blessings from their father and later from the Lawgiver Moses. [Therefore in Genesis 49:1-44 it is related how Jacob when about to die called his sons together and said to them prophetically,] "Gather yourselves together, and hear, O ye sons of Jacob, hearken to Israel your father: Ruben, my firstborn, thou art my strength, and the beginning of my sorrow: excelling in gifts, greater in command. Thou art poured out as water, grow thou not: because thou wentest up to thy father's bed, and didst defile his couch." In these words is mentioned only curse and denunciation and through this is implied a twofold knowledge of what ought to be done, one of which is to know what is right so well as not to do it and the other to know the evil offered to the imagination as a temptation. Thus Ruben is accused of sleeping with Bilhah, the handmaid of Rachel and his father's concubine. Because although he prudently knew that this was an evil to be avoided it offered a temptation to his heart's imagination and he defiled his father's bed. Thus although Reuben ought to have seen the truth about such worldly matters, Bilhah was abused for his lustful pleasure. Hence although the firstborn is and ought to be the greater in his gifts and born in the strength of his father, through lust Reuben wasted himself like water in the pleasures of the things of this world. Therefore his father chose that in this he should not increase, but decrease, since through the temptation of sensuality he had defiled his father's bed.

But the lawgiver Moses makes another point about rejecting evil and choosing the good when he relates in Deuteronomy 33:6 that Jacob in his dying prophecy blessed Reuben and said, "Let Ruben live, and not die, and be he small in number." For he ought to live since whatever contributes to life should be chosen and he ought not to die through a lust for evil, since he acknowledges it to be such. He ought, however to be few in the number of his descendants, since [although Jacob in the words already quoted had said that Reuben was his strength, "excelling in gifts, greater in command," that is, was quite prudent] one ought not to be too "prudent" [as Reuben was in deceiving his father] but place a limit on one's prudence as the Apostle says, Romans 12:3, "For I say...to all that are among you, not to be more wise than it behoveth to be wise, but to be wise unto sobriety, and according as God hath divided to every one the measure of faith," whence the Philosopher also says that "it is better not to know some things that are vile," and Romans 8:7, "The wisdom of the flesh is an enemy to God."

Of Simeon and Levi, who their father said [in his dying prophecy], Genesis 49:5-7, "Simeon and Levi brethren: vessels of iniquity, waging war. Let not my soul go into their counsel, nor my glory be in their assembly: because in their fury they slew a man, and in their self-will they undermined a wall. Cursed be their fury, because it was stubborn: and their wrath because it was cruel: I will divide them in Jacob, and will scatter them in Israel." This also is in large part a curse. For, as we said above, Simeon is interpreted "hearing" and signifies obedience to the Commandments. Levi, however, is interpreted "growing' and as we also said signifies fulfillment of the Counsels. Dinah, however, because of whom killing and death occurred, is interpreted "that judgment," that is, a judgment on the lascivious things of this world in which all living worldlings are imbedded. But after such a judgment, when concupiscence ought to be repressed by obedience to the Commandments and vowing to keep the Counsels, instead these brothers rose, boiling with indiscrete fury, and killed the Sichemites, that is, they slew them like a sin-offering and undermined their city walls, that is, the body which in its members is built like a city from its stones. [Similarly some imprudently to repress concupiscence kill the body] undermining it by indiscrete fasting. Such indignation against the body is severe and indiscrete since it makes hateful the father of sons of Canaan, that is the sons of this world, because worldly men, seeing such excessive austerity, are repelled from penances properly assigned [by their confessors] and hence remain in their sins. They are, nevertheless, [like the Sichemites were], "divided in Jacob," that is, counted among the soldiers of Christ as champions and are "scattered in Israel," that is, they are God-seekers, because having God before their eyes, all that they do, although irrational, is intended as worship of Him. And note that Simeon and Levi first induced these Sichemites to be circumcised, that is, as sinners to repent that they might be circumcised of their sins and be joined in company to the people of God, but on the third day when the pain of their wound was greatest, Simon and Levi killed them, because the first day is contrition, the second day confession which they endured well, but the third day is that of satisfaction and in that they were most gravely afflicted and therefore by the sword of indiscrete obedience and the fulfillment of a vow they perished and therefore the glory of Jacob did not pass on in their tribe nor his will in their assembly. Yet nevertheless because some did carry out all these matters discretely thus destroying the enemy in order to give life to a circumcised and united people by consecrating themselves to the Lord, Moses says neutrally of Levi in Deuteronomy 33:8-11, "Thy perfection, and thy doctrine be to thy holy man, whom thou hast proved in the temptation, and judged at the waters of contradiction: Who hath said to his father, and to his mother: I do not know you; and to his brethren: I know you not: and their own children they have not known. These have kept thy word, and observed thy covenant, Thy judgments, O Jacob, and thy law, O Israel: they shall put incense in thy wrath and holocaust upon thy altar. Bless, O Lord, his strength, and receive the works of his hands. Strike the backs of his enemies, and let not them that hate him rise." Much of this blessing elates to those who have taken on themselves the vow of the perfection of the Councils. First it pertains to their imitation of Christ as the true "holy one" who is the source of the perfection of their life and doctrine, since they have learned it from him and they have proved him faithful at the "Waters of Contradiction," [in the desert, cf. Deuteronomy 32:5] that is, as regards the renewal of poverty which has been contradicted by almost all. They have there "tempted," that is proved, that Christ is faithful since he does not permit them to lack any thing necessary for their salvation, as it says in Psalm 37:25, "I have been young, and now am old; and I have not seen the just forsaken, nor his seed seeking bread." For they have left father and mother and sisters and brothers for the sake of Christ. Second they are guardians of the pact with God which Jesus had made with them when he said, as we read in Matthew 10:37, "He that loveth father or mother more than me, is not worthy of me; and he that loveth son or daughter more than me, is not worthy of me." Third, they are praised and blessed because in the "wrath of the people," that is, in the wrath of God against the people, they offer before the Lord the "incense" of prayer which the Lord does not himself need but rather for others that they might better hear the message. These are indeed "holy ones" that because more than others they have left all things for the Lord attaching themselves to the works of perfection and placing a holocaust, that is, a sacrifice to be wholly burned upon the altar of God's mercy. Thus they immolate themselves, body and soul, in the fire of charity for the sake of God: offering themselves bodily in this fire through a vow of continence and abstinence and in soul by a vow of perfect obedience by also freely adding to the Precepts the fulfillment of the Counsels; and in both body and soul by the vow of poverty. And thus fourthly the "strength" by which they are able to do all this is blessed and their works graciously accepted and rewarded. Fifth, they "strike the enemy" by whom they are attacked "on the back" and keep striking them as long as they persist in their temptations and do not let the devils who hate them "rise above them" in joy that these holy ones have consented to them, the devils, in sin. This blessing [just explained] should be understood both of Simeon and Levi, since otherwise Simeon was not blessed by Moses.

Next, Genesis 49:8-12 says to his son Judah, "Judah, thee shall thy brethren praise: thy hands shall be on the necks of thy enemies: the sons of thy father shall bow down to thee. Judah is a lion's whelp: to the prey, my son, thou art gone up: resting thou hast couched as a lion, and as a lioness, who shall rouse him? The scepter shall not be taken away from Judah, nor a ruler from his thigh, till he come that is to be sent, and he shall be the expectation of nations. Tying his foal to the vineyard, and his ass, O my son, to the vine. He shall wash his robe in wine, and his garment in the blood of the grape. His eyes are more beautiful than wine, and his teeth whiter than milk." We have already explained that Judah is interpreted "glorifying," that is, an agent who is superior in grace and thus the action of grace is blessed in six ways that make Judah blessed in soul.

The first of these is in the praise of brothers, "Judah, thee shall thy brethren praise"; for the brothers of the soul are the angels who praise such a soul that acts in heart, in mouth, and works of grace, as the Apostle says in I Thessalonians 5:18, "In all things give thanks."

Second Judah is blessed, in that "thy hands shall be on the necks of thy enemies" thus he is blessed in his victories over his enemies for as it says [in the Parable of the Unjust Steward in] Matthew 18:28-29, "When that servant was gone out, he found one of his fellow servants that owed him an hundred pence: and laying hold of him, throttled him, saying: Pay what thou owest. And his fellow servant falling down besought him, saying: Have patience with me, and I will pay thee all. And he would not: but went and cast him into prison, till he paid the debt." Thus the ingratitude of the unjust steward to his master makes him impute the unpaid debt of his fellow servant as owed to himself Thanksgiving, however, exalts because of victory over the enemy, that is, the devils; it does not exalt in returning to sin.

Third, "The sons of thy father shall bow down to thee," thus Judah is blessed in the admiration of his mother's sons and this is understood of the older sons, Ruben, Simeon, and Levi who admire him, while to them are given gifts in knowledge and prudence in acting, as well as obedience and keeping of vows, this son conserves and multiplies in confessing and praising and giving thanks, lest that praise through ingratitude should be lost.

Fourth, the blessing says, "Judah is a lion's whelp: to the prey, my son, thou art gone up: resting thou hast couched as a lion, and as a lioness who shall rouse him? To the prey, my son, thou art gone up. The scepter shall not be taken away from Judah, nor a ruler from his thigh, till he come that is to be sent, and he shall be the expectation of nations," thus Judah is blessed in his prey and its possession. This "prey," however, is nothing other than acceptance of grace through violent seizure because thanksgiving accepts grace through the force of the generosity and piety of God and what those who give thanks have accepted they multiply and then conserve what has been multiplied. Whence it is also said in this blessing that a lion and even a lioness, which is said to be still stronger than a lion, rests in grace so that the devil does not dare to put them to sin and temptation. Because one who accepts such a grace but through sin is ungrateful to the giver of that grace, succumbs to that temptation and sin by the devil; which he does not who continually in heart, mouth and works gives thanks; in heart by devotion, in mouth through praise and the remembrance of benefits and in works through reverence, for thus no room is given to the devil. And therefore it is added that "the scepter" that is of the dignity of grace, "shall not be taken away" from Judah, "till he come that is to be sent," that is Christ, the glorifier of the soul in the day of death when it gets its reward, because then Christ, who comes to glorify the soul, "shall be the expectation of nations," that is of all who are his own.

The fifth blessing is on Judah, "Tying his foal to the vineyard, and his ass, O my son, to the vine. He shall wash his robe in wine, and his garment in the blood of the grape," is the flourishing of his "vineyard" and this is noted in two ways; first he is said to be "Tying his foal to the vineyard," because desire is rightly called a "foal' because it is as untamable as a young donkey and hence it is said to be tied to the vineyard, that is, to internal and external joy. To the vineyard, however, is also said to be tied the "ass," that is the body, which also because of its corruption needs to be tied to the same vineyard, as one can say with the Psalmist 84:3, "My heart and my flesh have rejoiced in the living God." What is be noted, however, about how the vineyard is flourishing is that Judah "washes his robe in its wine," and this wine has a further significance in that in having much wine he has the pure wine of eternal joy which this means and he also has red wine of the suffering and passion of our Lord Jesus Christ. Hence in Revelation 7:14, it reads of the Saints that they "have washed their robes, and have made them white in the blood of the Lamb." For the robe of charity is washed in blood. The crushed grape is the dead body of Our Lord Jesus Christ in which this robe is washed our charity because it is colored by the charity of his passion in so far as wet can imitate it. Hence it is also said of his passion in John 15:12, "This is my commandment, that you love one another, as I have loved you" and the next verse, "Greater love than this no man hath, that a man lay down his life for his friends."

The sixth blessing on Judah, "His eyes are more beautiful than wine and his teeth whiter than milk" refers to the purity of his intention and the efficacy of his preaching of praise, because the praises of Christ giving thanks to him return to those who sing them and these Judah announces. The purity of intention is praised by saying, His eyes are more beautiful than wine" and here "vineyard" is taken in still a third sense that it grows along side this world, and its wine touches the tongue through the grandiloquence of worldly knowledge which as such serves not God but ambition; and therefore the eyes of one who has them fixed on God are more beautiful than those turned to worldly pride. These "teeth' are those of the memory of the preacher by which he continually chews and then pronounces and again announces the grace given to him by God, which are whiter and cleaner than the milk of the newly converted infant in faith who does not yet give thanks, since by reason of the newness of its conversion it does not yet recognize the greatness of grace.

Hence Moses the Lawgiver in Deuteronomy 33:7 also says, "This is the blessing of Judah. Hear, O Lord, the voice of Judah, and bring him in unto his people: his hands shall fight for him, and he shall be his helper against his enemies," for the Lord hears nothing as acceptable as thanksgiving and the one who expresses it, that is, to his people and to the angels, because this is the work of the angels in heaven who sing in hymns to God and give him thanks, as it says in Luke 2:14, "Glory to God in the highest; and on earth peace to men of good will." Judah's "hands fight for him," because by "hands" is understood his works and by his continual works in worship he also offers thanks. God in this is his helper; yet also the action of thanksgiving is a help to actions of his hands, because the devil either tempts him through adversity and then he gives thanks for his trials, or the devil tempts him through prosperity and then he gratefully refers these gifts to the goodness of God and thus gives no occasion to the Tempter.

Father Jacob also blessed Dan the first son of Bilhah who signifies the first step in the contemplative life, when he says in Genesis

49:16-18, "Dan shall judge his people like another tribe in Israel. Let Dan be a snake in the way, a serpent in the path that biteth the horse's heels that his rider may fall backward. I will look for thy salvation, O Lord." We have already said that the name of Dan signifies the "judgment of reason" that we have about God through his creatures and through which only many know God. Dan's blessing on his tribe, therefore, is threefold: first in the judgment of his people, and just as the other blessings are each on a tribe, that is, a type of reason, Dan judges the people of God through a shining truth, namely, that it is a contemplative people, for thus also he judges through the traces and images of creatures he judges the judgment of the divine truth in Israel, that is in a people seeing God through the eye of contemplation. That judgment, however, is made "like a serpent in the path." That way, however, is that of created works, as it says in Job 40:14, "He is the beginning of the ways of God, who made him," that is the first and principle being among God's works. A "serpent" is a snake and this term is used for prudence' sake, because caution is necessary to be cautious in contemplation through creatures lest we take the creature for the Creator, as some have thought the beautiful gods to be in the likeness of the heaves and the stars as it says in Wisdom 13:2-3, "But [some] have imagined either the fire, or the wind, or the swift air, or the circle of the stars, or the great water, or the sun and moon, to be the gods that rule the world with whose beauty, if they, being delighted, took them to be gods." A *coluber* is a horned serpent and this snake is a coluber to signify prudence [and means a horned snake], and this is the wisdom of faith, having a horn by which it tosses off all that is heretical, that is, by the horn of reason enlightened by creation. Hence this serpent is also said to be "in the path" because the way of judgment through creatures is the common way. But faith is graded as the shorter way because it is sufficient in itself, as St. Augustine says, because the will of God is the cause of everything that is, and it seeks no other causes, even when it makes a judgment of reason which as regards creatures is often necessary. Hence the text says that the serpent in this path "biteth the horse's heels," because this horse is the philosopher who is proud in worldly science and girded for the wars of disputation, who snorts "Nonsense!" in contempt for all who are not skilled in wordplay. The "hoof" of such a philosopher by which he tramples down simple persons is the syllogism. And there are four such hooves, the syllogism, the enthymeme, the example, and the induction which are the four types of argument.

Dan wields these hooves of judgment in keeping with the faith since by the truth of faith he wholly tramples down such arguments and concludes the journey as the rider of this horse, that is, philosophical reasoning falls behind, that is, is eliminated, as Paul in Acts 13:34 eliminated the arguments of Dionysius the Areopagite as Peter also did he arguments of Clement, Martha, and Aquila, who were philosophers. But since the judgment which is made from the images of creature is not complete, therefore Father Jacob says, "I will look for thy salvation, O Lord," that is in revelation is more accessible.

Of Dan, it said that he was blessed by Moses saying, Deuteronomy 33:22, "Dan is a young lion, he shall flow plentifully from Bashan." This means Christ who was a young lion of the tribe of Judah, because as he perfectly confuted the Pharisees and Scribes who were glorying in their learning, so Dan in his manner confuted all the wise of this world who contradicted the faith, as the Apostles says II Corinthians 10:4-5, "For the weapons of our warfare are not carnal, but mighty to God unto the pulling down of fortifications, destroying counsels, and every height that exalteth itself against the knowledge of God, and bringing into captivity every understanding unto the obedience of Christ." He flows in reasons and arguments from "Bashan," a name that signifies a [swarm of] locusts and intends to say that coming from Bashan it flows more abundantly and philosophers and heretics are the locust swarms of this world whom as they confute each other so, Dan flows abundantly with reasons to defend the Faith.

Next Father Jacob blesses Nephthali, the second son of Bilhah, and notes the second grade of contemplation; for Nephthali is interpreted "width' and signifies the width of wonder. Jacob says in Genesis 49:21, "Nephthali, a hart let loose, and giving words of beauty," "Hart" is said to signify the wonder of speed for nothing happens quicker in the human heart than wonder: for what makes the human heart wonder does not await the questioning of reason nor draw back from the profundity of wisdom. Whence Nephthali is called "a hart let loose," because the order of reason does not await what arouses wonder. For we admire the things that please us even when we are not able to perfectly see their cause and they seem to us marvelous, so that these are what we especially contemplate. How the Redeemer, for example, is somehow both God and man in one person [John 1:14], how he could be born of a Virgin [Matthew 1:23], how he could have been poor [Mark 6:3], who if he thirsted did not request a drink from man [John 4:13], whose will covers the orb of the earth and all that is on it [John 10:30], how he, by bowing his head on the Cross, gave up his spirit [John 19:30], to whose nod of the head the whole world bows down [Philippians 3:21] and who within his head sees all [John 1:48]. For [as is related in Matthew 27:46-55] the rocks were shattered, the graves opened, the sun is darkened, the veil [of the Temple] was severed, the heart of the pagan centurion, though accustomed to seeing crucifixions, at Jesus' cry was softened and exclaimed, "Indeed this was the Son of God!" [Matthew 27:54] while others returned to the city striking their breasts [Luke 23:48]. Also how can death die and life be regained by rising? And how can many awake from the dust of the earth, some rising to eternal life, while others rise to see eternal damnation? And there are many other such questions. Thus "giving words of beauty" is simply to express the joy of such wonders in cries of jubilation, as the Apostle exclaims in Romans 11:33, "O the depth of the riches of the wisdom and of the knowledge of God! How incomprehensible are his judgments, and how unsearchable his ways!"

Of Nephthali Jacob said in Deuteronomy 33:23, "Nephthali shall enjoy abundance, and shall be full of the blessings of the Lord: he shall possess the sea and the south." The abundance which is enjoyed, that is, in which pleasure is taken, is the abundance of wonders of divine wisdom which are continually enjoyed and are turned over and we recite them to others so that they too may know the wonders of God. Hence it says "full of the blessings of the Lord," that is, with the blessings of the sacraments with which God has blessed us, for these are subjects of wonder by the consensus of faith along with Christ's Incarnation, Baptism, Resurrection, Ascension, and Coming at the Last Judgment, and therefore Nephthali is blessed with the possession of "the sea," that is Christ's Passion, since this is the work of our redemption. Nephthali will also "possess the south," the region of eternal light, which means that in contemplation he will wonder at the light that surrounds the Lord where are built the many mansions of heaven, for there rest the souls of the Saints.

Then Gad and Asher the sons of the concubine Zelpha, also received a blessing form their father Jacob. Gad is interpreted "happiness" and signifies the ultimate state of virtue in the completed will which is its perfection in God's will, good in regard to the Precepts and better in regard to the Counsels, and best in the consummate tranquility of virtue, so that it is no longer difficult to serve God but joyful and pleasurable so that it seems that the yoke of Christ is indeed "easy and its burden light." and therefore to come to him is not labor but refreshment. Hence Father Jacob said in blessing this perfect son [Genesis 49:19]: "Gad, being girded, shall fight before him: and he himself shall be girded backward," because this which is consummate virtue is "before him," that is before the neighbor, battling with the sword of the spirit which [as it says in Ephesians 6:17, is the "word of God"] casting down the enemies of the people of God and also battling against the temptation of the enemies attacking from behind, because those he has first saved from sin and freed from their enemies, he afterwards defends against the deceits of the Tempter.

Of him the Moses the Lawgiver says in Deuteronomy 33:20-21, "Blessed be Gad in his breadth: he hath rested as a lion, and hath seized upon the arm and the top of the head. And he saw his pre-eminence, which in his portion the teacher was laid up: who was with the princes of the people, and did the justices of the Lord, and his judgment with Israel." For "breadth" is the extension of all the virtues in which happiness consists, but in grace "he hath rested as a lion" over against his and their deceits, because Gad "hath seized upon the arm and the top of the head," that is, he has raised his arm of grace and strength and his head, that is, the summit of happiness, which consists in the perfect attainment of virtues, and "sees his preeminence," namely that he is no longer is troubled by concupiscence since sin no longer reigns in his mortal body. Instead Christ, the Doctor of justice, reposes in Gad's heart, as it did in [St. Paul] the Apostle when he gave to the people and to the world an example for them of God's justice. As he did, so must we do, for this is the same justice that God taught Israel. Thus the example of all virtue is in Christ and in the Apostle Gad in so far as it can be imitated as he did.

Asher, the second son of Zilpah, handmaid of Leah, is interpreted "blessed" and we think this signifies the zeal for conversion of souls that is born in a man after he has himself gained the virtues. For this is proper to consummate virtue that it wishes others to be like itself and therefore labors for their conversion, which is the only kind of true human beatitude that it is possible to attain in this life. Hence Father Jacob in blessing Asher says in Genesis 49:20, "Asher, his bread shall be fat, and he shall yield dainties to kings." The fat of the bread is the bread of the Divine Word which he who has zeal for soul constantly supplies as a delicacy for such kings as rule themselves as is experienced what is said in Psalm 119:103,

"How sweet are thy words to my palate! More than honey to my mouth."

Hence Moses the Lawgiver also says of Asher (Deuteronomy 33:24-25), "Let Asher be blessed with children, let him be acceptable to his brethren, and let him dip his foot in oil. His shoe shall be iron and brass. As the days of thy youth, so also shall thy old age be." Asher receives a blessing in his sons that in his zeal for souls he bore and was pleased in the many brothers whom he joined to himself in the brotherhood of grace. In the "oil" of the mercy of God he "dipped the feet" of his affections because those he converted mercifully received the pardon of their sins; but in the "feet" of his intellect he has "iron and copper," the iron of instruction that he might confute all heresies against his teaching and the copper of the sound of his preaching to the ears of the faithful for their instruction, but lest in caring for others, he neglect himself, it adds "as the days of thy youth" when he improved himself, lest he turn away from virtue and self-discipline.

Then the sons whom Leah conceived in a symbol of the active life also conceived and bore offspring who were themselves blessed by their father. In Genesis 49:14-14 Issachar was blessed thus, "Issachar shall be a strong ass lying down between the borders. He saw rest that it was good: and the land that it was excellent: and he bowed his shoulder to carry, and became a servant under tribute." Issachar which is interpreted "wages," we say signifies the office of the responsibility for preaching. He is called "strong" because he ought to arouse himself and others. He is called an "ass" not in the sense of stupidity but because of the carrying of burdens, because he who accepts the responsibility of preaching the word, ought to carry the burdens of others, as the apostles says in Romans 15:1, "Now we that are stronger, ought to bear the infirmities of the weak, and not to please ourselves," and Galatians 6:2, "Bear ye one another's burdens; and so you shall fulfill the law of Christ." The benediction says "lying down between borders" because he thinks partly of himself and partly of his neighbor, seeking for himself what is necessary for his salvation, yet does not neglecting was is useful for the salvation of his neighbor. What follows, "He saw rest that it was good," implies for what cause and what intention Isaachar preaches, for unless he sees the good that is eternal rest he cannot through his words invite others to that good; for unless he also knows the "excellent land" of the living, he will not defer earthly patronage in order to admonish others that really lasting inheritance is acquired only in that "excellent land of the living. And thus his preaching will be done only in service of payment, because when he furnishes his neighbor with preaching, he accepts a payment and a stipend for the conversion of souls.

Next is considered Zebulun, who is the last son of Leah and who signifies the courage of a doctor and bishop who in days of persecution ought to place himself as a wall for the house of Israel against men and demons. Hence in Genesis 49:13 Zebulun is thus blessed by Father Jacob "Zebulun shall dwell on the sea shore, and in the road of ships, reaching as far as Sidon." "The shore of the sea is solid grounds in persecution, for on the shore of the sea tempests are quelled because by doctors of the faith the floods of temptation ought to be quelled even on the dry land, that is, lest these floods submerge all even to the simplest of the people. In the marinas of fishing boats along the [Mediterranean] sea as it reaches up to Sidon, men are "fished," [as it says in Matthew 4:19, Jesus said to the Twelve, "Come ye after me, and I will make you to be fishers of men"], since the doctor's whole intention in preaching, in defending, and in guiding is that souls should be hunted and gain for Christ; whence also Sidon is interpreted "hunting."

In Deuteronomy 33:18-19 Moses the Lawgiver says of these two sons conjointly in their work, "Rejoice, O Zebulun, in thy going out; and Issachar in thy tabernacles. They shall call the people to the mountain: there shall they sacrifice the victims of justice. Who shall suck as milk the abundance of the sea, and the hidden treasures of the sands?" The "going out" of Zebulun is to visit the flock. The "tabernacle" of Isaachar is the tabernacle of the Church built not by man but by God in which these two are praised because the preacher and the doctor or prelate glory in the multitude of the faithful in the Spirit. For both sons call the people to "the mountain' of God, that is the heights of life, as in Genesis 19:17 the angel says to Lot, ["Save thy life: look not back, neither stay thou in all the country about:] but save thyself in the mountain [lest thou be also consumed."] So that there the people might offer themselves as victims of justice, since as it say in Psalm 51:19, "A sacrifice to God is an afflicted spirit: a contrite and humbled heart, O God, thou wilt not despise." For both inundations, or "abundance of the sea," pouring out in words and deeds, as it were, suck out the sweet milk of meekness and patience, collecting in them "treasures hidden in the sand," that is, in the anger of the foolish as Solomon says in Proverbs 27:3, "A stone is heavy, and sand weighty: but the anger of a fool is heavier than them both." For these are the treasures of precious pearls of suffering for the Lord's sake which the Lord hangs on Preachers, doctors, and Bishops, as it says in Psalm 21:4, "For thou, Lord, hast set on his head a crown of precious stones." In this benediction of these two brothers is completed [the description] of the perfection of the active life.

Joseph, however, who signifies the third grade of contemplation, is given a lengthy benediction by Father Jacob although he accepts it is not for himself but for his two sons. In Genesis 49:22-26 Jacob blesses him saying. "Joseph is a growing son, a growing son and comely to behold; the daughters run to and fro upon the wall. But they that held darts provoked him, and quarreled with him, and envied him. His bow rested upon the strong, and the bands of his arms and his hands were loosed, by the hands of the mighty one of Jacob: thence he came forth a pastor, the stone of Israel. The God of thy father shall be thy helper, and the Almighty shall bless thee with the blessings of heaven above, with the blessings of the deep that lieth beneath, with the blessings of the breasts and of the womb. The blessings of thy father are strengthened with the blessings of his fathers: until the desire of the everlasting hills should come; may they be upon the head of Joseph, and upon the crown of the Nazarite among his brethren." This benediction consists in four parts all of which relate, as we said above, to the illumination if the intellect which Joseph signifies: first the praise preceding the benediction, second the benediction which concerns the multiplication of graces, third in the confirmation of this benediction, and finally in a prophecy of future sanctity. Where each of these is noted will be evident in what follows.

The fourfold praise of Joseph...	Fecundity of offspring Beauty Patience in trials Manner of liberation from prison

Joseph's fecundity in offspring is mentioned when it says, "Joseph is a growing son." There are however two sons who are so to speak, sons of illumination, Manasses and Ephraim, but Manasses is interpreted "forgetfulness" which signifies the forgetting of this life which results when the intellect is illumined by the goods of the future life, as the Apostle in I Corinthians 12:2 says that he was raptured to the third heaven when his intelligence was illumined, and also says [in Philippians 3:13-14], "One thing I do: forgetting the things that are behind, and stretching forth myself to those that are before, I press towards the mark." Ephraim, however, is interpreted "fruitful," because when anyone looks to higher things with clearer eyes, so much more in the land of the living he scatters the fruits of good works and keeps doing so during his whole life as it says in Ecclesiastes 11:6, "In the morning sow thy seed, and In the evening let not thy hand cease [for thou knowest not which may rather spring up, this or that: and if both together, it shall be the better]."

These two sons, however, are blessed by their grandfather with crossed hands, because the right is imposed on the head of the younger son which is efficacious, since that one will remain in eternity in numerous works, while on the older son the left is imposed, as it says in Genesis 48:15-20 [". And Joseph seeing that his father had put his right hand upon the head of Ephraim was much displeased: and taking his father's hand he tried to lift it from Ephraim's head, and to remove it to the head of Manasses. And he said to his father: It should not be so, my father: for this is the firstborn, put thy right hand upon his head. But he refusing, said: I know, my son, I know: and this also shall become peoples, and shall be multiplied: but this younger brother shall be greater than he: and his seed shall grow into nations. And he blessed them at that time, saying: In thee shall Israel be blessed, and it shall be said: God do to thee as to Ephraim, and as to Manasses. And he set Ephraim before Manasses." The left was imposed on the hands of the elder son because forgetfulness of the present proceeds with time. For we are then able to remember safely when remembering something does not move us to depart from God but instead in every way moves us toward God. Thus Father Jacob [began his blessing by saying in] Genesis 18:15-16, "God, in whose sight my fathers Abraham and Isaac walked, God that feedeth me from my youth until this day, the angel that delivereth me from all evils, bless these boys: and let my name be called upon them, and the names of my fathers Abraham, and Isaac, and may they grow into a multitude upon the earth" as if to say, God, in whose sight as in the light of grace, my father walked in deeds of good merit, God also who nourished me on the bread of supersubstantial grace and the sacrament from the youth of baptismal innocence to perfect power according to virtue. Thus by the "angel of good counsel" [Jacob meant] Christ, the incarnate Word who saved him through his redeeming passion from all the evils which he had inherited from Adam. Hence with purity of words

Jacob blessed these boys by giving thanks and thus the name of the ancient Saints was affirmed and invoked over them in imitation of those holy ones that they might grow up multiplying goods works over the land of the living forever. The crossing of Jacob's hands signifies the exchange of eternal rewards for temporal merit, since here we live in the worship of God for the short time of our lives yet for this receive from God a life that is eternal.

The second thing that is to Joseph's praise is his beauty which is noted when the blessing says, "comely to behold; the daughters run to and fro upon the wall," for he had beauty of appearance, like the face of Moses that was so illuminated that the sons of Israel could not look at him because of the glory of his face, as it says in Exodus 34:30, ["Aaron and the children of Israel seeing the face of Moses horned, were afraid to come near."] So also Joseph walking daily in the light of the face of God and exulting in the name of God all day long, exalted in God's justice. And according to the Apostle in II Corinthians 3:18, "We all beholding the glory of the Lord with open face, are transformed into the same image from glory to glory, as by the Spirit of the Lord." Whence even the "daughters," that is, those not yet perfect in contemplation of soul, are said to have "run to and fro upon the wall," and the "wall" here is nothing other than our mortality which divides us from the contemplation of the eternal vision, as it says, in the Song of Songs 2:9, "My beloved is like a roe, or a young hart. Behold he standeth behind our wall, looking through the windows, looking through the lattices." The "wall of the city" is our mortal body, the "windows the light of our intellect," and the "lattices" are special revelations made through the Scriptures or through the angels on which wall or city wall the daughters "run to and fro," because imperfect souls are not yet able to see in the contemplation of the Lord what they desire because they admire it in others.

The third item in the praise of Joseph is his patience in trial and this is noted is in two points, namely, as to the cause of his trials and the way he is liberated from them. Thus the first cause of Joseph's trials was the exasperation and quarrels of his brothers when they accused him of the worst of crimes because he prophesied in a dream of the future truth. This serious crime of which all his brothers accused him for claiming an illumined intellect was that of hypocrisy and pretence which persons commit in action or in thought, not with pure intentions, but for the sake of praise. The dreams in which this is revealed according to Genesis 37:2-10 were also twofold: one, according to verses 9-10, was "'I saw in a dream, as it were the sun, and the moon, and eleven stars worshipping me.' And when he had told this to his father and brethren, his father rebuked him, and said: 'What meaneth this dream that thou hast dreamed? Shall I and thy mother, and thy brethren worship thee upon the earth?'" and the other, according to verses 7-8, was, "'Hear my dream which I dreamed. I thought we were binding sheaves in the field: and my sheaf arose as it were, and stood, and your sheaves standing about, bowed down before my sheaf.' His brethren answered: 'Shalt thou be our king? or shall we be subject to thy dominion?' Therefore this matter of his dreams and words ministered nourishment to their envy and hatred." The "sun" which shines in the day signifies the knowledge of Sacred Scripture, while the "moon" that governs the night signifies worldly science and both serve the knowing of the intelligence in contemplation, as it says in II Corinthians 4:6, "For God, who commanded the light to shine out of darkness, hath shined in our hearts, to give the light of the knowledge of the glory of God, in the face of Christ Jesus." The "eleven stars" are the small lights of secular doctrine: grammar, rhetoric, dialectics, geometry, arithmetic, music, physics, metaphysics, ethics and the sciences of positive and natural law, for these "stars" adore Joseph in so far as they are able to serve the illumination of the intelligence in contemplation. [In the second dream] the "sheaves" are the works of perfection in the gatherings of the harvesters of justice, which are said to be eleven since the Ten Commandments serve the unity of charity. They adore Joseph, because whatever he does in his works is done to render his intelligence open to truth. This matter of the dreams was tinder for the envy of the brothers and aroused their other feelings because although in this life we do not see the contemplative intellect to be satisfied by mere dreams, they can predict truths to the intellect at which we arrive slowly and imitatively and with some conjecture. Sometimes, however, we also sell the intellect, which ought to contemplate eternal verities, captive to the world [as Joseph's brothers old him in slavery] so that it, is occupied with the cares and worries of earthly matters. And thus his brothers were irritated against him and envied him; [as Jacob's blessing says: "They that held darts provoked him, and quarreled with him, and envied him."] So they dug a hole to cast him in alive, thus making the open hidden, the certain uncertain, not leaving the invisible visible. [In their accusations] the brothers were also supported by a woman, Joseph's mother, unfaithful in mind, that is, by vainglory, since although a woman according to the Apostle in I Corinthians 15:7, ought to be "the glory of her husband," in criticizing and accusing Joseph she was also given to earthly thoughts and turned away from the contemplation of heavenly things.

The fourth thing to be noted about Jacob's blessing is the way he was to be freed, whence the blessing in Genesis 49:22-26, says, "Joseph is a growing son, a growing son and comely to behold; the daughters run to and fro upon the wall. But they that held darts provoked him, and quarreled with him, and envied him. His bow rested upon the strong, and the bands of his arms and his hands were loosed, by the hands of the mighty one of Jacob: thence he came forth a pastor, the stone of Israel. The God of thy father shall be thy helper, and the Almighty shall bless thee with the blessings of heaven above, with the blessings of the deep that lieth beneath, with the blessings of the breasts and of the womb. The blessings of thy father are strengthened with the blessings of his fathers: until the desire of the everlasting hills should come; may they be upon the head of Joseph, and upon the crown of the Nazarite among his brethren." This says, "His bow rested upon the strong." What is "strong," as we read [in the apocryphal work], III Esdras 3:12, that Zorobabel said is the "truth" on which Joseph's bow rests, that is, the mendacity of vain thoughts is punctured by the arrows of the authority of Sacred Scripture, and "his hands were loosed," that is, his intellect and affections are dissolved, and this is done through the helping hand of the power of God who aided Jacob [better, Joseph] as true warrior in the fight against the envy of his brothers. Hence this applies to Joseph imprisoned in his captivity in Egypt, out of which he came forth as a "pastor" [shepherd, feeding the flock] with the fodder of truth. He also came out as a "stone of Israel" in solidity, that is, in the firmness of unchanging truth. For truth is the illumination of the intelligence which feeds and also grounds us on the rock which is Christ, thus making us stable so that the house of thought is not blown down by the wind of temptation and the rain of persecution but is founded on solid rock [Matthew 7:24-27].

Then Father Jacob makes a second benediction on Joseph, first invoking God the Father as his aid, from this that man cannot know the things that are above him without God's aid, [as [Jesus says in Luke 10:22,] "No one knoweth who the Son is, but the Father; and who the Father is, but the Son, and to whom the Son will reveal him." He blesses him "with the blessings of heaven above," that is, with the light of those dwelling in the heaven of contemplation, and "with the blessings of the deep that lieth beneath," that is the depths of wisdom, as it says in Psalm 36:7, "Thy judgments are a great deep," lying below in the depths of hell to which God condemned the proud angels and the men he had made from the dust of the earth that he might set them with princes where they would sit on seats of glory, for thus it is true what is said in Psalm 107:26, "They mount up to the heavens" in the benediction of the heavens, "and they go down to the depths," in contemplation of the pains of damnation "of their souls." As to the intellect "it wastes away in evils" by having compassion for the afflicted especially those in purgatory, as it says in Psalm 55:16, "Let them go down alive into hell," that is, through intellectual contemplation. "The "blessings of the breasts and of the womb" since through such intellectual contemplation they draw out what flows from other sources in teaching whence in entrails of charity conceive these truth as from the womb of piety and nourish them at the breasts of doctrine.

Next follows the third part of this benediction which is its confirmation, "The blessings of thy father are strengthened with the blessings of his fathers: until the desire of the everlasting hills should come; may they be upon the head of Joseph" in which it is noted that this benediction on Joseph is confirmed through the counsel that the deeds and words of the patriarchs in the contemplation of eternal life is to be imitated even until "the desire of the everlasting hills," [Psalm 76:5] that is, until he joins the choirs of angels on the eternal hills which with all the desire of his mind he desires. Then it will no longer necessary that the words and deeds of the patriarchs guide him in contemplation, since then the truth will appear before his open eyes. Hence they who claim to contemplate God by some novel manner of contemplation are to be reprehended, since their way of contemplating is found neither in the Sacred Scriptures nor does it follow the example of the Saints. There is no doubt that those who invent such novelties follow Satan and, as it says in II Corinthians 11:14, ["Satan himself transformeth himself into an angel of light,"] since these novelties the faith of Sacred Tradition has rejected as ridiculous.

Then Father Joseph prophesied sanctity for Joseph's progeny, saying, "and upon the crown of the Nazarite among his brethren." "Nazarite" is interpreted "florid" or "flourishing" and signifies the affections of sanctity which arise in the hearts of contemplatives when the intellect see the light of truth and the interior affections of the heart seeking joy in holiness began to flower: and this happens "on" the crown" of the heads of those among his brothers; because they occupy the eminence of life and mind in the place of other works of sanctity. They are at the "crown" because they will always achieve the purer and higher things of the mind. Moses the Lawgiver, however, when he blessed Joseph said, as we read in Deuteronomy 33:13-17, "Of the blessing of the Lord be his land, of the fruits of heaven, and of the dew, and of the deep that lieth beneath. Of the fruits brought forth by the sun and by the moon. Of the tops of the ancient mountains, of the fruits of the everlasting hills: And of the fruits of the earth, and of the fullness thereof. The blessing of him that appeared in the bush, come upon the head of Joseph, and upon the crown of the Nazarite among his brethren. His beauty as of the firstling of a bullock, his horns as the horns of a rhinoceros:with them shall he push the nations even to the ends of the earth. These are the multitudes of Ephraim and these the thousands of Manasses." This blessings touches on three things that are proper to an intellect illumined by God, of which the first is in what God is contemplated and these are especially eight things that he calls the "land" or region of the contemplating soul to be filled as it were with benedictions of God. The first of these is the "fruits of heaven," that is, the fruit of eternal beatitude. The second is the "dew of heaven," that is, the dew of grace as it says in Isaiah 26:19, "For thy dew is the dew of the light." The third is "the deep that lieth beneath," that is, eternal punishment. The fourth is "the fruits brought forth by the sun and by the moon,' that is the sacraments of the Church and of the Synagogue, since the Church is the "sun" while the Synagogue was only the "moon" because from it the sun of justice, Christ our Lord, was raised. Therefore these latter sacraments only symbolize salvation, while the former actually confer it. The fifth is "the tops of the ancient mountains," that is, eminence of the ancient patriarchs who like mountains were raised above the people of God that they might see the day of Christ and exult in it, as Jesus says in John 8:56, "Abraham your father rejoiced that he might see my day: he saw it, and was glad," and Psalm 114:6, "The mountains skipped like rams, and the hills like the lambs of the flock." The sixth, however, is the "the fruits of the everlasting hills," that is the fruits of the ranks of the angels. For these are the mountains and hills of Bethel to which the contemplative intellect leaps when it is illumined by certain joyful affections. Seventh is the "fruits of the earth, and of the fullness thereof," that is, the common contemplation of all that is good by all the Saints, since those Saints who in this world once lived and are still living are the beauty of all earthly things, since the earth is now plunged in evil and empty in the darkness because sin is upon it. The eighth and last note of this benediction [as it says in Exodus 3:2 is the blessing of "the Lord [who] appeared to him in a flame of fire out of the midst of a bush: and he saw that the bush was on fire and was not burnt]," that is, the Word Incarnate, because we recognize that the unburnt bush which Moses beheld is the praiseworthy virginity of the Mother of God in which shone the fire of God Incarnate not to consumed but to be renewed, yet which burn up all traces of sin and this blessing "comes on the head of Joseph," when it descends into his mind, since, as St. Augustine says, "'Head' stands for mind." It comes upon the "upon the crown of the Nazarite among his brethren," that is, upon him who is flourishing among his brethren, and who is no one else but Joseph who alone among his brethren flourished, because the intellect illumined by God more than any other affection of the soul puts forth a unique branch and flower.

The second thing the benediction touches on is the beauty which is noted in Joseph's face, as was previously explained, but here this is compared to the "firstling of a bullock and this "firstling" is not said here of time but from the principle of his generation, meaning that beauty of his face is like great generative energy of a bull, for a bull is a fecund animal and signifies spiritual desire in walking in the light of God and in his love in the desires of the secret bed of the conscience, as Jeremiah 31:13, says of the virgin Jerusalem and Sion that in the chorus of dancers "Then shall the virgin rejoice in the dance."

The third thing on which this benediction touches is the strength of the perception of truth is like "the horns of a rhinoceros," that stand for two kinds of truth, one that reveals the faith, the other that instructs in morals. A rhinoceros, however, is to said to be captured in the bosom of a virgin since the first truth descended into a Virgin's womb. A rhinoceros is also said to gesture with a horn on its nose because the horn of contemplative truth is perceived always to be had in the nose of discretion and comparison, as Jesus says in Matthew 10:16, "Be ye therefore wise as serpents and simple as doves" and with these horns "shall he push the nations even to the ends of the earth," because the infidels and sins attack the truth, while their opponents teach and enlighten. The ends of the earth from which these opponents are expelled are three in number that all earthlings seek in vain: the ambition for honor, the desire for pleasure, and the greed for riches. These are "the multitudes of Ephraim and these the thousands of Manasses," and it has already been explained how these apply Joseph's sons.

Finally comes the benedictions on Benjamin who signifies the ultimate grade of contemplation, that is, he symbolizes the excess of mind or rapture as in this benediction in Genesis 49:27 his Father Jacob says, "Benjamin a ravenous wolf, in the morning shall eat the prey, and in the evening shall divide the spoil." Those who know the nature of wolves say that their eyes have an inner fire so that they seem to shine in the dark. Similarly it is also customary that wolves secretly and swiftly attack and not openly. And this pertains to contemplatives who have the fire and light of God in their eyes so that even in the dark places of this life they can see heavenly truth and this swiftly as if seizing on it rather than merely touching it and hence are "ravenous" when they enjoy such felicity, as it is related in the Scriptures. "In the morning" is the matinal vision which according to St. Augustine is a vision in which the contemplative is caught up into the light of divine truth and there "eats the prey" since the joy of heavenly things is enjoyed in the manner of prey rather than of mere possession, since in this life of eternal vision what we may possess utterly transcends the limits of this human life. Hence the Scriptures call "prey" what is attained in this heavenly rapture." Vespers or "evening" is however, when contemplative persons return to the conscious knowing of this world and "divide the spoils" retained from heaven among their brethren, since whatever of God in heaven they hand as spoils for the use of their brethren. Thus St. Paul was raptured into paradise and tasted the prey of beatitude in the eternal light, but when he had returned at evening to soberness, spoke of these heavenly things among the perfect, that is, among his brothers, as he says in I Corinthians 5:13, "For whether we be transported in mind, it is to God; or whether we be sober, it is for you," as if to say, The raptures of the mind in God and their return to you are our gift to you since what we saw their in rapture we now teach you here in all sobriety.

When Moses also blessed Benjamin in Deuteronomy 33:12 said, "The best beloved of the Lord shall dwell confidently in him: as in a bride chamber shall he abide all the day long, and between his shoulders shall be rest." Benjamin is interpreted "most beloved of the Lord" who is with him in the place of the blessed, that is, leads him in the spirit to the third heaven. Benjamin also rests confidently in himself without terror of anxiety because of his tranquility of heart, as it says in Psalm 76:3, "And his place is in peace" [on Salem] that is, in contemplation in rapture of mind: "and his abode in Sion," that is, in eternity. Hence in eternity as in his wedding-bed, that is, he is said to dwell in his secret conscience, because such grace is given to persons only in the secret silence of solitude. And he rests "between his shoulders" because these are two branches of obedience, namely obedience with devotion, and with alacrity, since one who is never perfect in obedience and action is not able to live in the rapture of light

Thus the sons of this Valiant Woman rise from blessing to blessing through the benedictions of Jacob and the Lawgiver Moses.

§2

There follows a reflection on how the Valiant Woman's "**Children rose up, and called her blessed.**" Blessedness is defined by the Saints in three ways: For Cassiodorus in his *Commentary on the Psalms* says, "Blessed is he to whom all he desires comes to pass," while St. Augustine says, "Blessed is he who has all he wants and who wants nothing evil," and Boethius says, "Beatitude is the state of all that is good perfectly united." In the first way the Valiant Woman is most blessed in desire, in the second way in merit, and in the third in reward.

In the first of these ways she seeks and desires nothing but what is said in Matthew 6:33, "Seek ye therefore first the kingdom of God, and his justice, and all these things shall be added unto you." In the second way she has virtue and wishes nothing else but also wishes nothing evil. For as St. Augustine says, "Virtue is a good quality of mind by which one lives rightly and no one uses badly, which God works in us without us." In the third way the Valiant Woman has all that is good and that she loves and admires. For the good that is the whole good of the human person is the uncreated good as the Lord says in Luke 18:19, "No one is good but God alone," that is, no one is substantially good, having all goods in a perfect state to which nothing can be added. The Valiant Woman is blessed in the first way, but is more blessed in the second, and according to the third is most blessed.

What follows is "**her husband,**" add "has risen," "**and he praised her.**" That husband is Christ who enjoyed grace and perfect knowledge from the first moment of conception by his mother, as it says in Jeremiah 31:22, "The Lord hath created a new thing upon the earth: A woman shall compass a man." That one who is the husband of her soul is the witness of her praise and chastity. Praise, however, is nothing other than the glad preaching of her excellence. Hence her husband praises the Valiant Woman for three things: her usefulness, her dignity, and the admirable mysteries that God has worked in her: the usefulness of fertility, the dignity of virginal chastity, and the marvels of these mysteries: that as a virgin she conceived, as virgin bore, that she remained a virgin after her child's birth, and lives unto eternity as the Mother of God and of fertility, because the Virgin Mother conceived at a word. And so the word is fertile so that it brings forth offspring of good works and affections together and this is signified by the fertility of Hannah who it says [in I Kings 1:17, "Then, the priest, Heli said to her: Go in peace: and the God of Israel grant thee thy petition, which thou hast asked of him," and who obtained fertility in prayer. Hannah is interpreted "grace."

As to the Valiant Woman's dignity it says in Luke 1:48-49, "Because he hath regarded the humility of his handmaid; for behold from henceforth all generations shall call me blessed." For as Christ her son in the flesh did not take away the virginity of his virgin mother but sanctified it, so in spirit he conferred fertility on her and did not take away her virginity but rather consecrated her, for she is that "chaste generation which is extolled in praise in Wisdom 4:1, "O how beautiful is the chaste generation with glory: for the memory thereof is immortal: because it is known both with God and with men."

As to these wonderful mysteries, the Valiant Woman was not corrupted since whatever that was corrupted in her was restored. She did not make them the evils heavier, but by her heaviness in pregnancy lightened them. Although she did not take all suffering, she healed all the weaknesses and sorrow of our first mother Eve. Whence Isaiah 66:9 says in the name of God, "Shall not I that make others to bring forth children, myself bring forth, saith the Lord? Shall I, that give generation to others, be barren, saith the Lord thy God?" as if to say, "No!"

THE VALIANT WOMAN

OUTLINE OF CHAPTER XX

Many daughters have gathered together riches:
Thou hast surpassed them all. (v.29)

§1) The Acrostic Letter Res, ר, signifies wisdom in which the Valiant Woman is rich, though not in worldly goods
  1) What are these "Many daughters"? There are four kinds:
    1) Daughters by nature, like those of Jepthe and Lot, rejoice in husband and children
    2) Daughters of the world live in luxury, virgin in body but not in soul
    3) Daughters of the law serve God only in fear to be blamed by men if they vow chastity—the foolish virgins
    4) Daughters of grace are chaste in body and heart like Christ's Virgin Mother

§2) What riches do these daughters gather together
  1) Worldly women excel in the riches of nature which are in the number of children and works of mercy
  2) Worldly women excel in desire for the abundance of luxury and the pomps of Satan
  3) Worldly women also excel in riches of empty praise and pretended justice
  4) But those like the Valiant Woman excel in the riches of virtue and grace

§ 3) How has the Strong "surpassed them all"? In three ways:
  1) In dress as shown in Chapter 12
  2) In ornaments
    1) Shoes that signify examples of the patriarchs that protect our feet, i.e. feelings and will
    2) Little moons on garments that signify reflection on one's own personal defects
    3) Chains for the neck that connects us to Christ our Head and that signify
    4) Ornamental bands that cover the breasts and thus signify the chastity of heart and body
    5) Bracelets for the arms that signify the constancy and fortitude of good works
    6) Headdresses which contain the hair and signify holy meditations
    7) Combs that signify the thickness of thoughtful discussions
    8) Brassieres that guard modesty
    9) Ear rings that signify good listening to the Word of God
    10) Perfume vials that signify the odor of good works
    11) Ear-rings that signify obedience
    12) Rings signify the faith to husband and the marriage-bed
    13) Forehand jewels that signify the glory of Israel
    14) Changes of apparel that signify the diversity of personal relationships
    15) Short cloaks for warm weather that signify the modesty in posture and gait
    16) Fine linen for headdresses that signifies the shyness that especially becomes women
    17) Gold pins that signify holy fear that keeps conversation truthful

18) Mirror signifies Holy Scripture that portray the beautiful good and ugly bad
19) Ribbons to control the hair that signify the customs of the patriarchs that unite us
20) Fine veils that signify the joy of mind and body in the delight of the joy of the Holy Spirit

3) In fourfold riches:
1) The gift of the Valiant Woman's soul to the Father who is both father of the bride and of the true husband of the soul, and of her body in which she suffers for him.
2) The gifts of the Valiant Woman's dowry are the foretastes of eternal life.
3) The wedding feasts or graces of the Valiant Woman from Christ, her spouse
4) Her daily profit or joy that the Valiant Woman has in her great number of merits in action

CHAPTER XX

Many daughters have gathered together riches: thou hast surpassed them all. (v.29)

§ 1

RES ר. Res signifies "wisdom" and this superscription renders learned the one who hears of this wisdom. For it is prefixed to this verse lest he believe that the praise of this Valiant Woman is in regard to earthly riches and not in the riches of wisdom. For as it says later in Proverbs 31, verse 30, "Favor is deceitful, and beauty is vain: the woman that feareth the Lord, she shall be praised." and in Sirach 1:16, "The fear of the Lord is the beginning of wisdom." Therefore if the Valiant Woman has riches they are riches of divine wisdom and of this worldly pomp which are to be more blamed than praised.

The phrase "**Many daughters**" in this verse should be noted as regards three things; first, what or which are the manly daughters; second, how and how riches do they gather; third how in what has the Valiant Woman "surpassed them all." Concerning the first is should be noted that there are daughters by nature, daughters of the world, and daughters of the law, and daughters of grace.

Daughters of nature are those who put soul and will to the propagation of nature, supposing this to be best, namely to rejoice in children and husband. And these are signified by the daughter of Jephte, as related in Judges 11:37-39, "He made a vow to the Lord, saying: If thou wilt deliver the children of Ammon into my hands, Whosoever shall first come forth out of the doors of my house, and shall meet me when I return in peace from the children of Ammon, the same will I offer a holocaust to the Lord. And Jephte passed over to the children of Ammon, to fight against them: and the Lord delivered them into his hands...And when Jephte returned into Maspha to his house, his only daughter met him with timbrels and with dances: for he had no other children. And when he saw her, he rent his garments, and said: Alas! My daughter, thou hast deceived me, and thou thyself art deceived: for I have opened my mouth to the Lord, and I can do no other thing. And she answered him: My father, if thou hast opened thy mouth to the Lord, do unto me whatsoever thou hast promised, since the victory hath been granted to thee, and revenge of thy enemies. And she said to her father: Grant me only this which I desire: Let me go, that I may go about the mountains for two months, and may bewail my virginity with my companions. And he answered her: Go. And he sent her away for two months. And when she was gone with her comrades and companions, she mourned her virginity in the mountains. And the two months being expired, she returned to her father, and he did to her as he had vowed, and she knew no man," so that she left no descendants.

This is also signified by the daughters of Lot who, as related in Genesis 14:30-36. "And Lot went up out of Segor, and abode in the mountain, and his two daughters with him, (for he was afraid to stay in Segor) and he dwelt in a cave, he and his two daughters with him. And the elder said to the younger 'Our father is old, and there is no man left on the earth, to come in unto us after the manner of the whole earth. Come, let us make him drunk with wine, and let us lie with him, that we may preserve seed of our father.' And they made their father drink wine that night: and the elder went in and lay with her father: but he perceived not neither when his daughter lay down, nor when she rose up. And the next day the elder said to the younger: Behold I lay last night with my father, let us make him drink wine also to night, and thou shalt lie with him, that we may save seed of our father. They made their father drink wine that night also, and the younger daughter went in, and lay with him: and neither then did he perceive when she lay down, nor when she rose up. So the two daughters of Lot were with child by their father." Thus this is also signified by these daughters of Lot who feared they would lack children when they supposed the world had perished in the burning of Sodom and the five cities and so got him drunk and had intercourse with him lest the world come to an end.

These they seem to imitate who enter into and second and further marriages, for, as St. Augustine in his *De Civitate Dei* writes of a certain Roman woman who had twenty two husbands successively, and in Matthew 22:25 we read of a woman with seven successive husbands. And these daughters did not intend to sin, nor did they sin, but it is wrong that the reason of honesty should not have as much strength in a human person as has the force of chastity in some brute animals for it said that it is of the nature of the turtledove that after the first mate dies it does not admit a second, and this is praised in Judith 15:11 where it is said, "Because thou hast loved chastity, and after thy husband hast not known any other: therefore also the hand of the Lord hath strengthened thee, and therefore thou shalt be blessed for ever."

The daughters of this world are those who live always in luxury and pleasure-seeking and though they may remain virgin in body, in mind they are incestuous. losing their virginity of body by their external behavior by which they seduce the sons of God, that is clerics who have vowed themselves to chastity, as it says in Genesis 6:2, "The sons of God seeing the daughters of men, that they were fair, took to themselves wives of all which they chose." These are signified by the daughters of Madian [Moab] who were a scandal to the sons of Israel by eating of the sacrifices to idols and fornicating as it says in Numbers 25:1-2, "And Israel at that time abode in Settim, and the people committed fornication with the daughters of Moab. Who called them to their sacrifices. And they ate of them, and adored their gods." It is also signified by that "Jezabel" of whom it is said in Revelation 2:20, "I have against thee a few things: because thou sufferest the woman Jezabel, who calleth herself a prophetess, to teach, and to seduce my servants, to commit fornication, and to eat of things sacrificed to idols." For these are those women who, as it says in [Baruch 6:42-43], "The women also with cords about them, sit in the ways, burning olive stones. And when any one of them, drawn away by some passenger, lieth with him, she upbraideth her neighbor, that she was not thought as worthy as herself, nor her cord broken." These are those woman of whom it is said in Ezekiel 16:25, "At every head of the way thou hast set up a sign of thy prostitution: and hast made thy beauty to be abominable: and hast prostituted thyself to every one that passed by, and hast multiplied thy fornications," because a "passer by" is one who does not tarry, and that man is not lawful who is not bound by the chain of matrimony to his mate, and thse women are those of whom it says in Sirach 9:1ff, "Every woman that is a harlot, shall be trodden upon as dung in the way," and also Isaiah 3:16-17, "Because the daughters of Sion are haughty, and have walked with stretched out necks, and wanton glances of their eyes, and made a noise as they walked with their feet and moved in a set pace," that is, walk in chorus, "The Lord will make bald the crown of the head of the daughters of Sion, and the Lord will discover their hair," that is, those who ought to act like daughters of Sion, but through licentiousness are become daughters of this world.

These are also described in Proverbs, 7:7-20, "And I see little ones, I behold a foolish young man, Who passeth through the street by the corner, and goeth nigh the way of her house. In the dark, when it grows late, in the darkness and obscurity of the night, And behold a woman meeteth him in harlot's attire prepared to deceive souls; talkative and wandering, Not bearing to be quiet, not able to abide still at home, Now abroad, now in the streets, now lying in wait near the corners. And catching the young man, she kisseth him, and with an impudent face, flattereth, saying: I vowed victims for prosperity, this day I have paid my vows. Therefore I am come out to meet thee, desirous to see thee, and I have found thee." And she shows the beauty and softness of her bed, saying "I have woven my bed with cords, I have covered it with painted tapestry, brought from Egypt. I have perfumed my bed with myrrh, aloes, and cinnamon. Come, let us be inebriated with the breasts, and let us enjoy the desired embraces, till the day appear. For my husband is not at home, he is gone a very long journey. He took with him a bag of money: he will return home the day of the full moon," that is, he will not be back for a month and it is evident that these are the words of a mercenary adulteress.

The daughters of the law are those who serve God only with fear and empty intentions fearing that they will be blamed by men who will be irritated if they vow a vow of chastity. And these are those of whom Jeremiah in Lamentations 1:4 says, "her virgins are in affliction, and she [the city of Sion] is oppressed with bitterness." Because such women are always bitter in soul because they do not dare to ignore slander for whatever they pretend to have chastity in body and dress they expose it all through hypocrisy and empty praise to worse defilement. These are the foolish virgins related in

Matthew 25:8, whose lamps are extinguished when the Lord comes to the wedding. These are also those of whom Solomon says in Proverbs 11:22, "A golden ring in a swine's snout, a woman fair and foolish," for as a pig immerges from the mire with a golden ring in its nose, so women who pretend to have the beauty of a false religiosity represent the lust for praise, impious hypocrisy, and iniquity.

The daughters of grace are those who are chaste in body and in heart and holy intention and serve Christ in humility, having as their banner carrying leader the glorious Mother of God and his Son the Immaculate Lamb. The Apostle speaks of this in I Corinthians 7:34, "The unmarried woman and the virgin thinketh on the things of the Lord, that she may be holy both in body and in spirit" and Revelation 14:4 also says, "These are they who were not defiled with women: for they are virgins. These follow the Lamb whithersoever he goeth. These were purchased from among men, the firstfruits to God and to the Lamb." Whence St. Augustine in his book *On Holy Virginity* says that "the rest of the faithful [who have lost virginity, follow the Lamb, not whithersoever He shall have gone, but] so far as ever they shall have been able, but the more fortunate virgins exult more happily and reign more joyfully." And these are signified by the wise virgins, related in Matthew 25:1-13, who took up their lamps of clear chastity in body and accepted the oil of charity in the lamps of their heart and when death came entered with the Lord to the eternal nuptials in which they are made spiritually one with him, for as the Apostle says in I Corinthians 6:17, "The person who is joined to the Lord, is one spirit" with him.

§ 2

These daughters have "**gathered together riches**" of four kinds. First, they have gathered together riches of nature which are in the number of children and works of mercy. Second they have gathered together riches of desire which are in the abundance of luxury and the pomps of Satan. Third they have gathered together riches of empty praise and pretended justice. But fourth, they have gathered together riches of virtue and grace.

Of the riches of the daughter of nature which are in the number of children and works of mercy, it says in Job 1:2, "And there were born to him seven sons and three daughters" and it is also shown that Job was simple, upstanding, God-fearing, and withdrawn from evil. The daughters of nature are women who want to be married in the fear of God in this differ from the daughters of world, because as St. Augustine says, "marriage is a duty of nature. When the Gloss on Genesis 1:28 says that "God gave Adam two commands: one of nature and one of discipline." The first precept of nature is, "Increase and multiply, and fill the earth, and subdue it" for whose fulfillment God instituted marriage in Paradise. And the other precept of nature [is found in Genesis 2:16-17] is "Of every tree of paradise thou shalt eat." And the third precept is "But of the tree of knowledge of good and evil, thou shalt not eat. [For in what day soever thou shalt eat of it, thou shalt die the death."] The first precept of nature pertains to propagation [of the human race]; the second precept of nature to the sustaining of life; while the third precept of discipline pertains learning obedience. Thee are also the riches of Jacob who in Genesis 31:1, it says, "He [Jacob] heard the words of the sons of Laban, saying: Jacob hath taken away all that was our father's, and being enriched by his substance is become great." Yet Jacob took nothing from Laban except wives, sons, and sheep: and in sons is the abundance of progeny and in sheep the works of piety.

Of the riches of worldly daughters Revelation 18:7 it says of the Great Harlot that she boasts of her riches: "She saith in her heart: I sit a queen, and am no widow; and sorrow I shall not see," thus boasting of three things, namely her dignity and flower of honor when she says, "I sit as a queen," and the abundance of her lust or whoredom when she says, "I am no widow," since for one husband who is dead she has relations with a hundred or more others. Such a woman does not mourn over some loss because by her widowhood she procures for herself what is splendid and delicate. For these daughters the temple of God, that is the association of clerics and monks is full, as it says in II Maccabees 6:4-5, "For the temple was full of the riot and revellings of the Gentiles: and of men lying with lewd women. And women thrust themselves of their accord into the holy places, and brought in things that were not lawful. The altar also was filled with unlawful things, which were forbidden by the laws."

Of the riches of proud daughters Jeremiah 17:11 says, "As the partridge hath hatched eggs which she did not lay: so is he that hath gathered riches, and not by right: in the midst of his days he shall leave them, and in his latter end he shall be a fool." A partridge is said to be of such a nature that it sits on eggs not its own, but when this produces little birds when they hear the true mother who laid these eggs they immediately leave the bird the hatched them and follow the bird that laid their eggs. And thus it is with these foolish virgins who foster in appearance the virtue they do not nourish in their hearts. Thus produces riches in vain since much of the times when they believe that they are supported more by their works, they waste these works through empty praise. This happens to them in this life, yet in the newness of days after this life they still remain foolish virgins because the doors of the heavenly kingdom are closed against them [as it relates in Matthew 25:1-13.

The riches of virtue and grace, however, are the riches of the daughters of grace and these are true riches of which it says of Moses in Hebrew 11:25-26, "Rather choosing to be to be afflicted with the people of God, than to have the pleasure of sin for a time, Esteeming the reproach of Christ greater riches than the treasure of the Egyptians"

§ 3

Next is treated the phrase in the chapter text, "**thou hast surpassed them all**" as to how and in what the Valiant Woman has surpassed them all, and this in dress, ornaments, and riches. As to dress it says in Psalm 45:14-15 "All the glory of the king's daughter is within in golden borders, Clothed round about with varieties," and of this we have already said much Chapter 12 §1). As to ornaments however the Valiant Woman has many as listed in Isaiah 3:18-23, ["ornaments of shoes, and little moons, and chains and necklaces, and bracelets, and bonnets, and bodkins, and ornaments of the legs, and tablets, and sweet balls, and earrings, and rings, and jewels hanging on the forehead, and changes of apparel, and short cloaks, and fine linen, and crisping pins, And looking-glasses, [and lawns], and headbands, and fine veils."]

And first is considered "ornaments of shoes," and these are sandals which women have to adorn and protect their feet. The example of the patriarchs, should be noted, who left to us the leather of their works when they died in the Lord for the protection of our feelings and our will which are signified by the feet.

Second are the "little moons" which are little moons of gold hanging on the front of a garment as an ornament. Through "moon", however, is signified a reflection on one's own personal defects.

Third are the "chains" which adorn the neck and through these are signified the custody of discretion since as the neck joins the head to the body so our discretion ought to connect the whole body of our behavior to Christ the head.

Fourth are the "necklaces" [better, ornamental bands] which draw together the folds of hair and garments and protect the bosom lest an adulterer slip in his shameful hand and these signify the chastity of heart and body.

Fifth are the "bracelets" that are ornaments of the arms and signify the constancy and fortitude of good works.

Sixth are the "bonnets' or headdresses which contain the flowing down of the hair and signify holy mediations which bind illicit thoughts that are like tangled hair and prevent it from flowing down.

Seventh are "bodkins' or combs and they signify the thickness of our thoughtful discussions and distinctions so that what more often occupies our thinking.

Eighth are "ornaments of the legs" [better "of the breasts"] that is, bandages for the bosom that restrain the overflow of the breasts and signify the guarding of love lest it force itself as illicit love into the breast and heart; but after perfect and chaste love a woman's modesty which is in part in the breast is restricted and tamed.

Ninth are "tablets" [*murenulae*) or ear-rings that are ornaments to beautify the ears and signify good listening to the Word of God which hears what is like God. Hence in the Song of Solomon in one version we read, "We will make thee chains (*murenulae*) of gold, inlaid with silver," but in another "golden images."

Tenth is the "sweet-balls" or perfume vials which are small bottles filled with perfume and other scented material for a pleasant odor and these signify the odor of good works.

Eleventh are the "ear-rings" that are common ornaments for the ears and signify obedience.

Twelfth are "finger rings" that signify the faith to husband to the marriage-bed that especially mark what is called the ring-finger in which there is a vein that flows directly from the heart.

Thirteenth are "the jewels hanging on the forehead" which is the finest ornament of women and which signifies which in the Scriptures is called a "bud" [as in Isaiah 4:2, "In that day the bud of the Lord shall be in magnificence and glory, and the fruit of the earth shall be high, and a great joy to them that shall have escaped of Israel."]

Fourteenth is "the changes of apparel" and these are the diverse kinds and appearances of clothes in which is noted the various kinds of conversations according as one speaks diversely to different partners as the Apostles says I Corinthians 9:22, "I became all things to all men, that I might save all."

Fifteenth is the "short cloaks" which are fitting in warm weather and are thin and these signify the modesty that controls posture and gait.

Sixteenth is "the fine linen" which adorns the head and signifies the shyness that especially becomes women.

Seventeenth is the "crisping pins" which are golden needles fastening together and the borders of a cloak lest they part and these signify the holy fear which control and restricts the conversation of the Saints lest it become deceitful.

Eighteenth are 'looking glasses" in which women are accustomed to inspect themselves and these signify the understanding of Scripture in which are described both what is wicked and what is beautiful.

Nineteenth are "head bands' which are certain red ribbons by which a headdress is tied in back to control the size of the hair and signifies the customs of the patriarchs which like strings that are not easily broken and hold us together lest we fly apart.

Twentieth and last of these ornaments are the "fine veils" which are thin mantles which are highly decorative and cover the fine adorned woman and signify the joy of mind and body in the delight of the joy of the Holy Spirit.

These are the ornaments of chaste and modest soul which are taken away by the Lord from unchaste minds as it says in Isaiah 3:21, "And instead of a sweet smell" of good reputation "there shall be stench, and instead of a girdle" of gold mediation and chastity "a cord," of habitual sins that sent to hell," and instead of "curled hair" of inordinate thoughts "baldness" or open uncleanness of heart "and instead of a stomacher" which signifies, as we have said, the guardianship of a chaste love, "haircloth" namely the harshness of eternal punishment by which the incontinent soul is vested as with a hair shirt.

In riches all are wealthy in four degrees, namely in the size of the gift, and in the number of gifts in of her dowry, and in the excellence of the wedding gift, and in daily profit.

The gift of the Valiant Woman's soul is that which she gives to the Father who is both father of the bride and of the true husband of the soul, and this a vision of clarity and true love of him and also perfect understanding of him so that the whole of divinity is so enclosed in us that its goals are seen and that we have all that we see and love in him. Similarly the gift of her body is that for its weight agility is given and for its grossness is given subtlety or spirituality. For her mortality and ability to suffer she receives impassibility and for opacity or obscurity a light greater than seven suns.

The gifts of the Valiant Woman's dowry are what the woman receives as wedding gifts. And these are the things that here and now as foretastes of eternal life that are shown and given to us so that we can sustain our exile and more ardently desire its finish when through more experience we know the sweetness of what is everlasting.

The wedding gifts of the Valiant Woman which her spouse gives to his bride in sign of married love, is the glory which our human nature shall have from Christ the man. For this glory is given to us from the fact that Christ has espoused our nature and joined and wed with him in one person.

The daily profit is the joy which the Valiant Woman has in the great number of good merits she has in action.

And thus it is evident how this Valiant Woman surpasses many daughters of nature and this world in clothing, ornaments, and riches both of law and grace because more than all of them she has labored and served God.

OUTLINE OF CHAPTER XXI

**Favor is deceitful, and beauty is vain:
the woman that feareth the Lord, she shall be praised. (v. 30)**

§1)The Acrostic Letter Sin, שׁ, is interpreted "wound" yet the Valiant Woman is not praised for wounding hearts:
   1) By a deceitful image
      1) When the interior image of God is distorted by sin
      2) When the exterior image is a cosmetic and fashion facade
   2) By vain beauty, which even when truly beautiful, can hide a soul still in sin
   2) She will be praised, when redeemed from sin, for:
      1) Her interior soul is freed of sin, and recreated in faith, hope, and charity.
      2) Her exterior body remains as created in the praise of God its creator.
   3) Why will she be praised?
      1) Why only if she fears the Lord? For three reasons:
      1) Because by this fear she is humbled
      2) Because fear of God removes all blame and leaves the praiseworthy
      3) Because fear of God is the beginning of wisdom
§ 2) Why not now but in the future?
      1) No one should praised until dead, because they are still free to sin
      2) In this life God is praised in his Saints but the Saints are not yet praised.

CHAPTER XXI

**Favor is deceitful, and beauty is vain:
the woman that feareth the Lord, she shall be praised. (v. 30)**

§ 1

SIN שׁ. Sin is the twenty-first letter of the Hebrew alphabet and is interpreted "wound." As the acrostic letter it is set at the head of this verse because Solomon speaks here of two things for which this Valiant Woman is not praised but which are often accustomed to wound the human heart, namely, the image of woman and her beauty, as Daniel 13:56 said to the two elderly judges, "O thou seed of Canaan, and not of Judah, beauty hath deceived thee, and lust hath perverted thy heart," that is, the beauty of Susanna.

"**Favor is deceitful, and beauty is vain**," two things are to be noted in this verse, namely what the Valiant Woman is not praised for and what she is praised for. What she is not praised for is twofold: namely "favor" [or a false image] and vain beauty. It should be noted that this "image" is the exterior form of the body, while "beauty" is in the brilliance of color, and St. Ambrose says, "give praise when praise will not injure by flattery nor tempt the one praised to vanity," namely, that there is an image of creation, of recreation, and of likeness.

The image of creation is that in which man is created in the image of God as it says in Genesis 1:26, "God created man to his own image: to the image of God he created him" because man is rational as also is God. It also says in Sirach 16:1, "God created man of the earth, and made him after his own image."

This image is a resemblance in which we ought to imitate God in intelligence, remembering, and loving so that our memory should resemble God the Father, our intelligence the Son, and our loving the Holy Spirit: and so that we have God in our memory without forgetfulness, in our intellect without error, in our will without any bitterness of hatred, anger, envy, or other voluntary evils. For us in our will should be the tranquility of peace, in our intelligence the splendor of eternal light, and in our memory the immutability and completeness of eternity. Of this image it says in I Corinthians 15:49, "Therefore as we have borne the image of the earthly, let us bear also the image of the heavenly."

The image of this "new creation" is faith, hope, and charity. For charity which is mother and principle of all that is divine is attributed to God the Father; faith, however, to the Son, because in this world Jesus taught the faith; and hope is attributed to the Holy Spirit because he descends into the hearts of the faithful raising their hope to things on high. For faith opens the eyes, hope enlivens them, and charity focuses their attention. And concerning this image can be understood what is said in Romans 8:29, "For whom he [God] foreknew, he also predestinated to be made conformable to the image of his Son; that he might be the firstborn amongst many brethren."

The exterior image, however, is the disposition of the shape of the human body and about it Job 4:6 says: "There stood one whose countenance I knew not, an image before my eyes, and I heard the voice as it were of a gentle wind."

What follows is the adjective "deceitful," for both the intrinsic and extrinsic image are sometimes deceitful. The true image is interior when God is imitated and the image is the form of the reformed man who is Christ. The interior image is, however, deceitful when this image is deformed through sin, as it says in Psalm 73:20, "O Lord; so in thy city thou shalt bring their image to nothing."

The exterior image is true when it remains in the praise of God whose is praised as its Creator, as it says in Psalm 92:5, "For thou hast given me, O Lord, a delight in thy doings [creations]: and in the works of thy hands I shall rejoice." But this exterior image is deceitful when it is meretricious painting and a cosmetic facade or when it is hidden beneath some lying hypocrisy. Hence in Matthew 22:20 [Jesus looking at a coin] says, "Whose image and inscription is this?" because the Lord can raise this question to hypocrites and painted women in whose face is indeed the image that he created but a superscription is written over the image that God made and falsifies that which God had so well created.

The phrase "**and beauty is vain**" follows next in the chapter verse meaning that while the interior may be true the exterior can be vain. The interior consists in the beauty of the conscience as it says in the Song of Songs 1:4, "I am black but beautiful, O ye daughters of Jerusalem, as the tents of Cedar, as the curtains of Solomon." The "tents of Cedar" are beautiful within but their outsides are called "black." The "curtains of Solomon" in which the Ark was moved on the interior shine with gems and gleam back with gold, but do not pretend to be exteriorly much decorated. Thus also holy souls have within them the adornment and beauty of the virtues but outside have only humility and the homeliness of asceticism and abstinence and are "black" like the temples of the Lord that are much ornamented within but rather grim without. Hence it says in the Song of Songs 1:9, "Thy cheeks are beautiful as the turtledove's," for she has two cheeks, namely, innocence of conversation and maturity of manner, which are said to be like a turtledove's because chastity and faith are manifest in all her behavior and show themselves without the anger of malice.

As to the beauty of exterior vanity many evils follow it and have been recorded, such as in the story of Helen [of Troy] of whom the Philosopher says, "We should follow the advice of wise men that we should 'flee from Helen.'" Yet there have been certain holy women who were also beautiful in appearance, yet not vain because they did not exhibit their beauty to worldly lust. Such were Judith, Susanna, the three daughters of Job, Rebecca and others of whom we read in the Scriptures. [As it says in Job 42:14], "The daughters of Job were called, the names of one Dies, and the name of the second Cassia, and the name of the third Cornustibil [Hebrew; Jemimah (Turtledove), Keziah (perfume), and Keren-happuch (mascara jar)]" because of their beauty, since it is said in the next verse, "And there were not found in all the earth women so beautiful as the daughters of Job." But in all these is verified what it says in Judith 10:4, "The Lord also gave her more beauty: because all this dressing up did not proceed from sensuality, but from virtue."

§ 2

Next to consider is the second phrase of the chapter text where it says, "**The woman that feareth the Lord, she shall be praised**," concerning which there are two questions: Why does it say "will be praised" in the future? And why not now in the present? A woman who fears the Lord is to be praised principally for three things: first, because of this fear she is greatly humbled and hence is extolled in praise as it says in Romans 11:20, "Thou standest by faith: be not high-minded, but fear," that is, if you fear you will not desire a higher place.

The second question, "Why not now?", however, is answered by noting that the Valiant Woman is praised because her fear of God will purge away all that in her is now blameworthy; hence all that remains will be praiseworthy as in says in Sirach 1:27, "The fear of the Lord driveth out sin."

Third and final is the fact that fear of the Lord leads to perfect wisdom, fulfilling the Commandments and obedience, as it says in Psalm 111:10, "The fear of the Lord is the beginning of wisdom," and in Ecclesiastes 12:13, "Fear God, and keep his commandments: for this is all [the duty of] man."

And therefore since the fear of the Lord especially accomplishes these three things, David says in Psalm 34:12 that since nothing is more useful to us, "Come, children, hearken to me: I will teach you the fear of the Lord." Tobit the elder also taught his son even from infancy the fear of the Lord and to avoid all sin [Tobit 1:10] and therefore Psalm 34:10 commands "Fear the Lord, all ye his Saints: for there is no want to them that fear him." Hence also praise is not lacking to such God-fearers.

Next follows why it says this praise will be future and this is what the wise man says in Ecclesiastes 11:30 "Praise not any man before death" and St. Ambrose says, "give praise when praise will not injure by flattery nor tempt the one praised to vanity." Therefore in this life the Saints are not praised but instead God is praised in his Saints.

OUTLINE OF CHAPTER XXII

Give her of the fruit of her hands:
and let her works praise her in the gates. (v. 31)

§1)
1) The Acrostic Letter Thau, ת, means "sign" or the praise of the Valiant Woman's works for which she will be rewarded through the angels by God, her husband.
2) What reward is the Valiant Woman to be given? The twelve fruits of the Spirit in her labors.
    1) Charity that is the most perfect of these fruits for it is charity because:
        1) It is sharp and penetrates to the beloved's inmost being
        2) Fervid because never made tepid by worldly love
        3) Super-fervid continually boiling to evaporate in embrace of the Beloved.
    2) Joy in the sweetness of the Kingdom of God
    3) Peace that is the tranquility and quiet of the heart in the taste of God
    4) Patience of those who in this life get energy in hope of expected beatitude.
    5) Benignity is fiery goodness melting the heart to help one's neighbor.
    6) Goodness that truly shows we live in God and share ourselves with all
    7) Longanimity is equanimity in awaiting the fulfillment of the promises
    8) Mildness is a meekness that provokes no one nor is easily provoked by another
    9) Faith is certitude in the unseen
    10) Modesty is exterior and interior and both delight those who walk with God.
    11) Continency that has a threefold fruit (Matthew 13:8):
        1) One hundred in virgins
        2) Sixty in widows
        3) Thirty in married persons,
    12) Chastity as temperance with regard to physical pleasures
3) What is to be given to the Valiant Woman of the fruit of her hands which she uses in three ways
    1) To eat it (cf. Chapter IX) :the light of her search for wisdom is never extinguished in the dark of physical pleasure
    2) To plant it so as she will gain further merit
    3) To give thanks to God for it, since it all comes from his grace.
    4) Why is she praised in the gates?

§2)
1) There are six gates:
    1) The gate of life is birth which is principally fourfold:
        1) From the earth as Adam was created
        2) From Adam's rib as Eve was created
        3) From both Adam and Eve
        4) From Mary Ever-Virgin as was Jesus Christ
    2) The gates of death
    3) The gates of judgment where the elders and senators of the earth sit in judgment (see Chapter XIV)
    4) The gates of hell
    5) The gates of heaven

    6) The gates of paradise from which with Adam and eve we were exiled
2) Why is she praised in these gates?
    1) In the gate of this life she is praiseworthy through her remembrance of her lowliness
    2) In the gate of death she is praised for her security in faith
    3) In the gate of judgment she is praised by the wise for her good fame
    4) In the gates of hell she is praised for her victory over hell & the devil
    5) In the gates of heaven she praised by God
    6) In the gates of paradise she is praised because Eve closed them and Mary, the Valiant Woman, opened them
3) She is praised for her works for three reasons
    1) Most importantly because these works are the best witnesses to her life
    2) At the judgment only our works will count
    3) Our works are own and not any other creature's
    4) What is the Valiant Woman's, the Church's, praise? It is fourfold:
        1) The praise of God before the Holy Angels
        2) The Church will sit together at the table of God.
        3) They will share Christ's own joy
        4) They will receive the Kingdom and its Crown, as it says in Matthew 25:34, "Come, ye blessed of my Father, possess you the kingdom prepared for you from the foundation of the world.," to which may Jesus Christ, the Son of God, lead us, to whom is honor and glory for ever and ever. Amen

CHAPTER XXII

Give her of the fruit of her hands: and let her works praise her in the gates. (v. 31)

§ 1

THAU: ת, Thau is the last letter of the Hebrew alphabet and the epigram of this last verse. It is interpreted "sign" and notes the sign of praise and encomium which arises principally from the works of this Valiant Woman who is praised in this chapter. What is especially praiseworthy in her is indicated in John 5:36 where the Lord says, "But I have a greater testimony than that of John: for the works which the Father hath given me to perfect; the works themselves, which I do, give testimony of me that the Father hath sent me." Thau, however, is a sign of this Valiant Woman, for all who are not destroyed by the Destroying Angel are signed with this sign as Ezekiel 9:4 says, "And the Lord said to him: Go through the midst of the city, through the midst of Jerusalem: and mark Thau upon the foreheads of the men that sigh and mourn for all the abominations that are committed in the midst thereof," and thus this sign Thau signifies the sign of the Cross. [And in verse 5 it says "To the others he said in my hearing: Go ye after him through the city and strike: let not your eyes spare, nor be ye moved with pity]."For those redeemed by the Cross should be signed and marked with the Cross, as the Apostle says in Galatians 6:17, "For I bear the marks of the Lord Jesus in my body."

Next to be considered is the phrase **"Give her of the fruits of the works of her hands and let her works praise her in the gates**," Concerning this three things must be considered: to whom this verse is addressed as a command, what is to be given her, and why it is "in the gates" that she is to be praised and concerning the first of these considerations there are also three questions: To whom the command is address? What is to be given the Valiant Woman? Why should it be given her?

The command to give praise is addressed to the angels to whom God commits the Valiant Woman, as Husband to her as his wife, for the angels are ministers of God bringing to us what God has given us. As it says in Psalm 104:4 "Who makest thy angels spirits: and thy ministers a burning fire" and in Tobit 12:12 the angel Raphael says, "When thou didst pray with tears, and didst bury the dead, and didst leave thy dinner, and hide the dead by day in thy house, and bury them by night, I offered thy prayer to the Lord."

What is to be given is indicated when it says, "of the fruit of her hands," for "hands" are taken here for her works and their "fruits' are the foretaste of the Holy Spirit whose fruits that Spirit sometimes gives us here through the ministry of angels as a foretaste of blessedness. These fruits are twelve in number as enumerated by the Apostle in Galatians 5:22-23, "The fruit of the Spirit is, charity, joy, peace, patience, benignity, goodness, longanimity, mildness, faith, modesty, continence, chastity."

It is "charity," however, that is the most perfect of these fruits for it is charity that renews like the sweetness of fruit, and this is what [Pseudo-]Dionysius the Areopagite says when he writes that charity is "sharp, mobile, fervid and super-fervid": sharp because it penetrates the inmost being of the beloved; mobile because it continually ascends to the beloved; fervid because it is never made tepid by worldly love; and super-fervid because it continually boils so as to evaporate in embracing the beloved and this is the fire on Mount Sion and the forge of Jerusalem. For this becomes "fire" when we ponder on the Faith and the "forge" in which though truth we find peace.

The "joy" spoken of here is the gladness of the mind in the taste of the divine sweetness which beyond doubt is in the Kingdom of God, as the Apostle says in Romans 14:17, "For the kingdom of God is not meat and drink; but justice, and peace, and joy in the Holy Ghost."

"Peace" is made and enjoyed by the Saints and is the tranquility and quiet of the heart in the taste of God quieting all our restless desires and which the Lord gave and left to the Apostles, [as he says in John 14:27, "Peace I leave with you, my peace I give unto you: not as the world giveth, do I give unto you. Let not your heart be troubled, nor let it be afraid." But the peace the Lord gives is not what the world gives because in the world we are under many pressures; while in the Lord is the peace of which Psalm 85:9 says, "I will hear what the Lord God will speak in me: for he will speak peace unto his people: And unto his Saints: and unto them that are converted to the heart." And this is the peace of which the Apostle in Philippians 4:7 says, "And the peace of God, which surpasseth all understanding keep your hearts and minds in Christ Jesus," that is, that surpasses all sensible pleasure and guards the senses and intelligences of the Saints.

"Patience," as this fruit is here called, is constancy and equanimity of souls in their labors in this life who get energy from the hope for expected beatitude.

"Benignity" is fiery goodness when, namely, the good which in the heart begins to melt from the fire of charity in love for one's neighbors so that it becomes sweet in words and works in all that will aid them.

"Goodness" as a fruit of the Holy Spirit is the true goodness in the heart which shows that we live in God and share ourselves with all as God does, for as [Pseudo-] Dionysius the Areopagite says, "the good is diffusive and communicative of itself."

"Longanimity" is equanimity in awaiting the fulfillment of what has been promised.

"Mildness" is a meekness that provokes no one nor is easily provoked by others.

"Faith" is here not taken for that which, as the Apostles says in I Corinthians 13:12, "We see now through a glass in a dark manner; but then face to face," but, as the Gloss says on this text, for the certitude of what is unseen since a man is fed on the truth when he possesses it so that he knows it plainly.

"Modesty" is the becoming exterior and interior manner that delights a man who walks with God.

"Continency" has a threefold fruit, one hundred in virgins, sixty in widows, and thirty in married persons, [since as Jesus says in Matthew 13:8], " Other seed fell upon good ground: and they brought forth fruit, some an hundredfold, some sixtyfold, and some thirtyfold. He that hath ears to hear, let him hear."

"Chastity" here can be taken for an innate temperance as regards pleasure in food and others things that delight the body, according to which it is called after the chastisement of corporal pleasures as the Apostle says in I Corinthians 9:27, "But I chastise my body, and bring it into subjection: lest perhaps, when I have preached to others, I myself should become a castaway."

But note that to this Valiant Woman is given "the fruit of her hands" that is fruit as the reward of work. But there are some who pretend to have this sign in themselves externally but which they bite into and devour and these are the hypocrites who devour their work before it comes to fruition. Some, however, are sinners who have no fruit in their hands except perhaps acorns which like filthy swine they gobble up.

The next point concerns "what" is to be given to the Valiant Woman of the fruit of her hands and she is given it so she can use it three ways: eat it, plant it, and give thanks for what it demands.

As to "eating" it, Proverbs 30:18, as mentioned once before (Chapter IX § 1), says, "She hath tasted and seen that her traffic is good," and therefore the light of inquiry is not extinguished in the dark. St. Gregory the Great says, "Having tasted of the spirit he despises all flesh," that is physical pleasure. Thus when one is strengthened by a taste of food one can be made stronger in spirit to labor, as it is said of St. Paul, Acts 9:19, "And when he had taken meat, he was strengthened."

As to "planting" it, the Valiant Woman accepts the fruit as the reward of her labor but then sows the same seeds in the soil of her heart to reap a further reward. The grace which she accepts as the fruit of her labor she employs that it might further increase in merit and knows that according to the Apostle, II Corinthians 9:6, "He who soweth sparingly, shall also reap sparingly: and he who soweth in blessings, shall also reap blessings," and Ecclesiastes 11:6, "In the morning sow thy seed, and In the evening let not thy hand cease [for thou knowest not which may rather spring up, this or that: and if both together, it shall be the better."]

As for "thanksgiving," the Gloss on this text says that the Valiant Woman once she has collected these fruits, just as the Lord prescribes in the Law that first fruits must be brought to the Temple and to the High Priest, obeys this command to confess that the Lord has given her what he promised. Hence the Lord wills that everyone recognize the fruit of grace so that to that Giver of grace they might give thanks magnificently.

§ 2

The last phrase of the chapter verse is "**and let her works praise her in the gates**," in which three things are to be noted: where the Valiant Woman is to be praised, for what she is to be praised, and with what praise. "Where," it is to be noted, is "in the gates." "For what" she is to be noted is for her works. "By what praise" what is to be praised is by the testimony of her virtues and righteousness.

There are, however, gates to this life, and gates to death, and gates to judgment and there are also gates to hell, gates to heaven, and the gates of Paradise.

The gates to life are births, and birth is principally fourfold: namely, from the earth, from a rib, from a woman and a man, and of female virgin without a man. The first is of Adam, the second of Eve, the third both, and the fourth is the birth of Jesus Christ, when it says of Abraham in Genesis 15:13-16, "And it was said unto him: Know thou beforehand that thy seed shall be a stranger in a land not their own, and they shall bring them under bondage, and afflict them four hundred years. But I will judge the nation which they shall serve, and after this they shall come out with great substance. And thou shalt go to thy fathers in peace, and be buried in a good old age. But in the fourth generation they shall return hither." Of these gates is to be understood what is said in Job 5:3-4, "I have seen a fool with a strong root, and I cursed his beauty immediately. His children shall be far from safety, and shall be destroyed in the gate, and there shall be none to deliver them." This means that in this gate of birth through which they must enter into life they are seized and damaged in the first flowering of their lives as Isaiah 38:10 quotes Hezekiah, King of Judah, saying when he had recovered from sickness, "In the midst of my days I shall go to the gates of hell: I sought for the residue of my years," and further on in verse 12, "My generation is at an end, and it is rolled away from me, as a shepherd's tent."

Of the gates to death it is said in Psalm 127:5, "Blessed is the man that hath filled the desire with them [children]; he shall not be confounded when he shall speak to his enemies in the gate." For in death the demons as enemies of the human race labor greatly to confuse the dying person because in the gates of death a person finally perishes or gains [eternal life].

The gates to judgment are where the elders and senators of the earth sit in judgment, as Proverbs 31:23 says, "Her husband is honorable in the gates, when he sitteth among the senators of the land" and in the law it is prescribed that judges sit in the gates and discern just judgment [Deuteronomy 16:23, 17:8].

Of the gates to hell in Matthew 16:18 the Lord speaks to Peter saying, "That thou art Peter; and upon this rock I will build my church, and the gates of hell shall not prevail against it," and also in Psalm 24:7-9, "Lift up your gates, O ye princes, and be ye lifted up, O eternal gates: and the King of Glory shall enter in." This is what the angels and the holy fathers say about Christ when he descended into hell, as says the [apocryphal] *Gospel According to Nicodemus* V (21) [M. R. James translation], "Shut ye the hard gates of brass and put on them the bars of iron and withstand stoutly."

The gates to heaven are also referred to in Psalm 78:23-24, "And he had commanded the clouds from above, and had opened the doors of heaven," and Jeremiah 2:12-13, "Be astonished, O ye heavens, at this, and ye gates thereof, be very desolate, saith the Lord. For my people have done two evils. They have forsaken me, the fountain of living water, and have digged to themselves cisterns, broken cisterns that can hold no water." The heavens are "astonished" when the inhabitants of heaven are astonished. Its gates are "very desolate" when those who ought to enter heaven by another way wander into death. And this happens because people in sinning cause two evils, namely, by deserting the Lord in contempt and ingratitude and by digging empty cisterns of desolation through desire and labor for earthly things which do not contain refreshing water but filthy mud. And so it says in Psalm 118:19-20, "Open ye to me the gates of justice: I will go into them, and give praise to the Lord," and Jesus says in Matthew 7:13, "Enter ye in at the narrow gate: [for wide is the gate, and broad is the way that leadeth to destruction, and many there are who go in thereat."]

The gates to Paradise are those from which we have been exiled but before which it says in Genesis 3:24 that God "cast out Adam; and placed before the paradise of pleasure cherubim and a flaming sword turning every way, to keep the way of the tree of life." In all these gates the Valiant Woman is worthy of praise.

In the gates of nature or of this life the Valiant Woman is praiseworthy through her remembrance of the record of her lowliness, for she knows that she entered through this gate humbly and knows herself to be miserably weak in the real manner of her birth, since as Isaiah 40:6 says, "All flesh is grass, and all the glory thereof as the flower of the field."

In the gates of death she is praised for her security because, as the Apostle says Philippians 1:23, "But I am straitened between two: having a desire to be dissolved and to be with Christ, a thing by far the better," and again in II Corinthians 5:8, "But we are confident, and have a good will to be absent rather from the body, and to be present with the Lord," and as it says in Revelation 14:13, "Blessed are the dead, who die in the Lord. From henceforth now, saith the Spirit that they may rest from their labors."

In the gates of judgment in which sit the wise ones of this world disposing of this world, the Valiant Woman is praised for her good fame. For as it says in Ruth 3:11, "For all the people that dwell within the gates of my city, know that thou art a virtuous woman.' Besides her husband sits there who, as it was said before [in Chapter XIV], rises and praises her and her sons also spread the fame of her virtue.

In the gates of hell she is praised for her victory over hell because she has so triumphed over the devil that he is not able to shut the gates of hell on her; whence she has also gloried over death as Hosea 13:14 says, "O death, I will be thy death; O hell, I will be thy bite." For what this woman has in Christ, her husband, she also has in herself through merit, since she has even herself put hell to death by saving her herself and others whom she has converted from death.

In the gates of heaven the Valiant Woman is praised by the confession of true praise and the recognition of her blessedness by God Himself. Whence Jesus says in Matthew 10:32, "Every one therefore that shall confess me before men, I will also confess him before my Father who is in heaven."

In the gates of Paradise also the Valiant Woman is praiseworthy as the reward of merit. Adam wrongly yielded to temptation by transgressing God's commandment. Hence it is sung in the hymn to that strongest [Most Valiant] of Virgins that says "the gates of Paradise were closed through Eve and opened again by the Virgin Mary." Thus in all these gates this Valiant Woman is worthy of praise and not vainly because the preaching of her virtue is true.

The Valiant Woman is praised because of her works for three reasons: the first and most important of which is that these works are without exception the greatest witnesses to her life. A second reason is that only our works will count for us at the Judgment. The third reason is because our works are ours and not anyone else's.

The reason that our works are without exception the greatest witnesses to our life is evident from what the Apostle says, II Corinthians 5:10 "For we must all be manifested before the judgment seat of Christ, that every one may receive the proper things of the body, according as he hath done, [whether it be good or evil]" and the Athanasian Creed says, "At whose [Jesus Christ's] coming all men shall rise again with their bodies; and shall give account of their own works," and in Revelation 14:13, "For their works follow them." These witnesses are without exception the greatest because they never lie and fraud or deceit is never found on their lips. That Christ prefers the testimony of works to that of John the Baptist is clear from what he says in John 5:36, "But I have a greater testimony than that of John: for the works which the Father hath given me to perfect; the works themselves, which I do, give testimony of me, that the Father hath sent me."

The testimony of works is so great a witness of praise that if the whole world would gather and testify someone to be holy and praiseworthy and only a work of the accuser stood on the other side accusing the conscience, it would convict the accuser of being himself blameworthy and to be condemned. Similarly if all the creatures of God cried out against someone, accusing and condemning him, and only his good and holy works would excuse him and praise him and pronounce him innocent, that single witness of works more than all others, would be preferred by God. Although this seems very surprising it follows from what the Lord says in Matthew 18:16, "Take with thee one or two more: that in the mouth of two or three witnesses every word may stand," though this should be understood only of witnesses who review the case and search out every major exception. These witnesses are not able to be witnesses of the heart and life of a man unless through in terms of works and conscience and through God, who in the last judgment will be both witness and judge.

For then only works will stand in judgment, for there other assets, secular goods, friends, sons, parents, and all that is pleasing in this world must yield. The substance of this world will then be burned up in the great fire that will go before the Judge. A man's friends and sons and parents and other neighbors then will also stand to be judged and therefore cannot be witnesses. For if any one of them could be witnesses for another all would be excused. But all will stand together as for one trial in which all are to be judged, so that none are able to witness for another, as it says in Job 10:7, "There is no man that can deliver out of thy hand."

For only works reveal a person, as the Lord says in Matthew 15:18-19, "But the things which proceed out of the mouth, come forth from the heart, and those things defile a man. For from the heart come forth"...a different version says, "These are the manifest works of the flesh...evil thoughts, murders, adulteries, fornications, thefts, false testimonies, blasphemies," and these are said to be "works of the flesh" because they are from bodily concupiscence and will. Hence the Apostle says in I Corinthians 15:50, "Flesh and blood cannot possess the kingdom of God," and the Gloss says that this means "the work of flesh and blood," and John 1:13 says of the Saints, "Who are born, not of blood, nor of the will of the flesh, nor of the will of man, but of God."

Next follows the question "What is this praise?" and it is the testimony of virtue in which consists the honor of this Valiant Woman. For honor is the showing of reverence in testimony to virtue. The honor and praise of this Valiant Woman consists in four things that God does in honoring his Saints.

The first is their praise spoken from the very mouth of God before his holy angels, when in John 12:26 Christ says, "If any man minister to me, him will my Father honor," that is, he will announce to those in heaven that this person is worthy of praise.

The second is that they will sit together at the table of God for they are made a community that eats together. And the bread is the sweetness and goodness and truth which refresh us and that are the bread and nourishment of the angels, whence in Luke 22:29-30 Jesus before his passion says, "And I dispose to you, as my Father hath disposed to me, a kingdom; that you may eat and drink at my table."

The third is the sharing in Christ's joy which Christ happily and eternally enjoys with which he wills that we as his consorts who should enjoy with him, as he says in Matthew 25:21, "Well done, good and faithful servant, because thou hast been faithful over a few things, I will place thee over many things: enter thou into the joy of thy lord."

And the fourth kind of praise is in the reception of the kingdom and its crown, as it says in Matthew 25:34, "Come, ye blessed of my Father, possess you the kingdom prepared for you from the foundation of the world," to which may Jesus Christ, the Son of God, lead us, to whom is honor and glory for ever and ever. Amen.

Scriptural Index

Genesis
1:2 • 192
1:26 • 233, 343
1:27 • 233
1:28 • 337
1:31 • 96
2:6 • 213
2:10 • 213
2:16-17 • 337
2:21-22 • 286
2:23-24 • 29
3:12 • 29
3:15 • 7, 129
3:16 • 38
3:17-18 • 36, 162
3:24 • 354
4:3-4 • 148
4:3-16 • 131
4:7 • 92
4:8 • 228
4:15 • 276
4:21 • 204
4:23-24 • 276
6:2 • 334
6:14 • 62
6:15 • 109
8:11 • 84
9:25 • 206
10:8-10 • 263
10:8-9 • 276
10:15 • 277
14:15-16 • 76
14:30-36 • 333
15:1 • 190
15:13-16 • 352
18:2 • 152, 236
18:5 • 223
18:11 • 6
18:15-16 • 321
19:2 • 152
19:6 • 143
19:17 • 143, 319
22:1-8 • 94
22:4, 18
23:11 • 91
24:31 • 153, 288
24:63 • 17, 09
24:67 • 38
25:22 • 125
25:29-33 • 90
25:33 • 136
26:12 • 156
27:3-46 • 277
27:15 • 125
27:15-23 • 125
27:20 • 13
27:27 • 89, 176
27:39-40 • 101
28:17 • 288
29:1ff • 127
29:17 • 298
29:21-35 • 298
29:32 • 301
29:34 • 26, 302
29:35 • 302
30:1 • 38, 302, 303
30:1ff • 127
30:1-5 • 298
30:8 • 303
30:9 • 304
30:14-16 • 304
30:16 • 26
30:19-20 • 305
30:21 • 306
30:22-24 • 306
30:25-43 • 125
31:1 • 31, 337
31:21-55 • 126
31:31-35 • 127
32:1 • 15
32:24-30 • 8
33:24-30 • 125
34:1-2 • 306
34:25-26 • 107
35:16-19 • 307
35:2-3 • 176
36:24 • 12
37:2-10 • 322
37:3-4 • 181
37:14 • 14
38:7-10 • 5
39:4 • 53
39:33 • 301
39:6-20 • 138
41:14 • 178
41:18-22 • 300
43:31-34 • 79
48:15-20 • 321
49:1 • 180
49:1-44 • 307
49:5-7 • 308
49:8 • 128
49:8-12 • 311
49:11 • 99
49:13 • 69, 319
49:14-14 • 318
49:16-18 • 314
49:18 • 52
49:19 • 105, 317
49:20 • 71, 317
49:21 • 315
49:22-26 • 320, 324
49:27 • 328

Exodus
1:21 • 24
2:11-12 • 49
3:2 • 177, 327
3:21-22 • 31
3:29 • 198
4:6-8 • 169
7:8-14 • 141
8:19 • 144
8:28 • 58
9:24-25 • 259
9:28 • 58
9:31 • 48
12:35-36 • 31
15:5 • 65, 253
15:11 • 222
17:11 • 142
20:1 • 200
20:1-17 • 279
20:8 • 279
20:12 • 56, 279
20:13 • 280
20:16 • 280
20:17 • 280
20:18 • 18
28:6-28 • 205
33:11 • 116
33:20 • 307
34:30 • 322

34:32-35 • 50
Leviticus
  4:17 • 144
  15:2-4 • 5
Numbers
  6:4 • 71
  11:4-6 • 133
  11:32-34 • 163
  11:34 • 136
  12:1-15 • 164
  12:3 • 49
  14:28-29 • 163
  16:15 • 282
  21:6-9 • 163
  23:10 • 58
  24:6 • 107
  24:23 • 17
  25:1-2 • 334
  26:9-10 • 163
  32:35 • 95
Deuteronomy
  1:15 • 186
  3:28 • 223
  6:5 • 23, 93
  8:3 • 78
  9:10 • 144
  14:4 • 150
  16:23 • 353
  17:8 • 353
  23:21 • 200
  24:12 • 150
  32:5 • 310
  32:10 • 12
  32:22 • 258
  33:2 • 273
  33:6 • 308
  33:7 • 313
  33:8-11 • 309
  33:9 • 218
  33:12 • 24, 328
  33:13-17 • 326
  33:18-19 • 319
  33:19 • 69
  33:20-21 • 317
  33:22 • 315
  33:23 • 316
  33:24-25 • 318
Joshua
  1:3-4 • 18
  7:19 • 58, 269

7:21 • 188
15:19 • 52
Judges
  3:15 • 58
  3:15-30 • 291
  4:2-10 • 138
  4:18-23 • 138
  5:2 • 217
  5:9-11 • 217
  9:9 • 86
  11:30-40 • 93
  11:37-39 • 333
  14:14 • 198
  16:1-21 • 137
  16:3 • 75
  16:4-21 • 239
Ruth
  2:2 • 90
  3:11 • 354
  4:11 • 27
I Samuel
  2:8 • 187
  2:12 • 203
  2:12-15 • 136
  2:19 • 182
  2:25 • 215
  3:10 • 39
  4:11 • 136
  9:20 • 12
  12:2-3 • 50
  12:3 • 282
  14:27 • 90
  14:29 • 114
  16:14 • 131
  17:40 • 135
  18:9ff • 34
  18:27 • 77
  30:19 • 77
II Samuel
  2:5-7 • 223
  12:15-23 • 35
  12:3 • 47
  13:22-19:10 • 34
  16:1-2 • 173
  23:8 • 49
  23:11-12 • 90
  23:20 • 170
  24:1-17 • 34
I Kings
  1:17 • 330

2:12 • 224
2:19 • 191
3:1 • 224
6:31-32 • 88
7:7 • 167
10:4-5 • 236
10:22 • 69
10:23-24 • 222
11:1-9 • 239
12:1ff • 133
15:19 • 52
17:40 • 135
18:10 • 132
19:3-4 • 71
19:8 • 71
22:22 • 141
22:27 • 71
22:49 • 69
II Kings
  1:7-8 • 204
  4:1ff • 141
  5:10 • 287
  5:20 • 92
  5:20-27 • 203
  8:15 • 182
I Chronicles
  29:17-18 • 150
II Chronicles
  9:22-23 • 222
  14:11 • 225
  20:12 • 161
  20:17 • 231
  20:35-36 • 70
  20:37 • 70
  33:13-19 • 162
Tobit
  1:10 • 345
  2:19 • 27
  4:7 • 148
  4:9 • 148
  4:11 • 153
  4:12 • 225
  5:12 • 75 • 95
  5:13 • 232
  10:13 • 27
  12:12 • 87, 349
  12:13 • 34
Judith
  8:5-6 • 166
  9:1 • 53

10:2 • 301
10:4 • 345
13:7 • 223
13:10 • 107
13:11 • 301
15:10 • 25
15:11 • 185, 334
Esther
  1:3 • 79
  5:1-2 • 243
  5:2 • 273
  10:7 • 132
  11:6 • 132
  11:11 • 132
I Maccabees
  2:16 • 231
  2:19-22 • 217
  2:23-25 • 217
  2:24-25 • 106
  2:38 • 294
  2:62 • 240
  2:63 • 240
  3:52-54 • 161
  3:58-59 • 104
  4:47 • 288
  9:8-10 • 106
II Maccabees
  1:11 • 222
  4:7-10 • 92
  4:7-20 • 203
  5:24-26 • 227
  6:4-5 • 337
  6:13 • 87
  6:19-20 • 51
  6:30 • 51
  7:1-42 • 35, 218
  7:20-27 • 8
  9:13 • 58
  9:4 • 160
Job
  1:1 • 94
  1:2 • 336
  1:4 • 79
  1:25 • 222
  2:4 • 215
  3:7 • 74
  3:8 • 7
  3:13 • 286
  3:20-23 • 119
  3:22 • 284

3:23 • 95
4:3-7 • 160
4:4 • 223
4:6 • 344
4:18-20 • 164
5:3-4 • 352
5:11 • 197
5:18 • 87
6:6 • 114
6:16 • 171
7:1 • 3 • 285
8:13-14 • 225
8:21 • 243
9:7-10 • 299
9:24 • 192
9:30-31 • 172
10:7 • 356
11:26 • 30
12:4-3 • 245
12:7-10 • 299
12:11 • 114
12:18 • 204
13:7 • 202
14:1-2 • 62
14:2 • 160
15:21-23 • 216
15:26 • 214
15:29-30 • 230
16:2-3 • 153
17:13 • 261
17:14 • 261
18:5-6 • 121
19:3 • 127
19:6 • 204
20:15 • 156
21:13 • 292
24:19 • 171, 259
24:21 • 26
26:13 • 142, 202
27:19 • 135
28:7 • 283
28:17 • 120
29:15 • 271
29:17 • 77
29:20 • 142
29:21 • 271
30:1 • 200
30:16-20 • 252
30:17 • 74
31:1 • 57

31:12 • 177
31:17-18 • 149
31:21-22 • 149
32:19 • 100
33:23-24 • 11
36:25-26 • 18
37:17 • 176
38:22-23 • 169
38:24 • 101, 169
39:5-8 • 278
39:25 • 129
40:2 • 107
40:5 • 198
40:11 • 107
40:14 • 314
40:21 • 110
41:6 • 257
41:9-14 • 262
41:24 • 10
41:25 • 32
42:5-6 • 115
42:14 • 345
Psalms
  1:1 • 28
  1:2 • 51 • 95, 267
  1:3 • 85
  3:2-3 • 226
  4:8 • 99
  5:13 • 110
  8:2 • 223
  8:8 • 154
  10:17 • 272
  13:5 • 215
  18:12 • 13
  19:2 • 299
  19:10 • 219, 220
  19:15 • 267
  21:4 • 320
  22:19 • 139, 175
  24:3-4 • 166, 284
  24:7-9 • 353
  26:8 • 165
  26:13 • 192
  29:7 • 258
  30:7 • 160
  31:21 • 246
  32:5 • 269, 287
  34:9 • 37, 116
  34:10 • 346
  34:12 • 345

35:10 • 14
35:13 • 96
36:7 • 325
36:10 • 41, 213
37:11 • 192
37:25 • 39, 310
37:30-31 • 272
38:10 • 272
40:2 • 25
45:2 • 266
45:3 • 7, 39, 288
45:4 • 105
45:10 • 39, 167, 177
45:11 • 301
45:11-12 • 23
45:14 • 113
45:14-15 • 338
49:13 • 232
49:18 • 135
49:23 • 42
50:23 • 271
51:9 • 171
51:19 • 319
52:3-5 • 239
52:10 • 84
55:13-15 • 140
55:16 • 325
55:23 • 218
60:5 • 98
60:13 • 96
63:2 • 96
63:7-8 • 98
66:13-14 • 200
68:16-17 • 99
68:28 • 307
69:10 • 5, 66
69:32 • 302
73:20 • 344
73:23 • 130, 170
73:25 • 25, 267
76:3 • 329
76:5 • 325
76:11 • 8
76:12 • 200
77:20 • 249
78:18 • 215
78:23-24 • 353
80:6 • 70
81:17 • 268

83:11 • 164, 166
84:3 • 166, 312
84:8 • 116
84:11 • 41
85:9 • 189, 350
89:19 • 100
89:21 • 13, 87
89:22-23 • 109
89:32 • 87
91:1 • 102, 284
91:11 • 284
91:15 • 37
92:5 • 344
93:1 • 242
93:5 • 165
95:1 • 271
95:8-9 • 163
103:1 • 97
103:2-5 • 97
103:5 • 9
103:8 • 229
104:1-2 • 175
104:4 • 349
104:6 • 175
104:15 • 78, 99, 223
104:25-26 • 67
105:4 • 15
105:17-22 • 188
106:23-24 • 68
107:26 • 65, 325
109:4 • 140
110:1 • 257
110:3 • 35
110:4 • 140
110:4-5 • 36
111:5 • 20
111:10 • 218, 345
112:9 • 149
113:7-8 • 187
114:6 • 326
115:10 • 51
116:12 • 97
116:12-13 • 34
117:1 • 271
118:18 • 87
118:19-20 • 353
119:7 • 140
119:37 • 57
119:47 • 145

119:47-48 • 267
119:55 • 75
119:62 • 75
119:103 • 317
119:105 • 75, 118, 267
120:1 • 161
121:7 • 250
127:2 • 20
127:5 • 190, 353
130:7 • 20, 86
133:1-2 • 246
134:2 • 75
134:19 • 24
137:6 • 272
139:11-12 • 75
140:4 • 269
140:6 • 169
141:2 • 142
144:1 • 30
144:2 • 128
144:5 • 147
144:7 • 128
144:13 • 287
146:2 • 97, 271
147:16-17 • 168
149:5 • 10
149:5-6 • 241
Proverbs
1:24-29 • 244
1:5 • 63
3:9 • 148
4:18 • 278
4:26 • 281
6:6-11 • 293
6:9-11 • 67
6:27-29 • 177
7:7-20 • 335
7:10 • 85
7:21 • 85
9:1 • 290
9:5 • 78, 100
10:23 • 245
11:1 • 206
11:19 • 273
11:22 • 336
12:11 • 54
13:4 • 293
14:4 • 93
14:12 • 278

14:13 • 244
16:32 • 11
19:15 • 293
20:4 • 54, 293
21:5 • 293
22:13 • 293
22:29 • 94
23:34 • 64
23:35 • 227
24:30-31 • 91
25:15 • 228
26:1 • 27
27:3 • 319
27:9-10 • 56
28:13 • 269
28:19 • 293
30:7-8 • 128
30:18 • 351
30:30 • 108
30:31 • 105
31:10 • 3, 16
31:10-31 • xi, xii
31:11b • 29
31:21 • 47
31:23 • 353
31:29 • 113
31:30 • 332
37:3 • 66

Ecclesiastes
1:2 • 47
1:4 • 230
1:5 • 40, 213
1:7 • 42, 270
4:10-11 • 101
7:7 • 245
7:29 • 3
7:30 • 233
8:10 • 36
9:1 • 36
9:10 • 54, 94
10:18 • 54
10:19 • 155
11:1 • 17
11:6 • 321, 351
11:30 • 346
12:11 • 62
12:13 • 219 • 345
24:42 • 213
24:44 • 17
46:1 • 214

Song of Songs
1:1 • 38, 100
1:2 • 86, 93
1:4 • 344
1:5 • 140
1:9 • 53, 344
1:13 • 100
1:15-16 • 26
2:6 • 38
2:9 • 322
2:11 • 168
2:12 • 52
2:14 • 39, 288
3:1-2 • 15
3:4 • 9 • 16
3:7-8 • 104
4:4 • 30, 284
4:11 • 7, 177
5:1 • 78, 99
5:10 • 25, 289
5:14 • 58
5:2 • 24
5:6 • 40
6:3 • 232
7:1 • 4
7:5 • 183
7:10 • 25
7:11 • 91
8:1 • 23
8:2 • 9, 100
8:7 • 120

Wisdom
1:5 • 141
2:15 • 151
2:23-24 • 32
2:24 • 75
2:24-25 • 131
3:5 • 3
3:5-6 • 15
3:7-8 • 247
4:1 • 235, 330
5:1 • 231
5:8-10 • 69
5:18-22 • 259
5:20 • 109
5:21 • 110, 132, 206
5:23-24 • 260
6:16 • 268

6:26 • 271
6:7 • 149
7:1-4 • 62
7:2-5 • 181
7:8-9 • 266
7:11 • 20
7:25-26 • 206
7:28 • 267
8:1 • 19, 232
8:7 • 63
8:9 • 268
8:16 • 39, 164
9:10 • 267
9:14-15 • 37
9:15 • 15
10:1 • 130
13:1 • 96, 304
13:2-3 • 314
13:5 • 303
14:5 • 64
14:6-7 • 64
15:12 • 134
15:3 • 96
16:16-17 • 259
16:20-21 • 72
17:3 • 74
17:5 • 261
17:10 • 113
18:24 • 175

Sirach
1:1 • 53
1:16 • 332
1:27 • 345
3:27 • 151
4:35 • 173
4:36 • 150
9:1ff • 335
10:9 • 151
11:1 • 157
13:23 • 276
14:22 • 268
15:3 • 27, 72, 268
16:1 • 343
17:1 • 233
17:2 • 242
20:22 • 234
24:26-29 • 268
24:30-31 • 267
24:33 • 273
26:1 • 27

26:2 • 28
26:16 • 28
26:21 • 47
27:12 • 278
31:1 • 96
31:8-9 • 11, 155
31:12 • 97
32:24 • 55, 278
32:25-26 • 77
33:29-30 • 294
36:18 • 190
41:1 • 240
41:1-2 • 63
42:19 • 303
43:4 • 69
43:18-19 • 170
43:22 • 67, 168
43:26 • 68
44:5-6 • 52
45:9 • 203
46:1-2 • 106
47:21-22 • 137
48:1 • 50
50:1-2 • 242
Isaiah
  1:9 • 65
  1:14 • 294
  1:16-17 • 287
  1:18 • 172
  1:26 • 193
  2:3 • 271 • 280
  3:5 • 187
  3:14 • 134
  3:14-15 • 193
  3:16-17 • 335
  3:17-24 • 199
  3:18-23 • 338
  3:21 • 340
  4:1 • 78
  4:2 • 339
  5:1 • 99, 102
  5:8 • 134
  5:11 • 32
  5:18 • 32
  5:23 • 202
  6:1 • 49
  6:6-7 • 16
  6:8 • 271
  7:14 • 11
  8:3-4 • 76

8:16 • 200
9:3 • 31
9:5 • 77, 176
9:6 • 11
10:13 • 223
11:1-2 • 186
11:3 • 219, 220
11:14 • 30
13:22 • 66
13:8 • 254
14:9-10 • 261
14:11 • 255
14:19 • 253
16:1 • 102
16:9 • 101
19:9 • 47, 55
21:3 • 108
21:5 • 58
21:14-15 • 72
22:12 • 204
22:22 • 108
23:18 • 117
24:17 • 251
26:1 • 285
26:7 • 281
26:8 • 284
26:8-9 • 98
26:13 • 124
26:17-18 • 4, 219, 220
26:19 • 102, 326
28:20 • 25
28:5 • 21
30:1 • 55, 182
30:26 • 248
30:33 • 258
32:18 • 247
32:20 • 94
35:2 • 238
35:3-4 • 216
35:10 • 244
36:20 • 214
38:10 • 352
38:13 • 25
38:15 • 162, 286
40:6 • 354
40:29-31 • 8
40:31 • 8
40:67 • 240
41:5 • 204

41:7 • 232
42:8 • 31, 138
43:25 • 269
47:8 • 31
48:13 • 261
49:24-25 • 76
51:3 • 42
51:9 • 128
53:7 • 48
53:8 • 11
54:6 • 172
55:6 • 15
55:9 • 17
56:7 • 286
57:20-21 • 67
58:6 • 155
58:7 • 153
58:11 • 19
58:14 • 192
62:6 • 285
63:2-3 • 180
64:4 • 100
64:6 • 87
65:1 • 12
65:17-18 • 248
66:9 • 330
66:10-11 • 249
66:12-13 • 250
66:15 • 256
66:24 • 253, 255
Jeremiah
  1:13-14 • 300
  1:14 • 188
  2:11-13 • 14
  2:12-13 • 353
  2:21 • 102
  2:36-37 • 226
  3:1 • 28
  6:6 • 160
  6:16 • 277
  9:4 • 96
  9:23-24 • 239
  11:16 • 88
  14:8 • 15
  15:16 • 12
  17:11 • 337
  17:16 • 217
  18:9-10 • 36
  19:1ff • 91
  27:2-3 • 263

31:13 • 327
31:16-17 • 42
31:8-19 • 42
31:19 • 7
31:22 • 187, 330
32:6-15 • 91
32:7 • 89, 91
36:22-23 • 292
39:6 • 186
Lamentations
1:4 • 335
1:7 • 294
1:13 • 96
1:15 • 223
3:1 • 42
3:2 • 260
3:19 • 97
3:20 • 97
3:22 • 156
3:26 • 42
4:2 • 165
4:8 • 254
5:10 • 261
Baruch
3:14 • 162
3:16-19 • 277
6:42-43 • 85, 334
Ezekiel
3:18-21 • 5
4:13 • 292
9:4 • 348
16:3-5 • 189
16:10 • 175
16:25 • 334
28:16 • 130
28:17-18 • 32
32:27 • 255
46:23-24 • 288
48:31-34 • 187
Daniel
2:31 • 300
3:13-97 • 236
4:30 • 137
7:2-28 • 300
7:9-10 • 256
7:10 • 178
9:3 • 57
12:3 • 95
13:5 • 193
13:23 • 215

13:56 • 343
14:4 • 291
14:5 • 136
Hosea
2:6-7 • 28
2:16-17 • 26
4:14 • 199
6:3 • 41
6:5 • 231
6:6 • 200
12:3-4 • 125
12:7 • 206
13:14 • 190, 354
14:3 • 42, 270
14:7 • 85
Joel
2:1-2 • 248
2:10-11 • 119
2:11 • 248
Amos
3:15 • 292
4:2-3 • 251
4:10 • 253
5:20 • 255
5:23 • 294
8:11 • 72, 286
Micah
6:3-4 • 283
7:19 • 288
Habakkuk
2:1 • 145
2:2-3 • 17
Zephaniah
1:12 • 118
2:25 • 227
Zechariah
3:1-2 • 140
4:2-3 • 89
5:4 • 279
5:5 • 154
9:11 • 261
11:12-13 • 20, 91
12:7 • 223
14:4 • 88
Malachi
1:6 • 219
1:14 • 92, 148
2:7 • 51
Matthew
1:21 • 106

1:23 • 315
3:4 • 177, 204
4:1ff • 133
4:5 • 10
4:19 • 68, 277, 319
5:1-2 • 271
5:3-11 • 197
5:3-12 • 280
5:4 • 10, 192
5:5 • 52, 249
5:7 • 53
5:8 • 16, 95, 115
5:11-12 • 42
5:44 • 56
6:2 • 86
6:2-4 • 149
6:5 • 269
6:20-21 • 156
6:22 • 26
6:23 • 119
6:25-33 • 38
6:33 • 329
7:13 • 353
7:7 • 269
7:14 • 10
7:24-27 • 324
8:23-26 • 68
8:25 • 216
9:1 • 64
9:13 • 156
9:37-38 • 304
10:8 • 68
10:16 • 327
10:19 • 217
10:22 • 230
10:24 • 173
10:32 • 51, 354
10:37 • 310
11:12 • 10
11:29 • 48, 132
11:30 • 125, 273
12:29 • 10
13:18-30 • 90
13:41 • 91
13:43 • 247
13:45-46 • 117
13:45-46 • 47
13:8 • 200, 351
14:30 • 216

15:11 • 266
15:14 • 234
15:17 • 135
15:17-20 • 266
15:18-19 • 356
15:21-28 • 207
16:18 • 353
17:1-9 • 284
17:4 • 37
18:16 • 355
18:28-29 • 311
19:21 • 149, 302
19:27 • 280
19:28 • 191
19:29 • 157
20:2 • 20
20:6 • 54, 293
20:10 • 259
21:13 • 165, 286
21:8 • 88
22:2 • 281
22:13 • 264
22:20 • 344
22:25 • 334
22:25-29 • 185
24:12 • 7
24:12-13 • 230
24:30 • 256
24:37 • 248
24:45-47 • 15
25:1-13 • 120, 336, 338
25:8 • 336
25:11-13 • 120
25:14 • 117
25:21,23 • 244, 357
25:30 • 255, 260
25:33 • 14
25:34 • 53, 192, 357
25:34-35 • 191
25:35 • 87
25:40 • 199
25:41 • 120
25:41-45 • 191
25:42 • 257
26:26-29 • 40
26:36ff • 35
26:38 • 216
26:7 • 291
27:28 • 131
27:34 • 48, 97, 114
27:43 • 226
27:46-55 • 316
27:51-54 • 181
27:54 • 316
27:7-8 • 91
27:9-10 • 20

Mark
3:24 • 202
6:3 • 315
9:2-8 • 176
14:22-25 • 40
14:32 • 199
14:50-52 • 199
15:23 • 97
15:36 • 97
16:17-18 • 202

Luke
1:48-49 • 330
1:69 • 197
1:78 • 156
2:7 • 48
2:14 • 31, 138, 313
2:36-37 • 53
2:52 • 187
6:25 • 245
6:36 • 86, 156
6:38 • 246
7:36-39 • 290
7:37 • 291
9:5 • 138
9:62 • 94
10:22 • 324
10:29-37 • 77
10:30-37 • 86
10:34-35 • 282
10:38 • 285
10:38-42 • 236, 290
10:42 • 246
11:1 • 269
11:5-10 • 98
11:5-8 • 269
11:20 • 144
11:27 • 228
11:33 • 118
11:34-36 • 118
11:41 • 148
12:4-5 • 215
12:35 • 107, 205
12:37 • 105, 205
13:6 • 205
13:11-16 • 197
13:24 • 10
13:27 • 13
15:1ff • 12
15:6 • 101
15:7 • 126
15:8-9 • 118
15:11-32 • 173
15:27-28 • 262
16:9 • 117, 156
16:19 • 126, 137
16:19-31 • 85, 239
16:24-25 • 245
16:25 • 147
17:21 • 113
18:1 • 98
18:2-5 • 270
18:11 • 86
18:11-12 • 278
18:19 • 20, 329
18:24 • 134
18:35-43 • 95
19:8 • 156
19:12-13 • 117
19:23 • 282
20:5 • 108
21:19 • 10, 228
22:15-20 • 40
22:26-27 • 31
22:29-30 • 78, 190, 246, 356
22:42 • 48
23:28-30 • 256
23:36 • 97
23:43 • 162
23:48 • 316
24:13-35 • 40
24:15 • 268
24:26 • 37
24:29 • 153
24:32 • 39
24:39-43 • 116
28:22-23 • 215

John
1:1 • 48
1:2-3 • 299
1:5 • 119
1:13 • 356
1:14 • 19, 315
1:16 • 3
1:17 • 273
1:29 • 48, 172
1:48 • 316
2:17 • 304
3:18 • 191
4:13 • 316
4:17-18 • 185
5:3 • 287
5:28-29 • 41
5:33 • 121
5:36 • 348, 355
5:44 • 66, 129
6:15 • 207
6:27 • 294
6:33 • 61
6:48 • 72
6:52 • 61
8:44 • 202
8:56 • 326
9:1 • 34
9:2-3 • 204
9:7 • 287
10:9 • 19
10:30 • 316
11:10 • 75
11:33-44 • 290
12:3 • 291
12:26 • 250, 356
12:28-30 • 290
14:2 • 10, 76, 165, 174
14:27 • 350
14:30 • 10
15:12 • 313
16:13 • 9
16:16 • 40
16:24 • 269
16:33 • 10
19:23 • 49
19:23-24 • 175
19:24 • 139
19:29 • 97
19:30 • 316
20:11-12 • 147
20:14-19 • 40
21:3 • 68
21:6 • 68
21:7 • 105
21:15-18 • 93
21:15-19 • 52
21:18-19 • 205
21:19 • 180
Acts
1:19 • 91
2:3 • 273
4:13 • 231
4:28 • 225
5:1-5 • 93
8:18 • 92
8:18-24 • 203
9:15 • 217
9:19 • 223, 351
12:21 • 161
12:23 • 35
13:34 • 315
13:46 • 231
14:32 • 247
17:30 • 119
18:24-26 • 225
20:26-27 • 6
20:28 • 52
20:33-34 • 50, 282
27:14-14 • 67
27:17 • 66
27:24 • 51
27:29 • 64
27:41 • 63, 67
Romans
1:4 • 35
1:20 • 50
1:21 • 303
2:4 • 229
2:16 • 257
2:19 • 226
4:3 • 49
4:18 • 49
4:20-21 • 224
6:9 • 75
8:7 • 308
8:17-18 • 37, 242
8:24-25 • 227
8:29 • 343
8:29-30 • 35
9:1 • 202, 238
10:1 • 107
10:10 • 51
10:17 • 115
11:17 • 84
11:18 • 239
11:20 • 345
11:33 • 144, 303, 316
12:1 • 54
12:3 • 308
12:4-6 • 234
12:7-9 • 279
12:8 • 52
12:11 • 109, 176
12:17 • 237
12:20 • 57
13:1 • 200
13:10 • 108
14:1 • 287
14:17 • 113, 350
14:23 • 238
15:1 • 318
I Corinthians
1:12 • 113
2:9 • 100, 244
3:1-2 • 7, 78
3:18 • 94
4:5 • 257
4:7 • 239
4:13 • 66
4:17 • 242
4:55 • 190
5:6-7 • 37
5:7-8 • 78
5:13 • 328
6:2 • 194
6:12 • 237
6:17 • 9, 29, 336
6:20 • 170
7:28 • 263
7:34 • 52, 336
8:9 • 237
9:13-15 • 282
9:18 • 68
9:22 • 340
9:24 • 21
9:27 • 53, 96, 351
10:4 • 268

10:6-12 • 163
10:16 • 78
10:31 • 270
11:26 • 40
11:3 • 29, 38, 125
11:7 • 138
12:2 • 320
12:8-10 • 166
12:14-27 • 235
12:31 • 119
13:8 • 246
13:12 • 115, 350
13:13 • 236
15:7 • 324
15:10 • 41
15:33 • 143
15:49 • 343
15:50 • 356
15:52 • 254

II Corinthians
1:12 • 238
1:3 • 153
1:8-10 • 224
2:10-11 • 30
2:17 • 5
3:5 • 3
3:11 • 235
3:18 • 116, 322
4:17 • 37
4:5 • 5
4:6 • 323
5:7 • 15, 115
5:8 • 354
5:10 • 355
5:13-14 • 6
6:1 • 41
6:4-6 • 229
6:11-12 • 6
8:21 • 58
9:6 • 351
9:7 • 148
9:10-11 • 39
10:4-5 • 315
11:14 • 325
11:30 • 238
12:2-4 • 116
12:4 • 307
12:7-9 • 35
12:9f • 238
12:14-15 • 50

Galatians
1:8 • 201
2:20 • 41
3:5 • 3
4:4-5 • 17
4:19 • 5
5:17 • 66, 128
5:22 • 115
5:22-23 • 229, 349
5:24 • 127
6:2 • 318
6:8 • 165
6:10 • 173
6:14 • 53, 127, 174, 238
6:17 • 349

Ephesians
2:1-5 • 224
2:14 • 36
2:17 • 77
2:19 • 76, 174
3:11-12 • 226
3:16-18 • 70
4:29 • 84
5:8 • 119
5:19 • 271
5:25-27 • 38
6:12 • 65
6:16 • 109
6:17 • 317

Philippians
1:23 • 354
2:3 • 56
2:6-8 • 243
2:7 • 207
2:8 • 48
2:21 • 155
3:13-14 • 98, 321
3:18-19 • 135
3:21 • 316
4:1 • 305
4:7 • 350
4:8 • 237
4:18 • 109

Colossians
1:23 • 235
2:3 • 187
3:1 • 75
3:5 • 134

I Thessalonians
4:16 • 251, 257
5:2 • 247
5:18 • 42, 270, 311

II Thessalonians
3:7-10 • 293

I Timothy
1:17 • 139
2:5 • 70
2:8 • 142
2:9-10 • 39
2:12 • 237
2:15 • 38
4:7 • 143
4:8 • 151
4:13 • 145
5:5 • 53
5:8 • 53, 77, 174
5:20 • 100
5:23 • 128
6:7 • 62
6:8 • 128
6:9 • 134
6:17 • 201

II Timothy
1:6 • 42
3:8 • 141
3:12 • 8 • 65
4:1-2 • 51
4:2-5 • 201
4:7 • 130
4:7-8 • 242
4:8 • 21

Titus
3:5 • 87

Philemon
1:7 • 288

Hebrews
2:13 • 224
2:15 • 216
4:12 • 49, 110
4:15 • 283
5:12-14 • 78
6:6 • 139
6:7-8 • 93
6:9 • 226
6:13 • 249
6:13-15 • 229
6:16-20 • 36

6:18-19 • 64
10:28-29 • 14, 215
10:32-34 • 51
10:35-36 • 226
10:36 • 42, 227
11:1ff • 49
11:2 • 49
11:4 • 238
11:8 • 94
11:13 • 52
11:33 • 214
12:1-3 • 143
12:7 • 230
12:11 • 96, 288
12:12-13 • 143
12:15 • 42
12:29 • 74
13:1-2 • 150
13:2 • 288
13:3 • 287
13:7 • 56
13:17 • 200
20:34 • 148
James
1:4 • 228
1:17 • 139
1:20 • 131
1:25 • 267
3:2 • 273
5:1-3 • 201
5:10-11 • 229

5:20 • 304
I Peter
1:11 • 242
2:3 • 37, 114
2:4 • 116
2:9 • 283
2:13 • 56
2:13-15 • 199
2:23 • 48
3:15 • 287
4:6 • 128
5:7 • 218
5:8 • 198
5:8-9 • 285
II Peter
2:4 • 263
2:5 • 64
I John
2:16 • 126
2:20 • 9
3:2 • 115
3:17 • 150
4:3 • 141
4:18 • 219
Jude
1:9 • 140
Revelation
1:7 • 256
1:11 • 240
1:13 • 178, 205
2:7 • 240
2:11 • 240

2:17 • 240
2:20 • 334
3:1 • 36
3:5 • 241
3:12 • 241
3:21 • 242
4:26-27 • 241
5:10 • 187
7:14 • 312
9:6 • 253
10:5 • 248
12:7 • 130
14:13 • 190, 354, 355
14:13-4 • 130
14:4 • 336
16:13 • 141
16:9 • 255
18:7 • 337
18:21 • 253
19:8 • 183
21:2 • 39
21:4 • 20, 244
21:9 • 3
21:16 • 290
22:13 • 12

III Esdras
3:12 • 324
3:18-19 • 101
4:29-30 • 137

Non-Scriptural Index

Ambrose, St. • 11, 116, 235, 290, 343, 346
Anselm. St. , *Cur Deus Homo* • 11
Aristotle [The Philosopher] • [108,], 151, 176, 221, 232, 254, 285, 308, 345,
   History of Animals • 6
   Posterior Analytics • 85
   Nicomachean Ethics • 105
   Meteorologica • 167
Athanasian Creed • 98, 361
Augustine, St. • 4. 6, 63, 71, 92, 96, 102, 107, 109, 113, 127, 145, 171, 200, 218, 223, 230, 236-37, 246, 255, 262, 299, 314, 327-29
   Rule • xi, 286, 289
   On John • 19
   City of God • 163, 254, 334
   On Jude • 201
   Gloss on Jn 21:18
   On Christian Doctrine • 221
   De bono perseverantiae • 229
   On Matthew • 266
   Confessions: X • 271
   On holy virginity • 336-37
Basil the Great, St. • 96
   On Proverbs • 160,
   On Psalms • 258
Bernard of Clairvaux, St. • 264, 272
Boethius • 20
Cassiodorus • 244,
   Commentary on the Psalms • 329
Cicero • 106. 214, 220-24, 227, 229
   First Rhetoric • 273

Gloss • 27, 64, 75, 101, 118, 129, 143, 144, 181, 187, 191, 198, 238, 255, 271, 350, 352, 356,
   Jerome on Genesis • 2
   On Isaiah 4 • 78
   Gregory on the Gospels • 91, 119, 205,
   Of Augustine on Jn 21 • 205
   Of Ambrose • 235
   On James • 273
   On John • 286
   On Genesis • 337
Gospel according to Nicodemus • 353
Gregory, St. • 17, 28, 43, 75, 77, 85, 91, 95, 107, 114, 115, 119, 120, 136, 137, 162, 171, 205, 218, 351,
   Homilies on Ezekiel • 271
   Commentary on Job • 272
Isaac the Philosopher • 254
Isidore, St., *Etymologies* • 4
John Damascene, St. • 198, 221
Mary, Blessed Virgin • 138, 355
Plato • 24, 155, 167,
[Prayer of Manasses], • 162
Pseudo-Dionysius • 165, 256, 315, 349, 350,

www.ingramcontent.com/pod-product-compliance
Lightning Source LLC
Chambersburg PA
CBHW060106170426
43198CB00010B/787